4th EDITION

THE MINING VALUATION HANDBOOK

MINING AND ENERGY VALUATION FOR INVESTORS AND MANAGEMENT

Dr VICTOR RUDENNO

WILEY

John Wiley & Sons Australia, Ltd

First published in 2012 by John Wiley & Sons Australia, Ltd
42 McDougall St, Milton Qld 4064

Office also in Melbourne

First edition first published by John Wiley & Sons in 1998
Second edition first published by John Wiley & Sons in 2004
Third edition first published by John Wiley & Sons in 2009

Typeset in 11/13.8 ITC Berkeley Oldstyle Std Book

© Victor Rudenno 2012

The moral rights of the author have been asserted

National Library of Australia Cataloguing-in-Publication data:

Author:	Rudenno, Victor
Title:	The mining valuation handbook : mining and energy valuation for investors and management / Victor Rudenno
ISBN:	9780730377078
Notes:	Previous ed.: 2009.
Subjects:	Mine valuation — Australia.
	Mines and mineral resources — Valuation — Australia.
Dewey Number:	338.2029

Cover design by Rob Cowpe

Cover image (open pit mine): © iStockphoto.com/Pgiam

Figure 6.2 photo (A Mobile Drilling Rig): © Steve Lovegrove/Shutterstock.com

Figures 1.1, 1.2, 1.3, 4.1, 4.4, 4.5, 4.8, 4.9, 4.10, 4.11, 4.12, 4.13, 5.10, 8.1, 8.2, 8.3, 8.4, 8.5, 8.6, 8.7, 8.8, 8.12, 11.1, 11.2, 16.2, 20.2, 20.5 Microsoft Excel charts reproduced with permission from Microsoft.

Printed in China by Printplus Limited

10 9 8 7 6 5 4 3 2 1

Disclaimer

The material in this publication is of the nature of general comment only, and does not represent professional advice. It is not intended to provide specific guidance for particular circumstances and it should not be relied on as the basis for any decision to take action or not take action on any matter which it covers. Readers should obtain professional advice where appropriate, before making any such decision. To the maximum extent permitted by law, the author and publisher disclaim all responsibility and liability to any person, arising directly or indirectly from any person taking or not taking action based on the information in this publication.

CONTENTS

To my parents, who always encouraged and provided me with the opportunity to acquire the most valuable of all commodities: knowledge.

ACKNOWLEDGEMENTS

Once again I have been fortunate enough to have good friends and colleagues to help with the provision of ideas, information and proofing. For this edition my grateful thanks go to Bob Adamson, Rod Elvish, Warren Kreyzig, Michael Potter and Keith Skipper.

A number of people have helped with past editions, which have laid the foundations for this one. My thanks go to Andy Border, Howard Brady, Bob Cameron, Arron Collaran, Ann Diamant, Andrew Driscoll, Joel Forwood, Tim Gerrard, Tim Goldsmith, Phil Gray, Tim Knapton, Murray Kornweibel, Garry Lowder, Richard Kuo, Mick Lucas, Creagh O'Connor, Paul Pinnock, Peter Rose, Neil Seage, Trevor Sykes and Wayne Zekulich. A special thank you to Robert Champion de Crespigny for his kind words in the foreword of the first and second editions of this book.

And as always, to my wife Sue, I give my greatest thanks for her continued support and help in all my endeavours.

INTRODUCTION

Over the last 35 years, I have been fortunate enough to lecture to university students in mining engineering and geology, to industry practitioners at seminars and workshops, to students of the Securities Institute of Australia and Kaplan, to investors through the Australian Stock Exchange (ASX) and to fund managers around the world. I have often been asked if there is a text that covers the myriad related and interrelated financial issues in the resources industry. Although there are many good books that cover specific issues, some of which unfortunately are out of print, I was motivated to write the first edition in the form of a handbook in an attempt to bring everything into one easy-to-use reference work. In the second and third editions, as well as updating historical information, I expanded on some issues, added additional project examples and covered several aspects raised in reviews of the prior editions.

I have again tried to add new ideas and commentary, and where possible provided more up-to-date examples. However, although some examples may be a little old, I have kept them only because I have been unable to find examples that explain the point any more clearly. This updated edition once again goes further towards covering these issues, including more commentary on forecasting, real option theory and allocation of fundamental value. Hopefully the book will continue to act as a reference for those in the mining industry who are seeking information of a more financial nature, and for those in the finance industry who are looking for simple detail of the characteristics of the resources industry in a financial light. For the non-professional who is keen to invest in resource companies, this book will hopefully remove some of the mystique that often surrounds technical disciplines.

In attempting to cover a large number of issues, it is always difficult to decide upon the order of presentation. Often, to help explain an issue, it would be great to explain several subsidiary issues simultaneously. This is of course not possible, so please bear with the text and hopefully the worked examples will help make everything clear in the end. As far as possible each topic is self-contained so that those readers who have knowledge of a particular topic can move on to the next chapter.

Important issues have been highlighted with the heading 'Tip' so that they can be easily located; by important, I mean those issues that, in my experience, often play a key part in the equity market's appreciation of the value of a listed equity. That is not to say that this book is specifically designed with listed resource companies in mind, but it is the major area of experience from which I speak, and hopefully will be a suitable guide for both the professional and non-professional investor, as well as for management of resource companies who wish to get the most from their investment or project.

On occasions in this book I will refer to 'mining' and 'resources' interchangeably and, unless otherwise indicated, these will include both hard and soft rock mining and the hydrocarbon industries. A detailed glossary is provided at the end of this book. I also hope to provide many of the worked examples on my website, <www.revaluate.com.au>, to try to make it easier to understand how the myriad numbers were calculated. In chapter 8 I have provided cost curves, which I will occasionally update on the website with additional project data and indexed to a more recent date.

Since writing the third edition only three years ago, we have continued to see an amazing rollercoaster of fortunes in the equity markets, in particular in resources and in commodity prices. After suffering the global financial crisis (GFC) just before the publication of the last edition, the commodity markets recovered strongly, especially with the emergence of China and to a lesser extent India as economic powerhouses. Now as I write this text, the European credit crisis has unfolded and, if one can believe the International Monetary Fund, another depression is possibly around the corner! Hopefully this will not eventuate and, as you read these words in the coming months and years, most of the financial problems might have been resolved and resource stocks will once more be on the rise.

Finally, as always, the views and opinions expressed in this book are mine and mine alone. If you would like to send me a note on any of the issues raised, please feel free to email me at <victor@miningvaluation.com>.

Dr Victor Rudenno
Sydney
January 2012

CHAPTER 1
The resources industry

The mining and processing of raw materials have played a critical part in the development of modern civilisation. Towards the end of the twentieth century there was a subtle, but important change through the development of increasingly diversified multinational mining companies while leaving grassroots exploration to smaller resource companies. Indeed, the level of exploration and, importantly, exploration success declined significantly in the late 1990s and the impact of low commodity prices restricting the availability of funds saw a significant reduction in new mining operations.

What no one foresaw was the significant growth among developing nations, particularly China and to a lesser extent India, as they raced to increase the quality of life for their people, generally reflected in increasing per capita consumption of metals and energy. Figure 1.1 (overleaf) shows an Index of primary base metal prices since January 2004. The price rose slowly, and then there was a dramatic 100 per cent plus rise between 2005 and 2007, often referred to as the Super Cycle. The arrival in 2008 of the global financial crisis (GFC) showed just how fragile commodity prices could be, as they are directly linked to world economic growth. With expectations of recession and reduced consumption, commodity prices also fell, as shown in the commodity price index. However, by March 2009 commodity markets were on the rise again and after a 65 per cent price fall they had made up two-thirds of the lost ground in a matter of 24 months. More particularly, bulk commodities such as iron ore and coal have shown amazing strength, fuelled primarily by economic growth in China. Commentators and mining companies remain bullish at the outlook for commodity prices over the next few years, although during the latter part of 2011 the European economic crisis resulted in concerns over economic growth and a further weakening in commodity prices.

Figure 1.1: index of primary base metal prices, March 2004–September 2011

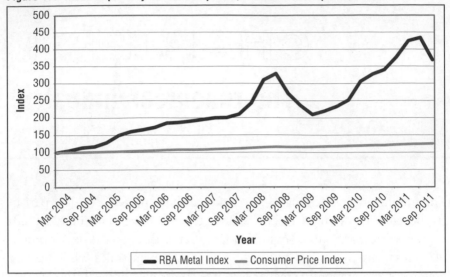

Higher commodity prices have meant that many previously discovered resource projects have now become economically viable. The mining industry is very capital hungry as a result of the large development costs and the high level of mechanisation necessary to ensure greater productivity through economies of scale. The removal of available funding by debt or equity markets should significantly curtail, if not totally prevent, the development of many new projects or major expansions in the near term, particularly those with high operating costs per unit of output. Some of the larger and better projects may yet proceed, but most likely only by companies that have funding available from their own balance sheets. This delay in new sources of commodities may go some way to offset reduced demand, but it will take time.

What resource companies do

The primary aim of resource companies is to find, develop and extract mineral resources. The definition of a mineral resource is an economic occurrence of an element in nature. There are a large number of minerals and many occurrences, but the trick is to find a deposit that is economic to mine. For the mining of mineral deposits we talk about ore, which is a naturally occurring concentration of minerals, and waste or gangue rock in which the ore is found. For hydrocarbon deposits, we talk about reservoirs in which oil or gas has been trapped in the pores of the rock that make up the reservoir.

Steps that resource companies generally undertake in the development of a new resource are:

» *Exploration*. A little over US$12 billion was spent worldwide in 2010 to find exploitable nonferrous minerals (nearly half for gold) and US$440 billion for exploration and development of oil and natural gas. Various techniques are employed to locate deposits, which, more often than not, are located below the surface with little or no surface expression (see chapter 5 for more detail). Successful exploration can result in a dramatic increase in the value of a company and is therefore of great significance to the equity (stock) markets.

» *Definition*. Once a mineral discovery has been made it is important to define the size of the orebody in tonnes and the grade or quality — for example, the amount of gold as grams per tonne of ore. This will ultimately set the parameters by which the deposit will be valued and hence the value to the company and, if listed, the company's share price.

» *Feasibility studies*. The economic viability of the resource project has to be established. Engineering and financial models of the project are constructed to determine, within a framework of commodity prices and exchange rates, the economic return that can be expected. If the return, generally by way of future cash flows, is sufficient to warrant the capital expenditure needed to develop the mine, then the project may go ahead.

» *Development*. If the feasibility study has justified the project, then access to the orebody is required either by open cut (open pit) or underground mining methods, or, in the case of oil and gas, through production wells. Infrastructure must be constructed to support the project — including transport, power and water facilities, and the processing plant. Often the remote location of a project will require the construction of a town or living quarters for the workforce.

» *Extraction*. The mineralised orebody or hydrocarbons must be removed from the surrounding (waste) rock. For open cut mines, where the orebody is close to the surface, large volumes of waste rock may have to be removed to expose the orebody. For underground mines, where the orebody is too deep to be exploited by open cut mining methods, a shaft or decline, or both, will be constructed to gain direct access to the orebody. For oil and gas fields a sufficient number of production wells will have to be drilled to adequately recover the hydrocarbons.

» *Processing*. Most minerals will require some initial on-site processing. For bulk commodities, such as coal, some upgrade may be needed to meet the quality requirements of the purchaser. For low-grade ores, concentration will be undertaken to reduce the amount of waste material within the ore, which would otherwise be transported to another location for further recovery of the economic element. An increasing number of mines are introducing technology that allows for the recovery of the economic element, such as copper, at the mine site itself.

» *Refining*. Concentrate sent from the mine site may undergo further processing, either by hydrometallurgical (liquid) or pyrometallurgical (heat) processes, or by a combination of both, to recover the saleable commodity. In the case of petroleum the oil will be refined to produce various products, such as diesel or petrol.

What makes resource companies different from industrials?

There are a number of significant differences between resource and industrial companies. These differences are unique to resource companies and require specific knowledge, hence the motivation for writing this book. That is not to say that industrial-based companies—such as those in the telecommunications industry, for example—do not have complex issues that require specialist knowledge that is often technical in nature. However, it seems easier for the public to relate to industrial companies, perhaps due to the familiarity they have with many of the products and issues that surround those types of industries. On the other hand, due to the isolation of mining projects, few members of the public have had the opportunity to visit mining sites and become familiar with the resources industry.

Volatility of share prices

Share price volatility for resource stocks has historically been greater than for industrials. Figure 1.2 shows the percentage monthly change in two Australian indices on the ASX—the S&P/ASX Industrials Index versus the S&P/ASX Materials Index, which contains the resource companies.[1]

Figure 1.2: S&P/ASX Industrials Index compared with S&P/ASX Materials Index, February 2007–December 2011

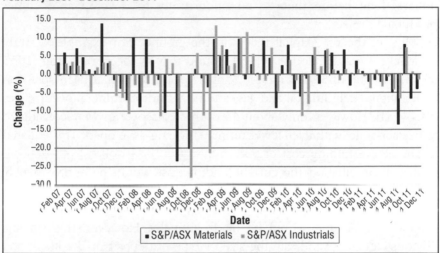

While the Materials Index has been more volatile than the Industrials over the last few years (based on ASX indices), Industrials appear to have overtaken Materials in volatility, although over the period shown in figure 1.2 (2007–2011) they have been quite similar. However, individual resource stocks can still show significantly greater price variation than Industrials.

The factors that influence the volatility are discussed later. The resources market can therefore provide a potentially higher return in the short term, but this is balanced by the higher risk—the resource stocks can fall more abruptly. For example, in figure 1.2 the largest one-month increase for the Materials Index was 13.7 per cent while the largest fall was 23.5 per cent.

1 An S&P/ASX index is a numerical value that is adjusted to reflect the net price change of all of the listed companies that make up that index. If the index rises by 1 per cent, this tells us that the total capitalisation of the quoted shares of the companies in the index rose by 1 per cent. Readers should note that a company may have on issue additional shares that for various reasons, such as vendor escrow, are not listed by an exchange such as the ASX and are therefore not included in the company's market capitalisation, which can lead to erroneous calculations regarding market capitalisations—a major fault of S&P/ASX indices.

Exploration

A unique feature of the mining industry is the need to explore in order to find and define an economic resource on which a mining project can be built. Industrial companies are not confronted with this difficulty. The success rate for exploration is also relatively low. For example, in the oil industry as a whole the success rate can be of the order of one in ten. A company therefore requires large amounts of risk capital (exploration dollars) long before there is an opportunity to develop an income-producing project.

Most of the risk capital is lost in the ground. For example, a study by Mackenzie and Bilodeau (1984) found that in the period from 1955 to 1978 a total of $1618 million (dollars of the day) had been spent on exploration (excluding oil and gas) and thousands of mineral occurrences discovered. However, only about 43 of these discoveries were considered to be economic, with even fewer ultimately being developed. This equated to an average finding cost of $38 million (in 1984 dollars) per deposit. Adjusted for inflation the current finding cost would be approximately $100 million. For 2011 the Australian annualised mineral exploration expenditure was approximately $4 billion, which suggests that some 40 economic discoveries could be made annually. However, this statistic obviously does not indicate the size or type of deposit or the likelihood that any would ultimately come to production.

Finite reserves

Any mineral resource has a finite volume, and therefore will have a finite life that will vary according to the production rate. This is a problem not usually confronted by industrial companies. Once they have a raw material supply (often provided by the resources industry) and a market for their product they are in theory able to operate for an indefinite length of time.

Following an exploration success, a mining company will undertake a drilling program to define the resource. As the number of holes drilled increases and additional information is obtained, the confidence level in the amount of ore (tonnage) or hydrocarbons (volume) available will also increase. Confidence will also grow in the quality or level of the economic element contained within the resource. The industry has a number of standards that define the operator's confidence (discussed in more detail in chapter 6). Reserves that are economically recoverable are classified as proven (high confidence) and probable (medium confidence). An example of a proposed copper mine is shown in table 1.1.

Table 1.1: project ore reserves for a proposed copper mine

Proven reserve	Probable reserve	Measured resource
Tonnage: 2 million	Tonnage: 3 million	Tonnage: 8 million
Grade: 1.2%	Grade: 1.0%	Grade: 0.8%
Copper: 24 000 tonnes	Copper: 30 000 tonnes	Copper: 64 000 tonnes

For this project the total reserve (proven plus probable) consists of 54 000 tonnes of copper metal dispersed within 5 million tonnes of rock (ore). There is additional ore that is classified as a measured resource—this has not been included within the reserve, as economic constraints have not been applied. The measured resource or some part of it may or may not become a reserve at a future date.

It is within these confidence levels of a finite reserve and resource (and those resources still to be converted to a reserve) that an economic decision will need to be made on whether to develop the project, knowing that the project will have a finite life.

Resource companies should always ensure that quoted reserves and resources are clearly defined, and investors should always check and ensure that they fully understand how the companies have compiled and quoted their figures.

Commodity price volatility

Resource stocks are exposed to greater external commodity price volatility than most industrial stocks. Most of the world's major exporters of raw mineral commodities are price takers rather than price makers. In other words, they rely on international commodity prices—in a very competitive market—which in turn are very much dependent on world economic activity and overall levels of supply, demand and inventories. For example, even though Australia is a major producer of mineral sands, their price is still dependent on international economic activity. The primary use of rutile is in the production of white pigment (due to its high titanium content) for the paint industry. The major consumers of paint are the housing and automotive industries, the largest being in the United States (US). Therefore the price of rutile is dependent on housing starts and car sales in the US, which are obviously beyond the control of Australian producers.

In figure 1.3 the US Consumer Price Index (CPI) and the previous Metal Price Index have been plotted since 2004. Although the CPI is not the best indicator of industrial prices, it does show a fundamental trend of ever-increasing prices in an inflationary environment. On the other hand, the prices received by resource companies are more volatile, and after a strong upward trend until June 2007 there was a dramatic downturn, caused by the GFC, which placed pressure on producers to reduce costs, alter operating procedures and, for some, close operations. While much of the lost ground had been recovered by mid 2011, recent uncertainty has again weakened commodity prices, as previously discussed. However, in real terms over the period shown, base metal prices are up 34 per cent, which equates to an annual real increase of 3.8 per cent since 2004.

Figure 1.3: CPI and Metal Price Index, January 2004–October 2011

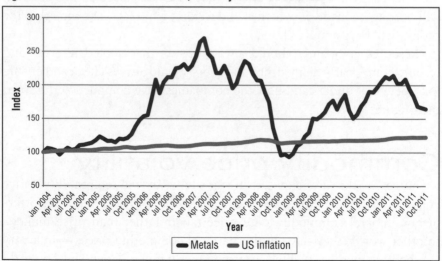

Because a large portion of sales are to overseas markets, and prices are predominantly quoted in US dollars, earnings for resource companies outside the US are also very much influenced by movements in their local exchange rate.

Capital intensity

The mining industry, by its very nature, is capital intensive. The factors that influence this high level of expenditure include:

» *Exploration.* As mentioned, considerable funds are needed to find and delineate mineral resources. Most of the $4 billion spent in Australia on mineral, oil and gas exploration each year does not result in new economic discoveries.

» *Economies of scale.* Given the relatively low value per unit of production due to low levels of value adding (raw commodities), it is necessary to move large tonnages cost effectively. The industry therefore often requires expensive and, at times, complex equipment. For example, the value per tonne of ore can range from a low of around US$15 to a high of US$750, with an average of around US$235, compared with an average price of US$325 per tonne of wheat and US$18 000 per tonne of wool.

» *Isolation.* Mining projects, including initial processing, are undertaken where the mineral reserves are found, often in remote locations. As a result, infrastructure (for example, roads, railways and townships) is developed in conjunction with the project, increasing the capital costs. An increasing trend in recent years to reduce this cost has been the provision of fly-in–fly-out facilities, where the workforce work on site, typically for 12-hour shifts for several weeks, before returning home for an extended break.

» *Power and water.* Critical requirements for all mining projects are power and water. Power in the form of fuel oil or diesel is required for the earthmoving fleets, while electrical power is required for the processing plant and electrically driven mine machinery such as longwall units in underground coalmines. Because of the isolation, a common mode of generating electrical power is by diesel electric generators. Obviously, if main grid electric power is available, it is preferred, as diesel-generated power is more expensive. The use of natural gas to generate electric power is increasing, given its lower operating cost, despite the higher initial capital cost. Mines are often located in arid areas and ensuring an adequate and reliable water supply may require considerable expenditure.

Figure 1.4 shows a typical distribution of capital costs for a base metal mine constructed in Australia. The distribution varies, depending on the location and type of mine, but it does highlight the additional capital cost for power and water (22 per cent), which is often not a consideration for industrial operations.

Figure 1.4: typical capital costs for a base metal mine in Australia

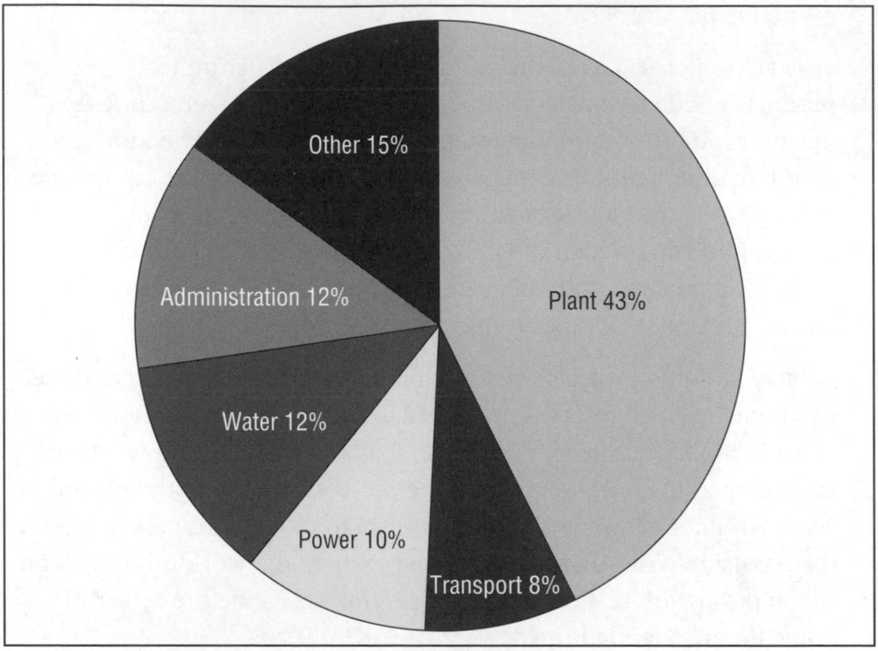

Environment

Protection of the environment is important for both industrial and resource companies. In Australia, for example, state and federal legislation has set increasingly high environmental standards. Within practical limitations, companies must ensure minimum impact on the environment. These measures increase capital and operating costs. Given the impact on the landscape, these costs can be very high for resource companies, as shown in table 1.2, although they only represent some 1 per cent of total current expenses for the mining industry.

Table 1.2: operating and capital environmental protection expenditure, 2000–01 ($ million)

	Mine site rehabilitation	Solid waste	Liquid waste	Air emissions	Other	Total
Operating	97.7	53.8	24.8	40.5	67.0	283.8
Capital	7.4	54.2	17.3	23.1	4.9	106.8

Source: 2003 Australian Year Book.

An environmental impact statement (EIS) is required for the development of new resource projects. The EIS describes the project and its impact on all aspects of the environment in detail. Some of the issues that will be addressed are the project's impact on water quality and use, noise, air quality and the landscape, and the disposal of waste.

Mineral processing can affect air and water quality, and also have a direct physical and visual impact on the land, caused by plant mine waste dumps and tailings dams. For an average mine the approximate levels of water consumption, carbon dioxide (CO_2) emissions and sulphur dioxide (SO_2) emissions per tonne of ore milled are shown in table 1.3. Obviously, other types of emissions may also occur. The CO_2 figure compares with a major iron ore open cut operation with minimal treatment and high economies of scale that produces some 3 kg of CO_2 per tonne of ore and overburden mined. Concern over the emission of greenhouse gases has resulted in the introduction of a carbon tax in Australia from July 2012. Under the scheme the cost per tonne of coal mined is estimated to increase by $3 for the introduction of a $23 per tonne of carbon tax, which will rise to $4.60 per tonne of coal for a carbon tax of $40 per tonne.

Table 1.3: environmental impact per tonne of ore milled

Water consumption (kilolitres)	Carbon dioxide emission (kg)	Sulphur dioxide emission (kg)
0.8 to 1.2	50 to 150	0.1 to 0.7

Sulphur dioxide emissions near residential areas can be of major concern, and additional equipment may be required to reduce these emissions.

Financial bonds are often required by governments to ensure remedial work is undertaken at the conclusion of the mining operation. The plant is removed and equipment and machinery are re-used at other sites. The waste dumps (overburden) will be contoured to resemble low hills and revegetated, so that they blend into the surrounding landscape as much as possible. An underground mine will generally be closed from the surface and present little, if any, impact on the surrounding environment. However, open cut mines are generally left open to perhaps fill with water and provide an artificial lake. It is not economically practical to refill the open cuts, although some portion of the pit may be filled with waste towards the end of the mining life if this doesn't interfere with the mining operation, or if suitably situated they may be used for landfill. Strip mines, such as those in coal mining, use the shallow open cuts as a disposal site for waste from the next sequence of mining. Due to the bulking of the waste, once it is mined, small hill-like structures are produced.

Tailings dams, which contain the waste residue from the mine plant (water and finely ground low-grade ore), are compacted, covered with soil and revegetated.

Land rights

The rights of traditional owners have become an increasingly important and complex issue in a number of international jurisdictions. Although industrial-based companies may also be faced with these issues, they are not as exposed as mining companies, which are often involved in exploration on land not covered under freehold title. See appendix B for more information on Australian land rights.

CHAPTER 2

A quick guide to financials

Valuation of listed securities and resource projects relies on the analysis of financial data. For those readers unfamiliar with the process it is important to provide a simple overview of the various parameters that make up the numbers. This should help make the detailed sections that follow more meaningful.

The principal aim of this type of analysis is to effectively forecast the future financial performance of the company, which most often relates to the future financial performance of the company's resource project(s). Each project needs to be categorised into its major financial components and, as more advanced studies are undertaken, the level of detail will increase substantially. The major financial components are:

» capital costs

» revenue

» operating costs

» other costs

» depreciation

» taxation

» cash flow.

We will look at these individually.

Capital costs

The costs of constructing a mine or developing a hydrocarbon field and associated infrastructure can be far ranging. The mine's capital costs will generally include the cost of developing access to the orebody—which, in the case of underground mines, includes such items as shafts—while for open cut mines it may include the removal of large volumes of waste material. Mining equipment to extract the ore will also be required; however, the use of contract mining should result in a reduction in capital costs associated with mining equipment. Most ores require some level of processing before sale. The processing can vary from simple concentrating to reduce the amount of waste material shipped, to more complex on-site processing, to the production of final saleable product.

For oil and gas projects, capital costs will include the installation of production wells to allow the hydrocarbons to reach the surface and on-site processing facilities to separate hydrocarbon products. Pipelines are often required for transportation of oil and gas from the field to refineries or market. For offshore developments, there is a requirement for production platforms with the hydrocarbons sent to shore by pipelines. For small fields, floating production, storage and offtake (FPSO) facilities are used, where the oil is stored in a modified oil tanker. Once full, the oil is then discharged into other tankers that take the oil to refineries.

Infrastructure costs may include such items as water and power supply, airports, roads and towns to house workers. The level of expenditure on capital costs can vary from several million dollars for very small mining operations to several billion dollars for very large projects. Indicative capital costs for recent or planned mining projects are discussed in chapter 8. The capital expenditure will be undertaken as quickly as is practical in order to get the project into production at the earliest date possible to gain access to the future cash flows. Subject to the size of the project and external factors, such as location and topography, the project construction can take from several months to several years.

Additional capital costs may be incurred at other times throughout the life of the project to cover the cost of replacing old equipment or for any operating changes or expansions. At the end of the mine life, fixed assets will probably be sold and the net cash received is termed the salvage value.

It is important to include in capital costs an allowance for working capital, which is the initial operating cost that will be incurred before the first revenues are received or when revenues are insufficient to meet costs. Therefore the working capital represents a timing difference between costs and revenue that may change over the life of the project. The working capital will be returned to the investors (or bank) at the end of the project life.

Revenue

Once the project is under way, mineral product will be sold to produce a revenue stream. The revenue is simply the price of the product at the point of sale multiplied by the quantity sold. Most commonly, the revenue is forecast on a yearly basis over the life of the project to determine the fundamental value. If forecasts of the company's profits are sought, then the revenue is often forecast over the first few years, or the next few years if already in production.

The obvious difficulty (or risk) is the inability to forecast commodity prices well into the future (see chapter 4). As most mineral commodities are sold in US dollars (US$), it is also sometimes necessary to forecast future exchange rates so that prices can be converted into the local currency.[1] The price realised for the product may not be the price quoted on international markets due to quality differentials and the deduction of additional processing charges.

Marketing costs, and perhaps costs of international transportation and insurance, may also need to be deducted. It is also necessary to forecast the quantity of commodity production, which will often be a function of the processing plant capacities and the varying grade of the deposit, or the yield or decline of the hydrocarbon field production over time.

Operating costs

Operating costs are made up of the day-to-day costs in the production and processing of the commodity. These costs include wages, consumable materials such as chemicals and explosives, transportation and power. Contract mining costs would also fall under the operating costs heading.

Operating costs can be considered as variable if they increase or decrease depending on the tonnage mined or treated. Examples of these types of costs include explosives, chemicals for mineral recovery, transport and power. Fixed costs are those costs that will not vary with moderate changes in the mining or milling rate, such as wages.

It is not uncommon for overall mining costs to be quoted on a tonne of ore mined or processed, or on a unit of finished product. For example, the open cut mining cost might be quoted at US$1 per tonne mined, while the cost to remove overburden might be US$2 per cubic metre. The

---

1 All currencies in this book are in A$ unless otherwise specified although at the time of writing the A$ was at parity with the US$.

processing cost to produce a saleable product could be US$15 per tonne of ore processed plus a further US$10 per tonne of concentrate for transport and port handling charges. Total costs can be quoted on a cost per unit of saleable product such as US$685 per ounce of gold (which would be total costs divided by gold produced) or US$15 per barrel of oil production.

Other costs
These can include non-mining or processing items such as state or federal royalties, leasing costs and project-related interest costs.

Depreciation
This is a non-cash item that allows in accounting terms for the recovery of capital expenditure over the life of the project for tax purposes. (More detail is provided in chapter 10.) The pre-tax income is reduced by the allowable depreciation of capital items and thus the state or federal tax payable is reduced.

Taxation
Tax is payable in most jurisdictions at varying rates and with different allowances. Some countries have federal, state and local taxes, as well as royalties. More information on tax rates is provided in chapter 10, and on royalties in appendix C—particularly for Australia, Canada, South Africa and the US.

Cash flow
This is the flow of cash from the project owners for the capital expenditure to get the project into operation (negative) and the flow of cash from the project to the owners after all costs (which should be positive).

Worked example
Table 2.1 illustrates a simplified operating and financial summary of a hypothetical operation. Each line in the table is numbered and the following comments describe the issues that need to be considered in each case.

Table 2.1: cash-flow model for a hypothetical operation

Line	Calculation	Year 1	Year 2	Year 3	Year 4	Year 5	Year 6
1 Capital cost ($m)	Estimate	−27	−31	—	—	—	—
2 Ore mined (kt)	Estimate	—	—	1100	1100	1100	900
3 Ore milled (kt)	Estimate	—	—	1000	1000	1000	800
4 Commodity produced (kt)	Estimate	—	—	18.0	16.2	14.4	10.8
5 Commodity price (US$/t)	Estimate	—	—	2500	2625	2756	2618
6 Exchange rate (US$: local currency)	Estimate	—	—	0.70	0.72	0.73	0.75
7 Realised metal price ($/t)	5 ÷ 6	—	—	3571	3646	3778	3491
8 Revenue ($m)	4 × 7	—	—	64.3	59.1	54.4	37.7
9 Mining cost ($/t)	Estimate	—	—	6.0	6.2	6.4	6.6
10 Milling cost ($/t)	Estimate	—	—	20.0	20.6	21.2	21.9
11 Total operating cost ($m)	2 × 9 + 3 × 10	—	—	26.6	27.4	28.2	23.4
12 Depreciation ($m)	sum of line 1 ÷ 4	—	—	14.5	14.5	14.5	14.5
13 Pre-tax income ($m)	8 − 11 − 12	—	—	23.2	17.2	11.6	0
14 Tax ($m)	13 × 0.30	—	—	7.0	5.2	3.5	0
15 Cash flow ($m)	8 − 11 − 14	−27	−31	30.7	26.5	22.7	14.3

The important points to note from this simple example are:

» $58 million of capital expenditure will occur over a two-year period to bring this hypothetical mine into production. This is a negative cash flow to the owners of the project (line 1). No allowance has been made for working capital to simplify the example.

» Ore will be mined and then treated in a plant to produce a saleable product. The tonnage milled does not have to equal the ore mined, as some low-grade material might be stockpiled. The mine life is a function of the mineable reserves and the processing rate.[2] The mine life of four years is very low and has been chosen only for convenience (lines 2 and 3).

» The saleable product produced, in this case metal, is priced in US$ that are converted to the local currency ($) by dividing the US$ price by the exchange rate.

» The revenue can be calculated, in line 8, by multiplying the metal price by the amount of metal produced.

» Mining and milling costs on a per tonne basis are provided in lines 9 and 10 respectively. By multiplying these by the quantity of ore mined and processed (shown in lines 2 and 3), the total cost is calculated in line 11.

» The annual depreciation is calculated by dividing the total capital expenditure by the four-year life of the mine. The equation is: $58 million ÷ 4 = $14.5 million.

» The taxable (or pre-tax) income is the revenue less costs less depreciation as shown in line 13. The tax payable is 30 per cent of the pre-tax income (line 14).

» The operating cash flow is the revenue less the operating costs less the tax payable. The depreciation is not subtracted, as it is a non-cash item, but rather an accounting value to determine the tax payable. The capital costs show up as negative items in the first two years.

---

2 For large porphyry copper mines a rule of thumb to estimate the mine life based on tonnage only was proposed by HK Taylor in 1978, which states that the life in years is: $6.5 \times$ the fourth root of the reserves R (plus or minus 20 per cent). For example, if the reserves are 50 million tonnes, then the life is: $6.5 \times \sqrt[4]{50} = 6.5 \times 2.659 = 17.3$ years, with a range of 13.8 to 20.7 years. The rule can also be displayed as yearly mine capacity $C = 0.147R^{0.75}$ from which we can derive the mine life by R/C, which comes to 18.1 years.

The example is simplistic at this stage; however, the various parameters that make up the cash flow will be expanded throughout the book. The two important questions that do arise are:

» Do the future positive cash flows justify the initial capital expenditure, given the project's risk and in particular the need to forecast into the future?

» What is the fundamental value of this project to the company and, if the company is listed, to its share price?

The first phase in the valuation process for the mining company is to conduct a series of increasingly detailed feasibility and engineering studies. These studies will more fully define the operating parameters of the project and the financial issues to determine the viability and value of the resource project. This is the subject of the next chapter.

CHAPTER 3
Feasibility studies

The *Oxford English Dictionary* defines feasible as 'practicable and possible'. For feasibility studies in resource projects, the practicable and possible relate not only to the physical aspects of resource exploitation (technical) but also to the economics of the project (financial). From the very start, when consideration is given to exploration for a mineral resource, money will have to be spent. At each stage, from discovery through development to production, increasing amounts of finance will have to be committed, and at each stage will have to be justified.

In the very early stages of exploration, the decision to proceed will be based more on a qualitative assessment of the risk of failure versus the financial reward from an economic discovery. Initially, the assessment of the potential economic value may be inferred from previous success in that particular geological environment. As more geological data are obtained, particularly from the drilling of the orebody or hydrocarbon structure, a clearer picture will become available of the size and quality (grade) of the deposit.

In some cases, when the grade or volume is uneconomic, a relatively quick decision can be made to abandon further exploration expenditure. However, if the initial exploration results are encouraging, further expenditure may be justified. The initial feasibility study could take the form of a back-of-the-envelope valuation. This is where, given the approximate grade and tonnage—or in the case of hydrocarbons the volumes and deliverability—it is possible to infer from previous experience the scale of the operation and the various economic parameters that could be expected.

Components

Take, for example, a gold discovery, where perhaps the initial drilling suggests the potential for several million tonnes of ore. There is a trade-off between the annual production rate, the mine life (tonnage divided by annual production) and the capital costs. Higher production rates will reduce mine life and also increase capital costs, while for debt purposes, a 5- to 10-year mine life would probably be preferred. A production rate of between 200000 tonnes and 400000 tonnes might be an initial estimate. If the estimate of average grade is low—around 1 to 2 grams per tonne—then a heap leach operation may be the only alternative due to its lower capital and operating costs. If the grades are 2 or more grams per tonne, then perhaps a conventional carbon-in-pulp operation could be contemplated.

The equity markets are often faced with valuing an exploration discovery from the very early stages, often before any initial valuation has been carried out by the company. Some examples of the risk and outcome are discussed in chapter 16. The market will also make assumptions about the potential value based on previous experience and make adjustments for the risk of an unsuccessful outcome. The market will seek more information on the discovery, asking many of the critical questions, when even the company may not know all the answers. The issues that an equity analyst would like addressed, but would not necessarily get an answer to, include those in table 3.1.

Table 3.1: issues with a new discovery

Hard rock	Solid energy	Oil and gas
Grade	Steaming/coking	Net pay
Tonnage	Tonnage	Area of closure
Recovery	Yield	Recoverable reserves
Mining rate	Mining rate	Production rate
Open cut/underground	Open cut/underground	Decline rate
Capital cost	Capital cost	Capital cost
Operating cost	Operating cost	Operating cost

The initial, back-of-the-envelope, scoping study or preliminary assessment is steadily refined by the company, as new data provide the confidence to move to a pre-feasibility study.[1] Continued expenditure on exploration and financial analysis could amount to many millions of dollars and therefore monitoring of the project's financial viability needs to be undertaken. The pre-feasibility study would start to incorporate estimates of the larger number of parameters that make up a reasonably robust financial analysis to within accuracies of around plus or minus 25 to 30 per cent. Engineers and geologists provide the first-pass estimates for:

» hard rock and solid energy prospects

  – best mine configuration based on current knowledge of the orebody

  – estimate of likely operating and capital costs

  – initial metallurgical studies (bench tests) to determine likely mill/washery design and likely recovery/yield

  availability of water, power transport and infrastructure requirements, and environmental issues

  – product markets and future commodity price profile

  – preliminary financial model.

» oil and gas plays

  – estimate of likely decline in production rates over the field life

  – estimate of likely operating and capital costs

  – continuing interpretation of seismic and well data to define volume of recoverable hydrocarbons

  – design of optimum field development and environmental issues

1 The Canadian National Instrument 43-101 (NI 43-101), which is a codified set of rules for public disclosure of information on mineral properties by Canadian listed companies, defines preliminary assessment as 'a study that includes an economic analysis of the potential viability of mineral resources taken at an early stage of the project prior to the completion of a preliminary feasibility study'; and preliminary feasibility study and pre-feasibility study 'each mean a comprehensive study of the viability of a mineral project that has advanced to a stage where the mining method, in the case of underground mining, or the pit configuration, in the case of an open cut, has been established and an effective method of mineral processing has been determined, and includes a financial analysis based on reasonable assumptions of technical, engineering, legal, operating, economic, social, and environmental factors and the evaluation of other relevant factors which are sufficient for a qualified person, acting reasonably, to determine if all or part of the mineral resource may be classified as a mineral reserve'.

- quality of, and associated by-products from, the hydrocarbon stream
- potential markets for gas products and future commodity price profiles
- preliminary financial model.

The pre-feasibility study will provide management with the first indication of the likely viability of the project. A critical decision point will emerge on the risk of spending potentially tens of millions of dollars progressing to the final feasibility study. It is very important that the results of the pre-feasibility study provide a balanced view of the likely outcome of the project, based on the data available at the time. Clearly an overly conservative estimate may prematurely kill off a viable project, while an overly optimistic assessment could result in significant financial loss.

The confidence level of the pre-feasibility study may still be relatively low, with accuracy in some areas of plus or minus 30 per cent. The evolution to the final feasibility study[2], also sometimes referred to as the definitive feasibility study (DFS) or bankable feasibility study (BFS), will cover all of the aforementioned issues, but further tests and engineering design work will increase the level of confidence towards accuracy of better than plus or minus 10 per cent.

Rough estimates of the costs and times for the different levels of feasibility studies are given in table 3.2.

Table 3.2: estimated costs and times for various feasibility studies

Studies	Cost	Time	Accuracy
Scoping study	$100 000s	Months	Low
Pre-feasibility	$ millions	Months	Fair
Final or bankable feasibility engineering design	$10 millions	Year(s)	Good
Construction phase detailed engineering	$ millions to $100 millions	Year(s)	Very good

2 NI 43-101 defines feasibility study as 'a comprehensive study of a mineral deposit in which all geological, engineering, legal, operating, economic, social, environmental and other relevant factors are considered in sufficient detail that it could reasonably serve as the basis for a final decision by a financial institution to finance the development of the deposit for mineral production'.

For those jurisdictions where the definitions of feasibility studies are not clearly set out, there can be considerable variation in terminology. Table 3.3 lists a number of studies by Australian listed mining companies. The first point to note is that net present value (NPV—see chapter 11) analysis is common at all stages. Secondly, inferred resources under the Joint Ore Reserve Committee (JORC) Code tend to be more common in the early stage studies, which would be expected, and that reserves are available for the BFS and DFS studies. Interestingly in some cases it appears only ore resources rather than ore reserves are published when BFS and DFS have been completed. And in some cases, after completing the scoping studies, companies are confident enough to miss the intermediate step of doing a pre-feasibility and go straight to the final feasibility stage.

Table 3.3: characteristics of feasibility studies carried out by Australian mining companies

Company name	Commodity	NPV	Reserve/ Reserve	Next stage
Scoping study				
Venturex	Copper	Yes	M&I&If	DF3
Argent	Silver, Lead, Zinc	Yes	M&I&If	—
Manas	Gold	Yes	I&If	FFS[1]
Energy and minerals	Uranium	Yes	If	PFS
Kasbah	Tin	Yes	I&If	PFS
Westgold	Gold	No[2]	No	DFS[3]
Marenica	Uranium	No	No	DFS
Argent	Silver, Lead, Zinc	Yes	M&I&If	DFS
Pre-feasibility				
FerrAus	Iron	Yes	Pr	DFS
Southern	Manganese	Yes	M&I&If	FES[4]
Avalon	Copper, Magnetite	Yes ± 30%	M&I&If	BFS
Peninsula	Uranium		I&If	BFS

(*continued*)

Table 3.3: characteristics of feasibility studies carried out by Australian mining companies (*cont'd*)

Company name	Commodity	NPV	Reserve/ Reserve	Next stage
Reed	Lithium	Yes ± 30%	I&If	BFS
Hazelwood	Tungsten	Yes	P&Pr	DFS
Feasibility				
Cortona	Gold	Yes	P&Pr	DFS
Chalice	Gold	Yes ±15%	I	—
Andean	Gold	Yes	I&If	—
Minemakers	Phosphate	Yes	Pr	—
Definitive feasibility				
Terramin	Zinc, Lead	No	M&I&If	—
Brocman	Iron ore	Yes	Pr	—
Aquila	Iron ore	Yes	M&I&Ir	—
Mineral Deposits	Mineral sands	No	P&Pr	—
Kentor	Gold, Copper	Yes	P&Pr	—
Platinum Aust	Platinum	Yes	M&I&If	—
Bankable feasibility				
Atomic	Coal	No	P	—
Vantage	Gold	No	P&Pr	—
Discovery	Copper	Yes	P&Pr	—
Republic	Gold	Yes	P&Pr	—
Meridian	Zinc, Lead	Yes	M&I&If	—
Independence	Gold	Yes	P&P	—

Notes: P = Proven Reserve; Pr = Probable Reserve; M = Measured Resource; I = Indicated Resource; If = Inferred Resource.
1 Full Feasibility Study
2 Cash flows determined
3 Detailed Feasibility Study
4 Full Feasibility Study mining inventory determined.

Costs are never known with certainty, and so a contingency allowance is applied to cover any cost overruns from unforeseen difficulties. The contingency can range from 5 to 15 per cent of the construction cost, but this can vary greatly depending on the perceived risks associated with the project and the technology applied to the recovery of the mineral commodity.[3]

Construction contracts that include project management by recognised contractors can also reduce the amount of contingency that may be required for major areas. The final feasibility study can include information on numerous parameters, some of which are listed in table 3.4.

Table 3.4: elements of a feasibility study

Section	Content
1 General	Summary and recommendations
	Mine location and description
	Development plan
	Plant product and capacity
2 Site	Topographical maps
	Soil/geology reports
3 Geology and mine	Geology
	Resource and reserves
	Geo-technical
	Mine plan
	Mine production schedule
	Mine equipment
	Mine services
4 Plant and infrastructure	Site plan
	Process flow sheets
	Energy balance

(*continued*)

3 A clear example of overruns in the construction cost was the Murrin Murrin nickel project in Western Australia where the capital cost in 1997 was originally estimated at $980 million, including $145 million of contingency. Due to the deleterious environment of high-pressure acid leach, redesign and equipment replacement resulted in the capital cost blowing out to $1695 million, swamping the allowed contingency.

Table 3.4: elements of a feasibility study (*cont'd*)

Section	Content
4 Plant and infrastructure (*cont'd*)	Material balance
	Heat balance
	Major equipment
	Minor equipment
	General arrangement drawings
	Detailed structural drawings
	Building and piping drawings
	Electrical drawings
	Management systems
	Equipment vendors
5 Environmental policy	Environmental policy and plan
	Environmental risks
	Health and safety risks
	Environmental impact assessment
	Environmental permits issued
	Environmental monitoring plan
	Statutory requirements
	Closure plan
6 Implementation	Project plan
	Project business systems
	Cash-flow forecast
	Construction work plan
	Construction contract configuration
	Construction schedule
	Future work
	Labour rates
	Labour productivity

Section	Content
7 Capital cost estimate	Construction equipment
	Major equipment bids
	Minor equipment bids
	Site preparation, earthwork
	Building foundations
	Equipment foundations
	Structural steel
	Cladding
	Architectural
	Mechanical
8 Operating cost estimate	Staffing levels
	Labour rates
	Consumable/utility consumption
	Maintenance supplies
	Spares
	Power and water unit costs
	Fuel unit costs
	Supplies and reagents unit costs
	Transport and logistics
	Working capital
	Sustaining/replacement capital
	Training
	Ramp up
	Insurances
	Escalation
	Foreign currency provisions
	Target accuracy

Source: Author, Mineral Engineering Technical Services Pty Ltd.

The financial analysis will pull all the relevant factors together to provide an estimate of the future stream of cash inflows and outflows. The impact of any debt would be incorporated and, after allowing for accounting treatments of capital expenditure, estimates would be made of any likely tax to be paid. With the advent of personal computers and sophisticated spreadsheets, the financial and technical analysis has become a much easier task.

The financial parameters were described in chapter 2, and the methodology is further expanded throughout the book.

A major objective of feasibility studies is to determine the profits and cash flow that will be generated for the equity holders. Various valuation methods, such as NPV, are employed to determine whether the future cash flows justify the financial expenditure.

Techniques such as sensitivity and probability analysis (see chapter 13) can also be applied to consider issues such as the project risk.

Corporate and project debt

A company may have the financial capacity to use its own balance sheet to raise corporate debt to help meet the costs of constructing the project. However, it is not uncommon for companies to arrange project debt so that a large portion of the capital costs is provided by lenders, where their primary recourse, should the project fail, is to seize the assets of the project itself and not the company's own balance sheet.

The advantage of using equity and debt for the company is clearly the capacity to construct and operate larger resource projects than it could manage from its own balance sheet. Additionally, the gearing effect increases the return to the equity holders. The improved return from the gearing is matched by increased risk for the equity participants.

As shown in figure 3.1, if the commodity price increases above the base case value (100 per cent; that is, the assumed best estimate of the commodity price in the feasibility study), then the equity holders derive the full benefit of a higher price by way of increased cash flow—hence the advantage of having part of the project funded by debt. However, if the price falls below the base case value, the equity holders' return will suffer first, as interest on the debt will have to be paid. Once the commodity price falls to 80 per cent of the base case feasibility study, there is no longer any return for the equity holders, while the bank still receives its interest. There is a point (70 per cent of the price) when there is insufficient operating cash flow to service the debt or provide a return on equity. The interest on the debt will accumulate until such time as the cash flows recover sufficiently for the payments to recommence.

Figure 3.1: project funded by debt

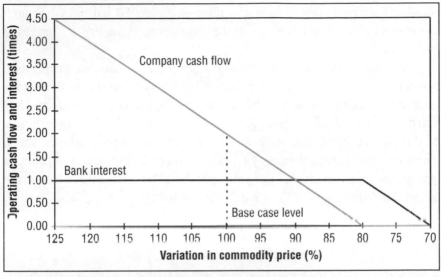

Obviously, the lenders also take some risk, although initially the risk is not as great as that taken by the equity participants, but the reward side is certainly less apparent. The lenders, therefore, have to be more risk averse and will seek to ensure that the project can be completed on time, within budget and, most importantly, that it will become operational at the planned operating levels. The lenders may seek different levels of completion guarantee from the equity participants and construction contractors.

To provide further comfort the lenders will look at the project cash flows and the requirement to service the debt and repay the principal. The lenders will want the cash-flow forecasts in the feasibility study to be well in excess of their requirements to provide a buffer against any deleterious impact on the project.

One financial test that lenders might apply is to compare each period's (say each quarter's) net cash flow with the financing costs to ensure that the cash flow is greater. This is the debt service coverage ratio. Another approach is to compare the present value of forecast cash flows available for financing for the remaining life of the project — or more commonly, the term of the financing—with the principal outstanding. These are the life of the project or life of the loan debt service coverage ratios. Depending on the perceived risk of the project, typical life of loan coverage ratios for mining projects vary between 1.5 and 2.0 times.

It is important from the bank's point of view that the company makes a success of the project to help ensure the repayment of debt and interest. Although the bank would have the mine and plant to fall back on, such assets invariably sell at a fraction of their initial cost if the project proves to be uneconomic.

The distinction between project finance (PF) and, as mentioned previously, corporate debt, is where the lender looks to the project's cash flow from which the loan will be repaid and the project assets are used as collateral. The risk of the transaction is measured by the creditworthiness of the project as the loan is non recourse to the owner's balance sheet. Therefore the parent company's balance sheet is not used; instead, a standalone entity or special purpose vehicle (SPV) owns and operates the assets. The advantages of PF include the following:

» its provision of capital allowing the corporate to own multiple projects

» its relatively low cost of finance

» its deep worldwide capital market, although this has contracted due to the current credit crisis.

The disadvantages of PF include:

» longer transaction time

» a higher fixed cost with restrictive covenants

» extensive hedging to mitigate commodity price risk

» an increased level of due diligence and frequent monitoring of technical performance

» a default with the lender gaining ownership of the asset.

A primary issue is in identifying project risks that include:

» reserves

» markets (off-take agreement) and commodity prices (hedging)

» construction time and costs

» operational costs

» political, labour and environmental issues

» ownership, tenure and tax.

To provide further security to the lenders most PF transactions require a debt service reserve account (DSRA) that provides a cash buffer representing principal and interest payments for a period from three to 12 months. If operational difficulties are encountered, the DSRA can be used to meet any shortfall before any equity payouts are made from the project.

The debt service coverage ratio (DSCR) is the ability for the project to repay debt periodically, defined as cash flow available for debt service (CFADS)[4] divided by debt service, where debt service = principal plus debt.

The periods can be quarterly, semi-annually, annually or some other forward-looking period. If the DSCR is less than one, then this implies that the project can't support the debt. This can be managed through one of the following:

» lower principal payments during lower CFADS

» grace period during which there is no obligation to repay principal

» the DSRA.

A PF loan would typically require that the DSCR does not fall below 1.2 times; a fall below this level would put the loan in default.

The loan life cover ratio (LLCR) is the number of times the discounted cash flow over the life of the loan can repay the outstanding debt balance. The issues to note are:

» the discount rate applied is usually the cost of debt

» for a steady cash flow the average DSCR over the loan life should be close to the LLCR.

A PF loan would typically require that the LLCR does not fall below 1.4 times; a fall below this level would put the loan in default.

Debt repayments may need to be tailored to ensure that the principal and interest are matched to the cash-flow pattern.

---

4 CFADS = net of revenue, operating costs, capital expenditure, tax and working capital adjustments.

Assuming a DSCR of 2.0, then DSCR = 2 = CFADS divided by (principal + interest); therefore, principal = CFADS / 2.0 – interest. So the principal payments can be modelled to meet the project's requirements.

For smaller resource projects a facility might be used where LLCR = NPV (CFADS over loan life) divided by debt balance; therefore, debt balance = NPV (CFADS over loan life) divided by LLCR. The principal draw down or repayment in each period is therefore governed by the target debt balance. Other conditions might also apply. The project life coverage ratio (PLCR) as per the LLCR is over the project's life rather than loan life and should not fall below 2 times.

Like the PLCR the reserve life coverage ratio (RLCR), is measured over the reserve life. Lenders can choose to disregard a proportion of the reserves in their determination of debt size and project evaluation, which is referred to as the reserve tail that provides lenders with a further buffer.

A cash sweep calculation is the time it would take to repay all the principal and interest from 100 per cent of the available cash flow — similar to a project's payback period.

Political risk insurance (PRI) is sometimes also required as part of the lending arrangements to cover against financial losses resulting from certain adverse political events including:

» expropriation of the project by the host country government

» war

» political violence

» currency inconvertibility and exchange transfer blockage.

Table 3.5 summarises a mining project where $50 million in equity capital is spent on project construction in year –1 (not shown in table 3.5), and in year 0 the remaining capital for the project of $50 million is provided by project finance plus $15.9 million for the establishment of a DSRA (year 1 principal and interest). Repayment of the loan is in five equal yearly instalments, plus interest on the outstanding amount at an interest rate of 9 per cent (an alternative would have been a yearly annuity of $16.94 million). A further $10 million of capital is required in year 3 to fund plant expansion, which will be funded by project cash flow. CFADS is determined for each year, as well as the DSRA to show the equity cash release available. Finally the DSCR and the LLCR are also calculated.

Table 3.5: hypothetical project financing

Year	0	1	2	3	4	5
Capital cost (debt component; US$m)	−50			−10		
Establishment of DSRA (US$m)	−15.9					
Tonnage (mt)		1.5	1.5	2.0	2.0	2.0
Grade (% Cu)		1.4	1.2	1.0	1.0	0.8
Price (US$/lb)		3.5	3.5	3.5	3.5	3.5
Revenue (US$m)		162.0	138.9	154.3	154.3	123.4
Operating costs (US$m)		−67.5	−67.5	−80.0	−80.0	−80.0
Treatment and refining charge (TC/RC; US$m)		−20.3	−20.3	−27.1	−27.1	−27.1
Royalty (5%; US$m)		−3.7	−2.6	−2.4	−2.4	−0.8
Tax (30%; US$m)		−18.1	11.6	10.4	10.4	−1.7
Working capital (US$m)		−10.9		−3.1		20.0
CFADS (US$m)		35.4	36.9	21.3	34.4	33.9
Scheduled principal (US$m)		−10	−10	−10	−10	−10
Debt balance (US$m)	65.9	55.9	45.9	35.9	25.9	15.9
Interest (9%) (US$m)		−5.9	−5.0	−4.1	−3.2	−2.3
Scheduled debt service (US$m)		−15.9	−15.0	−14.1	−13.2	−12.3
Funds available for DSRA (US$m)		19.5	21.9	7.1	21.1	21.5
Scheduled debt service (US$m)		−15.9	−15.0	−14.1	−13.2	−12.3
Target DSRA 1 yr fwd (US$m)		−15.0	−14.1	−13.2	−12.3	0.0
Shortfall DSRA (US$m)		0.0	0.0	0.0	0.0	0.0
Excess DSRA (US$m) (US$m)		0.9	0.9	0.9	0.9	12.3
Equity cash release (US$m)		20.4	22.8	8.0	22.0	33.9
DSCR		2.2	2.5	1.5	2.6	2.7
LLCR (9% discount)		1.8	1.6	1.7	1.2	—

Some of the other items that might be included in a term sheet (agreement between lender and project owner) include the following:

» term of the loan, which may include a grace period

» facility fee to be paid by the borrower to the facilitator (2.5 per cent of the facility amount)

» agency fee for administration of the facility (fixed amount per year)

» interest margin (percentage)

» interest rate—interest margin plus London inter-bank offer rate (LIBOR)

» default interest—interest rate plus, say, 2 per cent

» commitment fee—say 1 per cent of the undrawn balance of the facility

» taxes and charges—payable by the borrower.

When things go wrong

There are always risks associated with any feasibility study, as it represents the best estimate of an uncertain future. As an example, an oldie but goodie dates from November 1997, when the US mining company Pegasus Gold Inc. wrote off US$353.5 million of shareholders' funds after it closed the Mt Todd goldmine in the Northern Territory and put the mine on care and maintenance. This write-down was based on calculating the project's NPV, which proved to be significantly less than its book value (current depreciated level of previous expenditure).

The major problem in their case was not the gold price itself, which impacted negatively on the project's NPV, but the operating performance of the mine. The mine originally started as a heap leach operation in 1994, but was transformed to a carbon-in-leach operation by late 1996. The aim was to increase production from 60 000 ounces per annum to 200 000 ounces in 1997, then to 300 000 ounces in 1998, at an average cost of US$275 per ounce. Long-term production was to average 260 000 ounces per annum from a proven and probable reserve of 94.5 million tonnes at 1.07 g/t (grams per tonne) containing 3.3 million ounces. A crushing and grinding facility, flotation circuit, carbon-in-leach gold plant and 35 megawatt (MW) power plant was constructed at a cost of US$203 million to treat 8 million tonnes of ore per annum.

The following problems (which the company made public after the mine closure) became apparent after the mine reached steady state operations by the third quarter of 1997:

» The gold plant reached only 84 per cent of design capacity.

» Gold recovery was 74 per cent compared with the feasibility study figure of 84 per cent. The flotation circuit failed to recover an additional 8 per cent due to the impact of copper loading in the circuit.

» Crushed ore delivered to the plant circuit was larger in diameter at 3.1 mm compared with the feasibility study figure of 2.6 mm. This resulted in reduced gold recovery due to lower liberalisation due to smaller surface area.[5]

» Crusher throughput averaged 1065 tonnes per hour (tph) compared with the feasibility study figure of 1220 tph, although utilisation was higher at 80 per cent compared with 75 per cent. These factors resulted in higher wear rates and energy requirements for crushing, with the cost rising to US$1.72 per tonne, compared with the feasibility study figure of US$0.94 per tonne crushed.

» Power costs averaged US$0.052 per kilowatt hour (kWh), compared with the feasibility estimate of US$0.040, due to higher gas costs and increased consumption of 39 kWh per tonne, compared with the estimate of 34 kWh per tonne.

» Cyanide costs increased due to consumption of 0.86 kg per tonne of ore, compared with the original estimate of 0.68 kg per tonne.

» Contract mining costs increased to US$0.79 per tonne, compared with an estimate of US$0.69 per tonne, due to lower feed to the crushing circuit and increased drill and blast costs due to excess water associated with the ore.

» An updated ore reserve model resulted in a 7 to 10 per cent reduction in the ore grade compared with the original feasibility study.

The cumulative effect of these events was an increase in the estimated life of mine (LOM) cost to US$9.34 per tonne of ore processed, compared with

---

5 The larger the diameter of ground ore particles the lower the total surface area provided for the leaching of gold into solution.

the original forecast of US$8.18 per tonne. Average annual gold production was estimated to decrease by 30 000 ounces per year and cash costs to increase by an additional US$65 per ounce, which resulted in a smaller ore reserve and mine life. Additionally, due to the higher waste stripping required in the first two years of operation, minimal or negative cash flow was expected for those two years of operation.

From the information we can deduce the following additional operating parameters at the time of closure:

Mill throughput = 8760 hrs/yr × 80% crushing availability × 1065 t/hr

= 7.46 million tonnes per annum

Recovered grade can be estimated from the following:

Increased cost = US$9.34 − US$8.18 = US$1.16 per tonne

This equates to an increase of US$65 per ounce. Therefore, the average recovered grade can be estimated at (US$1.16 × 31.1 (grams per ounce)) ÷ US$65, which equals 0.56 grams per tonne, which was very much lower than the original estimated grade of 1.07 grams per tonne.

Long-term average mined grade = 0.56 g/t recovered/mill recovery of 74% = 0.76 g/t

An operating cash cost per ounce can be inferred from the above data. However, this would not give an accurate picture, as the mine did not operate at the new expanded capacity for the whole of 1997 and reached steady state only in the third quarter. The actual quarterly production figures and costs are given in table 3.6.

Table 3.6: actual quarterly figures for Pegasus Gold Inc. 1997

Three-month period	March 1997	June 1997	Sept. 1997
Gold production (ounces)	6100	4938	63 947
Cash operating cost (US$/ounce)	429	408	330
Total cash cost (US$/ounce)	429	414	330
Total cost (US$/ounce)	531	517	481

Clearly, the operating costs had blown out to totally unacceptable levels (compared with the budget of US$275 per ounce)—nearly every operating parameter failed to meet feasibility expectations. Management therefore engaged a contractor who recommended three actions to lower the cost: produce copper concentrates, screen before crushing, and a coarse ore reject system.

None of these procedures were considered able to reduce the costs to viable levels.

Tip

The most critical parameter is clearly the grade. Low-grade projects are much more sensitive to adverse movements in the commodity price or operating difficulties. The higher the grade, all other factors being equal, the safer the investment.

A question of forecasting or best guessing

As you have probably noticed from the preceding sections, and as you will see throughout this book, forecasting plays a pivotal role in the valuation of projects and mining companies. Forecasting, at best, is the art of estimating the most likely outcome for individual parameters. Financial tools are then used to determine the fundamental value of the company and, in the case of a listed company, we often compare the fundamental value with the share price to determine if the stock is a buy or a sell.

The role of the financial analyst is to dissect the economic relationships, to ascertain the likely trends and to translate these observations into the most likely outcome. For example, in the case of a resource company, the analyst might model the financial impact of a new mining project that is under development. The project will be made up of the numerous parameters previously discussed, and a best estimate (or forecast) is made of the financial outcome. The project's financial outcome is then translated into the likely impact on the company as a whole.

The risk is in the ability of the analyst (or the company's management or the marketplace) to forecast accurately the inputs into the financial model. There are no secret methods for forecasting accurately and in the end an element of good luck plays a part. However, experience, consistency and the application of the best procedures will help minimise any error.

In the Pegasus example, many of the forecasts and design estimates were not achieved, which resulted in a significant negative impact on the financial outcome of the project. What is somewhat unusual is that nearly all the errors had a negative impact on the financial results, with the only positive impact being the crusher utilisation, which was higher than originally expected. It is not uncommon for the errors in estimation to be both positive and negative, and, given the probability of events, the net effect often proves to be modest. In other words, the errors often tend to cancel each other out. By way of example, forecasts made by myself for an overseas company's interim profit results are compared with actual values in table 3.7.

Table 3.7: forecasting errors

	Forecast	Actual	Error (%)
Production (000s /t)	254.0	278.2	−8.7
Realised price ($/unit)	1801.0	1710.5	5.3
Revenue ($m)	457.5	475.9	−3.9
Operating cost ($m)	285.0	310.4	−8.2
Depreciation ($m)	52.0	48.5	7.2
Tax ($m)	60.2	56.7	6.2
Net profit ($m)	60.2	60.2	0.0

As table 3.7 shows, some significant errors were made, but, as luck would have it, they cancelled each other out and thus the forecast proved to be quite accurate.

For feasibility studies or company valuations it would be wrong to rely on luck to produce a reliable forecast on which important investment decisions have to be made. In later chapters techniques are discussed to help determine the veracity of the assumptions made, but there is no substitute for good data and a thorough understanding of the issues that might affect the eventual outcome.

CHAPTER 4
Commodity values and forecasting

Different commodities trade at different prices. The relative price difference between mineral commodities is a reflection not just of the current level of demand and supply, which has an impact on inventory levels and hence short-term price movements, but also of the relative scarcity of that mineral.

The scarcity — or, to put it a better way, the grade of materialisation — and to some extent the metallurgical complexity (and hence the cost to extract the commodity) are the major driving forces. Demand obviously plays a part as well. If the price is driven too high in the short term there will be substitution by other, cheaper commodities that can do the job, although perhaps not as well. If demand falls and prices become too low, then mines will close and production will fall. However, the overall commodity price rankings fall into a relative pattern of economic grades.

Table 4.1 (overleaf) lists the major mineral commodities, with typical market pricing listed in the second column. If the pricing is adjusted to US$ per tonne then, as shown in column three, the ranking of commodities in the table is in descending order. Gold is the most valuable at US$58.2 million per tonne, while the price of iron ore is US$230 per tonne. It can't be argued that high demand drives the relative price, as annual demand for gold is 4000 tonnes, while for iron ore it is 2.3 billion tonnes.

The difference in price lies in the relative grade or scarcity of the minerals and the difficulty in locating and processing them. As shown in table 4.1, for gold the average grade can vary between 0.0001 per cent for open cut mines and 0.0008 per cent for underground mines, while for iron ore the grades vary between 50 per cent and 65 per cent iron content. Additionally, it is easier to find an economic iron ore deposit than a gold deposit, and saleable gold needs to be recovered from the ore, while often minimal processing is required for the sale of iron ore. The barriers to entry are greater for iron ore, due to the high capital cost required for the infrastructure compared with gold, but this is compensated for by the very large economies of scale in dealing with a bulk commodity.

Table 4.1: major mineral commodities and their prices

Commodity	Typical pricing (US$)	Price (US$/ tonne)	Average mine grade (%)		Value per tonne of ore (US$)	
			Low	High	Low	High
Gold	1650/oz	58 185 600	0.0001	0.0008	58	465
Silver	30/oz	1 057 920	0.0015	0.003	16	32
Uranium	52/lb	114 608	0.1	0.3	115	344
Tin	9.50/lb	20 938	0.5	2	105	419
Nickel	8.80/lb	19 395	1	3	194	582
Copper	3.65/lb	8 045	0.5	2	40	161
Rutile*	2400/t	2 400	3	5	72	120
Aluminium	1.00/lb	2 204	25	35	551	771
Zinc	0.90/lb	1 984	3	10	60	198
Lead	0.90/lb	1 984	2	8	40	159
Oil	100/bbl	740	100	—	592	851
Coking coal†	235/t	235	75	85	176	200
Iron ore	2.30/unit	230	50	65	115	150
Steaming coal†	120/t	120	75	85	90	102

* Equivalent including ilmenite.
† Based on washery recovery.

The relationship between grade and price can be shown as in figure 4.1 by plotting, say, the low-grade average values against the price per tonne. A log-log scale has been used, given the large variation in values, and a linear trend is observed, although many relationships can approach linearity on a log-log scale. It would be incorrect to use figure 4.1 to predict price movements on the basis that all the commodities should lie on the line of best fit. As mentioned before there are other factors—such as ease of discovery, barriers to entry and metallurgical processing—that further influence the position of the commodity on the chart.

Figure 4.1: relationship between commodity grade and price

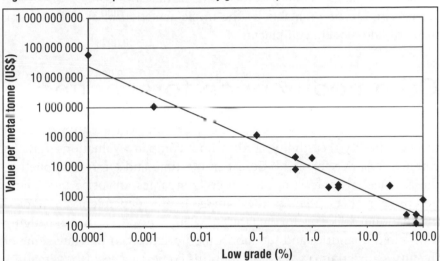

The final two columns of table 4.1 show the value per tonne of ore in the ground, based on the approximate low and high average grades. The interest in minerals by the equity markets, and to a lesser extent corporate entities, is often influenced by the current value in the ground and the forecast of that commodity's likely performance. For example, the average value of gold in the ground of between US$58 and US$465 per tonne of ore is very attractive given the low barriers to entry. Nickel projects have been keenly sought with the values of between US$194 and US$582 per tonne of ore, and even more so when the price of nickel reached US$54200 per tonne of metal in May 2007, which equates to between US$542 and US$1620 per tonne of ore! Obviously, the individual project economics have to be considered, and in particular the technology that needs to be employed, but the potential profits are quite significant. Aluminium looks attractive, but the process route is more complex where the raw commodity mined is bauxite, which has to go to a smelter to produce alumina and then on to a refinery to finally produce the metal. The costs of production are therefore relatively high, which requires a high in-ground value to justify mining and processing.

Oil projects continue to be keenly sought, due to the high value of the commodity, although it is not a question of grade per se, but rather of the level of recovery from the reservoir, as oil is not directly mined. For low-volume bulk commodities, such as iron ore and coal, which have massive reserves and large volumes of demand, significant economies of scale are required to be profitable by the implementation of efficient mining methods and modern equipment.

Commodity price forecasting

One of the most sensitive and, perhaps, most important factors in the valuation of a project or resource company is the future price of the commodity. Feasibility studies and company valuations rely on commodity price forecasts. Considerable time and effort is applied to the 'science' of forecasting. Resource companies are price takers and not price makers: that is, they are generally dependent on quoted international prices over which they have no control. The use of hedging for limited quantities and for short time horizons can mitigate some of the future uncertainty over price, but this comes at a cost (these matters are dealt with in more detail in chapter 9).

The likelihood is that any forecast will prove to be wrong over time, and the aim is to determine the most probable outcome based on information available at the time the forecast is made. Alternatively, such as in the case of an independent expert report, it may be more appropriate to forecast what the market is currently assuming, which may or may not be the same as the most probable outcome. The types of forecasting tools available are shown in figure 4.2.

Figure 4.2: price forecasting tools

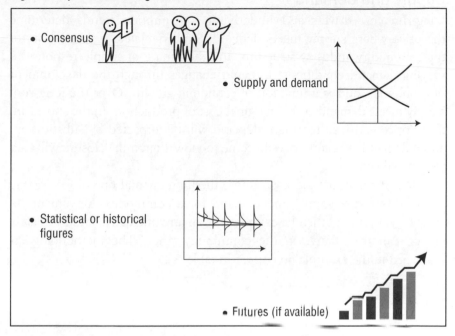

Consensus

There are numerous commercial suppliers as well as stockbroker analysts and economists who provide commodity price forecasts. The methods that they use individually to arrive at their forecasts may be varied, and in some cases unknown to the market, but as a whole (or on average) they may represent the market's view of likely future commodity prices.

Table 4.2 shows the consensus (average) forecast for gold and the standard deviation in June 2011 based on stockbroker estimates. One difficulty is that the number of analysts forecasting further into the future decreases rapidly and there are very few that provide long-term forecasts.

Table 4.2: broker consensus forecast for the price of gold, 2011–14

Nominal	2011(a)	2012(f)	2013(f)	2014(f)	LT(f)
Financial year price (US$/oz)	1376	1475	1455	1513	1500
Standard deviation (US$/oz)		129	186	150	150

Source: Author.

Supply and demand

Long-run cost drivers and underlying consumption trends determine the price where supply meets demand. Supply relates to the scarcity of the commodity, industry structure, and the timing of supply response to varying demand conditions. Demand changes through the development of economies, and is a function of economic growth. Over the long run, supply meets demand at the marginal cost of production. In the short run, if the price is driven too high, demand will be impacted by substitution, and if demand falls and prices become too low, then mine closure will lead to reduced supply.

The principal method is therefore the fundamental one of forecasting the world's future supply and demand for a commodity. Movements in inventory levels can then be estimated from any imbalance and ultimately so too can the change in the commodity price. The methodology is described in the example on copper in table 4.3.

Tip

Empirical studies of past forecasts have shown that the success rate for commodity price forecasting is very poor. The world commodity markets are very complex and, more often than not, some unforeseen event causes markets to take a direction other than the consensus view. This was clearly seen by the impact of the GFC on the demand for metals. Some forecasts are correct some of the time, but as a general rule it is best for projects to be low-cost operations and hence have the best natural insulation against falls in commodity price.

As discussed in chapter 14, for base and precious metal operations a cutoff grade is applied in defining what constitutes economic and non-economic ore. As a commodity price increases, cutoff grades fall and hence lower grade ore, which was not economic, becomes economic. Most mining operations are process-plant constrained so that the same amount of lower average grade ore is processed to produce less metal. Therefore in the short to medium term, mining operations produce less metal as prices rise, thus exacerbating the supply shortage, which is likely to be the primary reason for the price rise.

When prices fall, the opposite occurs and mining companies produce more metal to maintain revenue and this time put downward pressure on the commodity price cycle. In the longer term, higher prices will encourage substitution and new mining projects to come on stream, thus bringing balance into the market. On rare occasions, such as in the case of aluminium, major producers will shut down operations in the short term to help commodity prices recover.

Supply side

The supply side of the equation is more commonly the easier task to perform in fundamental analysis of commodity prices. On the micro scale, it is possible to forecast the likely change in commodity supply by listing all of the expected changes in current producing capacity. A simplified example for copper is shown in table 4.3. A similar approach can also be taken with smelting capacity to ensure that there are no bottlenecks in the production of copper metal. A difficulty that arises in predicting annual production of copper is the net contribution of China, Russia and secondary scrap supply.

Table 4.3: world copper mine production, 2011–12 (thousands of tonnes)

Project	Country	2011 (est.)	2012 (forecast)
Alumbrerra	Argentina	120	130
Andina	Chile	225	238
Antamina	Peru	310	379
Bingham Canyon	US	190	200
Buenavists	Mexico	180	250
Candelaria	Chile	170	180
Cerro Verde	Peru	270	290
Chino	US	32	52
Chuquicamata	Chile	400	400
Collahuasi	Chile	400	414
Cuajone	Peru	155	165
El Abra	Chile	145	130

(continued)

Table 4.3: world copper mine production, 2011–12 (thousands of tonnes) (*cont'd*)

Project	Country	2011 (est.)	2012 (forecast)
El Teniente	Chile	390	410
El Tesoro	Chile	95	100
Ernest Henry	Australia	85	50
Escondida	Chile	730	790
Grasberg	Indonesia	454	500
Highland Valley	Canada	100	105
La Caridad	Mexico	100	105
Los Pelambres	Chile	384	419
Lumwana	Zambia	161	167
Morenci	US	57	60
Mount Isa	Australia	158	160
Ok Tedi	PNG	130	135
Olympic Dam	Australia	187	182
Pampa Norte	Chile	270	280
Palabara	South Africa	73	74
Radomiro	Chile	450	450
Sossego	Brazil	95	100
Topuepala	Peru	125	130
Zaldivar	Chile	131	135
Other	—	10 019	10 720
Total		**16 800**	**17 900**

At best, estimates have to be made from anecdotal evidence, estimates of internal demand growth and the prospects of new mine developments. All these factors put together make the scenario shown in table 4.4.

Table 4.4: copper production scenario, 2011–12

	2011 (est.)	2012 (forecast)
World mine production	16 800	17 900
World scrap	3 700	3 550
Total availability	**20 500**	**21 450**

One further point to note is that mines have finite reserves and resources. In an environment of increasing metal prices, companies can consider increasing production through mine and plant expansion, if they have sufficient ore. Figure 4.3 shows the reserves, the resources and the inferred resources for approximately two-thirds of the world's production in 2006 (120 mines). At the then plant capacity, reserves and all resources would be insufficient by 2011 (assuming an infinite price). However, copper mining companies would not appear to have large tonnages of resources many times in excess of their reserve base that could be made available to meet increased capacity. That is not to say that some individual mines can't increase capacity because they do have significant additional resources, and that some mines may not have other targets and extensions to existing orebodies that have not been adequately defined by drilling to be included in their reserve and resource inventory.

Figure 4.3: copper mine reserves and resources, 2006–33

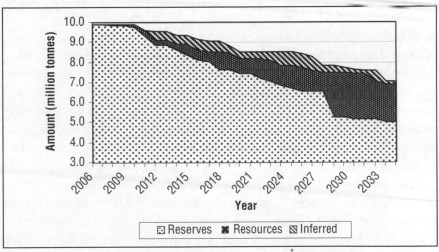

Demand side

There is, generally, a significant correlation between annual consumption and industrial production. Figure 4.4 shows the yearly percentage change for historical industrial production in the US. Although, as would be expected, there has been significant growth in the US economy over that time, in the short term there are both negative and positive cycles, such as 1989 to 1991 and 1992 to 2000 respectively.

Figure 4.4: percentage change for industrial production, 1983–2011 (US)

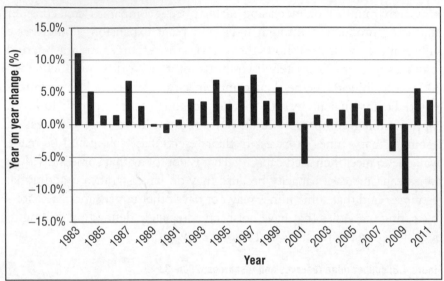

As industries grow, not only does the requirement for more raw materials increase, but also the intensity of usage (the amount of metal required to do the job) changes over time. The stage of development of an economy determines the pattern of demand growth where per capita metals demand moves along an S-shaped curve. The beginning represents the slow early phase of development, the middle represents the boom time, while the end represents a deceleration as demand matures. Demand is impacted by consumer stocking and destocking cycles, and speculative trade.

The difficulty is in determining likely world growth and the requirement for mineral commodities. Once an estimate is made it is possible to predict the change in world inventory levels, as shown in table 4.5. Estimates of true world inventory levels are also very difficult to determine, as much inventory may be held privately.

Table 4.5: changes in world inventory levels of copper, 2011–12

	2011 (est.)	2012 (forecast)
World supply	20 500	21 450
World growth (%)	3.9	4.3
World demand	20 067	20 930
Stock level	432.8	519.9
Stock to demand ratio (weeks)	1.12	1.29

The inventory levels can also be shown as a stock-to-demand ratio in weeks: in other words, the number of weeks of demand that current inventory levels (stocks) could meet if all production ceased. This is a relatively important ratio as there is a strong correlation between the ratio and the metal price. An example of London Metal Exchange (LME) inventories is shown in figure 4.5.

Figure 4.5: the effect of stock on copper price

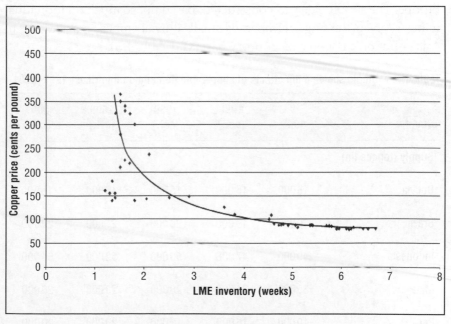

The relationship is by no means perfect, but it does show that if the stock-to-demand (liquidity) ratio increases then the copper price is likely to fall. Predictions of the future price could therefore be made. Table 4.5 shows that the stock-to-demand ratio for copper was expected to increase from 2011 to 2012. This suggests that if the calculations were correct the price of copper was likely to fall from an average of around US350¢ per pound in 2011 to US275¢ per pound in 2012, based on the scattergram in figure 4.5.

However, as mentioned before, the reliability of the prediction is dependent on the forecast for supply and demand as well as the price relationship. The supply side can encounter unexpected variations through the sudden closure of a mine or the discovery of a new high-grade, low-cost resource. On the demand side, economic dislocations, such as the Asian meltdown in the late 1990s, the 2008 GFC and the European debt crisis of 2011, can result in unforeseen declines in demand.

A further example of the difficulties that can arise with respect to the relationship between commodity prices and stock levels can be seen in a paper I wrote in the *Australian Mining Journal* (April 1999) on the price of tin. A supply and demand model was constructed with the industrial production (IP) forecast for the major consumers of tin — the US, Japan and Europe. The supply side was constructed, based not so much on individual mines — given the large number of small alluvial mines, particularly in Asia — but on a country-by-country basis (see table 4.6).

Table 4.6: example showing the effects of supply and demand on tin prices, 1997–2001

Country	1997	1998 (est.)	1999 (est.)	2000 (est.)	2001 (est.)
Supply (tonnes tin)					
Bolivia	15 000	15 000	15 500	16 000	16 500
Brazil	20 000	19 000	20 000	21 000	22 000
Indonesia	49 000	47 000	50 000	52 000	54 000
Malaysia	35 000	31 000	28 000	23 000	20 000
Peru	10 000	15 000	17 000	20 000	20 000

Country	1997	1998 (est.)	1999 (est.)	2000 (est.)	2001 (est.)
Supply (tonnes tin) (*cont'd*)					
Thailand	12000	14000	14000	14000	14000
Other	12000	11000	11000	10000	10000
China exports	25000	26000	28000	29000	30000
CIS exports	8000	8000	8000	8000	8000
USA strategic	11200	11000	11000	11000	11000
Total supply	**197200**	**197000**	**202500**	**204000**	**205500**
Demand (tonnes tin)					
US	38325	39706	41001	42321	44167
IP growth (%)	5.0	2.3	2.0	2.0	2.0
Japan	28003	28507	29077	29659	30252
IP growth (%)	4.1	1.8	2.0	2.0	2.0
Germany	20384	21077	21499	21929	22367
IP growth (%)	4.0	3.4	2.0	2.0	2.0
UK	10748	10877	11073	11295	11521
IP growth (%)	1.4	1.2	1.8	2.0	2.0
France	8404	8618	8808	8984	9163
IP growth (%)	3.8	2.5	2.2	2.0	2.0
Rest of Europe	22000	23500	25000	26000	27000
Other industrials	6500	6500	6600	6700	6800

(*continued*)

Table 4.6: example showing the effects of supply and demand on tin prices, 1997–2001 (*cont'd*)

Country	1997	1998 (est.)	1999 (est.)	2000 (est.)	2001 (est.)
Supply (tonnes tin) (*cont'd*)					
Developing countries*	51 000	53 000	57 000	60 000	63 000
Total	**185 386**	**191 797**	**200 067**	**206 896**	**214 280**
Reported stocks	45 889	48 491	49 707	48 259	43 869
LME stockpiles	11 000	11 624	11 915	11 568	10 516
Stock/Demand ratio (weeks)	12.9	13.1	12.9	12.1	10.6
LME price (US$/lb)	2.55	2.55	2.60	2.70	2.80
Actual price (US$/lb)	–	2.48	2.42	2.42	2.00

* Primarily Malaysia, South Korea, Taiwan and Thailand.

Once the change in expected inventories was forecast, the next job was to look at the historical relationship between stocks and prices on the London Metal Exchange (LME) and use the relationship to forecast tin prices. When the results were plotted on a scattergram, as shown in figure 4.6, two clusters became apparent. These could have been random, but on looking at the dates, two sequences were evident over the previous 16 months. The last eight months, during a period of high tin prices, showed a flatter line of best fit, while the previous eight months had a line of best fit that was much steeper, when stocks were higher. What this showed was the market adjusting for the tightness in inventories and anticipating either additional production to make up the shortfall in inventories and lower demand in the near term due to the high prices. The obvious questions when trying to forecast over the next few years were: which relationship to use and how would it change in the future?

Figure 4.6: scattergram of LME stocks and prices

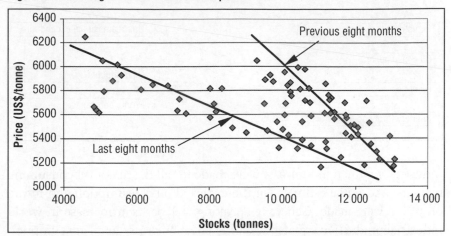

The results of the model are clear in that, having forecast modest price increases over the three-year forecasting period of the model (1998 was almost complete, but not all the statistics were available), the tin price fell dramatically in 2001. The primary reason was that industrial production had fallen that year as the world economies weakened and demand fell. The result was the closure of many smaller operations in Asia. With increasing demand over recent years, a shortage of supply developed by late 2006, as old alluvial mines failed to come back on stream, has resulted in significant price increases to this day.

By way of further illustration of the pitfalls of commodity price forecasting, I developed the following model in 1994 to predict future oil prices. As a first step, a number of important relationships were established:

» There was a very close linear relationship between world industrial production and consumption of oil.

» A reasonable correlation existed between world oil consumption and the oil price.

» A strong correlation existed between the price of oil and the level of upstream capital expenditure (exploration and oil field development). It was therefore possible to forecast the level of future capital expenditure based on forecast oil prices and installed production.

The relationship can be shown graphically (see figure 4.7, overleaf).

Figure 4.7: oil industry relationships

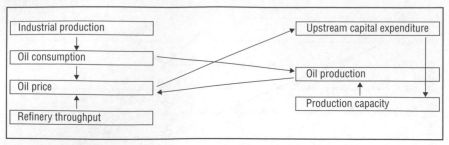

Industrial production forecasts were made for all the major oil consuming markets, and initial estimates of the expected oil consumption and future oil prices were made. Generally speaking, a 1 per cent increase in world industrial production equated to a 0.5 per cent increase in oil consumption and a US$1 per barrel price increase.

Once the future oil prices had been predicted it was possible to forecast upstream capital expenditure, and thus future installed production capacity. The model revealed a shortfall in installed production capacity by 1997, and in particular in 1998. The future oil price was therefore increased in small increments to increase capacity until forecast demand was met. The results of the forecast for the West Texas Intermediate (WTI) oil price per barrel — shown including and excluding Iraqi production, and the subsequent actual prices — are listed in table 4.7.

Table 4.7: forecasts and actual prices for oil, 1994–98

	WTI oil price (US$/bbl)				
	1994	**1995**	**1996**	**1997**	**1998**
Original forecast	17.53	18.73	20.33	22.73	24.15
Excluding Iraqi production	17.53	18.73	23.63	29.33	30.75
Actual price	17.21	18.42	22.16	20.61	14.43

The forecasts, particularly in the case of no Iraqi production, were too optimistic for 1997 and again too optimistic for 1998. This is consistent with most forecasts, and perhaps underestimates the ability of the resources industry to meet production requirements. Although the forecasts for industrial production and consumption were reasonable, supply was more easily met from existing production facilities than originally anticipated. The constraining factor of upstream capital expenditure did not materialise as expected, particularly among the OPEC nations.

More importantly, non-OPEC production increased more rapidly as prices rose. Other factors—such as seasonality, trade restrictions and declining economic conditions in Asia and Russia—also played a major part in oil price volatility. Since then we have seen higher than expected demand particularly from China and some level of price speculation resulting in significant oil price increases, peaking at US$147 per barrel by July 2008. The advent of the GFC and the prospects of weaker global growth have resulted in a significant fall in the price of oil, but it is still well above historical levels.

Statistical—mean reversion

Volatility is an observable trait of commodities and it is this volatility ironically that adds much to the value of resource projects and mining companies, as we will see in chapter 15. As discussed previously, the aim is to provide at best a meaningful forecast of commodity prices. The Monte Carlo methodology, which is discussed in chapter 13, involves the random selection of values from a statistical distribution of a particular parameter, often based on previous observations, to generate in this case likely future commodity prices.

For most natural phenomena the forecast of possible outcomes results in a normal distribution. A normal distribution is a symmetrical curve with the highest probability or likely outcome (mode) equal to the average (mean) and where 50 per cent of the observations are lower, and the other 50 per cent of observations higher, than the mean (mode). In other words the distribution is bell shaped, as shown on the left of figure 4.8 (overleaf). Because commodity prices cannot be negative, the distribution of possible random commodity price forecasts results in a log normal distribution, as shown on the right of figure 4.8. The log normal distribution is not uncommon when exploration samples are collated and in other cases where you can't have negative values. The log normal assumption is also important when it comes to valuing company stock options, which are discussed in more detail in chapter 15.

Figure 4.8: normal and log normal distributions

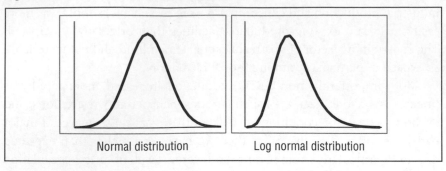

Normal distribution   Log normal distribution

As the log normal distribution is skewed to higher values, the application of this model to commodity price forecasting can lead to forecast values increasing to ever-higher prices over time, which in some ways is consistent with the assumption that inflation should result in higher prices. This is perhaps more likely in the case of share prices rather than commodity prices, where technology advances (reduced intensity of usage) may mitigate the likelihood of a positive long-term trend. However, historical observation and the conservative nature of forecasters often result in commodity price forecasts eventually returning to historical long-term averages. A good example of this long-term average is the copper price over the last five years, as shown in figure 4.9.

Figure 4.9: five-year copper price 2006–11

Although volatile, the price began and ended at around US$3.40 per pound over the five-year period. If we make the assumption that this will continue to happen over the next five years or more, then we can model five-year simulations of future copper prices on, say, a quarterly basis as shown in figure 4.10. Only 10 simulations and the average in bold are shown. Each of the simulations is a mean reversion process with the same price volatility as the historical data and represents a possible forecast of future prices. The simulations show that the average reverts to the price target of US$3.40 per pound with a similar frequency (half-life) as the historical data.

Figure 4.10: 10 copper price simulations over five years (average is shown as bold line)

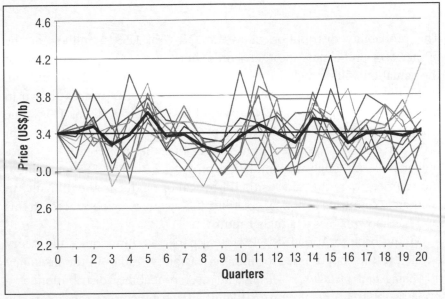

If the net present value (NPV) for a project is calculated for each price simulation and repeated many times, a cumulative distribution of the possible NPV outcomes can be generated as shown in figure 4.11 (overleaf), which is based on 5000 simulations. This is a simplified Monte Carlo simulation for a project where the only variable is the commodity price, assuming that the future price will exhibit a mean reversion to the historical long-term price (US$3.40), volatility and half-life. Note this is a major assumption that could prove to be far from the actual outcome.

Figure 4.11: example of NPV cumulative probability distribution for a project

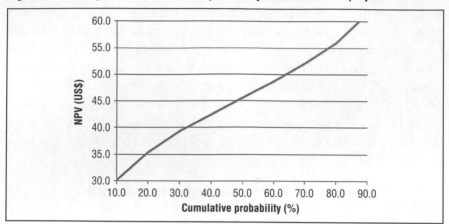

The probability distribution shows an NPV of US$45 million at the 50 per cent probability: in other words there is a 50 per cent chance that the valuation will be higher than US$45 million based on the simulation. If the future copper prices were to repeat the historical prices shown in figure 4.9, then the resultant NPV would be US$32.5 million. This value equates to a probability of 15 per cent in figure 4.11 or an 85 per cent (100 per cent – 15 per cent) probability that the project would have a higher NPV. Although the simulation provides a similar NPV outcome if future prices were the same as the historical ones, due to the difficulty in accurately capturing historical volatility, the mean reversion process in this case has shown a bias to a higher return.

Going back to April 1982, I wrote a paper on a random walk theory applied to the copper price for mining feasibility studies in the *Institution of Mining and Metallurgy — Transactions*. A probability distribution of a project's internal rate of return (IRR) was determined, not too differently from the Monte Carlo analysis described in chapter 13. For historical yearly average copper prices, statistical tests were undertaken which showed that the yearly changes in the copper price were normally distributed with a specific mean and standard deviation. It was this statistic that was used for the Monte Carlo simulation to predict future random prices to generate a probability distribution of the project's IRR.

However, to get a more statistically reliable distribution of yearly changes it was necessary to remove an apparent upward trend in the copper price. Both linear and log trends were tested. As stated in the paper, the acceptance of the continuation in the price trend would be up to the analyst doing the feasibility study. The trend had a material impact on the overall IRR, but not on the spread of the resulting probability distribution of possible outcomes (this assumes of course that the historical yearly price differences will be the same in the future).

The year-end copper price since 1982 has maintained an even higher volatility, and a larger positive yearly trend due to the recent and significant price increase. Figure 4.12 (overleaf) shows the adjusted (trend removed) yearly changes. To undertake a feasibility study, an assumption is made, as is often the case, of a steadily increasing commodity price (nominal terms). This assumption ignores the past reality of highly volatile commodity prices particularly in recent years, and so runs a significant risk. The application of sensitivity analysis does not check for volatility, but rather the risk of choosing the wrong starting price or trend.

One final observation: there are almost as many negative price moves as there are positive, and importantly there are few trends, except for the periods from 2003 to 2006 (positive), and 1995 to 1998 (negative). In other words, changes in commodity prices can be dramatic from year to year and don't have to show any meaningful cycles. This observation was also made for the copper prices prior to 1982.

Tip

Given the availability of cheap computer power, it may be worthwhile undertaking a simple Monte Carlo analysis of a project applying only the distribution for commodity price changes. The distribution may be based on the past, which could prove to be an unreliable substitute, but it certainly beats just a linear trend.

Futures

Hedging through the use of futures is discussed in more detail in chapter 9, but simply, futures contracts provide a mechanism whereby the seller and buyer of a commodity can agree in advance to undertake a transaction for a fixed amount of a commodity at a fixed price at some time in the future. This would suggest that futures could provide a mechanism for estimating future commodity prices. The difficulty is that futures contracts are not available for all commodities and those that are may extend for only a short time relative to the life of the mine.

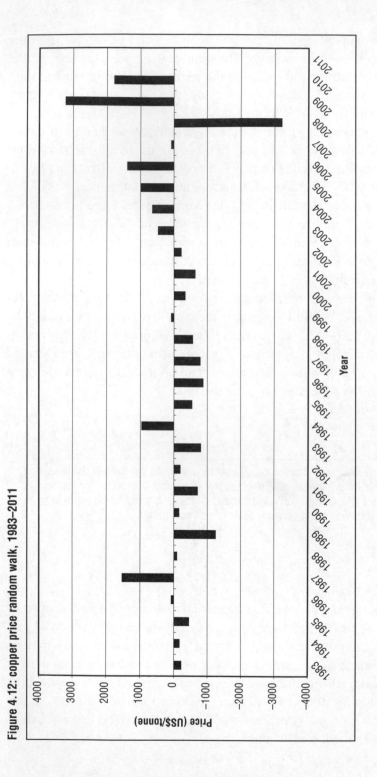

Figure 4.12: copper price random walk, 1983–2011

More importantly, forward curves are generally not good predictors of future prices. Figure 4.13 (overleaf) shows the spot LME copper price between October 2010 and October 2011 — a very volatile time for commodities. The first futures curve shows that the forward price for copper as at 4 January was in backwardation (declining) and falling to a price of US$4.05 per pound in 27 months. The three-month forward price was US$4.41, but three months later the spot price (price on the day) had fallen to US$4.27. The forward curves don't vary significantly from the spot price on the day and by October 2011 the forward curve was in contango (increasing) initially, but then back into backwardation.

Some commentators argue that the forward price curves should be used in forecasting future commodity prices for financial modelling, as they supposedly represent the best estimate based on all available information at that point in time. The view is that failure to use the forward curve, particularly for gold where it is always in contango, may undervalue the company and hence provide an arbitrage situation for a hostile takeover. The difficulty, as well as the forward curves being a poor forecast of future prices, is that forward markets are not available for all commodities. Further, for valuation purposes the forward curves may not represent the consensus view of investors in a particular equities market, and, in the case of a takeover, the view of the bidder.

In the case of gold the forward price curve relates to interest rate differentials rather than a market view of supply/demand and where the price might go. This is critical for gold, as while futures contracts for other commodities and exchange rates might reflect a market consensus of likely future prices, in the case of gold they do not!

In any forecasting process the best estimates of future operating outcomes are used to determine a project's valuation. The valuation, particularly if it is a public report, needs to be stationary for a reasonable time frame. In other words the valuer must be able to say 'Here is my valuation and I believe it will be valid for a reasonable length of time to allow investors time to make a decision based on that valuation.' Although commodity prices might change from day to day, the valuer has decided on a future price scenario that will not change as a result of those day-to-day price changes as long as there is no unexpected catastrophic event.

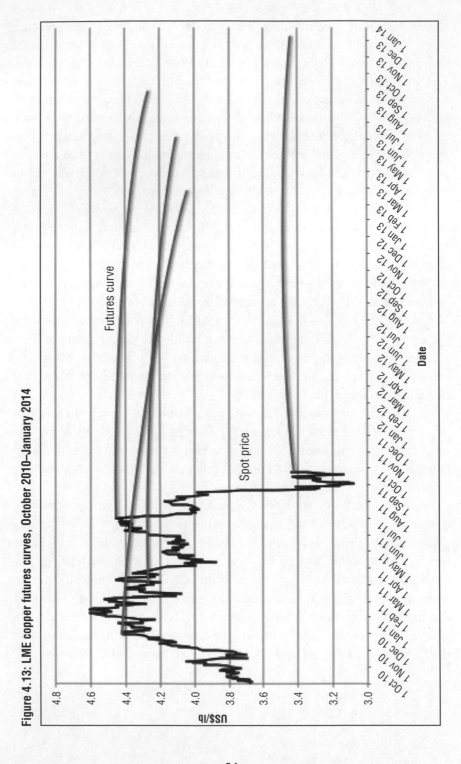

Figure 4.13: LME copper futures curves, October 2010–January 2014

If future price curves are used for the commodity price determination, and the futures price curve is the best estimate based on all information on that day, then it is reasonable to assume that, if the next-day future price curve, based on the best available information, changes, then so must the project valuation. The valuer can't argue on the one hand that the future price curve on the day of the valuation is the best estimate available of all information and then the next day argue that the best available information should not be included, particularly since the valuation could be very sensitive to the movement in the next day price change, as it can impact all along the price curve. The problem therefore in using a future price curve is that it doesn't allow for a stationary forecast price assumption.

CHAPTER 5
Resource project considerations

In determining the value of a resource project, and ultimately the value of a resource company, it is important to have an understanding of the major components that make up the project and its financial parameters. Chapters 5 to 7 provide a basic overview of the following issues:

» *Exploration.* The techniques employed to find a mineral or hydrocarbon prospect. This is followed by sampling procedures to define the grade/quality and size of the resource.

» *Reserves.* The methodologies used to determine the amount of minerals or hydrocarbons that can be economically recovered, given the sample information and data provided in the exploration program.

» *Classification of reserves and resources.* The standards for defining the differences between a resource and a reserve (economically recoverable portion of a resource), and applicable confidence levels as set by organisations such as the Joint Ore Reserve Committee, the Canadian Securities Administrators and the American Society of Petroleum Engineers.

» *Mining and hydrocarbon production.* The various methods for the extraction of near-surface and deeper mineral deposits. The technology employed for oil and gas production is also explained.

» *Mineral processing.* The procedures for separating the valuable ore-forming minerals from the as-mined products and concentrating the ore minerals in order to reduce the tonnage to be transported to smelters and refineries where the valuable commodity will finally be recovered to meet consumer market specifications. For oil and gas, this is the on-site processing undertaken to separate some of the hydrocarbon streams and deleterious products.

» *Infrastructure*. The mine and mineral processing plant and additional facilities such as power, water, transport, port facilities, communications and accommodation.

» *Smelting and refining*. The process for recovery of the metalliferous commodities from the mineral concentrate produced at the mine. The most common form is smelting of sulphidic ores, followed by a refining process to produce a marketable product. Alternatively, an increasing number of hydrometallurgical processes are being employed on the mine site to produce a finished product directly.

» *Marketing*. Marketing and its role in the initial viability of the project.

In chapter 20 there will be more detailed information provided on a commodity-by-commodity basis.

Exploration

The first and often most critical stage in the evaluation of a mining company is its exploration program. Its importance, and potential impact on the market value of a resource company, cannot be underestimated (examples of the impact of exploration results on company values and share prices are given in chapter 16). It is also one of the most difficult assessments to make due to the lack of hard data.

The value-added component of a significant exploration success can be many times the initial value of the company. As important as it is to the firm, it is difficult to predict the likely outcome of an exploration program in advance, particularly for investors outside the company. However, it is important to be aware of some of the basic exploration principles and terminology in dealing with resource companies.

Exploration can be divided into several key components, which are usually applied in the following sequence:

1 regional studies and area selection

2 airborne and ground reconnaissance

3 detailed ground (surface) evaluation

4 sub-surface evaluation—exploration drilling.

The key objective is to locate drillable targets (most often hidden below unmineralised surface deposits such as soils, alluvium, laterite or overlying strata (such as thick sediments or volcanics) by using a judicious combination of techniques appropriate to a particular geologic environment that provide the best chance of defining an economic resource in a cost-effective manner. The interplay of methods is highlighted in figure 5.1.

Figure 5.1: geological exploration methodology

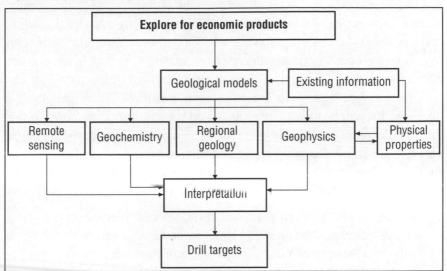

Regional study

The first phase that companies generally undertake, once they have decided on the appropriate mineral(s) to target, is to review existing literature, mines department publications and open files, and any generally available information that might highlight those areas that are prospective for the type of mineral sought. A good address or tenement location can be important because if known economic mineral deposits are nearby then the chances of success in adjacent geologically similar areas should be greater.

Regional geological maps, either existing or compiled from available data, are studied and interpreted to identify the rock types in the area; certain rock type assemblages are favourable for specific types of mineral occurrences. Exploration tenements are then acquired (by application, joint venture or purchase) over selected areas of favourable rock types.

Airborne reconnaissance

On-the-ground reconnaissance (large-scale geological mapping and geochemical sampling) carried out by field geologists can be supplemented by interpretation of aerial photographs and satellite imagery. In some instances, the orebody may outcrop at the surface, providing an easier means of location. However, more often than not, because most near-surface deposits have been discovered, the deposits will be blind (i.e. hidden or buried) and their detection will require some form of sub-surface exploration. As well as utilising aerial photography and satellite imagery, large-scale information can also be gathered using methods such as airborne geophysics (magnetics, electromagnetics, radiometrics, gravity) and airborne detailed imaging (such as side-looking radar).

The ultimate aim is to locate some form of visual or geophysical anomaly that can be further investigated on the ground or offshore. To this end, reconnaissance airborne geophysical methods (with follow-up ground surveys) are employed in detecting and then mapping the surface changes in the Earth's surface magnetic and gravimetric fields and radiometric signals that are generated by an underground (blind) orebody, as follows:

» *Magnetic survey*. The Earth's natural magnetic field interacts with magnetic mineral contained in a rock, inducing magnetism. The strength of the rock's magnetism is related to the amount of magnetic minerals (predominately magnetite—Fe_3O_4) present, often associated with igneous and metamorphic rocks. The aeromagnetic data are processed by removing the Earth's natural magnetic field to reveal anomalies in magnetic signature. In the Southern Hemisphere the high portion of the anomaly is located to the north and the low to the south of the magnetic body, and the reverse applies in the Northern Hemisphere. The position and size of the anomaly obviously depends on the depth, position and size of the magnetic body. Most magnetic surveying is now done by aircraft for both reconnaissance and detailed surveys.

» *Gravimetric surveys*. These measure variations in the Earth's gravity field. Variations are due to the density of underlying rock, with the least dense being sedimentary and the most dense extrusive igneous (basalt). Very dense and heavy minerals will also cause local variations. The effectiveness of this method can be up to 10 kilometres in depth. Proprietary airborne gravity survey methods are increasingly utilised. More accurate gravimetric surveys are conducted on the ground.

» *Radioactive surveys.* These measure the decay of radioactive elements, particularly gamma rays, which are emitted from three radioactive elements: uranium, thorium and potassium. Those areas where geological processes have concentrated minerals may concentrate radioactive elements that emit an anomalous gamma-ray reading where up to 90 per cent of measured gamma rays are received from the top 30 centimetres of the ground. Measurements can be done both from the air and on the ground.

More exotic techniques include sniffing for escaping oil and gas on the ocean's surface, using electronic sensors to detect the presence of hydrocarbons and highlight potential hydrocarbon targets, and geobotanical sampling to locate areas where plant roots have collected anomalous metals indicative of a blind mineral deposit.

Surface evaluation

Most of the reconnaissance exploration methods discussed before are also used on the ground to increase resolution. Geochemical surveys of streams, soils and subsoils (using, for instance, pits, trenches or shallow drill holes) are frequently the first step in detailed surface exploration work programs. Geological observations are made and recorded as geochemical sampling is undertaken so that geological maps and cross-sections may be built up and interpreted as the sampling progresses. Geological interpretations rank the anomalous geochemical results and prioritise geochemical anomalies for follow-up activities. Additional surface exploration methods include electrical and electromagnetic geophysical methods to test polarisation, conductivity and subsurface geochemistry for minerals, and seismic surveys for oil and gas, including:

» *Electrical and electromagnetic methods.* These are used to map variations in the polarisation (induced polarisation or IP) and the conductivity (electromagnetics or EM) of the sub-surface. For induced polarisation methods, a current is applied directly to the ground on the surface, while in electromagnetic methods, electromagnetic fields are generated in wire loops (either on the ground or suspended from a helicopter), which induce an electric current in the ground. Induced polarisation is principally used to detect large porphyry copper deposits where metallic sulpide minerals are disseminated throughout a large volume of rock. Fresh rock (unexposed) is generally a poor conductor, but metallic minerals are good conductors so the electromagnetic techniques are often applied in the search of the smaller copper, lead and zinc massive sulphide deposits, with effectiveness ranging to a depth of several hundreds metres.

» *Geochemistry*. Sampling and specialised chemical analysis of soils, some superficial deposits and stream sediments can be applied to map the chemical make-up of the soils and rocks on the ground in order to determine abnormal chemical patterns on the basis that metal ions have been dispersed from mineral deposits by erosion, or have migrated to the surface (by weathering processes or ground water circulation) from the buried mineral deposit, producing a surface geochemical anomaly. However, different elements have different mobility, so the anomaly may not contain the metal the survey is searching for, but rather pathfinder elements such as arsenic for gold.

» *Seismic survey*. For oil and gas deposits in sedimentary basins, seismic surveys are most commonly employed. The process involves firing an explosive charge or pneumatic pulse that sends a signal into the ground. The time for the reflections, from different density layers, to reach the surface is measured and translated into depth using estimates of the relative density of the sedimentary sequences to provide an image of the underground layers and structures.

Ultimately, the vast majority of exploration targets will require some form of drilling to reach down to the deposit and remove a sample that will help determine the quality, and hence the value, of the mineral commodity, and ultimately the size or tonnage or volume of the deposit.

It is perhaps worthwhile at this stage to mention the terminology of oxide and primary ore often applied to metal sulphide deposits. The oxide zone is that portion of the orebody that is above the water table (weathered). The oxide zone that has been in contact with oxygen for a long time differs in mineralogy, is generally lower in specific gravity and may be softer than the minerals of the deeper primary zone, which is below the water table and not affected by weathering. Most primary ore minerals (particularly the sulphide minerals) are stable only in anaerobic dry environments (no contact with air or oxygen). Changes in the level of the water table, plus rainwater (containing dissolved oxygen), dissolve sulphide minerals, causing them to precipitate as metalliferous oxides in the oxide zone.

The water also becomes acidic, increasing the rate at which the ore is dissolved. The most common base metal oxides include:

» copper—malachite, azurite

» iron—goethite, hematite

» lead—anglesite, cerussite

» nickel—gaspeite, garnierite

» zinc—smithsonite.

Acidic water, rich in dissolved metals, may move down through the oxidised zone and deposit the metal in a narrow band, which is just below the water table and is called the supergene zone. If formed, this is often the highest grade part of an ore deposit, although it may be small in tonnage given the thin nature of the deposition. The most common minerals found in supergene zones are:

» copper—chalcocite, bornite

» lead—supergene galena

» nickel—violarite

» zinc—supergene sphalerite, wurtzite.

For a brief summary of the geology of different types of mineral ore deposits, see appendix D.

Sub-surface evaluation—exploration drilling

Any anomalous areas indicated by the airborne and surface reconnaissance needs to be further tested and outlined in greater detail by exploration drilling. For resource companies and investors, it is the exploration drilling of a potential mineral deposit that holds the most interest and excitement in mineral exploration. Due to the major differences between the metals, coal, and the oil and gas sectors, they are covered under separate headings.

Metal and coal sector

Listed exploration and mining companies are generally required to release to stock exchanges, such as the ASX, those exploration results that may have a material impact on the share price in order to maintain a fully informed market. Companies also release important exploration results in their quarterly reports. A typical release might look like table 5.1 (overleaf).

Table 5.1: exploration drilling summary

Hole number	Northing	Easting	Interval from–to (m)	Intercept (m)	Grade (units/t)
10500	10000	500	50–65	15	4.5
10600	10000	600	55–62	7	3.8

The company may have drilled a number of exploration holes of which details for two (and perhaps they are the best two) have been released. The information generally takes the form of indicating the location of the hole (on a map, for instance), its inclination (angle), the interval below the surface at which the mineral was intercepted, the length of intersection (and preferably the true width of the mineralisation) and the grade or quality of the mineral intersected. (The level of detail provided can vary significantly between companies.)

In the example in table 5.1, the first hole, number 10500—which was located at a northing of 10000 and an easting of 500—hit the orebody 50 metres from the surface and drilled through the mineralised zone, which had a thickness of 15 metres. Assaying of the sample recovered over the 15-metre intercept was 4.5 units per tonne of ore. In the case of coal, the grade may relate to a number of quality parameters such as ash and sulphur.

The method used to drill down to and recover samples from the orebody is generally one of the following:

» *Rotary air blast (RAB)*. This is not unlike the way a home handyman's hammer drill is used to drill a hole into masonry or brickwork. A tungsten bit drills down towards the target and drill cuttings are blown back up the hole and collected as they reach the surface. This method is the cheapest, but the accuracy is the lowest. Drill cuttings arrive intermittently at the surface, providing a low level of confidence about their true location down the drill hole, and because they travel up the hole in contact with the rocks already drilled through, they are almost always contaminated by the up-hole rocks.

» *Reverse circulation (RC)*. In this process the drill bit is similar to the RAB drill (see figure 5.2) but the drill cuttings are forced up the hollow centre of the drill bit by compressed air or fluid. This is more expensive than RAB, but the accuracy is markedly increased due to the effect of immediately forcing the cuttings into the drill stem at the depth from which they are cut; this effectively cuts out up-hole contamination and also provides a well-controlled depth measurement. The accuracy is such that suitably controlled RC drilling is now extensively used to block out mineral resources and, in appropriate circumstances, ore reserves. On account of the large size and weight of RC rigs (compressors and dual-tube drill rods) their use is limited to areas that have reasonable vehicular access.

» *Diamond core drilling.* This is the time-honoured method of sampling mineral deposits, and it has been in use since the nineteenth century. Narrow, thin-walled drill tubes are used to support and rotate a diamond impregnated bit which cuts an annulus (the space between the drill pipe and the open hole formed by the drill bit) in the rock. This results in the cutting of a solid core of rock which passes through the hollow centre of the diamond bit and is collected in a special tube immediately behind the dill bit. When the tube (usually 2 metres in length) is full, it is withdrawn up the inside of the drill tubes using a wire cable winched by the drill rig. At the surface, the tube is opened and the rock core is placed in a special core tray. This is the most expensive drilling technique, but the most accurate. A solid core (from which samples can be taken) is recovered that provides geologists and engineers with a visual and physical picture of the underground mineralisation and host rock. Diamond core drilling also provides an excellent sample from a known underground location that can be used for metallurgical and geotechnical studies.

Figure 5.2: reverse circulation

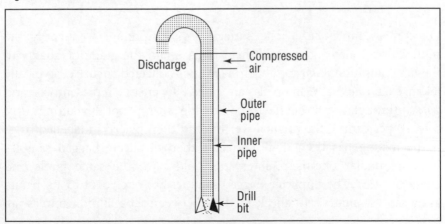

There are different size cores that can be drilled, the more typical sizes are listed in table 5.2. Larger cores can provide better data, but are more expensive to acquire generally due to the higher cost of the larger equipment and to the amount of power required by the drill rig.

Table 5.2: diamond core drill core sizes

Size	Inside (core) diameter (mm)	Outside (hole) diameter (mm)
AQ	27.0	48.0
BQ	36.5	60.0
NQ	47.6	75.7
HQ	63.5	96.0
PQ	85.0	122.6

Tip

Investors should be wary of estimates of resources based on RAB drilling alone, due to the low order of accuracy. For continuous bulk commodity orebodies, such as coal, it is not such a major issue. RC drilling is the more common drilling method, but it is important that there is strong correlation between RC results and any nearby diamond core drilling results. Twinning of selected RAB or RC holes with diamond drill holes is necessary good practice.

Once the samples reach the surface, it is important to identify the mineralised zones and sample them to ascertain the grade or quality of the mineralisation. RAB and RC drill cuttings collected at surface, typically taken over one-metre intervals, are mixed to ensure representivity and passed through a splitting device to provide a sample of the cuttings (say, 5 to 10 per cent of the original weight) and then placed in labelled bags. If the mixing has been done correctly, then duplicate bagged samples for a particular one-metre interval should have the same grade and characteristics. The duplicate bagged samples are often sent to a separate assay lab for analysis to check for bias between labs. Blind samples are also sent to the same lab to check its own internal consistency, and spare sample(s) are kept in case more checks are later required.[1]

For diamond core drilling, the core is photographed, geologically logged and sections marked for sampling. The samples are obtained by cutting (splitting) the core along the long axis, generally using a diamond impregnated circular saw system. One half is placed in labelled bags and dispatched for assaying and the remaining core is kept in storage (usually at the project site) as a record. Before a batch of samples is dispatched from the field, blind samples and company standards are inserted into the batch as assay control measures.

Oil and gas

The method employed in drilling an exploration and appraisal well for oil and gas is on a much larger scale than exploration for metal and coal deposits due to the very large depths involved, from hundreds to many thousands of metres. For example, a tungsten hardened tri-cone drill bit may be used—with an initial diameter of up to 1 metre—which turns and grinds away the rock. Drilling muds (mixture of water and clay and often polymers) are circulated through the centre of the hollow steel drill string, which connects the bit to the surface to lubricate the cutting, transport rock cuttings to the surface and place pressure on the bottom of the hole to prevent any blow-out of high pressure gases that may be encountered on the way. Weighting materials can be added to the mud to increase hydrostatic pressure and allow safe drilling.

The drilling mud has a specific density defined by the amount of clay added and therefore an increased hydrostatic head over that for pure water. For example, adding 10 pounds of clay per gallon, the weight of the column at 2000 feet is approximately 1000 pounds per square inch (psi). If the pressure of the reservoir is greater than 1000 psi at that depth, then it is said to be over-pressured; if the pressure is less then it is termed 'under-pressured'.

The drill cuttings and the mud return to the surface up the annulus, where samples are caught. Rock chips are examined under a microscope so that their mineralogy and potential reservoir characteristics, including

1 Unless careful checking procedures are in place fraudulent results may be released to the market. For example, in January 1997 the Busang gold deposit in Indonesia was estimated to have had a resource of 70 million ounces. Shortly thereafter, it was found to contain no significant amounts of gold, making it one of the largest mining frauds in history. Nearly all the core over two-metre intervals was crushed and assayed, so that check samples were not available. The samples were also tampered with by the addition of gold (salting). With poor procedures making independent verification of results difficult, only proper supervision could have limited the potential for a hoax of this magnitude.

porosity, can be described and to observe if they have traces of visible oil. The samples are tested under ultraviolet light, as oil is very fluorescent; the company might report the occurrence of strong fluorescence, which may be an encouraging sign. Drilling mud is also analysed for any gas or volatile hydrocarbons, which are reported as gas shows. However, these reports may prove only that at some time oil and gas were present in the reservoir, and this may no longer be the case.

After drilling to a certain depth, steel casing will be placed in the hole and cement forced between the casing and the sides of the well. A smaller diameter bit will then be lowered down through the narrower casing to recommence the drilling operations. These operations may be repeated a number of times before the total depth of the well is reached. Figure 5.3 shows a typical time versus depth chart for an oil and gas exploration well, including changes in casing diameter and several well logs and production tests before the well was plugged and abandoned.

On entering the reservoir sands or areas of interest, a diamond coring bit may be used to take a vertical core (termed a whole or full diameter core) for porosity and permeability tests, which are important parameters in assessing a reservoir's quality, as well as in forming a geological interpretation. Less accurate, but cheaper, is the side wall core, which is recovered from a tool lowered down the hole on a cable. Small horizontal core plugs are collected from the wall of the well and a sample of rock recovered from areas of interest defined by electric logging after the section has been drilled. The presence of oil and gas in the pores of the rock can affect the physical properties of the rock.

Electric logs are acquired by lowering instruments down the well to measure a range of physical properties such as electrical resistivity, radioactivity, self-potential and sonic velocity. The relative differences for alternate rock types are shown schematically on an exaggerated scale in figure 5.4 (on p. 80). Originally the instruments were lowered down the hole by wireline after the drill string had been removed; nowadays the instruments are part of the drill string and are located behind the drill bit as it drills through a section of interest. Logging tools today have become very sophisticated in measuring and evaluating a vast array of wellbore properties.

Ultimately it is important to undertake a test that recovers hydrocarbons to provide the engineers with a sample of reservoir fluid and a closer approximation of the reservoir's likely performance under full commercial production. One test is a wireline formation interval test where a test chamber is lowered by wire to the reservoir, and, using expanding rubber packers above and below, is sealed against the well walls. Valves are opened to allow any fluids to flow into a chamber where 10 to 15 litres of fluid might be collected, providing not only a sample, but also the rate of flow and pressures over a very short period. A drill stem test (DST) is more expensive and more time consuming, allowing the flow of hydrocarbons to surface; again it uses packers to isolate the zone. Fluids are allowed to enter the pipe and flow to the surface where rates, pressures and temperatures are measured and samples taken.

Figure 5.3: oil and gas exploration drilling depth versus time (drilling time curve)

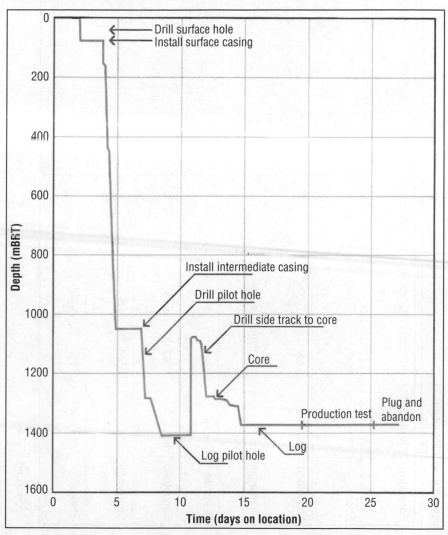

Figure 5.4: well log results

Formation	Permeability	Porosity	Content	Penetration rate	Gas shows	Neutron log	Density log	Resistivity log	Gamma ray log
Shale	Very low	High	Water						
Limestone	Low	Low	Water						
Sandstone	Low	Medium	Water						
Dolomite	Medium	Low	Water						
Sandstone	High	Medium	Gas						
Sandstone	High	Medium	Oil						
Shale	Very low	High	water						

Increasing ⟶

Finally, a full production test can be employed where the hydrocarbons are allowed to flow to the surface under controlled conditions often for extended time periods. The pressure and volume of fluids are measured, oil is collected and gas is flared (burnt). An open hole test is performed where the hole has not been cased, while if the zone is behind casing, perforations are blasted through the steel casing to get access to the reservoir. After a time the test will be stopped (shut in) to allow pressure to build up and then reopened for another measurement. This will provide further information on permeability; the reservoir's production potential is indicated by the time it takes for the pressure to rebuild between tests.

The costs of exploration can vary widely, depending on the type of exploration, location and topography of the site. Table 5.3 lists the indicative costs for a range of different exploration methodologies.

Table 5.3: indicative costs of exploration

Exploration method	Costs
Airborne geophysics	$25/km for aeromagnetics to $125/km for gravity (excluding mobilisation)
Satellite imagery	$25 to $50/km^2
Ground geophysics	$50 to $2000/km
Soil geochemistry	$10 to $20/sample (analysis only)
Rock, RC sample or diamond	$20 to $50/sample
Air photo interpretation	$200 to $500/km^2
RAB drilling	$20 to $25/metre, including sampling to a depth of approximately 60 m
RC drilling	$50 to $100/metre, including consumables (excluding mobilisation) to a depth of approximately 300 m
Diamond core drilling	$100 to $200/metre depending on hole diameter and depth, including consumables (excluding mobilisation) to a depth of approximately 1000 m
Onshore seismic 2D	Up to $10 000/km
Offshore seismic 2D	$2000/km

(continued)

Table 5.3: indicative costs of exploration (*cont'd*)

Exploration method	Costs
Onshore seismic 3D	$40 000/km^2, subject to terrain
Offshore seismic 3D	$20 000/km^2
Onshore oil and gas drilling	$1000/m (for average vertical depths of 3000 m)
Offshore oil and gas drilling	$3000 to $4000/m

Confidence level

It is important to understand that exploration results help build a picture of, and hence confidence in, three critical aspects of the mineralisation: the grade, the volume or mass, and the continuity of the orebody. The confidence level will increase as the number of data points increases. However, the number of data points required for a specific confidence level will vary greatly, depending on the geology and type of mineralisation under investigation. Figure 5.5 illustrates that lower grade type deposits can be homogeneous. Although bulk commodities, by their very nature, do tend to be more consistent, they have to be of economic size and location.

Figure 5.5: geological continuity and homogeneity

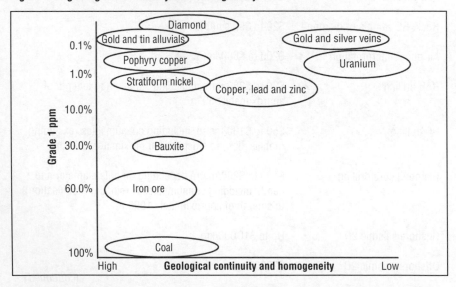

The continuity or homogeneity of the orebody is important in assessing the potential of a resource. In figure 5.6, two exploration holes have been drilled with similar mineral intercepts. The question is whether these two initial intercepts represent two distinct orebodies or a continuation of the same orebody. Geological interpretation and further drilling would ultimately resolve the issue.

Figure 5.6: exploration holes

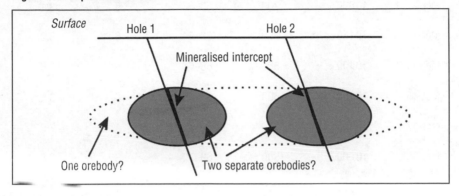

Calculating resources

Of critical importance is the translation of drill results for a deposit into a resource base. The exploration information available to the public will often be in the form shown in table 5.4 (overleaf). From this information, plus the market's general understanding of similar deposits, the company may be rapidly re-rated on the back of the published results.

Consider the results in table 5.4. The exploration results released to a stock exchange are often the best encountered and therefore the table may not be a complete list of drilling results. The company may indicate that, from geological interpretation and the other drilling results not listed, the orebody may be open (mineralisation may still continue) in a certain direction, which may be tested at a later date by further drilling. In the results shown the mineralisation deepens in a southerly and easterly direction, and becomes thinner and lower in grade in that direction.

Table 5.4 exploration results

Hole number	Northing	Easting	Interval from–to (m)	Intercept (m)	Grade (units/t)
Met-256	10 000	500	50–60	10	4.5
Met-26	10 200	600	53–62	7	3.8
Met-27	10 000	700	55–60	5	3.1
Met-1575	10 150	750	58–64	6	3.2
Met-15	10 100	500	60–66	6	3.0
Met-16	10 100	600	63–69	6	3.1
Met-17	10 100	700	66–70	4	2.9
Met-05	10 000	500	69–72	3	2.8
Met-06	10 000	600	71–73	2	2.5

Figure 5.7 shows a plan of the drill holes. It should be noted that the drill holes will probably not be drilled vertically, but at an angle, with the objective of intersecting the orebody at right angles, so that the intercept is close to the true width of the mineralisation. Companies will generally release the azimuth (compass direction) and the inclination (to the horizontal) for each of the drill holes.

Figure 5.7: drill-hole plan

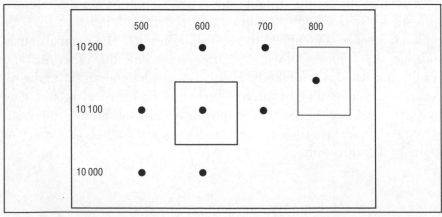

Analysts and the market will try to deduce a value from the exploration results. The orebody is likely to be more complex than the simple pattern of drilling would suggest; however, the first step is to determine the tonnage of the orebody by multiplying the volume by the ore's specific gravity (SG). Specific gravity (water has an SG of 1 and therefore 1 cubic metre weighs 1 tonne) varies greatly between different orebodies, depending on the type of mineral being sought. For example, coal seams have an SG of around 1 and lead–zinc orebodies have SGs of around 3.

Assume for the moment that the orebody defined by our drilling diagram has an SG of 2.5, or in other words 2.5 tonnes per cubic metre. For each hole an area of influence has to be applied. The area of influence is the area for which the exploration hole's thickness and grade will be applied. An area of influence, which is a square centred around the hole, is shown for hole Met-16 (coordinate 10 100N 600E) with the boundaries equidistant from the next hole.

As the holes are 100 metres apart, the size of the square is 100 by 100 metres. The thickness of the square is 6 metres (thickness of the drill intercept in table 5.4), therefore the volume of the block is:

Volume block Met-16 = 100 × 100 × 6

= 60 000 cubic metres

The tonnage is estimated at:

Tonnage block Met-16 = 60 000 × 2.5 (SG)

= 150 000 tonnes

This procedure can be carried out for each hole. The difficulty arises at the boundary where it is not clear whether the orebody stops abruptly (a fault) or if the mineralisation continues for some distance. Without further information, assume that each block has an area of influence of 100 square metres. A further difficulty arises for hole Met-1575. Perhaps, due to terrain difficulties, the drilling rig was forced to move out of line with the other holes and hence its area of influence could be considered differently. One example is shown where the area of influence is arbitrarily selected at 75 metres wide by 100 metres long.

The mineral content can then be determined by multiplying the grade per tonne by the number of tonnes. A summary is shown in table 5.5 (overleaf).

Table 5.5: mineral content

Hole number	Area (m²)	Volume (m³)	Tonnage (t)	Grade/Tonne (unit)	Metal content (units 000s)
Met-25	10 000	100 000	250 000	4.5	1125.0
Met-26	10 000	70 000	175 000	3.8	665.0
Met-27	10 000	50 000	125 000	3.1	387.5
Met-1575	7 500	38 000	190 000	3.2	608.0
Met-15	10 000	60 000	150 000	3.0	450.0
Met-16	10 000	60 000	150 000	3.1	465.0
Met-17	10 000	40 000	100 000	2.9	290.0
Met-05	10 000	30 000	65 000	2.8	182.0
Met-06	10 000	20 000	50 000	2.5	125.0
Total	87 500	468 000	1 255 000	28.9	4297.5

It is unrealistic to assume that the orebody will look like the group of somewhat disjointed ore blocks described above. Further, we have applied the grade obtained from a drill hole that is only several centimetres in diameter, over areas of influence covering thousands of square metres. Clearly, this is a major leap of faith and relates to a concept of statistical confidence level in an ore resource, which will be more fully discussed.

The areas of influence need not be squares with just one sample in the middle. As figure 5.8 shows, the areas can be triangular, square or rhomboid where an average of the corner holes can be used as the value for the area of influence. Intrinsically, and statistically, the confidence in the grade for the area of influence (or perhaps more correctly the block of ore) is higher when the average of more than one hole is used in determining the grade.

Figure 5.8: areas of influence

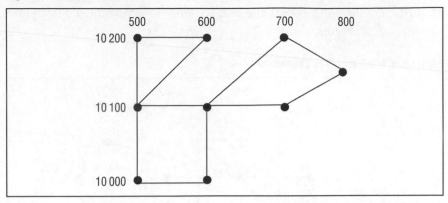

If the statistical confidence increases as more data are used in the estimation of the grade of a block, then why not use a very large number of sample points? There are two issues that need to be considered. First, by taking a large number of samples for grade determination of each block, it will tend to smooth the grade for the blocks and provide a false picture of the grade variability of the deposit and the impact of different cutoff grades (see chapter 14). Taking it to extremes, using all the data to estimate each block would result in the same value for each block, which in turn would be the average of all the data and each block would have the same grade.

Second, it might be reasonable to assume that exploration holes near a block of ore might have some correlation with the grade of that block. But the further away you move from that block, the less likely it is that a relationship would exist, until a certain point was reached where an exploration hole no longer played a role in the determination of that block's grade.

Geostatistical estimation and kriging

Consider figure 5.9 (overleaf), where a block has been selected for grade estimation. The average value of each of the nearby exploration holes could be used in determining the grade. Alternatively, assuming that exploration holes closer to the block are more highly correlated, a weighted average of the grade could be used, where the weighting is a function of the distance. The weighting could be based on an inverse of the distance so that the weighting would be lower for more distant points. This would result in a linear weighting, so perhaps the square or the cube of the inverse distance could be employed to reflect the considerably lower confidence of more distant sample points.

Figure 5.9: block for grade estimation

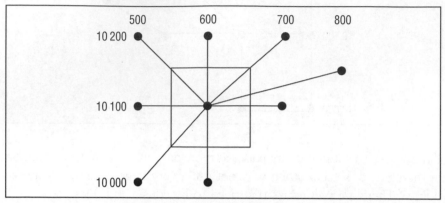

The aim is, therefore, to select a non-linear weighting that minimises the error associated with the grade estimate for the block.

The procedure for calculating the optimum weighting is called kriging after the South African geostatistician Daniel Krige, who, in 1980, was the first person who attempted to obtain the optimum weightings. The procedure for kriging is beyond the scope of this book, but the steps involved include:

1   *Generate a semi-variogram.* This graphically depicts the spatial relationship between data points, which are generated by calculating half the average squared difference in grade between any two points over a specific distance. The relationship is also conducted over a specific direction to determine if the variogram changes in different directions. If this does occur the deposit is said to be anisotropic. To generate meaningful semi-variograms adequate data points are required and a meaningful relationship needs to exist. For more highly variable or nuggetty deposits, such as gold, the semi-variogram may be more difficult to generate. Some degree of interpretation is required in fitting one of the standard models, which generally consist of: a nugget value, which is an estimate of the point grade variability; a sill, which is the lowest level of correlation; and a range, the distance beyond which there is no further correlation. Figure 5.10 shows a spherical semi-variogram with a range of 6, a nugget of 0.2 and a sill of 1.0.

2   *Simultaneous equations (kriging)*. For a selected point or ore block the distance to each exploration data point within the range of the semi-variogram is calculated and a gamma value determined from the semi-variogram model. A set of simultaneous equations is then solved that determines the set of weighting factors to be applied to each of the exploration points, which minimises the statistical error for the weighted average grade of that point or block. The weighting factors add up to 1 and the simultaneous equations include a factor for the size of the block if applicable. As well as generating a grade value for the point or block, a measure of statistical error can be generated.

3   *Back-testing and ore resources*. To check the validity of the semi-variogram model, and to optimise the model, it is possible to krige a known data point (excluding the known value) and compare it with the actual value. The ore blocks are then kriged and the total ore resources calculated. It is important to take into account the deposit's geology, as it is possible to krige a block that is within range of known data points but outside the mineralised zone, and hence phantom ore resources can be generated. Different-sized blocks can be selected, with larger blocks having lower theoretical statistical errors. Generally, smaller blocks allow for better grade resolution, but the error increases. It is best to use blocks no smaller than the selected mining unit, which conform with the selectivity of the mining fleet that will be employed in extracting the orebody.

Figure 5.10: spherical semi-variogram

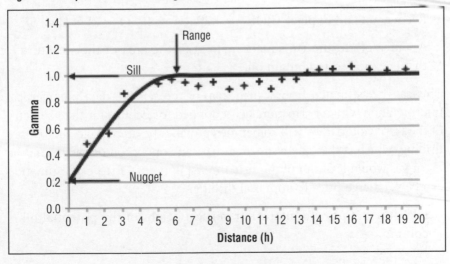

A number of different kriging procedures have been developed, including disjunctive kriging, indicator kriging and conditional simulation. However, simple kriging has the greatest application in ore resources determination.

Tip

The application of geostatistics by mining companies in the determination of ore resources is an optimum approach that minimises theoretical error. It effectively gets the most out of the available data. If data are insufficient or poor, it cannot improve the result—like the old adage 'garbage in, garbage out'.

Estimating oil and gas resources

The estimation of oil and gas resources is somewhat different from the case of hard rock mining. In most cases, due to the sedimentary environment for oil and gas accumulations, seismic data are available. This provides a visualisation of the underground structures. It is therefore possible to map the structure in terms of areal extent and thickness. Once a volume is established it is possible to estimate the theoretical quantity of oil or gas, or both, in place. The equation for estimating the possible recoverable barrels of oil is as follows (the terms are explained in the following pages):

Recoverable oil in place (ROIP) = $6.29 \times A \times NP \times P \times RF \times HS \times SF$

A = area of closure (in square metres) or the area of the structure that is expected to contain oil.

This can be estimated from a plan map of the seismic data plus vertical interpretation with a correction factor applied to account for the geometry of the trap. Companies will sometimes provide the area of closure, before drilling, which is the maximum area that can contain oil or gas before the oil or gas would leak out of the structure (spill point). Errors of estimation can be very large prior to appraisal drilling.

NP = the net pay (in metres) or vertical height of the potential oil column.

Initially this is estimated from the seismic and geological data derived from other wells in the particular sedimentary basin. It is an interpretation of the average thickness of the likely sands that would hold the oil. Sometimes it is quoted as a net-to-gross ratio that is the proportion of the total column that can produce hydrocarbons.

P = the porosity (as a fraction) of the oil or gas bearing sandstone.

The sandstone is made up of fine particles with voids or space (which potentially contain the oil) between the particles, which is designated as the porosity. Typical porosity ranges between 1 per cent and 40 per cent, with most common levels at around 15 per cent to 30 per cent. Permeability, which is the ability of the hydrocarbon to flow through the voids, is also important but is incorporated in the recovery factor.

RF = the recovery factor (as a fraction), which is the proportion of oil or gas that is recoverable from the reservoir.

This is ultimately a factor of the rock's permeability (ability of hydrocarbons and water to flow through the rock) measured in millidarcies (range of 1 mD to many darcies with typical levels in excess of 100 mD), and the pressure and driving forces such as water or gas in solution that will dictate the amount recovered. Factors such as oil properties and reservoir geometry can also influence the recovery factor. For oil fields typical recovery factors are between 10 per cent and 40 per cent, and up to 70 per cent, while for gas it commonly ranges between 50 per cent and 80 per cent.

HS = hydrocarbon saturation (as a fraction), which represents the proportion of oil present with water (found in all reservoirs in varying levels of saturation).

This is estimated by well logs with typical levels of 50 to 90 per cent.

SF = shrinkage factor (as a fraction), which is the reduction in volume recovered on the surface; sometimes the formation volume factor is used, which is the inverse of the SF.

Oil volume shrinks due to the loss of lighter fractions into the associated gas phase that goes out of solution as the pressure drops from the reservoir to the stock tank. Values commonly range from 0.50 to 0.95. In the case of a gas well, some shrinkage may occur due to the presence of non-combustibles such as CO_2, and condensates, and the removal of intermediate fractions such as propane and butane. However, due to reduction in pressure at the surface, gas expands from 50 to 350 times, depending on depth and composition of the gas. Hence a gas expansion factor is used.

The product of these factors results in the total recoverable cubic metres of hydrocarbons. The factor of 6.29 represents the number of barrels of oil in a cubic metre. By excluding the 6.29 factor, the equation equals the number of cubic metres that can then be converted to cubic feet of gas (as used in gas reservoirs) by multiplying by 35.3, or megajoules (a unit of energy) by multiplying by 93.3 (although this figure can vary depending on the calorific value of the gas). This figure then has to be adjusted for the change in pressure using the gas expansion factor mentioned before.

The veracity of the assumptions in estimating the ROIP can only be established once an exploration well has been drilled. The first confirmation will be if there are any hydrocarbons present. Evaluation of the reservoir by logging and testing will establish the quality of the reservoir (porosity and permeability) and the net pay zone. To confirm the areal extent of the reservoir will probably require the drilling of one or more appraisal wells.

Consider figure 5.11, where seismic interpretation and other exploration wells in the area predict the following:

Figure 5.11: prediction of recoverable oil in place

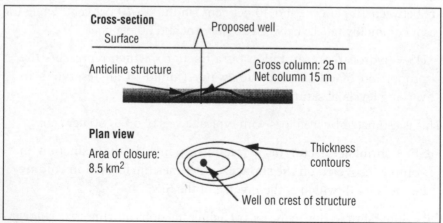

Note: not to scale.

The volumetric approach can be described as deterministic, but it is possible to use a stochastic or probability approach using the same methodology. Industry practice is to use continuous probability distributions of the likely outcome rather than a point value for a number of the parameters and combine them to determine a probability distribution of the resources. The most common approach is to use a Monte Carlo simulation (we will discuss this in chapter 13).

At a later stage, when there is sufficient pressure and production history from one or more wells to allow for the prediction of likely trends, it can be used to predict future performance and hence resources. Although probabilistic approaches can be applied, the common practice is to use a deterministic approach. Three methods are briefly described here.

» *Decline-trend analysis* is used to estimate resources on the basis of reasonably well-defined behaviour of production rate or oil cut performance characteristics. Usually used for single well analysis, this method is extrapolated until an economic limit is reached, with such estimates usually at the 90 per cent confidence level (P90) and sometimes at the 50 per cent confidence level (P50).

» *Material-balance* treats the reservoir as a tank and assumes conservation of matter whereby the pressure behaviour of the reservoir in response to the withdrawal of fluids is analysed in steps. There has to be sufficient pressure, volume temperature and production data of all fluids, and the reservoir must have reached a semi-steady state condition (pressure declining at a constant rate) or a steady state (pressure held constant—for example, aquifer drive or water injection at rates to provide voidage replacement) for the method to be applied.

» *Reservoir simulation* represents the reservoir as a set of interconnected tanks, each containing rock and fluid properties. Material balance calculations are performed for different cells, allowing for the migration of fluids via the use of Darcy's flow equation. The development plans and operating conditions are superimposed on the system, where a good relationship is required between observed history and the simulated performance to provide reliable results.

Test of wells

Listed oil and gas companies are required to make releases to stock exchanges that provide information on the success or otherwise of an exploration well. If the well is unsuccessful, then it will be plugged and abandoned. However, during the drilling of the well, as potential hydrocarbon reservoirs are reached, the company may provide some information on the thickness of the reservoir and the net pay (that proportion of the reservoir that has permeable sands that may flow oil and gas).

The results of any test may in some cases cover several zones, with only the combined results provided, which will make it difficult for the market to be certain whether all the zones are commercial. Stronger flow rates are obviously more commercially significant. Flow rates may also decline over time so that short testing periods, where the flow rate doesn't have sufficient time to stabilise, may be misleading.

Information on pressure may be provided, and often a small choke (a valve that controls the flow rate at the top of the well) may restrict the rate of flow from the reservoir. It is important that the flow rates and pressures are maintained during testing to indicate that there is a good driving force behind the reservoir for future production. The recovery of water during the test may indicate that it is near the oil/water contact — that is, the point where the oil is located just above the water.

While drilling the well, mud will be pumped down to ensure that reservoir pressure will not force the drill string out of the well and result in oil or gas blowing out at the surface, as is often shown in the movies. If the pressure from the mud is too great, it may be forced into the reservoir and cause damage. Therefore any mud acquired during testing may suggest excess mud pressure during drilling and potentially a damaged formation.

Table 5.6 lists typical ranges for the testing of oil and gas flow rates that may be announced to a stock exchange for both onshore and offshore wells.

Table 5.6: testing of oil and gas flow rates

	Oil (barrels per day)		Gas (million m^3 per day)	
Quality	Onshore	Offshore	Onshore	Offshore
Fair	300–1000	2000–5000	0.1–0.2	0.3–0.7
Good	1000–3000	5000–8000	0.2–0.5	0.3–1.0

Exploration success rates on a regional basis are quite varied, with some companies achieving zero success while a few fortunate companies have managed a near perfect success rate, generally in basins where they have been operating for many years. Once a discovery has been made the structure will probably have to be further appraised by additional wells to prove the resources and the economic viability of developing the field.

The average exploration and appraisal well success rates over 10 years for four areas are shown in table 5.7.

Table 5.7: average exploration and appraisal well success rates

Success rates	North West Shelf[†]	Zone of Cooperation[‡]	Papua New Guinea	Cooper Basin[§]
Exploration (%)	27	6	16	32*
Appraisal (%)	50	63	60	77*

*Includes a large proportion of gas wells.
[†]North West Shelf is located offshore from the northern part of Western Australia.
[‡]Zone of Cooperation is located offshore between the Northern Territory and the island of Timor.
[§]Cooper Basin is in central Australia.

Source: APEA, ABARE, Mines and Energy SA, and others.

Figure 5.12 shows onshore and offshore wildcat petroleum discoveries in Australia over time. Although technologies continue to improve the chances of success, the diminution of petroleum accumulations is possibly reflected in the downward trend from 40 per cent to 30 per cent over the 10-year period.

Figure 5.12: wildcat exploration success rates, 2000–09

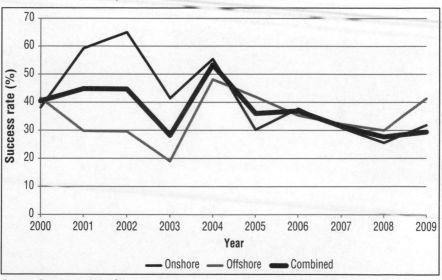

Source: Geoscience Australia.

The cost of exploration will depend on the size of rig required to drill the well. For offshore drilling, costs will depend on the depth of water and the duration to complete the well, as costs are based on a daily charge. For deep-water wells that require a drillship or semisubmersibles, the charges in the US vary from $250 000 to $450 000 per day. To this must be added additional on-costs that can double the price, so that a 100-day well could cost between $50 million and $100 million. Onshore wells are much cheaper and will depend on the depth of drilling. Costs for gas wells can range from $1 million for a well to 1500 metres and up to $10 million for a 7000-metre vertical well. The last 10 per cent of a deep gas well can account for up to 50 per cent of the total cost.

Tip

For commercial considerations wells may be put on tight hole, where no information will be provided until all testing is complete. Even information provided during testing will often be limited and difficult to interpret. More often than not, initial expectations of the size of potential recoverable hydrocarbons tend to be reported as higher than the final outcome due to the complexity of reservoir structures and deliverability.

CHAPTER 6

Classification of resources and reserves

The Joint Ore Reserves Committee (JORC), which was established in 1996 by the Australian Institute of Mining and Metallurgy (AusIMM), the Australian Institute of Geoscientists and the Minerals Council of Australia, has set a code for the classification of mineralised orebodies—the Australasian Code for the Reporting of Exploration Results, Mineral Resources and Ore Reserves (JORC Code 2004).

A number of other jurisdictions have introduced similar codes for the reporting of resources and reserves including:

» *Canadian Institue of Mining (CIM)* — CIM Standards on Mineral Resources and Reserves — Definitions and Guidelines (2000)

» *Institution of Mining Engineers of Chile (IIMCh)* — Certification Code for Exploration Prospects, Mineral Resources and Ore Reserves (2004)

» *Joint Committee of the Venture Capital Segment, Lima Stock Exchange Peru* — Code for Reporting Mineral Resources and Ore Reserves (2003)

» *PMRC Committee* — Philippine Mineral Reporting Code for Reporting of Exploration Results, Mineral Resources and Ore Reserves (2007)

» *South African Institute of Mining and Metallurgy (SAIMM)* — South African Code for the Reporting of Exploration Results, Mineral Resources and Mineral Reserves in South Africa (SAMREC 2007)

» *Institute of Materials, Minerals & Mining (IMMM)* — Code for Reporting of Mineral Exploration Results, Mineral Resources and Mineral Reserves (2001) (the standard for the UK, Ireland and Europe)

» *Society for Mining, Metallurgy and Exploration (SME)* — SME Guide for Reporting Exploration Results, Mineral Resources and Mineral Reserves (2007) (the US standard).

In 1994 the Committee of the Council of Mining and Metallurgical Institutions (CMMI) was formed with representatives from most of the aforementioned institutions to integrate the minimum standards of the other codes. In 2002 the Committee for Mineral Reserves International Reporting Standards (CRIRSCO) worked to produce the International Reporting Template (2006), which is currently an advisory code only.

As every orebody is unique, and the total exploration data may represent as little as one-ten-millionth of the total resource, the classifications are much more qualitative than quantitative. The codes recognise the unique nature of each orebody, the data available and the relevant economics. They are not prescriptive in nature, unlike the reporting codes of Russia and China, which are discussed briefly at the end of this section.

For the purposes of describing the primary aspects of various codes, the JORC Code will be used in this chapter, as most of the critical issues are common to all the codes. The level of enforcement of the codes is subject to local jurisdictions, but generally codes have become part of the listing rules of the national stock exchanges for the purpose of reporting of resources and reserves by publicly listed mining and energy companies. The most important requirement of companies in the release of their resources or reserves to an exchange, such as the ASX, is that the release is based on information compiled by a 'competent person' or in some jurisdictions a 'qualified person'. In the case of hydrocarbon reserves, the person must be qualified in the appropriate discipline. A competent or qualified person (engineer or geoscientist) in minerals is generally one who is a corporate member of an approved institution and has at least five years of relevant experience in the estimation of that style of mineralisation.

Definitions

In situ mineral occurrences may be defined as a resource if the deposit is of a concentration of intrinsic economic value and placed into one of three categories depending on the level of confidence that can be applied:

» *Inferred resources* are defined where tonnage, grade and mineral content can be estimated with a low level of confidence and when there are insufficient data to confirm continuity of the resource.

» *Indicated resources* are defined where tonnage, densities, shape, physical characteristics, grade and mineral content can be estimated with a reasonable level of confidence and when there are insufficient data to confirm continuity of the resource, but sufficient where the mineralisation's continuity can be assumed.

» *Measured resources* are defined where tonnage, densities, shape, physical characteristics, grade and mineral content can be estimated with a high level of confidence and sufficient data are available to confirm continuity of the mineralisation.

Importantly a resource is defined as having 'reasonable prospects for eventual economic extraction', which implies that excluding those portions of mineralisation that are of such low grade that they would be unlikely to be mined and treated economically must be considered. Therefore some cutoff grade, which defines that point in grade terms where blocks of ore with less than the cutoff grade are unlikely to prove to be economic, should be applied (see chapter 14 for a full discussion).

Companies can report on exploration targets in terms of target size and type. However, targets must be expressed in such a way that the information can't be misrepresented or misconstrued as an estimate of a resource or a reserve.

An ore reserve is defined as the economically mineable part of a measured or indicated mineral resource. It includes diluting materials and allowances for losses, which may occur when the material is mined. Appropriate assessments and studies have been carried out, and include consideration of and modification (modifying factors) by realistically assumed mining, metallurgical, economic, marketing, legal, environmental, social and governmental factors. These assessments demonstrate that at the time of reporting that extraction could reasonably be justified (2004 JORC Code). This is obviously a stricter interpretation of the economic viability of a block of ore than the more general one applied to a resource.

The reserves are divided into two categories:

» *Probable reserves* are the economically mineable part of indicated and in some circumstances measured resources, and so the confidence level is the same as that defined for the indicated category. Diluting materials and allowances for losses that might occur through mining must also be included and demonstrate that extraction could be reasonably justified.

» *Proven reserves* are the economically mineable part of measured resources and therefore the confidence level is similar to that defined for the measured category. Diluting materials and allowances for losses that might occur through mining must also be included and demonstrate that extraction could be reasonably justified.

The relationship is shown in figure 6.1.

Figure 6.1: relationship between identified mineral resources and ore reserves

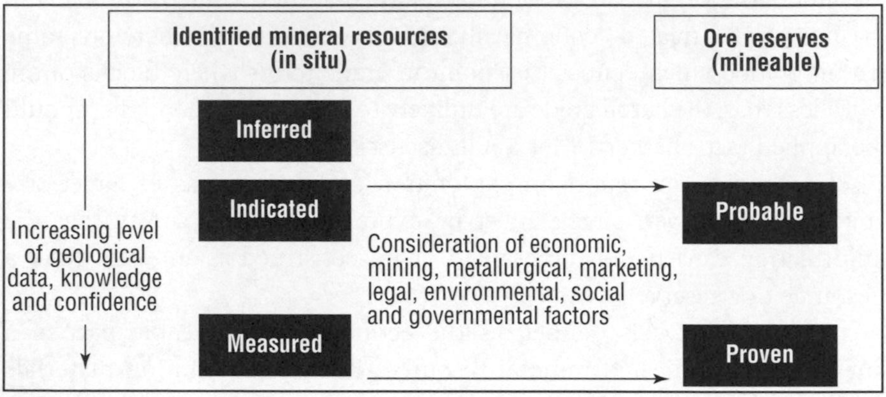

Source: AusIMM.

A more graphical presentation is provided in figure 6.2, where an artificial economic horizon has been applied to define economic and non-economic ore. As the number of drill holes increases so should the confidence level. To the left of the figure, where the drilling is more dense, the non-economic zone is a measured resource and not a reserve, while the section above the economic level is a proven reserve. Where the drilling is less dense to the right, we have a probable reserve above the economic limit and an indicated resource below the economic limit. Further infill drilling could convert the measured resource to a proven reserve and the indicated resource to a measured resource.

Figure 6.2: converting resources to reserves

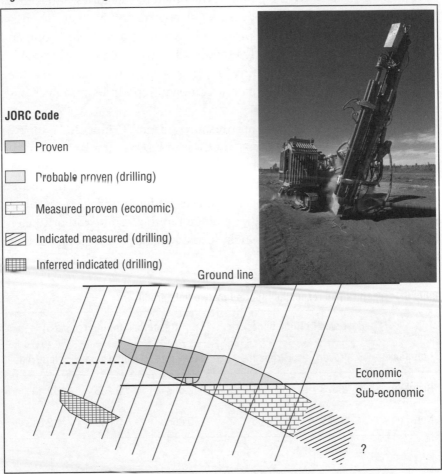

For the purposes of valuation it is preferable to use proven and probable reserves, but the resource base may still represent a significant value to the company. Many listed companies that have only resources may still have significant market value on the basis that over time a proportion of the resources may become reserves and ultimately be mined. The difficulty confronting an investor, or for that matter a valuer, is what proportion of the resources are likely to convert into a reserve and also what additional resources are still to be found through continued exploration.

Listed companies are required to publish their reserves in accordance with the code. One area of confusion sometimes does arise in the reporting of results. As mentioned in chapter 1, the different categories of resources and reserves should, wherever possible, be reported on an exclusive basis (resources which exclude that proportion which is a reserve). Company reports should clearly show and detail the different categories of resources and reserves to prevent any confusion. Investors should ensure that they fully understand the way in which a company reports its resources and, more importantly, its reserves.

Table 6.1 lists the reserves and resources as at 30 June 2011 for two gold producers. In Resolute's case, the proven reserves are larger than the measured resources, so it is probable, although not stated by the company, that the resources exclude reserves. However, in Norton's case, the proven and probable reserves are less than the measured and indicated resources, so the reserves may or may not be included in the resources. Fortunately, Norton states that the resources include reserves, but not all companies are that helpful.

Table 6.1: reserves and resources reported by two gold producers

	Reserves (million ounces)		Resources (million ounces)		
Company	Proven	Probable	Measured	Indicated	Inferred
Resolute	2.573	1.901	0.565	2.238	2.141
Norton	0.056	1.006	0.065	3.263	2.613

Diamond exploration

Due to the extremely low grade encountered in diamond exploration (0.05 to 2.00 carats per tonne) and the value component attributable to the diamonds, additional reporting requirements are set by the

JORC. Principally, exploration reports must specify the total number and weight (carats) recovered in the exploration sampling program. The type and size of samples and the lowest sieve size used must be specified. Microdiamonds smaller than 0.4 mm in size can be omitted. Resources and reserves for diamonds must report valuations of trial bulk samples.

Reporting coal resources and reserves

The following definitions have been set under the JORC Code:

» *Inferred resource class 1* — where the points of observation (no greater than 4 km apart) allow for estimation of coal thickness and general coal quality.

» *Inferred resource class 2* — where there is limited information, and thus assessment may be unreliable. May be expressed in ranges such as 10 to 100 million tonnes.

» *Indicated resource* — where the density and quality of data points (no greater than 2 km apart) allow a realistic estimate of coal thickness, quality, depth and in situ tonnage that will not vary significantly upon more detailed exploration.

» *Measured resource* — where the density and quality of data points (no greater than 1 km apart) allow a reliable estimate of coal thickness, quality, depth and in situ tonnage sufficient to allow detailed mine planning, costing of extraction and market specification.

» *Mineable in situ reserves* — where detailed mine planning has been applied to measured and indicated resources.

» *Recoverable reserves* — these are the tonnages of mineable in situ reserves that are expected to be recovered. If dilution is applied, the total equates to the run of mine (ROM). A recovery factor must be applied to obtain the recovered reserves; however, if a specific factor cannot be determined, then 50 per cent should be used for underground and 90 per cent for open cut mining.

» *Marketable reserves*—these are the tonnages of coal that will be available for sale. If the coal is sold raw it will be the same as the recoverable reserves, while if it is beneficiated (washed) then a yield has to be applied.

The relationship between resources and reserves is shown in figure 6.3.

Figure 6.3: relationship between coal resources and reserves

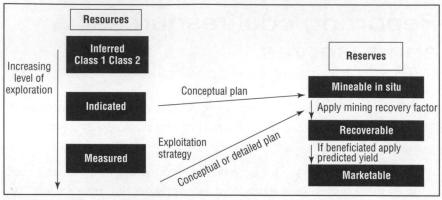

Source: AusIMM.

Russian reserves and resources[1]

Whereas the codes mentioned provide a consistent framework, which ultimately relies on a competent person to implement, the Russian code aims for total objectivity (see figure 6.4).

Figure 6.4: Russian reserve and resources code

Reserves				Undiscovered resources		
Groups by economic viability						
On-balance (economic)		Off-balance (potentially economic)				
Reserve/Resource categories by degree of geological and economic/technological knowledge				Predicted resources categories by degree of justification		
A	B	C_1	C_2	P_1	P_2	P_3

---

1 For more details see Steven Hanley *The Russian Reserves and Resources Reporting System* <www.imcinvest.com/pdf/Russian_reserves_8.pdf>.

The Russian system developed in the 1960s provides the entire process for exploration, resources calculation and reporting. Mineral resources are divided into seven categories — for fully explored reserves or resources (A, B, C_1), evaluated reserves or resources based on loose exploration grids and limited data (C_2) and prognostic resources which are generally defined outside areas that have been explored in detail and based on data only from trenches, geochemical and geophysical surveys (P_1, P_2, P_3).

Deposits are also categorised by their complexity from Class I to IV and their size and shape from Group 1 to 5. A Class I deposit has no structural complexity, uniform thickness and homogeneous grades. Each succeeding class is more complex: Class IV is an extremely complex structure, with extreme variations in thickness and in grade distribution. Group 1 deposits are large, simple in form, with uniform distribution of minerals, while normal density of drill holes would allow the definition of A and B reserves. Each succeeding group classification is smaller in size and with more complex form: Group 5 consists of small pocket deposits; category A and B reserves cannot be established; and only category C reserves can be established, by systematic prospecting.

The closest direct comparison of the Russian versus the western systems is as follows:

A, B $\approx$ Proved reserve/Measured resource

$C_1 \approx$ Proved or Probable reserve/Indicated resource

$C_2 \approx$ Probable reserve/Indicated resource/Inferred resource

$P_1 \approx$ Inferred resource

$P_2 \approx$ Reconnaissance mineral resource

$P_3 \approx$ No equivalent

Chinese reserves and resources

The current Chinese classification is summarised in figure 6.5 (overleaf). The first digit of each code indicates the level of economic viability: 1 = economic; 2M = marginal economic; 2S = sub-marginal economic; 3 = intrinsic economic; ? = economic interest undefined. The second number indicates phases of feasibility assessment: 1 = feasibility study; 2 = pre-feasibility study; 3 = geological study. The third number indicates geological assurance: 1 = measured; 2 = indicated; 3 = inferred; 4 = reconnaissance. The addition of the letter b = before the deduction of extractable quantities lost in the process of designing and mining.

Figure 6.5: 1999 Chinese reserve and resource classification

		Total identified mineral resource			Undiscovered resources
		Measured	Indicate	Inferred	Reconnaissance
Economic	Feasibility	Proved extractable reserve (111)			
		Basic reserve (111b)			
	Pre-feasibility	Probable extractable reserve (121)	Probable extractable reserve (122)		
		Basic reserve (121b)	Basic reserve (122b)		
Marginally economic		Basic reserve (2M11)			
		Basic reserve (2M21)	Basic reserve (2M22)		
Sub-economic		Resources (2S11)			
		Resources (2S21)	Resources (2S12)		
Intrinsic economic		Resources (331)	Resources (332)	Resources (333)	Resources (334)?

Reporting oil and gas reserves

Oil and gas reserves and resources are generally set by definitions set out in the Petroleum Resources Management System (2007) sponsored by the American Society of Petroleum Engineers (SPE), the American Association of Petroleum Geologists (AAPG), the World Petroleum Council (WPC) and the Society of Petroleum Evaluation Engineers (SPEE). As with other codes, there has been an evolutionary process with this US-centric approach. The current code is shown in figure 6.6.

Figure 6.6: petroleum reserves and resources

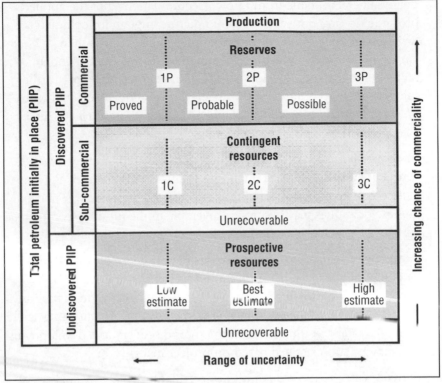

Source: Figure from p. 7 of 'Guidelines for Application of the Petroleum Resources Management System', SPE, November 2011 Copyright 2011 SPE. Reproduced with permission of the copyright owner. Further reproduction prohibited without permission.

The definitions in the Petroleum Resources Management System can be summarised as follows:

» *Production*—the cumulative quantity of petroleum that has been recovered at a given date.

» *Reserves*—those quantities of petroleum commercially recoverable from a given date forward under defined conditions. Reserves must be discovered, recoverable, commercial and remaining, based on the development project(s) applied. Reserves are further categorised in accordance with the level of certainty associated with the estimates and may be sub-classified based on project maturity or characterised by development and production status.

» *Contingent resources*—those quantities of petroleum estimated to be potentially recoverable from known accumulations, but the applied project(s) is (are) not yet considered mature enough for commercial development due to one or more contingencies, such as there are currently no viable markets, or commercial recovery is dependent on technology under development. Contingent resources are further categorised in accordance with the level of certainty associated with the estimates and may be sub-classified based on project maturity or characterised by their economic status.

» *Unrecoverable resources*—that portion of discovered or undiscovered petroleum initially in-place quantities that is estimated, as of a given date, not to be recoverable by future development projects. A portion of these quantities may become recoverable in the future as commercial circumstances change or technological developments occur.

» *Prospective resources*—those quantities of petroleum estimated to be potentially recoverable from undiscovered accumulations by application of future development projects. Prospective resources are further subdivided in accordance with the level of certainty associated with recoverable estimates assuming their discovery and development and may be sub-classified based on project maturity.

» *Proved reserves*—those quantities of petroleum which, by analysis of geoscience and engineering data, can be estimated with reasonable certainty to be commercially recoverable, from known reservoirs and under defined economic conditions, operating methods and government regulations. If deterministic methods are used, the term reasonable certainty is intended to express a high degree of confidence that the quantities will be recovered. If probabilistic methods are used, there should be at least a 90 per cent probability that the quantities actually recovered will equal or exceed the estimate. Often referred to as 1P or as 'proven'.

» *Probable reserves*—those additional reserves that are less likely to be recovered than proved reserves, but more certain to be recovered than possible reserves. It is equally likely that actual remaining quantities recovered will be greater than or less than the sum of the estimated proved plus probable reserves (2P). In this context, when probabilistic methods are used, there should be at least a 50 per cent probability that the actual quantities recovered will equal or exceed the 2P estimate.

» *Possible reserves*— those additional reserves that are less likely to be recoverable than probable reserves. The total quantities ultimately recovered from the project have a low probability to exceed the sum of proved plus probable plus possible (3P) reserves, which is equivalent to the high estimate scenario. In this context, when probabilistic methods are used, there should be at least a 10 per cent probability that the actual quantities recovered will equal or exceed the 3P estimate.

The industry will more often quote 2P reserves, meaning the total of proven and probable reserves. However, given the nature of oil and gas exploration, some companies will apply probabilistic estimates to the amount of recoverable gas or liquids that might be ultimately recovered. As mentioned, the guidelines for proven reserves state there should be at least a 90 per cent probability that the quantities recovered will be equal to or greater than the estimate; for probable reserves there should be a 50 per cent probability, while for possible reserves there should be at least a 10 per cent probability. These are sometimes referred to the P90, P50 and P10 reserves respectively, as shown in figure 6.7.

Figure 6.7: probabilistic reserves definition

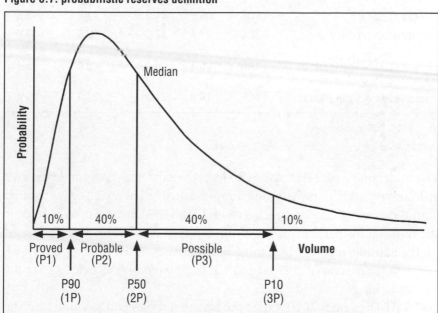

The reserves of the massive offshore North West Shelf gas project, which supplies domestic gas to Western Australia and produced seven million tonnes of liquefied natural gas (LNG) each year for the Asian market, were quantified in December 2000 as shown in table 6.2.

The table shows the reserves at the confidence levels of 85 per cent, 50 per cent and 15 per cent. The company was 85 per cent confident that there were at least 35.5 trillion cubic feet (TCF) of gas in place and that of this amount 27.4 TCF or 77.2 per cent would be recovered when the project was developed. The confidence of achieving higher reserves is lower as less conservative factors are applied to the known geological and engineering database. At a confidence level of 50 per cent (P50) the gas in-place increases to 41.9 TCF, which is close to the expected gas in-place. At a low confidence level of 15 per cent, gas in-place of up to 48.4 TCF could be estimated. After production of 6.4 TCF, the new reserves are shown.

Table 6.2: gas reserves of the North West Shelf, December 2000

Categories	Units	P85	P50	Expectation	P15
Original					
—gas in-place	TCF	35.5	41.9	42.0	48.8
— expected recovery	TCF	27.4	32.5	32.6	37.8
Production to 1 Jan 2001	TCF	6.4	6.4	6.4	6.4
Reserves as at 1 Jan 2001	TCF	19.8	24.5	24.6	29.4

Note: TCF = trillion cubic feet.

Source: Woodside bidder's statement, December 2000.

The reader might note that at the P85 level the expected recoverable reserves at 1 January 2001 plus the production to date totalled 25.2 TCF compared with the original expected recovery of 27.4 TCF. This variation would be the result of further refinement of the ultimate recoverable reserves based on the additional years of production data. Also, of the original 35.5 TCF of gas in-place some 71 per cent (25.2 TCF) would be recovered over the operating life of the fields.

By 31 December 2010, the approximate reserves and resources for the North West Shelf were as shown in table 6.3.

Table 6.3: reserves and resources of the North West Shelf, December 2010

Proven reserves (TCF)	Probable reserves (TCF)	Contingent resources (TCF)	Total (TCF)
12.8	1.4	0.7	14.9

Note: TCF = trillion cubic feet.

Over the intervening period a total of about 7.4 TCF of gas has been produced. Adding this number to proven and probable resources as at December 2010 provides a P50 figure of 22.3 TCF compared with the P50 figure of 24.5 TCF in 1 January 2001, suggesting that there has been some downward revision of resources over the 10-year period.

It should be apparent to the reader from the descriptions given that reserve estimation is an inexact science. It is ultimately dependent on the amount of information available, the quality of that information and correct interpretation and product price assumptions. Reserves are often the most critical part of any project valuation and hence company assessment, yet incorrect estimates are made. Ultimately, it comes down to the reserve variability of a project and a trade-off between the amounts spent on gathering data and reaching a point where the increased confidence no longer outweighs the added cost.

CHAPTER 7
Mining and hydrocarbon recovery

Once a discovery has been made, properly assessed and determined to be economic, the next step is to mine the reserve to recover the valuable commodity. The method employed to get access to the resource will depend on its location and orientation relative to the surface and on the mineral characteristics and value of the commodity.

Surface mining

For orebodies located near the surface, access may be gained without the need to go underground. There are a number of advantages to mining from the surface, principally lower cost, but there are limitations and the type of surface mining applied can vary.

Open cut

Where an orebody is located near the surface and is vertical in nature, it may be economic to excavate the ore and surrounding waste material (rock) directly from it. Due to the instability of the surrounding waste rock it is not possible to mine with vertical walls, and therefore the open cut or pit walls will need to be battered to an angle where they are stable. Therefore, for every tonne of ore mined, a certain amount of waste material will also need to be mined and removed to the waste dumps.

In figure 7.1 (overleaf), ore blocks 1 and 2 have already been mined. Block 3 is next in line to be mined, and from the diagram it is apparent that 12 waste blocks will have to be removed to gain safe access to the ore. Each waste block in this case is approximately half the size of the ore block so that for every tonne of ore mined a total of 6 tonnes of waste will be removed (assuming the ore has the same specific gravity as the waste), for a waste-to-ore ratio of 6:1. A similar observation for block 2 shows the ratio at 5 and for the lower block 4 the ratio is 7.[1]

Figure 7.1: open cut mining

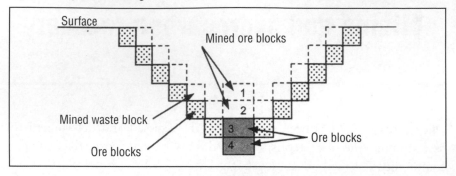

As the orebody gets deeper, the waste-to-ore ratio increases. It is therefore not uncommon for mining companies to pre-strip (remove additional waste) in the early years of the operation, to balance out the amount of annual waste removal so that major increases in the mining fleet are not required in the later years of the operation.

Some of the pre-strip mining costs may therefore be capitalised (carried forward) and brought to account in the profit and loss accounts in later years to smooth out the costs. However, from a cash flow point of view, higher negative cash flow might occur in the earlier years due to the pre-stripping.

Even allowing for pre-stripping, eventually the amount of waste removal will reach a stage where the cost of removing the waste will outweigh the revenue from the ore, and the open cut will no longer be economic. The break-even point, generally on a tonnage basis, can be defined as:

Break-even waste ratio = revenue per tonne of ore less cost to mine, treat and sell divided by cost per tonne of waste.

---

1 The aim is to design the pit to optimise the economic return or net present value (NPV). In practice there will be a large number of blocks made up of waste, low-grade and economic parcels. The sequencing and inclusion of economic blocks defined by the cutoff grade (which is discussed in chapter 14) within the confines of an open cut model can be optimised by applying algorithms such as Lerchs Grossman and floating cones. In simple terms the methods identify which blocks should be mined based on which have the highest total value subject to the required pit slope for a given set of costs and price. With the availability of cheap computer power, numerous commercial packages are now available that will design the optimum pit configuration.

For example, if the revenue per tonne of ore is expected to be $20 and the cost to mine that tonne, to treat it and to recover and sell the saleable commodity is $13 per tonne and the cost to remove one tonne of waste is $1, then:

$$\text{Break-even waste ratio} = \frac{(20 - 13)}{1} = 7$$

Therefore in figure 7.1, block 4 may be the last economically recoverable block from the open cut as the waste-to-ore ratio is 7 and any deeper blocks will have a higher ratio.[2]

The mining method will involve a cycle of:

» sampling to define the ore and waste boundaries

» drilling and blasting of the ore and waste, unless they are soft enough to rip or dig without blasting

» loading and hauling the ore and waste separately, commonly with the use of large front-end loaders or electric shovels and haul trucks[3] (see table 7.3 on p. 117 for indicative capital costs)

» dumping of waste on waste dumps and delivering the ore to a crushing circuit where it will be crushed to a manageable size of, say, less than 175 mm in diameter.

As with any type of mining operation there is always the likelihood that not all of the ore will be recovered (some may remain in the open cut and some may end up in the mine waste) and the possibility that some of the waste will be included as ore (dilution) due to the irregular ore/waste boundaries and the selective mining unit unable to discriminate at a fine enough level. Indicative recovery and dilution rates for typical open cut operations are around 90 per cent and 5 per cent respectively.

Table 7.1 (overleaf) lists the advantages and disadvantages of open cut mining when compared with underground mining.

---

2 One additional cost that can be argued for, but is not included in the above calculation, is a return on capital invested. However, given that we are interested in the maximum waste-to-ore ratio, which should occur at the end of the open-cut mine life, the servicing of the capital should no longer be an issue, and maximising total cash flow would be the objective. In the case of optimum cutoff grades, which can be calculated throughout the life of the project, return on capital is important (see chapter 14).

3 The Caterpillar 797F can haul 363 tonnes with a rated power of 4000 hp/2983 kW with each tyre costing up to $100 000 in the spot market.

Table 7.1: open cut mining compared with underground mining

Advantages of open cut	Disadvantages of open cut
Cheaper and simpler to mine	Large waste disposal issue
Economies of scale	Potential for higher dilution
Lower capital cost per annual tonne	Greater environmental impact
Safer working environment	Oxidation of ore
Higher ore recovery	Adverse weather conditions

Strip mining

For bedded type deposits, such as coal, where the mineralised zone (seam) is relatively flat dipping and close to the surface, a variant of open cut mining called strip mining may be used. Most commonly, large draglines are employed that are able to remove large volumes of overburden (waste) from on top of the mineral seam. The bucket capacity of a dragline can vary from 10 to 100 cubic metres with a 50 cubic metre dragline able to move approximately 10 million bank cubic metres per annum. (A bank cubic metre is the volume of material before it is stripped as, once stripped, the material will bulk and increase in volume due to the increased voids of air.)

The mineral is then mined by conventional means. The process is repeated in a parallel fashion with the overburden (waste) placed into the previously mined strip of mineralisation. Often, the mineralised beds will dip in one direction at right angles to the parallel strip mining, and therefore the amount of overburden removed will increase over time. Thus the waste-to-ore (stripping) ratio will increase over time and an economic break-even stripping ratio will also be reached, at which point the mine may have to go underground, close or wait for better economic conditions.

The recent and dramatic growth in the production of mineral resources has seen a significant increase in the demand for new mining equipment, which has resulted in a subsequent increase in delivery time from manufacturers. Rio Tinto provided estimates in the increase in delivery time in the first half of 2008 (see table 7.2).

Table 7.2: equipment delivery times, Rio Tinto estimates, 2008

Equipment type	Normal delivery time (years)	New delivery time (years)
Grinding mills	1.6	3.6
Draglines	1.5	2.9
Barges	2.0	2.7
Locomotives	1.0	2.2
Power generators	1.0	2.0
Wagons	1.0	2.0
Rope shovels	0.8	2.0
Reclaimers	1.5	2.0
Tyres	0.3	2.0
Large haul trucks	0.3	2.0
Crushers	1.4	2.0
Ship loaders	0.7	1.8

Some current indicative capital costs are listed in table 7.3.

Table 7.3: indicative capital equipment costs

Equipment	US$m approximate
72 m^3 electric dragline	122.5
42 m^3 diesel hydraulic front shovel	17.0
40 m^3 front-end loader	9.5
363 tonne haul truck	6.5
Tracked electric rotary drill 310 mm holes	6.0

(*continued*)

Table 7.3: indicative capital equipment costs (*cont'd*)

Equipment	US$m approximate
4 m³ diesel hydraulic backhoe	5.0
190 000 l water truck	4.0
634 kW bulldozer	2.3
7.3 m blade grader	2.3
Fuel and lube truck	0.9

Alluvial mining

Alluvial deposits are those deposits that occur through the re-deposition of minerals by water or wind. For example, hard rock gold deposits or kimberlite diamond pipes may be eroded by wind and water over many millions of years. The gold grains and diamonds are then transported down old rivers and subsequently buried in ancient river terraces. Another common example is ancient beaches, where the sands (including heavy mineral sands) were deposited by wave action, until the oceans receded and left the ancient beaches many kilometres inland.

The major advantage of these types of deposits is that the valuable minerals are already separated into fine sizes and therefore generally require no crushing or grinding, which greatly reduces the capital and processing cost. However, the mineralisation is often spread out over large areas (and hence volumes) so that the grades are often very low, and at times can be quite erratic. Gold grades are often less than 1.0 gram per cubic metre, diamonds less than 0.4 carats per tonne and heavy mineral sands around 2 per cent to 4 per cent. (Successful alluvial goldmining operations run by public companies are quite rare, given the low and variable grades and the difficulty in adequately managing the operations.)

Given the loose consolidation of the mineralisation the most common form of mining is to use a dredge. The dredge sits on its own artificially made pond and uses a bucket wheel or suction cutter head that breaks up the ground and brings material to the surface for treatment by gravity processes to separate the valuable commodity. The waste material is placed behind the dredge into the pond to fill it, while the dredge and pond move forward into the newly mined area. Thus the mining and initial processing plant can move cheaply over large areas to treat the ore material. The capital cost of a 150 tonne per hour suction cutter dredge only would be in the order of US$20 million. Dry alluvial mining can also be undertaken where no pond is utilised.

Underground mining

For mineral deposits that are too deep to be mined economically by surface mining methods, access and mining of the orebody is achieved through underground methods. The mining methods employed will vary depending on the shape, size and orientation (vertical or stratiform) of the orebody, its depth and the competence of the orebody, and the surrounding waste rock.

Typical deposits

The first step is to gain access to the orebody. Depending on its type and shape, and the surface topography, one or more of several methods might be employed.

As shown in figure 7.2, access to the underground orebody can be by a decline that is made up of a circular or zigzag of roadways, with say a 12 per cent incline, which might start at the base of an open cut if one exists, or from the surface if the orebody is not too deep. A stage will be reached where it is more cost-effective to sink a shaft and then drive across to the orebody and construct underground inclines for access to its different levels.

Figure 7.2: underground mining

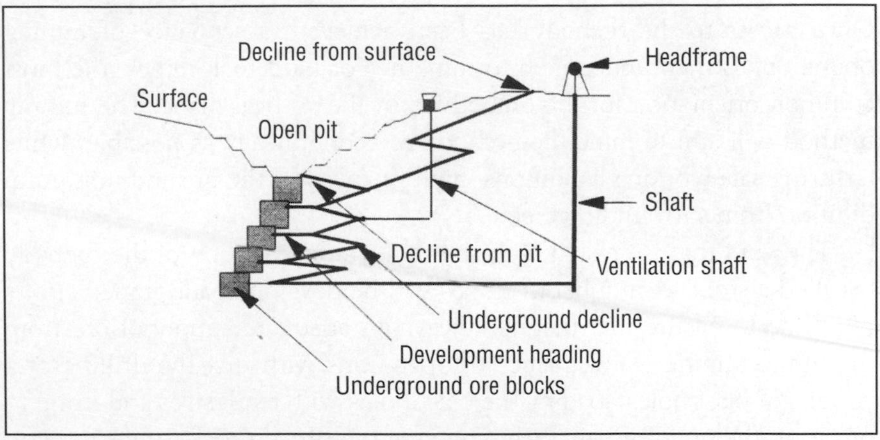

Note: not to scale.

The declines may have a height and width of between 4 and 5 metres on average (sufficient for the passage of small dump trucks and other equipment) and, depending on ground conditions, cost about $4000 to $6000 per linear metre. The cost of sinking shafts will also depend on the shaft's diameter and ground conditions — the larger the diameter the greater the cost, but the greater the tonnage of ore that can be hauled to the surface. Typical shaft diameters vary from 4 to 7 metres with costs of between $20 000 and $30 000 per metre of depth. The shaft and declines represent permanent access to the orebody, and therefore are capital costs that will be depreciated over their operating life or the life of the mine.

A large number of other capital items will be required to develop the mine, including:

» headframe, winder, skips and cages to haul the ore, men and materials in the shaft

» if chosen, underground crushing facilities to reduce the size of ore hauled and increase the tonnage for a given haulage volume

» underground ore passes that allow the mined ore to be moved by gravity to the base of the shaft for haulage to the surface

» ventilation raises and fans to ensure adequate ventilation for shaft, decline and underground development

» pumping facilities to remove excess water from the mine

» underground services, including power, compressed air and water.

Once access to the orebody has been achieved, a sequence of mining operations is then undertaken to mine it. For hard rock mines, the most common orientation for the orebody is in the vertical plane. The mining method will aim to mine the orebody as economically as possible, while ensuring safe working conditions, high recovery of the ore and minimum dilution from surrounding rock.

The void that is created with the removal of a section of the orebody is called a stope. A number of stopes will be developed and mined at any one time to ensure that there is always an adequate supply of ore from the mine. Mining is a sequence of operations with first the drilling of a pattern of blast holes, loading the blast holes with explosives and firing to break up the ore or waste, then removing the broken rock (mucking) and repeating the sequence. The mining at any one stope will generally be in an upward direction, blasting the competent rock above (back). A number of alternative underground mining techniques are employed in the industry, including, but not limited to:

» *Cut and fill.* Ore is removed from the stope and then partially refilled from the surface with fine waste (and sometimes with the addition of a small amount of cement) and some 25 to 35 per cent of water, which is then allowed to drain off. Enough room is left so workers and equipment can stand on the waste, and the ore above can then be drilled and blasted in the next cycle, removed and then filled again with fine waste. This method is applied where the ore is reasonably competent, but the irregular rock walls require support from the fill. The method allows for relatively low dilution and can be applied to long and wide orebodies. Given the cyclical nature of the operations there is down time while the fill cures so that more than one stope is required for continuous operations. Production rates are of the order of 500 to 1000 tonnes per day (tpd), while recovery and dilution are around 85 per cent and 5 per cent respectively.

» *Shrinkage stoping.* As ore is blasted, it will expand from the voids created between the broken pieces of ore. The extra volume created can be removed from the stope. Broken ore is left in the stope to provide support for the rock walls. The miners can then stand on the remaining broken ore and drill the ore above, with the process once again repeated. It is important that the walls are competent and there is a distinct contact between the ore and waste rock. The orebody should be dipping at least 55° and be 1.2 m to 4.5 m wide with production rates around 200 to 800 tpd, while recovery and dilution are around 90 per cent and 10 per cent respectively.

» *Sub-level caving.* This is done best with steeply inclined orebodies of medium width in relatively weak ground. A series of sub-levels are developed to the orebody and then an initial vertical slot is mined and removed into which successive slices of ore are blasted and fall into the adjacent previously blasted slice of ore. The broken ore in the upper sub-levels is drawn from lower level stopes as mining progresses. The method is low cost and highly productive (5000 to 15 000 tpd), while recovery and dilution are around 85 per cent and 15 per cent respectively.

» *Block caving.* If the orebody is sufficiently undermined it will start to cave in, and may continue to do so as ore is removed from the bottom. This mining method is cheap but requires that the orebody fracture into small enough pieces and that the rock walls do not fail and dilute the ore. Pre-development of the stope is required before mining commences. The method is the lowest cost per tonne and highest production rate (30 000 to 60 000 tpd) for underground mining, while recovery and dilution are around 95 per cent and 15 per cent respectively.

» *Sub-level open stoping.* As with block caving, open stopes remain after mining, so ground conditions have to be good to minimise dilution. High productivity (1500 to 5000 tpd) and recovery can be achieved, but it requires considerable development, although much of this development is in the orebody.

» *Open stoping.* the stope is left open and unsupported. Ore is blasted into the open stope and withdrawn and thus the stope will become increasingly large in size. Obviously, competent host rock is required to avoid excessive dilution.

A number of alternative underground mining techniques are employed in the industry. Figure 7.3 shows the relative operating and capital costs for different mining methods.

Figure 7.3: underground mining capital investment

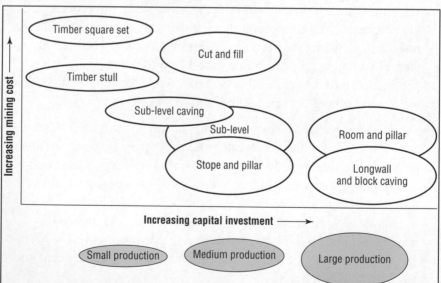

Stratiform or tabular deposits

For bedded deposits such as coal, which have a horizontal orientation, the mining methods employed vary to the extent that the roof, or back, has to be supported initially during the mining process. Access to the orebody can once again be achieved by decline or shaft as shown in figure 7.4.

Figure 7.4: access to horizontal deposits

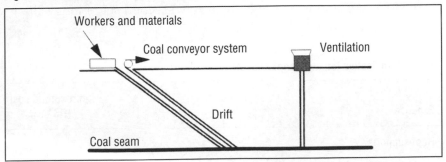

Due to the shallow nature of Australian coalmines, it is common for a continuous decline or inclined drift to be employed. Coal can then be transported to the surface using a conveyor belt system along the length of the drift. The extraction of coal generally involves one of several methods.

» *Room-and-pillar mining.* Consists of continuous miners, which have rotating drums with steel picks, cutting the coal to form roadways and crosscuts at right angles. Pillars of coal are left to provide roof support Towards the end of the mine life the pillars may be extracted, and the roof or back is allowed to fall in a controlled manner.

» *Longwall mining.* Employed to increase productivity levels, especially given the low dollar value for coal. Continuous miners are employed to develop panels, or rectangular blocks of coal some 300 metres wide by 1000 metres long. A longwall miner cuts coal back and forth from across the panel, retreating towards the front end of the panel. The roof is held in place above the miner and armoured face conveyor (AMC) by hydraulic jacks or longwall supports. As the miner moves forward the roof or back is allowed to collapse where the longwall miner had previously stood. The method is generally limited to seam thickness of 5 to 6 metres. Indicative longwall capital costs for a 300 m longwall are provided in table 7.4 (overleaf).

» *Longwall top coal caving (LTCC).* Developed in China where it is used for thicker seams with recoveries of some 75 to 80 per cent from seams 5 to 9 metres (and potentially to 12 metres) in thickness, and results in production rates of 15 000 to 25 000 tonnes per day from a 3-metre-high longwall. Basically, the coal above the section of coal removed by the 3-metre-high longwall is allowed to cave in and onto a second AFC, which travels behind the first AFC and is protected by its own second set of longwall supports (see figure 7.5).

Table 7.4: indicative longwall capital costs

Expense	Approximate cost (US$m)
Roof supports	90.0
Chain conveyor	27.0
Shearer	6.0
Electricals	12.0
Other	15.0
Total	**150.0**

Figure 7.5: conceptual model of longwall top coal caving (LTCC) system

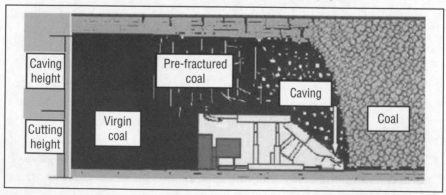

Source: Conceptual Model of LTCC System (after Xu, 1999) © Professor Bruce Hebblewhite.

Mine scheduling

Planning and scheduling the best order for developing and mining an orebody is an important part of the exploitation of a mineral resource. As described in chapter 6, the orebody can be seen as a number of discrete ore blocks that will be mined in sequence. The sequence of mining will be planned by the mining engineer, subject to the shape and orientation of the orebody as interpreted by the geologist. Obviously, for an open cut mine the lower ore blocks can only be mined after the higher zones are removed, and for an underground orebody, access will be subject to underground development. The scheduling will have several objectives in mind:

» to ensure worker safety and the long-term integrity of the mine

» to apply economic cutoff grades to define mineable ore

» to provide a continuous and adequate supply of ore

» to maintain a steady grade to meet the processing plant's requirements to help ensure optimum mill recovery

» to maximise the economic return from the mine.

Table 7.5 shows the January 2011 planned life of mine (LOM) schedule for the Amayapampa gold project in Bolivia. Mine production varies over the LOM, due to such factors as ore hardness, accessibility and equipment capacity, while the waste will also vary depending on the stripping ratio applicable at that time. The ore milled will remain relatively constant at the maximum plant capacity (24/7), but ore hardness may result in some variation. Grade will fluctuate depending on where mining operations are currently under way as the orebody is not grade homogeneous. Finally recovery will vary 74.1 per cent to 85.8 per cent depending on the grade and mineralogy of the ore delivered to the mill.

Table 7.5: life of mine (LOM) schedule for the Amayapampa gold project, Bolivia, 2011

	Year								
	0	1	2	3	4	5	6	7	8
Ore mined (kt)	470	2008	2923	2676	3514	2989	3144	1947	1314
Waste (kt)	2134	4280	6141	11534	11214	5682	4651	2249	647
Strip ratio (×)	4.54	2.13	2.1	4.31	3.19	1.90	1.48	1.16	0.49

(continued)

Table 7.5: life of mine (LOM) schedule for the Amayapampa gold project, Bolivia, 2011 (*cont'd*)

	Year								
	0	1	2	3	4	5	6	7	8
Ore milled (kt)	–	1665	2700	2700	2700	2700	2700	2416	1303
Grade (g/t)	–	1.39	1.55	1.16	1.31	1.16	1.29	1.19	1.41
Recovery (%)	–	74.1	83.2	80.2	84.7	82.8	85.3	84.9	85.8
Gold (koz)	–	55	112	81	96	84	96	78	51

Note: kt = kilotonnes; koz = kilo ounces.

Oil and gas drilling

The recovery of oil and gas is different from the mining of hard and soft rock. The oil or gas, or both, is contained in a porous rock such as sandstone (not in a cavernous void). Development/production wells are drilled into the hydrocarbon-bearing reservoir (see appendix D for more detail) to optimise the extraction. Each of the wells will be cased in steel to ensure that the well's integrity is maintained. As shown in figure 7.6, at the appropriate level(s) where the reservoir(s) are located the steel casing will be perforated to allow the hydrocarbons to flow into the well. It is important that other non-hydrocarbon horizons are not perforated, as this may allow the ingress of unwanted fluids and the possible escape of hydrocarbons. With modern technology, wells can be vertical or horizontal.

Figure 7.6: casing perforations

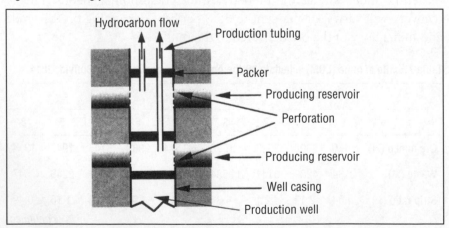

Primary oil production is obtained from the reservoir's own pressure driving the hydrocarbons to the surface. However, this may only result in partial oil recovery of 15 to 25 per cent of the field (although lower recoveries may be encountered). Secondary recovery techniques include the re-injection of water or gas recovered from the reservoir, through separate wells, to maintain or increase reservoir pressure. Gas lift is employed as artificial lift, whereby the gas is sent separately down to the bottom of the oil-producing well to lift more oil to the surface. Down-hole pumps can also be used to pump oil to the surface.

An example of decline rates is shown in figure 7.7 for the offshore Laminaria and Corallina projects in offshore Australia. Production started in November 1999 and reached a peak in March 2000, and then declined. Case 1 was based on the recovery of 152 million barrels of oil and assumed that all of the 2P reserves would be recovered with some remedial workovers (reconditioning of production wells) and that some additional possible reserves (3P) would be recovered through increased infill drilling in 2002 and 2003. Case 2 was based on the recovery of 118 million barrels of oil, which allowed for infill drilling in 2001 and 2000, but assumed that not all of the 2P reserves would be recovered based on lower recovery factors.

Figure 7.7: production profiles for the Western Australia offshore Laminaria and Corallina projects, 2000–11

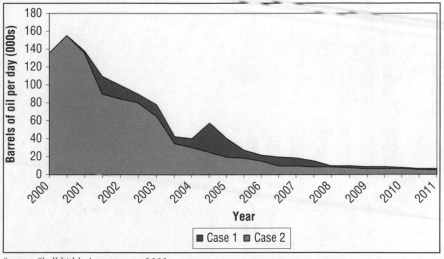

Source: Shell bidder's statement, 2000.

An important aspect of oil production is the decline in oil production over time due to falling pressure and increasing water production. Remedial action may be taken to mitigate the decline rate; however, production will decline over the life of the field at a geometric rate. Common practice in investment analysis is to use a 15 to 20 per cent per annum decline rate when specific details are not known and assume that some 20 to 30 per cent of the field's reserves are produced in the first 12 to 18 months of production.

As an example of the potential impact of remedial work, the Taylor field, in southern Queensland Australia, commenced production in May 1988 and by June 2010 was producing 28 barrels per day (bpd) of oil, 41 bpd of condensate and 2.4 (million standard cubic feet per day (mmscfd) of gas. To increase recoverable oil, a remedial program was planned, which consisted primarily of adding three new infill wells and retrofitting electric submersible pumps to five of the existing eight producers. The program was expected to increase recoverable oil from 0.224 to 0.759 million barrels and gas from 1.29 to 5.9 billion cubic feet (Bcf). The new production forecast is shown in figure 7.8.

Figure 7.8: Taylor production forecast, June 2011–26

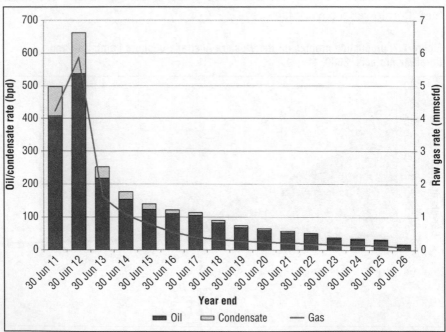

Source: Taylor Production Forecast, from p. 299 of the *Mosaic Oil Scheme Booklet*, released 6/9/10, reproduced with permission.

Marketing

A necessary aspect for any mining project is the marketing or sale of its mineral product. The product can be categorised into four primary types, as shown in table 7.6. Some mines will produce a crude product that requires little treatment and in most cases involves large tonnages sold on long-term evergreen contracts with prices renewed each year or shorter quarterly price renewals. A typical example would be iron ore, where prices have risen sharply in recent years to US$3.00 per metric tonne unit, or US$180.0[4] per tonne of lump ore with iron content of 60 per cent. For many mines producing concentrates, particularly for precious and base metals, terminal markets may exist where prices are determined by supply and demand on a daily basis. The sale of concentrates can be related to these publicly quoted prices. As the product sold is in the form of a concentrate, the price received by the mine needs to be adjusted for the cost of smelting the concentrate and refining the metal, with credits for valuable by-products and penalties applied for any deleterious elements in the concentrate.

Table 7.6: categorised products

Saleable product	Primary examples
Crude ore	Iron ore (lump and fines), unwashed coal, bauxite
Concentrates	Iron ore pellets, washed coal, alumina, copper, lead, zinc, nickel, tin, tungsten, titanium
Smelter ore	Pig iron, coke, alumina, blister copper, crude lead, nickel matte
Refined product	Steel, refined base metals

Mineral and hydrocarbon processing

Most minerals will require some amount of initial on-site processing. This concentrates the mineral in the ore and reduces the amount of waste that is transported off site. Processing involves crushing, grinding and concentrating the ore. Bulk commodities may require washing or

---

4 $3.00 × 100 × 0.6.

screening into specified size fractions. A concentrate may undergo further processing, either by a hydrometallurgical process which involves an aqueous solution, including leaching, precipitation or pressure reduction, or by pyrometallurgical processes, which involve high temperatures, such as roasting, smelting and converting, or a combination of both, to recover the saleable commodities. The steps include:

1 Physical reduction by crushing and grinding to allow liberation of the valuable mineral from the waste.

2 Concentration of the minerals by separation from the waste.

3 Downstream hydrometallurgy or smelting and refining, or both.

Mineral processing varies, depending on the type of ore, the different products to be recovered and the form in which the products are sold. The first phase of processing ore is normally the comminution circuit, which consists of crushing and grinding. The object is to liberate or separate, from within the ore, the valuable mineral, which can be microscopic in size. Total liberation may not be possible, as the cost of grinding may become prohibitive; however, achieving surface exposure of the valuable mineral or element is important.

The crushing phase generally uses jaw, gyratory or cone crushers, which break pieces of ore from as large as 1 metre in diameter to less than several centimetres in diameter. Capital costs can vary with ore characteristics and throughput from $500 000 to maybe $50 million including conveying, screening and stockpiling. A combination of crushers and screens that size the product can be used to ensure that the final product is below a certain size specification. High-pressure grinding rolls or vertical shaft impact crushers are finding increasing use to reduce particle size to below around 2 mm. The next phase is grinding, which will reduce the ore to the consistency of powder with particle sizes of less than, say, 75 microns (0.075 mm, the width of human hair). Crushing is generally less costly than grinding. In some cases ultrafine grinding will reduce particle size to below 10 microns. This is usually preformed on an intermediate concentrate rather than the whole ore.

Generally the grinding circuit is made up of a combination of mills that may be autogenous (AG), semi-autogenous (SAG), rod mills and ball mills. The mills are large rotating drums where grinding media (that is, rock itself, steel rods or balls) are used to grind the ore (see figure 7.9). The rotating action causes a cascade of ore and balls or rods that finely grind the ore. Very large diameter rotating mills that increase this cascading action are now commonly used. In AG, larger pieces of competent ore act as media, cascading over themselves. In SAG, some large-diameter balls are added as the media. Cyclones or screens may be used to ensure that oversized particles return to the circuit to be properly ground. Over time the steel balls or rods will wear down, which will add some iron to the ground ore. Consumption of iron balls/rods varies depending on the ore hardness, with typical rates of around 0.5 to 1.0 kg per tonne of ore. In ultrafine grinding, sand or ceramic media may be used.

Figure 7.9: cascading ball mill load

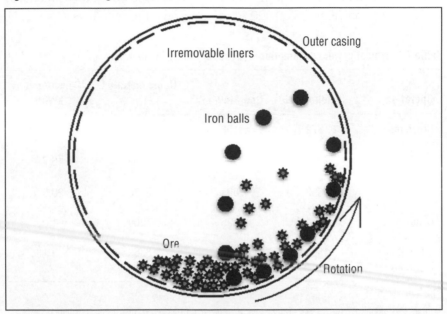

Large quantities of energy are required in this stage of the operation (and can therefore represent the largest component of operating costs). The strength of rock is quoted as a work index, which is used to calculate the amount of power required to grind the rock in kilowatt hours per tonne (kWh/t). Typical work indices for base metal ores range around 10 to 15. Where ultrafine grinding is required, power consumption can go as high as 150 kWh/t, so ultrafine grinding is normally used in regrinding of intermediate concentrates to minimise the tonnage required to be ground.

The equation that converts the work index (Wi) kWh per tonne to power consumed W is given by:

$$W = 10 \, Wi \, ((1 \div P^{0.5}) - (1 \div F^{0.5}))$$

F is the feed size in microns and P is the product size in microns; thus, if the feed size is 15 000 microns (15 mm), the product is 800 microns (0.8 mm) and Wi = 13, then:

$$W = 10 \times 13 \times ((1 \div 800^{0.5}) - (1 \div 15\ 000^{0.5})) = 3.5 \text{ kWh/t}$$

On-site power costs will vary, depending on the source, from approximately 3.5¢ to 30¢ per kWh.

An example of the relative amounts of power consumed in the operation of a base metal mill is shown in table 7.7. The Rosebery Mill in Tasmania at the time was processing 700 000 tonnes of lead, zinc and silver ore.

Table 7.7: typical power consumption — Rosebery Mill, Tasmania

Operation	Installed kW	Operating kW	Hours operated per year	Consumption kWh/t
Crushing	272	163	4800	1.1
Grinding*	2030	1500	7780	16.7
Flotation	2692	1694	8470	20.5
Mine fill	224	95	7200	1.0
Effluent treatment	1800	248	8760	3.1

*Includes regrind.

Source: Woodcock, JT (ed), 1980. *Mining and Metallurgical Practices in Australasia*, published by The Australasian Institute of Mining and Metallurgy: Melbourne. Monograph Series No. 10, 1980, included with permission of the AusIMM.

The next phase is often one of concentration of the mineral in an on-site mill or, in the case of coal, a washery. The primary modes of concentration are discussed in the following pages, but readers should refer to chapter 20 for more detail on individual commodities.

Gravity concentration

Gravity can be applied where the valuable mineral has a significantly different relative density (RD) (formerly referred to as specific gravity or SG) from the gangue or waste material. For example, heavy mineral sands have an RD of from 4 to 5, compared with the remaining sands, mostly made up of quartz, which have RDs of around 2.6. Spirals, jigs and tables utilise the high RDs to recover the heavy mineral sands. For the coal industry, where the RD of coal is around 1 and the RD of the gangue is 2 to 3, heavy media separation is utilised. A medium (often water and magnetite) is made of an RD between that of the coal and the gangue material so that the coal will float and the waste will sink.

Obviously, some coal that is still bonded to the gangue may sink and will be lost. The resulting proportion of coal that is recovered is called the yield, and this ranges from 75 to 90 per cent. Gravity concentration is often used to capture coarse gold as a gravity concentrate, leaving only the more readily leached fine gold to pass to cyanide leaching. Knelson and Falcon concentrators or in-line pressure jigs are commonly used in this application.

Froth flotation

Froth flotation was developed in Australia and is used worldwide throughout the metalliferous mining industry. The method relies on the attraction or repulsion of chemically coated mineral particles to bubbles of air. An agitated tank or cell is filled with ore that has been ground with water to form a slurry. Appropriate chemicals are added and air is introduced into the tank through the impeller, which creates fine bubbles that rise to the surface. The chemicals cause the small particles of the valuable mineral to attach to the air bubbles, which then float to the surface. Gangue (or waste) particles either are not attracted to or are repelled by the air bubbles. The bubbles (froth) and the mineral are collected at the surface. Different chemicals are used to both attract and repel specific minerals so that concentrations of different minerals can be achieved.

The degree of concentration and the amount recovered will depend on the complexity of the mineralogy and the success of the grinding in liberating the valuable minerals from the gangue. The increase in grade for, say, chalcopyrite copper ore of 1 per cent copper content could typically be 25 per cent copper content in the concentrate.

At the same time as concentrating the ore, some economic mineral will be lost with the waste product. Thus the mill recovery is very important, with typical values ranging from 85 to 95 per cent. The aim of concentration is to reduce the amount of waste included in the concentrate that is to be transported off-site, and in the production of smaller particle sizes to assist in the further processing and recovery of the metal. Flotation cells are also employed in the coal industry to increase yield.

Figure 7.10 shows indicative recoveries for different head grades for the primary base and precious metals. It is more common, however, to generate flotation curves showing concentrate grade versus recovery, although this will vary from project to project because of varying head grades and mineral mixtures. The concentrate grade is significant, as it impacts on the financially important aspect of treatment and refining charges (see the section on smelting and refining).

Figure 7.10: indicative recovery factors

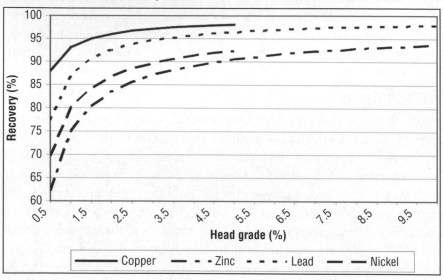

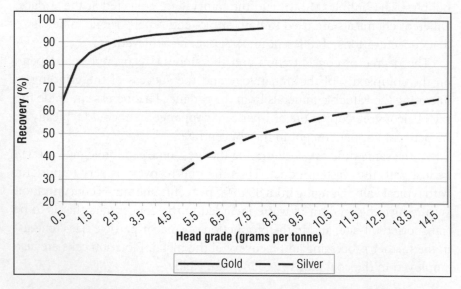

Magnetic and electrostatic

Minerals with high magnetic susceptibility are attracted to magnets, while minerals that are good conductors can be influenced by electrostatic fields. A good example of the application of these processes is in the mineral sands industry. Heavy mineral sands are made up of four primary minerals: ilmenite and monazite, which are susceptible to a magnetic field, and zircon and rutile, which are not. Rutile and ilmenite are conductors; therefore, the ilmenite can be separated from the monazite and the rutile from the zircon. Thus all four heavy minerals can be recovered from a heavy mineral concentrate by a dry process through a combination of magnetics and electrostatics.

Wet high intensity magnetic separation can be used where magnetic susceptibility can be induced by a very high magnetic field. An example of this is the separation of hematite from shale minerals.

Ore sorting

Some minerals will react differently from their associated gangue minerals when sensed by a variety of sensors. Valuable minerals can be distinguished by a differentiation in colour, with some minerals fluorescing under ultraviolet light or X-rays, and some can be distinguished by their response to near infrared spectroscopy. These differences can be used for sorting purposes. For example, diamonds can be made to glow with X-rays, and scheelite fluoresces. Similarly, sulphide minerals can be separated from non-sulphide minerals by conductivity sorting. Usually individual gangue particles are blasted from their trajectory with an air blast to sort the rocks containing valuable minerals from the waste.

On-site hydrometallurgical recovery

Further processing of concentrates to recover the metal, in particular for base metals, is often carried out off site at smelters and refineries. There is an increasing trend towards processing directly to metal on site, in order to reduce both costs of transportation and the reliance on third-party processing.

Gold

In nearly all cases, gold is recovered on site by gravity separation and the leaching or dissolving of gold from the gold ore with cyanide. The cyanide dissolves the gold and associated silver and other metals, which are then further concentrated by using activated carbon to load the solution until suitable concentrations of gold in cyanide are achieved. Where the gold is slow to leach, additional chemicals may be added, such as lead nitrate, which reduces filming over the exposed gold surface, allowing increased recovery of several per cent.

The gold is more often than not dissolved in tanks that contain the cyanide; however, where grades are low—say, below 1 gram per tonne—the ore is heaped on leach pads, where the cyanide percolates through the heaps (that is, heap leaching).[5] The gold is then recovered from the solution by electrolysis, with the gold plating onto iron electrodes and then recovered from the iron by melting in a furnace. The gold, which is often a dore (a mixture of gold and silver), is sent off to a refinery to be purified to international standards (99.99 per cent).

Figure 7.11 shows the daily assayed grade (light line) from the Higginsville gold plant in Western Australia with a seven-day moving average (dark line). For the June quarter, ore from the new Trident mine resulted in increased grades. Reconciliation of gold produced from the plant shows a higher average grade particularly for the months of May (6.2g/t) and June (6.0g/t) than those assayed going into the plant. The daily volatility and differences in reconciliation are not uncommon where it is difficult to gain truly representative samples of the mill feed. This is particularly the case where gold occurs in relatively coarse size fractions (commonly known as spotty gold).

Copper

Oxide copper and some sulphide copper ore will readily dissolve in sulphuric acid. Most chalcopyrite ore, the most common form of copper minerals (70 per cent of world reserves), is an exception to this. For copper minerals that can be dissolved in sulphuric acid, copper metal can then be recovered

---

5 This method allows for lower operating and capital costs, but may result in lower recoveries over a longer cycle time. An important aspect of heap leaching is the ability to maintain a steady flow of the leaching solution (leachant) through the heap. The heap needs to be sufficiently robust to withstand the process and the material stacked in such a way that there is minimal migration of fines towards the bottom to prevent blockages. Also, the bottom materials must be able to support the weight of the material stacked above. Clearly, the flow of leachant, which needs to get to all parts of the heap, could be greatly impacted and the overall recoveries reduced. Premature binding of heap material as well as slumping may occur, causing the heap to collapse. The use of heap leaching extends to gold, copper, nickel and uranium.

by solvent extraction and electro-winning—often termed SX-EW, which refers to the process of solvent (organic) extraction from a dilute solution to concentrate the electrolyte followed by electro-winning (electrolysis).

Figure 7.11 Higginsville gold plant assay grade, July 2008–09

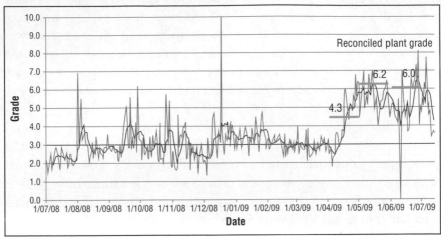

Source: Figure 3 from the Avoca 2009 Annual Report, p. 8, reproduced with permission from Alacer Gold.

Nickel

Under the right conditions, nickel will also dissolve in sulphuric acid or ammonia and, through a more complex process than copper, including leaching under high temperature and pressure, can be recovered as a metal through a final stage of electrolysis. A number of Australian projects using high-pressure acid leach of laterite nickel deposits have been developed and work continues in the development of lower temperature and pressure processes.

An approximate estimate of the capital cost for electro-winning (adjusted for inflation from the AusIMM *Cost Estimation Handbook,* 1993) is given by the formula capital cost = US\$22 000 × (tpa)$^{0.95}$, where tpa equals the tonnes of metal produced per year.

Mineral and metallurgical problems

As with any complex process, things can go wrong. Sometimes it may be a result of insufficient investigation of the mineralogy, lack of adequate pilot testing of the processing circuit or the failure of selected equipment in the plant. All of these can lead to reduced recovery, increased costs and closures that can have a devastating impact on the project economics.

For example, the $750 million expansion of Newcrest's Telfer goldmine in 2004 resulted in significantly lower gold recoveries than originally estimated. Once mining started it was found that the metallurgy was more complex in the supergene zone of the orebody and high-grade gold was associated with high arsenic and pyrite. To keep the arsenic levels low enough to meet customer requirements for the gold/copper concentrate produced, pyrite was sent to the tailings dam, resulting in an unexpected, significant loss of gold.

Another example was the initial plant throughput of OM Holdings Bootu Creek manganese mine in 2004, which ran at only 57 per cent of plant capacity due to deficiencies in ore-handling design of the heavy media separation plant. Fine ore caused blockages at the crushed ore reclaim feeders beneath the crushed ore stockpile, and so a temporary bypass feeder had to be installed with ore fed by excavators as well as upgrading of the tailings pumps. An additional $5.3 million was subsequently allocated to design a permanent solution, with an apron feeder and new surge bin replacing the crushed ore stockpile. Rectification was completed 18 months after first production.

In the case of Titan Resources' Armstrong nickel mine, after removing 2.5 million bench cubic metres of waste from the open cut in late 2004, the first shipment of ore (1.91 per cent nickel), and a subsequent second shipment to the nearby Kambalda nickel concentrator, failed to meet the ore purchase agreement for toll treating due to excess levels of non-sulphide nickel ore as a result of partially oxidised material being mixed with sulphide material. Testing of ore at the open cut showed that although non-sulphide ore was at a level that would now meet the ore purchase agreement, the ratio of iron to magnesium oxide (Fe:MgO) was outside specification. Previous test work had shown that the Fe:MgO ratio did not meet specification, but good recovery of nickel to concentrate was achieved. However, the database on which the economic valuation of the mine development had been based gave no quantification of the Fe:MgO ratio and subsequent grade control drilling showed that all of the open cut resource would probably not meet specification. Within two months of the first ore shipment the mine was closed.

Oil and gas processing

On-site processing of oil and gas is carried out prior to delivery and downstream processing. The hydrocarbons are gathered from the numerous wells within the field(s) to the main processing plant inlet, where the oil and gas are separated by utilising their different densities. Gas leaving the separation system can in some cases be flared (burnt). Otherwise, the gas is first treated to remove any water by absorption with glycol. Liquefied petroleum gases (LPG), such as ethane, butane and propane, are then commonly removed by using refrigeration to condense them out of the gas stream. The remaining gas (methane) can then be sent by pipeline to gas markets or used for gas lift or reservoir recompression.

The oil is stabilised by the removal of gas in the separation section. Any remaining water that may be present in an emulsion form is then removed by chemical or electrostatic means prior to shipment. Any separated water is treated for residual contaminates before it is discharged back into the environment or re-injected into the reservoir.

Some indicative onshore gathering, treatment and transport cost statistics provided by the South Australian Mines and Energy Department (*Economics of Gas Gathering and Processing in the Cooper Basin 1997*, <http://www.pir.sa.gov.au/__data/assets/pdf_file/0004/28615/RB97_034.pdf>) and adjusted for inflation show that reasonable tolling costs to access the existing Cooper Basin facilities (there is only one such facility) would be about US\$2.10 to US\$3.00 per million cubic feet of gas (mmcf), while the marginal cost to toll treat would be around 67¢ per mcf of raw gas. The cost of processing liquids would be about US\$115 to US\$150 per cubic metre or US\$18.00 to US\$22.50 per barrel.

Calculating the cost in, say, the Permian Basin of the US is more complex, as there are a number of operating facilities, but indicative figures are similarly provided in the same document based on production of, say, 2 million cubic feet per day (mmcf/d) declining at 10 per cent per year over four years (the expected third-party's payback period) for the total production of 2.0 billion cubic feet (bcf). The costs are estimated as follows:

» *Gas gathering*—assume a 10 cm diameter pipe over 7 km using a rule of thumb of US\$3000 per cm-km equals US\$1 496 000 divided by 2.0 bcf equals US 9.8¢ per mcf.

» *Compression*—assume three stages of compression to get the pressure from 200 kPa (kilopascals) to 6700 kPa, which would require approximately 375 kW. Using a rule of thumb of installed capital costs of US$1000 per kW for one stage, US$1300 for two and US$1600 for three, the capital cost comes to US$770 000. Assuming annual operating costs are US$150 per kW, then the total four-year cost is US50¢ per mcf.

The total gathering and compression costs come out to about US60¢ per mcf. If removal of CO_2 is required, as well as dehydration, then the charge for these volumes could add a further US30¢ per mcf.

Infrastructure

The amount and cost of infrastructure required for a resource project will be dependent on the location and specific project parameters. The mine site will be designed to accommodate the requirements of mining the resource, and treatment and transport of the saleable product. The level of on-site processing, and hence the level of infrastructure required, will be based on economic considerations.

Access

Access to and from the mine site will include roads, most likely an airstrip, possibly a rail loop or dedicated rail line, port facilities, and oil and gas pipelines for hydrocarbon developments. These modes of transport will be used to provide a workforce and materials for the construction and then continued operation of the mine. Additionally, finished mine product will be transported to market. The size and cost of this infrastructure will depend on the commodity volumes involved, from relatively small quantities of gold flown out from the mine site to millions of tonnes of iron ore railed each year to coastal ports.

Power

Power in the form of electricity is a major requirement for the processing and, to some extent, the mining of the orebody. Where possible, mine sites will aim to connect to a nearby power grid to obtain cheaper electricity. Of course, the cost of the power may be prohibitive if the supply is inadequate or the capital cost of transmission lines and the subsequent transmission losses are too great. Given the relative isolation of mining operations, it is not uncommon to generate electricity by diesel electric generators, which, due to the high cost of diesel fuel, will cost several times as much as conventional grid power. The construction of additional gas pipelines, particularly in Western Australia, the Northern Territory and Queensland, has provided an alternative supply of power to generate electricity, and can be less than half the cost of diesel electric.

A 1 million litre per year diesel consumption, which would generate some 5 GWh (gigawatt hours), is equal to approximately 41 terajoules of gas. The cost of the gas would be equal to the field price, which might be around say US$4 per gigajoule (Gj), plus the delivery cost. The delivery cost is usually made up of three components: toll charge, capacity reservation and throughput charge. The toll charge is a fixed fee per gigajoule, while the capacity reservation charge is a fee per kilometre of transmission line along which the gas has to be transported. These two fees are then often adjusted by a load factor, which is a ratio of the average volume to the maximum volume required per period, to allow for variable gas demands. The throughput charge is a charge per gigajoule per kilometre of transportation. For example, the charges for, say, 1000 km transmission with a load factor of 0.85 are shown in table 7.8.

Table 7.8: example of delivery costs

Delivery cost		US$/Gj
Toll charge		0.40
Capacity reservation charge	$0.0028 × 1000 km	2.80
Sub-total		3.20
Load factor	divide by 0.85	3.79
Throughput charge	$0.00106 × 1000 km	1.06
Total delivery cost		**4.85**

Take or pay provisions are often part of the supply contract, which sets a minimum volume the user has to purchase, irrespective of whether the gas is used during that period. A credit for unused gas may be provided for the user, but the minimum will have to be paid to ensure a cash flow to the pipeline owner to help fund the construction. The total cost of US$8.85 per gigajoule compares with a cost of approximately US$45 to US$55 per gigajoule for diesel excluding operating efficiencies. Capital costs for diesel generation are of the order of $1.5 million per megawatt, while gas-fired generators are some 10 to 20 per cent more expensive. With the current high cost of oil, gas-powered generation is very attractive when it is available.

The approximate cost of construction of a short/small-diameter gas trunk line from a main transmission line to a mining project can be calculated using the following equation, where the capital cost equals the pipe length in kilometres times the pipe diameter in millimetres times US$1400. For example, a 250-mm pipeline over 50 kilometres would cost approximately US$17.5 million. The difficulty with this approximation is that it does not take into account the gas pressure, internal and external diameter of the pipe and compressor stations. The Australian Gas Association (AGA) has provided a number of models, which can be used to arrive at a more accurate forecast (Australian Gas Association, 1992). A simple version (adjusted for inflation) for pipelines of less than 500 mm outside diameter (od) in remote locations is:

$$\text{Capital cost} = (0.42 - 0.000458 \times od + 0.000003 \times od^2) \times L$$
where L = the pipeline length in kilometres

For this example the cost is estimated at US$25.3 million compared with US$17.5 million.

Water

Water is critical to the on-site processing of most ores, dust suppression for mining, and for workforce needs. As Australia is the driest inhabited continent in the world, the water supply should always be assessed when considering the viability of a mining project. Typical consumption rates for mineral processing (assuming recovery of water from tailings) are of the order of 500 litres per tonne of ore processed. Water may be sourced from rivers, dams and underground reservoirs such as the Great Artesian Basin.

It is also common practice to reclaim and recirculate process water, with the addition of make-up water to replace losses. In some cases, such as uranium mining, the project will have a no-release system where all water that is collected in the processing area is retained and not discharged into the environment. Evaporation ponds are used to regulate the excess water accumulation.

Waste dumps and tailings

For open cut and strip mines, the removal and placement of waste material can be a major component of the operations, given the large volumes that can be involved. For strip mining, the waste will most often be placed into the previous strip, groomed and then revegetated as part of the mine's rehabilitation program. Provisions may be made to pay for the rehabilitation, but little in the way of infrastructure costs would be required. For open cut mines, suitable sites may need to be prepared for the dumping of waste. The cost of constructing waste pads to ensure proper ground stability and prevent acid rock drainage may be treated as a capital cost that would be depreciated over the operating life of the pad.

Tailings dams are required to contain the waste material obtained from the processing of the ore. The tailings are generally a fine slurry of waste material. The tailings are stored in tailings dams that are designed to allow for the compaction of the waste and the evaporation or decanting of the associated water. Costs associated with the construction of tailings dams and impervious walls are also depreciated over their useful life. Costs of rehabilitation on mine closure may also be incurred.

Towns

For mines in remote areas where there are no existing towns to provide accommodation and amenities, the mining company will often be required to provide a settlement. An increasing trend is for fly in–fly-out arrangements, where the workers will remain on site and work continuously (that is, 12-hour shifts) for several weeks before flying back to other population centres for extended breaks. A village and messing facilities (as a minimum) will then be required on or near the operation.

Smelting and refining

The application of high temperatures will result in the melting of the ore concentrate. Fluxes are used to lower the required temperatures. The heavy base metals then sink to the bottom of the furnace and waste and fluxes float off as slag.

Due to the complex nature of minerals, other elements may also be melted (or dissolved in a hydrometallurgical process), which can adversely affect the ultimate recovery and purity of the metal. The refining process will therefore use a variety of technologies to purify the metal. More specific processes of smelting and refining are briefly described in chapter 20.

Smelting

Smelting is the primary method of removing the wanted metal from the mine's concentrate by the application of heat in a furnace. The waste or unwanted materials are either burnt off in vapour or bled off as a liquid slag. The process usually involves reduction (the removal of oxygen from the ore) with the application of a reducing agent, such as coke. Additionally, fluxes are added to bond with waste materials to produce liquids or slag at the furnace temperature. The metal will have a different relative density from the slag and will therefore separate, which allows for the removal of slag from the furnace. The heat source in the furnace can be sulphur from a sulphide concentrate; coal, coke or gas in a blast furnace; or electricity in an electric arc furnace.

As an example, consider the case of copper concentrates, which may have grades of between 20 and 57 per cent. Prior to the advent of flash furnaces, sulphide concentrates (produced from refractory ores) were commonly roasted.[6] This involved the burning of the concentrate with oxygen (and perhaps a flux such as silica) to produce SO_2, which is a waste product and if released can be responsible for the production of acid rain. The SO_2 can be converted to sulphuric acid or combined with the blast furnace gases for further processing. The product from the roasting section is often referred to as a sinter. As well as reducing the level of sulphur, the sinter plant should also produce a product suitable for the next phase. A typical example is shown in table 7.9.

Table 7.9: copper concentrate and sinter grade

	Cu (%)	S (%)	Fe (%)	SiO$_2$
Mixed concentrate input	23	30	33	8
Sinter produced	40	7	27	20

6 Ferro-oxidans bacteria can be used rather than directly oxidising the ore: the bacteria act as a catalyst in the oxidation of refractory ores (bioleaching). Temperature and acidity have to be controlled to allow the bacteria to convert the sulphur in the pyrites into sulphuric acid, which further aids in the dissolving of the base metal such as copper into the acid liquor.

The sinter plus coke (9 per cent of the charge) is then placed or charged continuously into a smelter blast furnace to produce a liquid copper matte, which is a mixture of mainly iron and copper sulphides, usually containing 45 to 70 per cent copper, and liquid slag. The slag is granulated in cold water and the molten matte is sent to a converter to produce blister copper. At the converter, copper scrap, molten copper matte and silica are heated to white metal (Cu_2S), with the slag removed, thus increasing the copper content of the blister copper, as shown in table 7.10.

Table 7.10: copper concentrate and blister grade

	Cu (%)	S (%)	Fe (%)	SiO$_2$
Copper concentrate	57	24	12	2
Blister copper	98.8	1.1	0.1	—

The blister copper plus high-grade scrap copper are placed in an anode furnace. Compressed air is introduced into the molten charge for a fire-refining treatment where the oxidising treatment results in removal of such elements as iron, lead and sulphur by slagging and gas evolution. The molten copper, now with a grade of around 99 per cent copper, is then cast into anode shapes ready for the refining process by electrolysis.

Alternatively, flash furnaces are now more commonly used to produce blister copper directly from concentrates with typical grades as shown in table 7.11.

Table 7.11: flash furnace grade of matte and blister copper

	Cu (%)	S (%)	Fe (%)	SiO$_2$
Copper matte	48	21	22	0.3
Blister copper	98.5	0.2	0.1	—

In this process, dried concentrate and silica flux are introduced to the top of the furnace. Enriched air containing 80 to 90 per cent oxygen is injected into the furnace burner with 80 to 90 per cent of the sulphur acting as a fuel and converting into a gaseous phase in the following reaction:

$$Cu_2S + 2Cu_2O \rightarrow 6Cu + SO_2$$

The blister and slag form in the settler of the blast furnace at an operating temperature of 1270°C.

Refining

The cast copper anodes are placed in electrolytic cells in a tank house with stainless steel as the cathodes. The electrolyte is made up of a sulphuric acid solution through which a current of approximately 300 A/m^2 is passed. The composition of the electrolyte is shown in table 7.12.

Table 7.12: refining electrolyte copper grade

	Cu	Free H$_2$SO$_4$	Arsenic	Nickel
Concentration g/Litre	42–50	175–190	10–15	15–18

The copper anodes dissolve and are plated onto the stainless steel cathodes. The cathode copper, with metal grades of up to 99.99 per cent copper, is removed at regular intervals. Anode slimes containing precious metals fall to the bottom of the cells and are collected for recovery of the precious metals.

Treatment and refining charges

As described, sophisticated processes are required to produce a saleable metal product. Materials and energy are required in the various processes that must ultimately be paid for prior to the sale of the metal. Details of the various smelting and refining charges for custom or full treatment of different metals are set out in chapter 20. Ore concentrates are normally sold to a smelter net of treatment and refining charges, which vary between minerals and with the quality of the concentrate. The treatment charge is per tonne of concentrate, and the refining charge is per unit of contained metal. Thus the higher the concentrate grade, the lower the TC per unit metal. The refining charge is independent of concentrate grade.

The typical terms include a reduction in the amount of metal paid for and a treatment and refining charge (TC/RC). A price participation (PP) formula is included to increase the TC/RC if the metal price is above a set level and, conversely, to decrease the TC/RC if the metal price is below the set level. Refining charges may also be applicable for any precious metals and penalties applicable for undesirable (dirty) elements such as antimony, bismuth, arsenic and mercury. The following is based on a copper concentrate:

» *Payable metal.* Payment is made for 96.5 per cent of copper content of the concentrate or a minimum deduction of 1.1 per cent. Any gold content is paid for, after deducting 1 gram per tonne of concentrate (g/t), plus 90 per cent of silver content is paid after a minimum deduction of 30 g/t concentrate.

» *Treatment and refining charge.* The treatment charge is generally quoted as a fixed deduction per tonne of concentrate. This charge has fluctuated widely in the past, with current treatment charges at around US$70 per tonne of concentrate (although spot contracts can be lower). Refining charges are based on the metal content of the concentrate and are typically around US7.5¢ per pound of copper metal. For average concentrate grades, this equates to approximately US20¢ per pound or US$438 per tonne of metal.

» *Price participation.* US2¢ per pound for each additional 10 per cent increase in the copper price above a base price of US130¢ per pound.

» *Refining charges and penalties.* Refining charges for payable gold can be of the order of US$5, and for silver US 45¢ per ounce. Penalties are varied and negotiable. For example, in the case of arsenic an additional charge of US$3 for each 0.1 per cent above 0.2 per cent content in the concentrate may be payable.

Example

	Copper	Gold	Silver	Arsenic
Concentrate grade (%)	25	2	100	0.3
Price	US$7750/t	US$1750/oz	US$35/oz	—

Payable metal

Copper = 25% × 96.5% = 24.15% or 25% − 1.1% = 23.9%, therefore = 23.9%

Gold = 2 − 1 = 1 g/t

Silver = 100 × 90% = 90 g/t or 100 − 30 = 70 g/t, therefore = 70 g/t

Total payable for metal per tonne of concentrate

US$7750 × 0.239 + US$1750 × 1/31.1 + US$35 × 70/31.1 = US$1987.3

Treatment charge/refining charge per tonne of concentrate

Treatment charge = US$70 per tonne of concentrate

Refining charge = US$0.075 × 2204.6 × 0.239 = US$39.52 for refining

Total charge = US$109.52

Price participation charge per tonne of concentrate

Participation charges are often not included when concentrates are in strong demand.
(7750/2204 − 1.3)/1.13*10 × US$0.02 × 2204.6 × 0.239 = US$179.58

Refining charge

Gold (US$5/oz) = US$5 × 1/31.1 = US$0.16

Silver (US$0.45/oz) = US$0.45 × 70/31.1 = US$1.16

Penalties

Arsenic = US$3 (arsenic level 0.1% above 0.2% cutoff)

Total deduction = US$(109.52 + 179.58 + 0.16 + 1.16 + 3) = US$290.72

The net smelter return is therefore US$1987.30 less US$290.72, or US$1696.58 per tonne of concentrate. If the price participation factor is excluded the net smelter return is US$1876.16 per tonne. This compares with the gross metal value (price times metal content) of US$2162.58 per tonne. It is therefore crucial in any financial analysis to ascertain the correct saleable value of the mine product.

Consider the following example for a copper concentrate. Some of the larger mining companies, such as Xstrata in Australia, undertake their own smelting and refining. Some of the indicative costs for copper cathode production and lead bullion (which includes silver, which must be refined later) at Mount Isa are shown in table 7.13.

Table 7.13: indicative costs for copper cathode production and lead bullion at Mount Isa

Copper	
Smelter rate	0.955 million tonnes/annum
Concentrate grade	28%
Recovery	95%
Anode production	0.245 million tonnes/annum
Smelting operating cost	$290 per tonne
Refining cost	$90 per tonne anode
Lead bullion	
Smelter rate	0.325 million tonnes/annum
Concentrate grade	56.5%
Recovery lead	94%
Recovery silver	97%
Smelting operating costs	$230 per tonne

Source: MIM Information Memorandum, May 2003.

The mining, processing and recovery of a valuable mineral can be a complex and expensive exercise from both the capital required and the ongoing operating costs. The issue of costs is covered in more detail in the next section. Although much is said by investors about the geology and reserves of a deposit, less discussion occurs when it comes to the likely recovery factors and the ultimate product that might be derived from the deposit. The importance of mineral processing and metallurgy for any project should not be underestimated.

CHAPTER 8
Indicative capital and operating costs

The amount of information available for any valuation can vary considerably depending on the stage of development and the level of access to in-house information. The following sections provide information that may help you estimate some capital and operating costs for mining projects. It must be stressed that these numbers are very approximate and do not account for the specific aspects of any individual project.

Indicative capital costs—rule of thumb

The capital cost to develop a mine is dependent on a range of issues. These issues include but are not limited to:

» the type of mineral—metal, bulk or hydrocarbon

» whether the mine is underground or open cut

» the existing infrastructure—power, town site, airport, roads and rail

» the water and power supply

» the topography—terrain and availability of suitable areas for mine facilities, tailings dam, waste dumps and water dams

» the climate—the impact of rain, snow, ice, humidity and temperature.

The estimation of capital costs is thus a complex issue that requires adequate and detailed information about a particular deposit. This level of information is often not available to the market, so approximate values or rule-of-thumb estimates are used in placing a value on a resource project. A gauge of the order of magnitude of capital costs can be obtained from published information. For commodities such as coal and oil, where there is little secondary processing, the cost is in units of mine production.

For commodities where considerable secondary processing is required, such as base metals, the cost is often shown on a per-tonne-milled or -processed basis. For goldmines it is common for the cost to be quoted per ounce. Appendix E lists details of 223 Australian resource projects, covering numerous commodities planned or under development. A summary of the range of capital costs is shown in table 8.1.

Table 8.1: capital costs summary

Commodity	Capital costs range/unit of annual production
Black coal	$10/tonne to $671/tonne
LNG	$194/tonne to $5 000/tonne
Coal seam methane	$3m/Pj to $10m/Pj
Copper	$1833/tonne to $14 400/tonne
Gold	$104/ounce to $2430/ounce
Iron ore	$13/tonne to $720/tonne
Lead–Zinc	$310/tonne to $3889/tonne
Mineral sands	$250tonne to $1233/tonne
Nickel metal	$1800/tonne to $59 204/tonne
Uranium	$91/t to $313/t

To provide readers with additional indicative capital costs on a global perspective, I have included in figures 8.2 to 8.4 (see pp. 154–56) US$ cost curves based on more than 350 mining development projects located in over 60 countries around the world. The cost curves have been indexed to the end of 2011 (as shown in figure 8.1), one for the capital costs based on a weighed average of US steel, wages and energy indices and one for operating costs based on diesel, wages and chemical indices. As capital and operating costs are based in US$ the indices should adjust for relative inflation rates between the US and the country where the project is located.

Figure 8.1: capital and operating index, November 2004–11

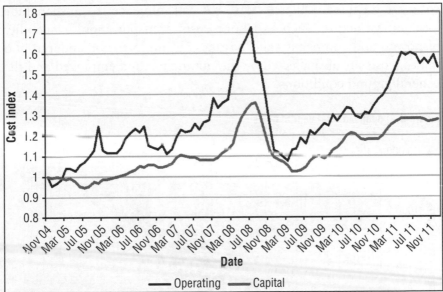

Costs curves for mining projects do exhibit economies of scale or power curves, which when plotted on log-log charts present themselves as straight lines, as shown in the charts to follow. As well as providing the two parameters for calculating the cost, the number of examples used and the goodness of fit are also shown.

There is considerable noise or scatter, as all mining projects are different even within one type of commodity, and using the same mining method and metallurgical process. Readers should therefore be mindful when using these charts, as they provide only a rough guide for new mining projects. The line of best fit can be considered the average value for a given production rate, although there can be quite a large variation around the mean. The projects include base metal, precious metals, coal, uranium and iron ore.

Capital costs are shown in figures 8.2 and 8.3 for open cut and for underground operations (the equation for the best line of fit is shown below each chart). The open cut chart is based on total tonnes (millions) mined per annum (mtpa): that is, total ore plus waste. As the production volumes increase the capital costs increase, but at a declining rate. A project cost can vary for a given throughput due to factors such as the amount of metal refining on site; this has been limited primarily to gold refining and solvent extraction, and electro-winning (SX-EW) for copper. For major base metal projects no smelting and refinery costs are included. Other factors that can influence the cost include local infrastructure, such as labour costs, transportation, availability of power, and complexity and hardness of the ore. For underground mines, costs are also affected by the mining method employed and the general ground conditions.

Figure 8.2: open cut total capital costs

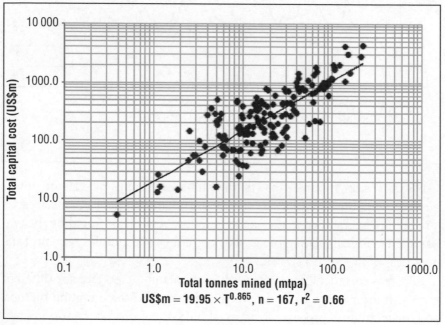

$$US\$m = 19.95 \times T^{0.865}, \; n = 167, \; r^2 = 0.66$$

Figure 8.3: underground total capital costs

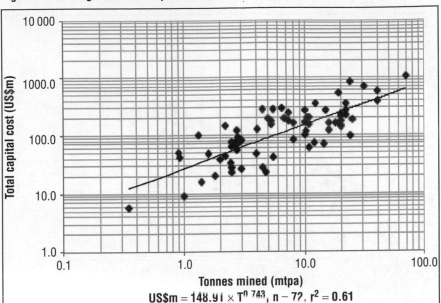

$$US\$m = 148.91 \times T^{0.743}, n - 72, r^2 = 0.61$$

Nearly all of the mines in this study have some level of on-site processing. As mentioned, most of the mills produce a concentrate for base metals or gold bullion on-site. Plant costs for a given throughput will also vary depending on the process involved, hardness of ore and energy costs (see figure 8.4, overleaf). The plant costs can be subtracted from the total capital costs to get an estimate of other capital costs.

Figure 8.4: treatment total plant capital costs

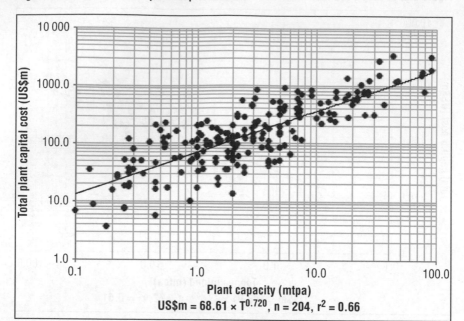

$$US\$m = 68.61 \times T^{0.720}, n = 204, r^2 = 0.66$$

Indicative operating costs—rule of thumb

Operating costs, like capital costs, will vary depending on location, mining and metallurgical factors. Two mines producing identical quantities of a resource product can have quite different operating costs; however, the order of magnitude of operating costs will often be related to the size of the operation. Additionally, there is often an economy of scale (exponent) so that the larger the operation the higher the absolute cost, but the lower the relative cost on a unit basis.

As with the capital costs, I have added US$ operating cost curves, which are based on more than 350 mining development projects located in over 60 countries. Total operating costs are shown in figure 8.5 for open cut and figure 8.6 (overleaf) for underground operations. As with total capital costs the open cut chart is based on total tonnes mined per annum: that is, total ore plus waste. Operating costs for a given size of operation will also vary for the same reasons as capital costs. Additionally, consider an open cut mine with combined ore and waste production of 10 million tonnes per annum (mtpa). This could be made up of either the processing of 1 mtpa of ore and 9 mtpa of waste or 4 mtpa of ore and 6 mtpa of waste. As the cost to mine waste is less than the mining and treatment costs for the ore, the cost per tonne is likely to be higher for the latter, if all other factors are equal. Variation in underground operating costs will also be influenced by the type of mining method employed and factors such as shaft haulage versus declines.

Figure 8.5: open cut total operating costs

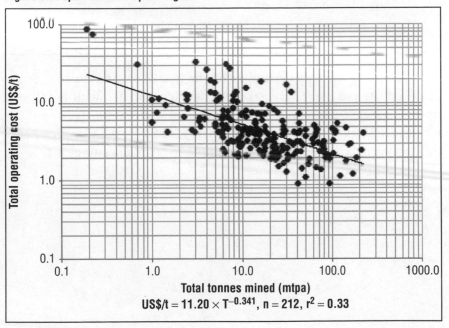

$$US\$/t = 11.20 \times T^{-0.341}, n = 212, r^2 = 0.33$$

Figure 8.6: underground total operating costs

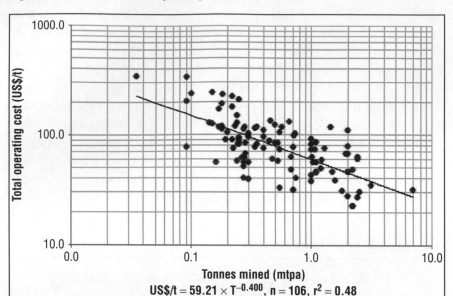

Treatment costs will vary depending on the type of ore and the complexity of the on-site process. Low costs are generally associated with heap leach operations while the high-cost operations, for a given tonnage, are those where metal is produced on site, particularly SX-EW (see figure 8.7). Again mill treatment costs can be subtracted from the total operating costs to get an estimate of other mining costs.

Figure 8.7: treatment plant total operating costs

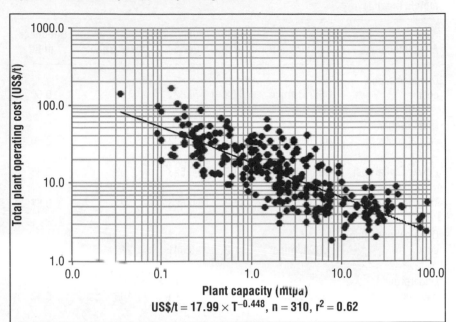

$$US\$/t = 17.99 \times T^{-0.448}, \; n = 310, \; r^2 = 0.62$$

Visit my website <www.miningvaluation.com> for more up-to-date charts.

I have also provided cost curves in table 8.2 for additional parameters based on data obtained from all projects and for those based on gold and base metals only.

Table 8.2: cost curves for additional parameters and for gold and base metals

All commodities	Output/input	Constant	Power	Observations	Goodness of fit
Open cut total capital cost	US$m, mtpa	19.95	0.865	167	0.66
Underground total capital cost	US$m, mtpa	148.91	0.743	72	0.61
Treatment capital cost	US$m, mtpa	68.61	0.72	204	0.66

(*continued*)

Table 8.2: cost curves for additional parameters and for gold and base metals (*cont'd*)

All commodities	Output/input	Constant	Power	Observations	Goodness of fit
Open cut capital cost	US$m, mtpa	6.62	0.821	138	0.60
Underground capital cost	US$m, mtpa	86.42	0.732	57	0.50
Power capital cost	US$m, mtpa	6.98	0.528	33	0.45
Tailings capital cost	US$m, mtpa	4.63	0.665	21	0.67
Open cut operating cost	US$/t, mtpa	11.2	−0.341	212	0.33
Underground operating cost	US$/t, mtpa	59.21	−0.4	106	0.48
Treatment operating cost	US$/t, mtpa	17.99	−0.448	310	0.62
Power operating cost	US$/t, mtpa	4.91	−0.454	39	0.46
Open cut direct operating cost	US$/t, mtpa	20.88	−0.39	132	0.34
Underground direct operating cost	US$/t, mtpa	36.67	−0.428	85	0.40
Gold					
Open cut total capital cost	US$m, mtpa	13.73	0.914	76	0.70
Underground total capital cost	US$m, mtpa	168.74	0.796	28	0.55
Treatment capital cost	US$m, mtpa	63.5	0.608	95	0.50

Indicative capital and operating costs

All commodities	Output/input	Constant	Power	Observations	Goodness of fit
Open cut capital cost	US$m, mtpa	6.15	0.937	60	0.76
Underground capital cost	US$m, mtpa	90.45	0.807	25	0.55
Power capital cost	US$m, mtpa	7.19	0.587	19	0.34
Tailings capital cost	US$m, mtpa	7.26	0.227	14	0.70
Open cut operating cost	US$/t, mtpa	4.07	−0.254	59	0.29
Underground operating cost	US$/t, mtpa	58.07	−0.343	52	0.29
Treatment operating cost	US$/t, mtpa	15.34	−0.498	146	0.55
Power operating cost	US$/t, mtpa	3.61	−0.512	19	0.47
Open cut direct operating cost	US$/t, mtpa	6.76	−0.244	96	0.27
Underground direct operating cost	US$/t, mtpa	40.12	−0.361	42	0.25
Base metals					
Open cut total capital cost	US$m, mtpa	26.41	0.875	67	0.75
Underground total capital cost	US$m, mtpa	132.13	0.702	34	0.63
Treatment capital cost	US$m, mtpa	80.81	0.683	86	0.71
Open cut capital cost	US$m, mtpa	9.59	0.87	58	0.55

(continued)

Table 8.2: cost curves for additional parameters and for gold and base metals (*cont'd*)

All commodities	Output/input	Constant	Power	Observations	Goodness of fit
Underground capital cost	US$m, mtpa	70.42	0.629	21	0.53
Power capital cost	US$m, mtpa	6.27	0.768	15	0.54
Tailings capital cost	US$m, mtpa	3.99	0.922	6	0.43
Open cut operating cost	US$/t, mtpa	5.05	−0.298	61	0.39
Underground operating cost	US$/t, mtpa	50.32	−0.466	54	0.51
Treatment operating cost	US$/t, mtpa	18.37	−0.425	140	0.66
Power operating cost	US$/t, mtpa	6.68	−0.373	21	0.30
Open cut direct operating cost	US$/t, mtpa	14.52	−0.394	85	0.40
Underground direct operating cost	US$/t, mtpa	32.52	−0.362	35	0.33

If an operating cost is known for one type of operation, then an estimate can be made for a different-sized operation by applying the exponents shown in table 8.3 as quantified by Mular (1982). It must be stressed that these are only a rule of thumb where the new cost equals the ratio of production to the power of the exponent. For example, if the cost to mine a 1 million tonne per year operation is $20 per tonne, then using the average cost exponent of 0.6, the estimated cost for a 2 million tonne per year operation would be:

$$\$20 \times (\tfrac{1}{2})^{0.6} = \$20 \times 0.66 = \$13.2 \text{ per tonne}$$

Table 8.3: exponents for estimating operating costs

Operation	Estimated cost/capacity	Exponent
Open cut labour costs	Tonnes per annum mined	0.5
Open cut mine supplies	Tonnes per annum mined	0.5
Underground mine labour	Tonnes per annum mined	0.7
Underground mine supplies	Tonnes per annum mined	0.9
Treatment plant labour	Tonnes per annum mined	0.5
Treatment plant supplies	Tonnes per annum mined	0.7
Open cut mine and mill electric power	Tonnes per annum mined	0.5
Undorground mine and mill electric power	Tonnes per annum mined	0.7
Average cost	**Annual capacity**	**0.6**

Cost curves

A further consideration when investing in projects or resource companies, given the volatility of commodity prices, is the project's position on the cost curve. Clearly the lower the operating cost the better the chances of economic survival during times of depressed commodity prices. Figure 8.8 (overleaf) shows a cost curve for some Australian coalmines. For the lower quartile, the average operating cost is about US$36 per tonne, including costs of transport to port and loading.

Figure 8.8: operating cost curve for Australian coalmines

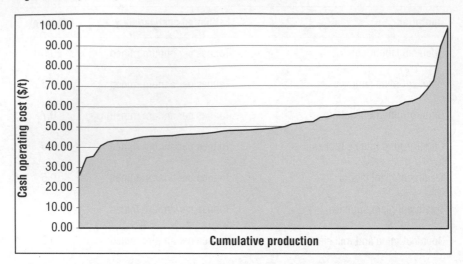

Operating costs on a per tonne basis can vary widely, depending on the level of washing required and the resultant saleable coal (yield), the productivity level and the distance to port.

A number of case studies follow. These are intended to provide information on important aspects that should be considered when undertaking company or project valuations.

MIM coal operations — transport costs

MIM Holdings Limited was a major producer of coal and base metals in Australia; it is now owned by Xstrata Holdings Pty Ltd. Its coal operations in 2003 consisted of the Oaky Creek No. 1 and North underground mines, and an open cut mine, which together produced some 9 million tonnes (Mt) of clean coal per annum. The Collinsville operations consisted of a number of open cut mines producing 5.5 million tonnes of clean coal per annum. The Newlands operations consisted of both underground and open cut operations, producing 8 million tonnes of clean coal per year. Some of the salient operating statistics are listed in table 8.4.

The operating costs for Oaky Creek were the highest as the majority of production was sourced from underground; however, a major contributing factor was the cost of transportation via rail, which again was highest for Oaky Creek. Sustaining capital costs were higher for more complex underground operations and major project capital costs were high for Newlands due to development of another underground mine.

Another planned MIM development was the Rolleston project, which contained recoverable reserves of 173 million tonnes. Plans called for a $250 million open cut producing 8 million tonnes of run of mine (ROM) coal with a strip ratio of 6.8 bench cubic metres (bcm)/ROM tonne. Production was expected to start in mid 2004, ramping up to full production by October 2005. Two 88 m^3 draglines were proposed with typical waste removal by dragline (64.5 per cent), throw blasting (15.5 per cent), dozer assist (8.5 per cent), and truck and shovel (11.5 per cent).

Table 8.4: MIM coalmine operating costs, 2003

Life of mine	Unit	Oaky Creek	Collinsville	Newlands
Production				
ROM	Mt	196.7	64.0	105.0
Saleable	Mt	142.4	56.4	87.0
Operating costs (total)				
Mining	Mt	2961	1016	1490
CHPP	Mt	419	67	176
General	Mt	3.43	—	206
Rail, port and marketing	Mt	1675	294	601
Rehab and closure	Mt	137	23	20
Total	**Mt**	**5536**	**1401**	**2492**
Operating costs (unit)				
Mining	$/ROM t	15.05	15.88	14.18
Mining	$/saleable t	20.74	17.96	16.91
CHPP	$/saleable t	2.94	1.19	1.99

(*continued*)

Table 8.4: MIM coalmine operating costs, 2003 (*cont'd*)

Life of mine	Unit	Oaky Creek	Collinsville	Newlands
General	$/saleable t	2.40	—	2.34
Rail, port and marketing	$/saleable t	11.73	5.20	6.82
Rehab and closure	$/saleable t	0.96	0.41	0.22
Total capital costs	$/saleable t	38.77	24.76	28.29
Sustaining	Mt	474	35	252
Major project	Mt	65	15	449

Note: ROM = run of mine; CHPP = coal handling and preparation plant.

Source: MIM Information memorandum, May 2003, included with permission of AMC Consultants Pty Ltd. Figures and plans were current at the time the report was prepared.

The estimated operating costs per tonne of coal loaded on rail cars are listed in table 8.5. Additional costs of transport and port charges are not included. The operating charges are low when compared with the other operating mines as no washing of the coal was planned.

Table 8.5: Rolleston projected operating costs per tonne, 2005

Item	Average unit cost
Clearing $/bcm	2.05
Drill and blast $/bcm	0.37
Truck and shovel waste removal $/bcm	1.52
Dragline $/bcm	0.43
Waste total $/bcm	0.77
Coalmining $/ROM t	0.80
Pit services $/ROM t	0.30

Item	Average unit cost
Rehabilitation $/product t	0.10
Coal handling $/product t	0.45
Other costs $/product t	2.16
Total direct $/Product t	**10.06**

Source: MIM information memorandum, May 2003, included with permission of AMC Consultants Pty Ltd.

Creston molybdenum project — contract mining versus owner operator

The following example is taken from the 2009 capital and operating cost estimates for the proposed Creston molybdenum project in Mexico. The costs were prepared for both contract mining and owner-operator mining. The capital costs for owner-operator mining were US$104.2 million compared with contractor mining, where the owner would have to spend only US$51.8 million. This reduction is because the contractor would supply its own mining equipment. On the reverse side, the cost of mining would be higher if the contractor was selected, as the contractor needs to service the cost of the mining fleet and make a profit. One item that does stand out is the cost of pre-stripping the open cut. The capitalisation of the larger operator costs for removal of the waste as well as site mining support and staff costs is the reason the capital cost is higher if a contractor is used (see table 8.6).

Table 8.6: project capital costs for the proposed Creston molybdenum project in Mexico, 2009

Expense	Owner-operator (US$ million)	Contractor supplied (US$ million)
Drilling	5.10	—
Loading	21.50	—
Trucks	31.10	—

(*continued*)

Table 8.6: project capital costs for the proposed Creston molybdenum project in Mexico, 2009 (*cont'd*)

Expense	Owner-operator (US$ million)	Contractor supplied (US$ million)
Support equipment	8.70	2.40
Blasting	0.20	—
Maintenance	0.50	0.10
General services	0.30	0.30
Communications	0.01	0.01
Other	0.40	1.60
Pre-stripping	26.80	42.60
Contingency	9.50	4.70
Total	**104.20**	**51.80**

The operating costs on a tonne moved basis (approximately 40 million tonnes of ore and waste per annum) are shown in table 8.7. Whereas the owner-operator costs are US$1.156 per tonne, the inclusion of a contractor increases costs to US$1.846 per tonne.

Table 8.7: project operating costs for the proposed Creston molybdenum project in Mexico, 2009

Expense	Owner-operator (US$/t moved)	Contractor supplied (US$/t moved)
Drill	0.095	—
Blast	0.159	—
Load	0.171	—
Haul	0.503	—

Expense	Owner-operator (US$/t moved)	Contractor supplied (US$/t moved)
Pits, roads and dumps	0.172	0.037
Maintenance	0.027	0.013
General services	0.029	0.026
Contractor	—	1.770
Total	**1.156**	**1.846**

The decision for the mine's owner was whether the capital cost saving of US$52.4 million outweighed the additional operating cost of US$0.69 per tonne moved. This can be determined by calculating the NPV of the additional operating costs and comparing them with the additional capital costs. As mentioned previously, the owner of a mine may find it too difficult to fund additional capital costs and may therefore choose contract mining even if it does not maximise the NPV. The current owners of the project, Mercator Minerals, plan to develop the mine with owner-operator equipment.

Gold and platinum

For the goldmining sector, costs are often quoted on a per production ounce basis, which can vary significantly on a quarter-by-quarter basis as the level of gold production changes. For example, the operating cost may remain stable at, say, US$35 per tonne of ore treated; however, if the recovered grade drops from 3 g/t to 2.5 g/t, then the cost will increase from US$362.8 per ounce (31.1 grams per ounce/3.0 × US$35) to US$435.4 per ounce (31.1/2.5 × US$35).

A number of examples follow, which show the major cost components for operating goldmines. In the first two examples, shown in tables 8.8 and 8.9 (overleaf), for open cut gold mines in Western Australia, the costs on a per tonne basis and total annual cost are converted to dollar per tonne of ore milled. The mill is often the production bottleneck and can be a point of comparison, but still needs to be converted to cost per ounce produced. Readers might like to do the sums where Bluebird had a cost of $511 per ounce, while Nimary was $280 per ounce. The crucial difference was the grade.

Table 8.8: Bluebird Gold Mine operating costs to June 1997

		$/t milled
Waste mined (mtpa)	10.30 (est.)	
Ore mined (mtpa)	2.60	
Ore milled (mtpa)	2.70	
Average head grade (g/t)	1.57	
Estimated recovery (%)	98.20	
Gold production (oz)	128 840.0	
Mining cost ($/t ore plus waste)	1.22 (est.)	5.81*
Sampling cost ($/t ore mined)	0.88	0.85
Milling cost ($/t milled)	7.85 (est.)	7.85
Administration cost ($/t milled)	1.78 (est.)	1.78
Development cost ($/t mined)	4.23	4.07
Exploration cost ($/t milled)	4.04	4.04
Total		**24.4**

* Includes cost of mining waste at a strip ratio of 3.96 (10.3 ÷ 2.6).

Source: St Barbara Mines Limited 1997 annual report.

Table 8.9: Nimary Gold Mine operating costs for 1998–99

	$/t milled
Waste mined (bcmpa)	12.20
Ore mined (mtpa)	1.20
Ore milled (mtpa)	1.25
Average head grade (g/t)	4.78

		$/t milled
Estimated recovery (%)	92.00	
Gold production (ounces)	175 000	
Mining cost	$31.3m	25.04*
Milling cost	$14.5m	11.60
Administration cost	$3.2m	2.56
Total		**39.20**

*Includes cost of mining waste at a strip ratio of 10.2 (12.2 ÷ 1.2).

Source: Independent valuation for Eagle Mining Corporation NL Part D takeover response.

Big Bell goldmine — providing all the facts

Most of the examples in this section are based on public data provided by company responses to hostile bids. Even so, the information provided is often incomplete, and although salient factors are provided, they are often averages over longer time frames, or a group figure that provides less detail, and quite often important factors are missing altogether. The investor is required to rely on the 'expert' in terms of valuation, but this begs the question of why the expert needs to provide any information at all, unless the information provided to the investor is there to give him or her the opportunity to test the expert's assumptions. Obviously, companies are reluctant to provide truly commercially sensitive information, and so sensitivity tables or charts can be provided that offer the investor a limited look at the impact of different assumptions on valuation.

One case where detailed information was provided was in the defence by Australian company New Hampton Goldfields Limited in its takeover by Harmony Gold in February 2001. A summary of New Hampton's valuation was produced, which is shown in table 8.10 (overleaf). The points to note are that as well as the assets in the two mines and exploration areas, the company had an interest in the listed company Croesus, some cash and a gold hedge book that could be sold at the time for $5.5 million, and which, importantly, was not included in the valuation of the mining assets.

Against these assets were net liabilities of $32.3 million that were made up of receivables, trade creditors and bank borrowings. Another important item to subtract is the present value of future head office expenses that would be necessary to run New Hampton if it remained an independent company. These costs include such items as listing and board fees, which are not part of the day-to-day administrative fees at the mine site.

Table 8.10: New Hampton summary of assessed fair market values, 2001

	Preferred assessed values ($000)
Big Bell gold operations	43 200
Big Bell exploration	4 700
Jubilee gold operations	38 800
Jubilee exploration	9 200
Other mineral assets	3 580
Total mineral assets	**99 480**
add investment in Croesus	8 701
less other net liabilities	(32 264)
add cash	3 347
less borrowings	(13 716)
add hedge book	5 500
less future corporate overheads	(11 500)
Total equity value (non diluted)	**59 548**
add proceeds from listed options exercised	17 782
add proceeds from unlisted options exercised	3 054
Total equity value after options	**80 384**
Number of shares (000)	205 023

	Preferred assessed values ($000)
add listed options exercised (000)	77 313
add unlisted options exercised (000)	11 500
Diluted number of shares on issue (000)	293 836
Value per share (undiluted)	$0.29
Value per share (fully diluted)	$0.27

Source: Included with permission of Harmony Gold Australia Pty Ltd.

The major assets of New Hampton were the Western Australian Big Bell and Jubilee goldmines. Table 8.11 shows a summary of the detail provided for Big Bell, which is more than adequate for the market to undertake its own assessment of its value. A similar table was provided for Jubilee with an NPV of $42.7 million. Sensitivity analysis was carried out and preferred values determined, as well as values for the exploration potential.

Table 8.11: Big Bell goldmine revenue and costs, 2001–07

	Unit	2001 2nd half	2001–02	2002–03	2003–04	2004 05	2005–06	2006–07	Total
Underground production	kt	504	1 500	1 950	2 100	1 726	1 400	450	9 630
Grade	g/t	3.32	3.22	3.59	3.19	3.19	3.74	4.63	3.43
Contained gold	koz	53.8	155.1	225.0	215.3	176.9	168.5	67.0	1 062
Open cut production	kt	923	1 586	780	—	—	—	—	3 289
Grade	g/t	2.26	2.33	2.18	0	0	0	0	2.28
Contained gold	koz	67.2	67.2	54.8	—	—	—	—	241

(continued)

173

Table 8.11: Big Bell goldmine revenue and costs, 2001–07 (*cont'd*)

	Unit	2001 2nd half	2001–02	2002–03	2003–04	2004–05	2005–06	2006–07	Total
Mill throughput	kt	1 500	3 000	3 000	3 000	3 000	3 000	970	17 470
Grade	g/t	2.6	2.77	3.03	2.45	2.14	2.13	2.56	2.52
Recovery	%	91%	91%	91%	88%	86%	85%	86%	89%
Recovered gold	**koz**	**114.7**	**243.2**	**265.1**	**207.3**	**178.4**	**175.7**	**71.9**	**1 256**
Revenue @ A$483/oz	k$	55 381	11 7483	12 8021	10 0136	86 179	84 862	34 736	60 6797
Govt royalty	k$	1 369	2 907	3 170	2 473	2 124	2 091	800	14 936
Other royalties	k$	0	0	—	84	—	—	289	373
Underground op. cost	k$	1 188	32 837	45 676	47 227	37 883	32 863	21 962	234 636
Open cut op. cost	k$	1 066	21 846	9 991	—	—	—	—	46 903
Milling cost	k$	13 268	27 471	28 277	28 249	27 393	26 640	8 363	159 661
Admin. cost	k$	3 435	6 871	6 602	4 809	3 954	3 206	1 051	29 927
Engineering services cost	k$	2 295	4 590	4 504	3 933	3 661	3 422	1 111	23 516
Total operating cost	**k$**	**51 622**	**96 522**	**98 221**	**86 774**	**75 014**	**68 222**	**33 576**	**509 951**
Cost per ore tonne milled	$/t	34	32.17	32.74	128.93	25.00	22.74	34.62	29.19
Cost per recovered oz	$/oz	450	396.82	370.57	418.55	420.43	388.29	466.87	405.91

Indicative capital and operating costs

	Unit	2001 2nd half	2001–02	2002–03	2003–04	2004–05	2005–06	2006–07	Total
Underground capital	k$	500	8800	500	1700	500	4000	500	16500
Open cut capital	k$	0	—	—	—	—	—	—	0
Mill capital	k$	500	1000	750	750	2500	—	—	5500
Exploration costs	k$	0	325	100	300	500	90		1315
Mill/mine salvage value	k$	0	—				—	6773	(6773)
Closure costs	k$	0	—					9682	9682
Total non-op. cost	**k$**	**1000**	**10125**	**1350**	**2750**	**3500**	**4090**	**3409**	**26224**
Tax paid	k$	0	632	7554	2318	1323	1221	0	13048
After-tax cash flow	k$	2759	10204	20895	8294	6342	11329	(2249)	57574
Discount @ 9% pa	k$	2759	9362	17587	6404	4493	7363	(1341)	46627

Source: 'New Hampton Goldfields Limited-Specialist Report on Mineral Assets of New Hampton Goldfields Limited', included with permission of Westgold Resources Limited.

New Hampton also had on issue listed and unlisted options, which gave the holder the right to subscribe for ordinary shares at a predetermined or exercise price by a certain date. As the bidder also made an offer for the options, the expert included them as if they were exercised, and as if the company had received the benefit of the cash for the exercise of those options. However, on some occasions bidders might not make an offer for the options, in which case they may or may not be included as above, depending on whether they are likely to be exercised in the course of the bid. If the cost to exercise the options is greater than the price to be received for the ordinary shares, then it is highly unlikely that the options would be exercised, and therefore they would be ignored. In the reverse case, if it makes economic sense for option holders to exercise, then they would be included.

East Kundana — permanent openings

The Western Australia East Kundana gold deposits, made up of both open cut and underground reserves, were located within a short distance of the Kundana mine and its processing facilities. The following information comes from the Gilt Edge Mining Part B takeover response in December 1999. A database of 203 reverse circulation and 10 diamond drill holes, creating a database of 7317 assays was used in conjunction with inverse distance square and indicator kriging (see chapter 5) to determine the appropriate tonnage and grade for blocks 5 metres by 20 metres by 10 metres in depth. The grade tonnage curve for the resource is shown in figure 8.9.

Figure 8.9: East Kundana grade tonnage relationship

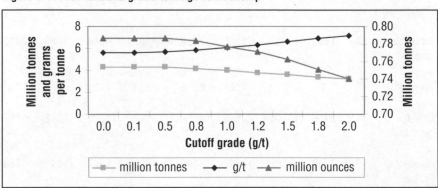

An important aspect of any ore reserve determination is the application of the appropriate specific gravities (densities) for each block. The densities used are shown in table 8.12.

Table 8.12: East Kundana specific gravities

Specific gravities	Tonnes per cubic metre
Transported cover	2.00
Zone of complete oxidation	2.00
Highly weathered zone	2.25

Specific gravities	Tonnes per cubic metre
Moderately weathered zone	2.45
Slightly weathered zone	2.60
Fresh bedrock	2.75

Table 8.13 shows the operating costs, based on a mill throughput of 500 000 tonnes per annum.

Table 8.13: East Kundana operating costs, 1999

Operating cost items	Cost
Ore processing	$13.5/t milled
Haulage (approx. 28 km)	$3.50/t milled
Administration	$2.00/t milled
Supervision and rehabilitation	$0.50/t milled
Grade control	$0.75/t milled
Open cut mining cost	$1.89/t milled
Underground stoping cost	$20.00/t mined
Underground haulage cost (diesel)	$2.70/t/km
Underground level development	
Waste (5.5 × 5.0 m)	$1800/m
Low-grade ore (3.5 × 4.5 m)	$1600/m
Ore (3.5 × 4.5 m)	$1600/m
Rising in waste (1.4 × 1.4 m)	$1000/m
Rising in ore (3.0 × 3.0 m)	$1500/m

(*continued*)

Table 8.13: East Kundana operating costs, 1999 (*cont'd*)

Operating cost items	Cost
Ground support (2.4 rebar)	$70 each
Main decline (5.5 × 5.0 m)	$2200/m
Vent and escapeway x cuts (5.5 × 5.0 m)	$1800/m
Vent and escapeway raises (2.4 m dia.)	$200/m
Other (pump bay)	$1800/m

Source: Gilt Edge Mining Part B, Dec. 1999.

The underground costs show that, for permanent openings such as the decline, the costs for a given cross-section of 5.5 by 5.0 metres is the highest at $2200 per metre advance, as more permanent ground support such as concreting would be employed.

More mechanised methods, such as the drilling of ventilation raises, cost at least $200 per metre. The underground mining costs were also estimated based on good ground conditions and moderate mine water inflows of less than 10 litres per second. The decline was designed for a one-in-seven gradient (for every 7 metre horizontal advance the decline would go 1 metre deeper). The underground long-term access cost was estimated at $10.9 million. The initial surface capital costs were estimated at a total of $4.28 million over two years, as shown in table 8.14.

Table 8.14: East Kundana surface capital costs, 1999

Items	Year 1 ($m)	Year 2 ($m)
Site access roads	0.100	0.150
Flood protection	—	0.050
Fencing	0.020	—
Evaporation ponds	—	0.350
Office and civil works	0.075	0.075

Indicative capital and operating costs

Items	Year 1 ($m)	Year 2 ($m)
Main haul road	1.000	—
Ventilation foundation	—	0.100
Miscellaneous	—	0.120
Power	0.030	—
Potable water	0.030	—
Process water	0.020	0.020
Underground dewater pipeline	—	0.150
Surface communication	0.075	0.075
Underground communication	—	0.140
Office building	0.100	0.150
Office fit-out	0.050	0.070
Contractor office	0.050	0.050
Change rooms	—	0.20
Workshop	0.050	0.200
Mine rescue	0.050	0.250
Vehicles	0.100	0.100
Primary ventilation fans	—	0.160
Total	**1.750**	**2.530**

Source: Gilt Edge Mining Part B, December 1999.

Henty and Paddington goldmines — underground versus open cut

The high-grade Henty goldmine in Tasmania was discovered in 1982 and gold was first produced in 1996. The annual production of 90 000 ounces of gold from the treatment of 200 000 tonnes of ore came from mechanised narrow-vein methods. Cut and fill was used in the narrow sections where the ground conditions were poor, while up-hole benching methods were used in the wider sections. As at June 2001 the reserves were 298 000 tonnes at 12.8 g/t, while the resource was 1.417 million tonnes at 9.2 g/t.

The forecast production schedule for 2002 and beyond is shown in table 8.15. Although the proven reserves provided for little more than one year's operation, the independent valuation at the time considered that it was likely given previous results that most of the resources would be converted to reserves as further drilling and development were undertaken. Underground production was also expected to increase, which would require further capital costs for underground development and plant expansion. One reason for this expansion was the likelihood of lower grades requiring increased capacity to help maintain gold production.

Table 8.15: forecast production schedule for Henty and Paddington goldmines, 2002–06

| | | Year to June | | | | |
	Units	2002	2003	2004	2005	2006
Ore mined	kt	220	250	320	350	350
Total ore milled	kt	225	250	320	350	350
Grade	g/t Au	13	9.0	9.0	9.0	9.0
Recovery	%	97	95	95	95	95
Gold recovered	kozs	94	68	89	96	96
Capital costs						
Mine development	$m	14.2	4.8	7.8	0.3	—
Processing	$m	2.1	1.6	0.3	—	—

Indicative capital and operating costs

	Units	Year to June				
		2002	2003	2004	2005	2006
Other exploration	$m	1.6	0.6	—	—	—
Operating costs						
Mining	$m	13.5	14.8	18.0	19.3	19.3
Processing	$m	5.9	6.2	7.2	7.7	7.7
Administration and exploration	$m	3.4	3.5	3.5	3.6	3.6
Total site cash costs	**$m**	**22.8**	**24.4**	**28.7**	**30.5**	**30.5**
Unit cost per tonne treated	$/t	101	98	90	87	87
Unit cost per ounce	$/oz	243	359	322	318	318

Source: Delta Gold information memorandum, November 2001.

The Paddington open cut goldmine commenced operations in 1985, and the plant progressively expanded to a throughput capacity of 3.4 mtpa. By June 2001 the reserves were 9.9 million tonnes at 2.5 g/t, and the total resource was 68.8 million tonnes at 2.0 g/t. Due to the age of the operations, by 2001 the existing pits were nearing the end of their economic lives, necessitating extensive cutbacks (removal of overburden) to access the deeper ore, plus the development of some lower grade satellite orebodies. The major development was the Havan pit, which was designed to go to 160 metres with a stripping ratio of 8:1. Contractors undertook all mining.

The mining schedule in table 8.16 (overleaf) assumes that 3 million tonnes of the large but low-grade resource base is converted to reserves. Given the nature of numerous gold materialisations within economic trucking distance of the plant (use was made of multi-trailer trucks with haulage costs ranging from $2.50 to $3.75 per tonne), it was likely at the time that the plant's life would extend beyond that forecast in table 8.16. The mine development costs included capitalised waste stripping, while the mill capital costs included $2.5 million for a cone crusher, $5.5 million for a tailings dam and $5.5 million for mill sustaining capital. Approximately 28 per cent of mill costs were related to maintenance.

Table 8.16: Paddington goldmine forecast production schedule, 2001

| | Units | Year ending June | | | | |
		2002	2003	2004	2005	2006
Ore mined	Mt	2.5	2.3	2.4	2.2	0.5
Total ore milled	Mt	2.9	3.0	3.0	2.5	0.5
Grade	g/tAu	2.3	2.1	2.3	2.7	2.5
Recovery	%	95	95	95	95	95
Gold recovered	kozs	208	196	214	205	34
Capital costs						
Mine development	$m	6.9	19.4	7.8	13.6	0.3
Plant and equipment	$m	8.0	4.5	4.0	4.0	2.0
Sustaining capital	$m	1.0	1.0	1.0	1.0	1.0
Operating costs						
Mining and ore cartage	$m	28.1	24.9	31.4	28.0	6.3
Processing	$m	26.6	27.0	27.0	22.6	4.1
Administration and other	$m	4.3	4.3	4.3	4.3	4.3
Total site cash costs	**$m**	**58.9**	**56.2**	**62.7**	**54.9**	**14.7**
Unit cost per tonne treated	$/t	20.3	18.7	20.9	22.0	29.4
Unit cost per ounce	$/oz	283	286	293	268	432

Source: Delta Gold Information memorandum, November 2001.

Note from the tables the cost per tonne of ore treated and the cost per ounce at Henty when compared with the Paddington open cut operations.

It is only the high gold grade that has enabled the economic recovery of gold from the high-cost-per-tonne Henty mine, while it is the large volume throughputs to get the economies of scale that allowed the low-cost-per-tonne Paddington mine to continue operating.

Groundrush goldmine — using existing infrastructure and contractors

The Western Australian Groundrush gold deposit, previously owned by Normandy Mining, is located some 45 kilometres from the Tanami Mine Joint Venture owned by Otter Gold Mines and AngloGold Ashanti. Normandy arranged to pay a usage fee that would give it sole use of the existing plant and infrastructure at Tanami. The terms of the agreement were $5 million per year plus $5/t for any additional ore treated above 1.0 million tonnes (Mt) for a period of three years, plus an option to extend one more year. The resource and reserves at Groundrush as at June 2001 are shown in table 8.17.

Table 8.17: Groundrush goldmine resources and reserves, 2001

Resource	Indicated		Inferred		Total	
	Mt	g/t	Mt	g/t	Mt	g/t
	3.15	4.7	1.84	4.31	4.99	4.5
Reserve	Proven		Probable		Total	
	Mt	g/t	Mt	g/t	Mt	g/t
	—	—	3.15	4.7	3.15	4.7

Source: Normandy Target statement, November 2001.

A contractor was hired to undertake the open cut mining, which involved the use of 100-tonne and 175-tonne excavators, and a fleet of 85-tonne trucks. Metallurgical tests showed a recovery of 97 per cent for the oxide ore and 94 per cent for primary ore, with an average life of mine recovery schedule of 93 per cent. Initial throughput was 1.0 million tonnes per annum, reducing to 800000 tonnes as the ore increased in hardness. Some additional capital costs were required, and the operating costs are summarised in table 8.18 (overleaf).

Table 8.18: Groundrush goldmine capital and operating costs, 2001

Capital costs	$m	Operating costs	Unit
Processing	1.4	Mining contractor $/t	12.2
Site infrastructure	1.7	Ore haulage $/t	3.22
Haul road	2.8	Other pit costs $/t	1.78
Other	4.9	Processing $/t	17.10
Rehabilitation	3.9	Administration $mpa*	1.2
Sustaining	0.9	Plant usage fee $mpa	5.0
Total	**15.5**		

*$mpa = million dollars per annum.

Assuming a three-year mine life, the obvious question is whether the total usage cost of $15 million is more cost-effective than constructing a new plant. With a reserve of 3 million tonnes, it would be difficult to make a commitment to a large plant capable of processing the ore over such a short time period as three years. It is likely that a smaller plant of, say, 500 000 tonnes with a mining life of six years would be seen as a more reasonable alternative.

Although capital costs might be lower for the smaller plant, the advantages of short mine life and the ability to use the surplus capacity of a nearby plant, even allowing for the increased haulage costs, would be enticing. The mine life summary of operations is shown in table 8.19.

Table 8.19: mine life summary, Groundrush goldmine, 2001

	Unit	Operating parameters
Ore milled	kt	3147
Gold grade	g/t	4.7
Gold production	ounces	444 000
Mining operating cost	$m	38.7

	Unit	Operating parameters
Process operating cost	$m	53.8
Admin and other costs	$m	35.0
Total operating cost	$m	**127.5**
	$/t milled	40.51
	$/ounce	287.16
Total capital cost	$m	**15.5**
	$/t milled	4.93
	$/ounce	34.91

In the November 2001 Normandy target defence statement the NPV of the project at a 6 per cent discount rate was forecast at a very healthy $58 million, based on a gold price of US$270 per ounce and an exchange rate of US$:A$ = 0.50. If we assume a mine life of six years, as suggested previously, and that a dedicated plant were built, which would save the $5 million yearly fee and the ore haulage cost, then to maintain the NPV of $58 million the most that could be spent on the plant would be $7 million. This of course assumes that other costs remain constant. It is likely that the lower economies of scale would increase some operating costs. However, it is unlikely that a suitable plant could have been acquired and installed for as little as $7 million.

Browns Creek mine—even the best laid plans

The Australian-listed Hargraves Resources NL was taken over by the South African mining company Durban Roodepoort Deep in late 1999. Hargraves' primary asset was the underground Browns Creek gold and copper mine in Australia, which commenced underground operations in 1995. Detailed financial forecasts on the mining operations were provided in Hargraves Resources 1999 Part B Statement (see table 8.20, overleaf). The mine at the time had four years of mine life based on the forecast production rates but, surprisingly, given the detail provided, was not valued separately from the company's other assets (an estimate based on supplied data would suggest an NPV of $25 million). The risks associated with the ongoing Browns Creek operations were considered low by the independent expert, who stated: 'in particular, operating risks such as production rate, geotechnical security, operating and capital costs, and metallurgical recovery are considered to be very low'.

Table 8.20: Browns Creek mine forecast financial detail

	Unit	2000 (10 months)	2001	2002
		Year ending 30 June		
Ore mined	t	382 000	450 000	288 000
Head grade	Au g/t	5.79	5.79	5.50
Head grade	Cu %	0.40	0.40	0.39
Contained A	oz	71 110	83 769	50 927
Contained Cu	t	1 528	1 800	1 123
Stockpile recovered	t	0	0	23 800
Head grade Au	g/t	0.00	0.00	4.50
Head grade Cu	%	0.00	0.00	0.39
Contained Au	oz	0	0	3443
Contained Cu	tonnes	0	0	93
Ore treatment				
Dry treatment factor	%	98.5	98.5	98.5
ROM ore treated	t	376 270	443 250	283 680
Stockpiles treated	t	0	0	23 800
Total treated	t	376 270	443 250	307 480
Au recovery to ore	%	47.0	48.5	48.5

Indicative capital and operating costs

		Year ending 30 June		
	Unit	**2000 (10 months)**	**2001**	**2002**
Au recovery to concentrate	%	42.0	41.2	41.2
Cu recovery	%	92.6	92.6	92.6
Recovered Au in ore	oz	33 422	40 628	26 369
Recovered Au in concentrates	oz	29 866	34 513	22 400
Total recovered Au	oz	63 288	75 141	48 770
Recovered Cu in concentrates	tonnes	1 415	1 667	1 126
Target Cu concentrate grade	%	35	35	35
Concentrate production	tonnes	4 043	4 762	3 217
Concentrate Au grade	g/t	229.8	225.4	216.6
Recover Ag in ore and concentrate	oz	75 819	90 018	58 426
Production from dore				
Gold production	oz	63 288	75 141	48 770
Silver production	oz	37 910	45 009	29 213
Cu paid	%	96.5	96.5	96.5
Deductions				
Copper TC	US$/dmt*	66.50	73.00	76.00
Copper RC	US$/dmt	49.50	54.34	56.57
Freight	US$/dmt	74.75	74.75	74.75
PP	US$/dmt	0.00	0.00	0.00
Au refining	US$/dmt	36.04	35.36	33.96

(*continued*)

Table 8.20: Browns Creek mine forecast financial detail (*cont'd*)

		Year ending 30 June		
	Unit	2000 (10 months)	2001	2002
Ag refining	US$/dmt	2.87	2.90	2.77
Total	**US$/dmt**	**229.67**	**240.35**	**244.06**
Unit operating costs				
Mining	$/t	27.10	28.60	29.48
Treatment	$/t	7.36	7.56	7.56
Maintenance	$/t	4.03	4.14	4.14
Administration	$/t	2.27	2.34	2.34
Environment/Rehabilitation	$/t	0.92	0.95	0.95
Laboratory	$/t	0.66	0.67	0.67
Geology	$/t	0.99	1.02	1.02
Total operating costs				
Mining	$000s	10 352	12 870	8 490
Treatment	$000s	2 769	3 351	2 145
Maintenance	$000s	1 516	1 835	1 174
Administration	$000s	854	1 037	664
Environment/Rehabilitation	$000s	346	421	269
Laboratory	$000s	248	297	190
Geology	$000s	373	452	289
Total site costs	**$000s**	**16 459**	**20 263**	**13 222**

		Year ending 30 June		
	Unit	2000 (10 months)	2001	2002
Capital costs				
Mine development	$000s	2361	1900	500
Reserve/Resource drilling	$000s	439	500	0
Tailings dam	$000s	695	800	0
Plant sustaining	$000s	0	300	300
Total	**$000s**	**3495**	**3500**	**800**

*Dry metric tonnes

Source: Part B Statement Hargraves Resources NL, 1999, included with permission of DRD.

The orebody was steeply dipping within a flat-lying limestone, which contained large aquifers. In late 1999, while blasting a production stope, a massive aquifer was broken into and large volumes of water entered the mine. The pumping station was unable to cope and, after all equipment was rescued, the mine flooded completely within a few days. The mine remains flooded to this day and, although the mining equipment and the plant were salvageable, they represented a small portion of the intrinsic value of the mine.

Brisas gold project—changing feasibility

The Brisas gold and copper project is located in Venezuela. Table 8.21 (overleaf) shows key statistics on the project from two feasibility studies, one in 2006 and a later one in 2008. Although operating parameters had not changed significantly over the two-year period and inflation played a part in increasing costs, there were a number of operating changes that had a greater influence, both positive and negative. Again this highlights the dynamic characteristic of any mining project and the need to finetune the feasibility studies until first production.

Table 8.21: Brisas gold and copper project operating parameters, 2006 and 2008

	Unit	2006	2008
Reserves	mt	484.6	482.7
Gold grade	g/t	0.67	0.66
Copper grade	%	0.13	0.13
Mill rate	mtpa	25.6	24.8–27.4
Gold price	$/oz	470	600
Copper price	$/lb	1.80	2.25
Capital cost			
Mine	$m	76.6	59.0
Mill	$m	241.5	314.7
Infrastructure	$m	65.8	67.8
Tailings	$m	23.8	38.3
Owner's cost	$m	55.6	63.4
Pre-stripping	$m	18.3	16.7
Indirect including EPCM	$m	97.0	127.6
Contingency	$m	59.4	43.8
Total	$m	**638.0**	**731.3**
Operating cost			
Mining	$/t	2.08	2.68
Processing	$/t	2.59	3.00
Administration	$/t	0.42	0.43
Transport	$/t	0.34	0.43

	Unit	2006	2008
Smelting & refining	$/t	1.02	1.08
Total	$/t	**6.45**	**7.62**
Cost per ounce	$	1.26	1.20
NPV at 5% discount	$m	780	1 290

Mine savings ($17.6 million) were a result of increasing the pre-production period from nine months to 17 months and thus reducing the amount of equipment required for pre-stripping.

The mill cost increased ($73.2 million) due primarily to an increase in the size of the SAG mill from 36 to 38 foot diameter, costing an extra $33 million plus an additional $16.2 million for other flotation and grinding equipment. Costs increased for cyanide destruction ($5.2 million), reagent facilities ($5.2 million), and compressed air and water ($3.0 million).

Tailings cost increased ($14.5 million) due to additional earthworks. Owner's cost increased ($7.8m) mostly due to increases in costs for earthwork and additional environmental/social programs. EPCM cost also increased ($18.4 million) due to additional work and changes in currency exchange rates. However, contingency costs decreased ($15.6 million) due to greater accuracy of cost estimates and the placing of orders on long lead items.

Mining costs increased ($0.60/t) due to price escalations and an increase in the strip ratio. Processing costs increased ($0.40/t) again due primarily to price escalations and increased consumption of electricity. The electrical rate increased 5 per cent to approximately $0.031 per kWh. Transportation costs increased ($0.09) for the gold-copper concentrate. Smelting and refining costs increased ($0.04/t) due to the 2006 negotiated smelter terms where the price participation cost was higher as a result of the increased copper price.

Brisas is one of the largest undeveloped gold/copper deposits in the world. So why, after its owner, Gold Reserve Inc., spent US$300 million on feasibility studies and was ready to commence mine construction, has the project not proceeded? In 2008 the Venezuelan government revoked Gold Reserve's authorisation and in late 2009 the company filed for arbitration by the World Bank, which is still awaited. Even the best feasibility studies don't necessarily predict all eventualities and financial outcomes.

Zimplats — platinum refining costs

Table 8.22 summarises the operating performance for Zimplats' open cut Ngezi platinum operations in Zimbabwe, which were linked by a 77-kilometre road to its Selous Metallurgical Complex, which produced a high-grade matt. The matt in turn was sold to Impala Refining Services Limited, from which the company received the contained value less refining costs.

Table 8.22: operating performance for Ngezi platinum operations, 2003

	Ore milled			Matt production
	Grade (g/t)	Concentrate recovery (%)	Recovery to matt (%)	Contained metal
Platinum	1.66	84.7	98.5	97 524 oz
Palladium	1.37	85.4	98.5	81 152 oz
Rhodium	0.14	88.4	98.5	8 584 oz
Gold	0.24	68.2	98.5	11 353 oz
Nickel	949.7	77.4	96.0	1 545 tonnes
Copper	549.3	82.7	96.0	955 tonnes
Revenue				US$86 448 000
Operating cost				
Mining	US$12.31/t			
Transport	US$2.80/t			
Milling/Flotation	US$4.23/t			
Smelter	US$2.20/t			
Administration	US$1.98/t			
Matt transport	US$0.07/t			

	Ore milled			Matt production
	Grade (g/t)	Concentrate recovery (%)	Recovery to matt (%)	Contained metal
Royalty	US$1.15/t			
Total operating cost				**US$54 180 000**
Refining cost (author est.)				US$2 520 000
Refining cost (author est.)				US$600/t

Source: Zimplats response document, July 2003.

The total 2003 costs for the open cut were forecast at US$56.7 million, while the direct operating cost (see table 8.22) came to US$54.18 million. If we assume the difference to be the cost to refine the 4200 tonnes of high-grade matt produced at the smelter, then the refining cost is US$600 per tonne. This may seem high compared with other refining costs, but the process is metallurgically complex and the matt can certainly afford the cost given a contained metal value of US$20 583 per tonne.

Base metal mining

Additional public information on operating and capital costs for selected base metal projects is given in the following pages.

Australian nickel mining — bedding down new technology

For planned nickel operations in the late 1990s, excluding cobalt credits,[1] the lowest quartile was expected to have costs of less than US$1.50 per pound (see figure 8.10, overleaf).

---

1 By-product credits are revenues received for minor commodities that might also be recovered and are included in the metal sold. For example, copper orebodies might also contain minor amounts of gold for which some value will be derived by the mine owners. Some owners will deduct the credits from their mining costs to show a lower operating cost, but these additional revenues should be included in the mines' total revenue.

Figure 8.10: cash operating cost estimates for Australian nickel operations

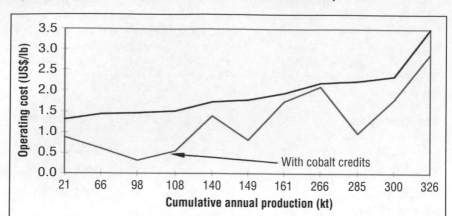

Cobalt credits refer to the cobalt that can be produced as a by-product from the production of nickel. The value of the cobalt is then subtracted from the operating costs to obtain the net cost of nickel production. There was considerable public information on the proposed development of several lateritic nickel projects; the details of their feasibility studies are shown in table 8.23. Since then, Cawse, Murrin Murrin and Ravensthorpe have gone into production and encountered severe operating difficulties that have resulted in increased operating and capital costs and reduced output. Initial production from Ramu commenced in late 2011.

Table 8.23: details and costs for five Australian laterite nickel projects, 1997

Open cut mines	Cawse	Marlborough	Murrin Murrin	Ravensthorpe	Ramu
Waste mined (mt)	6.7	6.7	24.0	3.0	—
Ore mined (mt)	1.20	2.25	6.50	2.00	3.80
Ore treated (mt)	0.6	1.8	3.5	1.0	3.0
Ni grade (%)	1.60	1.70	1.28	2.10	1.16

Indicative capital and operating costs

Open cut mines	Cawse	Marlborough	Murrin Murrin	Ravensthorpe	Ramu
Co grade (%)	0.12	0.08	0.11	0.09	0.10
Ni recovery (%)	92	92	85	92	94
Co recovery (%)	92	69	78	92	93
Ni produced (000s t)	9.0	28.2	38.0	19.3	32.7
Co produced (000s t)	0.7	1.0	3.0	0.8	2.8
Operating costs $/t treated					
Mining	11.7	5.2	12.9	7.6	5.6
Acid	—	15.2	—	16.0	10.5
Solvents	—	0.4	—	—	—
Reagents	38.8	—	—	14.0	—
Consumables	18.2	18.3	—	8.5	3.1
Power	—	2.7	—	7.7	4.5
Labour	13.3	5.3	—	16.0	—
Maintenance materials	5.0	7.7	4.3	9.5	—
Administration and sales	4.1	2.2	3.8	2.7	10.7
Tailings	—	0.5	—	—	—
Transport	—	—	—	—	2.0
Processing	—	—	25.2	—	13.4
Total	**91.1**	**57.4**	**46.2**	**82.0**	**49.8**

(continued)

Table 8.23: details and costs for five Australian laterite nickel projects, 1997 (*cont'd*)

Open cut mines	Cawse	Marlborough	Murrin Murrin	Ravensthorpe	Ramu
Capital cost $m					
Mine plant and equipment	3.1	18.4	17.0	5.4	29.9
Processing plant	189.3	249.3	342.9	180.1	477.6
Tailings circuit and/or disposal	—	7.5	16.8	—	143.9
General facilities	22.5	120.8	315.1	64.8	101.3
Temporary facilities	—	4.5	11.8	—	38.6
Engineering services	26.1	50.0	80.7	28.0	118.7
Owner's cost	31.9	—	29.5	—	77.0
Contingencies	13.0	48.0	144.9	18.0	148
Working capital	20.8	—	21.3	20.0	28.3
Total	306.8	498.5	980	327.8	1163.3

Source: Company reports, Murrin Murrin offering memorandum 1997; Centaur offering memorandum 1997; Highlands Pacific prospectus 1997.

Emily Ann and Maggie Hays—nickel sulphide projects

These two projects are located within 3 kilometres of each other in Western Australia, and the original development plan was to see Emily Ann developed first as an open cut mine, followed by Maggie Hays as an underground mine accessed by an incline. Three process routes were investigated—the capital and operating costs for both projects are shown in table 8.24. The first consisted of producing a conventional nickel sulphide concentrate (sale of concentrate). The second would use the

BioNICR process that produces a refined nickel sulphide concentrate on-site (refined concentrate on site), which would be toll-treated to produce nickel and cobalt. The third process would see the production of refined nickel sulphide concentrate off-site (refined concentrate off-site).

The Emily Ann project was ultimately accessed by a decline and commenced production of nickel concentrates in late 2001. The Maggie Hays project was approved for development in early 2003, and first production occurred in late 2004. The original production rates were:

» Emily Ann—565 000 tpa at 3.4 per cent Ni for 3.5 years assuming 90 per cent recovery of ore with 25 per cent dilution.

» Maggie Hays—1.25 mtpa at 1.5 per cent Ni for 7.5 years assuming a 1 per cent Ni cutoff grade.

Lower mill rates for Emily Ann were achieved: 220 996 tonnes were processed in 2002, with an average grade of 3.12 per cent Ni. Plant modifications in 2003 for the later introduction of Maggie Hays saw capacity increase to 320 000. Ultimately, the traditional nickel sulphide concentrate route was chosen, which had a lower capital cost but would result in lower value concentrate.

Table 8.24: Emily Ann and Maggie Hays nickel sulphide projects—costs, 1997

Key parameters	Sale of concentrate	Refined concentrate on-site	Refined concentrate off-site
Capital cost $m			
Feasibility study	12	12	12
Mining development			
Emily Ann	72	72	72
Maggie Hays	52	52	52
Mining replacement capital			
Emily Ann	Nil	Nil	Nil
Maggie Hays ($1.5m pa)	12	12	12

(*continued*)

Table 8.24: Emily Ann and Maggie Hays nickel sulphide projects — costs, 1997 (*cont'd*)

Key parameters	Sale of concentrate	Refined concentrate on-site	Refined concentrate off-site
Infrastructure	34	34	34
Concentrator	39	39	39
BioNICR plant	—	160	120
Process replacement capital	2	9	9
Total	**223**	**390**	**350**
Operating cost $/t ore			
Mining $/t			
Emily Ann	48	48	48
Maggie Hays	35	35	35
Concentrating $/t ore			
Emily Ann	48	48	48
Maggie Hays	15	15	15
BioNICR plant $/t ore			
Emily Ann	—	47	25
Maggie Hays	—	21	11
Road freight to port	35	35	35
Administration ($m pa)	3	4	4

Source: Independent expert's report for QNI Pty Ltd and Billiton merger, 1997.

Cerro Matoso operations — variable and fixed costs

Identification of variable and fixed costs is an important part of modelling the project and company valuation. If a sensitivity analysis of variations in annual production is undertaken, then the resultant changes in costs can be modelled more accurately.

As an example, consider the Cerro Matoso nickel operation in Colombia — the fixed and variable costs for 1998 are shown in table 8.25. Note that the values are given per pound of nickel produced, which is grade dependent. It would be best, if possible, to convert to tonne of ore processed so that any variation in tonnage would properly affect the variable cost. It is possible that variations in grade can also affect costs but to a lesser extent.

Table 8.25: Cerro Matoso nickel project — fixed and variable costs, 1998

Costs	Operating costs (US$m)	Unit cost (US$/lb nickel)	Percentage of total
Variable costs			
Electricity	31	0.52	32.5
Gas	4	0.07	4.4
Consumables	10	0.16	10.0
Contracts	1	0.02	1.3
Total	**46**	**0.77**	**48.2**
Fixed costs			
Labour	19	0.33	20.6
Supplies	7	0.12	7.5
Contracts	15	0.25	15.6
Other	8	0.13	8.1
Total	**49**	**0.83**	**51.8**
Total	**95**	**1.60**	**100.0**

Source: 1998 QNI Pty Ltd target statement.

Frieda River copper project — variable production schedules

The development of the Frieda River project in Papua New Guinea proposed a mining rate of 46 mtpa, a milling rate of 1 mtpa of gold ore and 26.1 mtpa of copper ore, for the production of 364 000 ounces of gold and 224 000 tonnes of copper. The relevant capital and operating costs are shown in table 8.26.

Table 8.26: Frieda River copper project — capital and operating costs, 1997

Capital cost	US$m	Operating cost/tonne milled	US$
Mine plant and waste dump	169.0	Mining	1.40
EPCM engineering services	138.9	Waste dumps	0.34
Process plant	550.8	Gold plant	0.76
General and temporary facilities	103.2	Copper metal plant	2.52
Tailings dam and pipeline	77.4	Tailings	0.13
Power supply	180.4	Power	1.43
Roads, airport and wharf	56.9	Roads and airstrips	0.01
Other	240.4	Metal sales	0.76
Contingencies	139.3	Administration	1.29
Total	1656.3	Total	8.63

Source: Highlands Pacific Ltd Prospectus, 1997.

It is not unusual to assume that operating statistics are constant for the mine life. The operating costs might be varied to reflect the impact of inflation. However, the production schedule may vary as a function of the orebody and the optimum economic development of those reserves. In the case of the Frieda-Nena project, the production schedules were expected to vary over three discrete periods, as shown in table 8.27.

Table 8.27: Frieda-Nena production schedule, 1997

Key parameters	Units	Project year		
		2003	2011	2018
Ore and waste mined	000s t	46 000	66 500	92 000
Gold ore milled	000s t	1 000	1 000	0
Copper ore milled	000s t	26 100	34 200	40 000
Gold produced	oz	364 000	330 000	296 000
Copper produced	t	224 000	226 000	166 000
Operating costs	US$ million	281	325	250

Source: Highlands Pacific Ltd Prospectus, 1997.

El Tesoro copper mine — falling head grades

The El Tesoro copper mine is a flat-lying copper deposit capable of open cut working in the Atacama Desert in Chile, 150 kilometres north of the Escondida mine. Reserves in 1997 were 155 million tonnes of copper ore with an average grade of 0.93 per cent copper. Being located in such a dry environment, water is of prime importance. Nearby bore water was to be developed to provide up to 164 litres per second (the plant would require 530 litres per tonne of ore processed). Power requirements were for a maximum demand of 26 MW with total requirements of 192 GWh per year. The capital costs to develop a mine of this size — which was to include agglomeration, heap leaching, solvent extraction and electro-winning — were estimated at US$250 million, plus a further US$64.3 million to expand the project, as shown in table 8.28.

Table 8.28: capital costs for mine development, 1997

Production	Years 1–5	Years 6–10	Years 11–15	Years 16–20	Total
Mined (mtpa)	5.4	7.8	8.9	8.8	154.4
Av. grade (% Cu)	1.4	1.0	0.8	0.7	0.93

(*continued*)

Table 8.28: capital costs for mine development, 1997 (*cont'd*)

Production	Years 1–5	Years 6–10	Years 11–15	Years 16–20	Total
Waste (mtpa)	16.0	24.4	15.8	8.2	321.4
Strip ratio	3.0	3.1	1.8	0.9	2.1
Recovery (%)	77.0	73.3	66.5	62.1	70.2
Copper (tpa)	59 300	59 300	47 400	36 200	1 011 100
Costs US$/t processed					
Mining/Geology	2.93	2.64	2.04	1.65	2.24
Labour	0.99	0.68	0.64	0.62	0.73
Energy	1.22	1.03	0.82	0.72	0.96
Acid	1.20	1.40	1.50	1.41	1.51
Reagents	0.84	1.40	1.50	1.41	1.51
Water	0.37	0.38	0.40	0.39	0.42
Materials	0.58	0.52	0.46	0.42	0.51
Administration	0.75	0.59	0.53	0.51	0.58
Marketing/Freight	0.85	0.61	0.42	0.33	0.52
Total	**9.73**	**8.52**	**7.38**	**6.53**	**8.11**
Costs US¢/lb Cu					
Mining/Geology	11.11	15.73	18.12	18.14	15.48
Labour	4.02	4.02	5.43	6.83	5.08
Energy	5.62	6.13	7.00	7.97	6.68
Acid	5.10	8.36	12.78	15.61	10.46

Production	Years 1–5	Years 6–10	Years 11–15	Years 16–20	Total
Reagents	3.55	4.04	4.83	5.34	4.44
Water	1.58	2.25	3.41	4.32	2.89
Materials	2.47	3.08	3.92	4.64	3.53
Administration	3.06	3.51	4.74	5.86	4.29
Marketing/Freight	3.60	3.60	3.60	3.60	3.60
Total	40.11	50.72	63.83	72.31	56.45

Source: Data from Equatorial Mining NL—Independent director's recommendation and Part B Statement in Relation to the Offer by Quay Mining Pty Ltd, reproduced with permission of Equatorial Mining Limited.

From the marketing costs it is apparent that the operating costs are in constant dollars. Fortunately for the project, as the grade of the deposit decreases over time as the open cut gets deeper, the stripping ratio declines. It is still necessary, however, to increase the ore production in later years to keep the costs down. Nevertheless, although the cost per tonne processed does go down due to the higher throughput, the cost per pound of copper produced goes up from an initial level of US40.11¢ to US72.31¢ due to falling head grade and poorer recoveries. Actual operating costs per pound of copper in the first quarter of 2003 were US$0.406 (cash) and US$0.543 (total).

Tip

It is important to know how the base case values might change over the life of a project, particularly for those projects where the grade and operating profiles are likely to have a material impact on the future cash flows.

Gunpowder copper mine—benefits of value add

Copper was first mined from the Queensland Gunpowder Mine in 1926, but it was in the late 1990s that copper was won by solution from the Mammoth underground mine (now the Mt Gordon mine) and heap leaching of surface ore from Mammoth and the Esperanza open cut mine. The copper was then recovered by solvent extraction—electro-winning (SX-EW).

By 1998—following a 1997 feasibility study, which concluded that the existing Gunpowder operations could be enhanced—it was decided to further expand the Esperanza open cut ($29 million for a pre-strip) and then go underground to mine a resource of 5.38 million tonnes at an impressive grade of 7.8 per cent copper. A low-pressure, low-temperature autoclave whole-ore leach and SX-EW plant at a cost of $93 million was constructed due to the high level of pyrite in the ore. Recoveries of 90 per cent were expected, with the production of 50 000 tonnes of copper metal per year (see table 8.29). The oxygen-based autoclave leaching process and SX-EW are very energy intensive, representing 38 per cent of direct operating costs (58 per cent SX-EW; 12 per cent oxygen plant; 12 per cent leaching; and 7.5 per cent grinding).

Table 8.29: Gunpowder copper mine—production and costs, 1998–99 and 1993–2003

Key parameters		Open cut	Total 1998–99	Under-ground	Total 1999–2003
Waste mined	(bcm)		8 605 385		240 820
Ore mined	(bcm)		180 045		157 175
Total waste and ore	(bcm)		8 785 430		397 995
Tonnes ore	(Dry tonnes)		683 931		617 000
Grade	(% Cu)		7.4		9.0
tonnes produced	(Cu)		44 290		50 000
Mining costs		$/tmined	$000s	$/tmined	$000s
Assays		0.37	251	0.43	265
Drill and blast		0.57	390	1.33	818
Load and haul		0.75	515	2.95	1 820
Ground support		0.00	0	0.30	182
Day works		0.23	154	0.30	183

Indicative capital and operating costs

Key parameters		Open cut	Total 1998–99	Underground	Total 1999–2003
Supervision		2.00	1366	1.15	709
Mining on costs		0.40	275	0.23	144
Amortisation		12.67	8664	15.37	9486
Depreciation		0.38	258	0.37	226
Care and maintenance U/G		0.28	193	0.29	177
Ore stock movement		(0.22)	(149)	(0.01)	(4)
Total mining costs		17.42	11917	22.70	14006
Total cost US¢/lb		8.18		8.80	
Processing costs			$000s		$000s
Crushing — operating	$/t ore	1.10	750	1.13	697
Crushing — maintenance	$/t ore	0.57	389	0.73	451
Grinding — operating	$/t ore	3.08	2103	3.49	2155
Grinding — maintenance	$/t ore	1.70	1160	2.17	1340
Tailing — operating	$/t ore	0.20	135	0.18	114
Leaching — operating	$/t Cu	154.46	6841	138.59	6929
Leaching — maintenance	$/t Cu	80.33	3558	73.16	3658
Heap leaching	$/t Cu	5.96	264	0.83	41
Solvent extraction — operating	$/t Cu	71.78	3179	49.73	2487
Solvent extraction — maintenance	$/t Cu	8.24	365	8.40	420
Electro-winning — operating	$/t Cu	270.77	11993	211.71	10585

(*continued*)

Table 8.29: Gunpowder copper mine—production and costs, 1998–99 and 1993–2003 (*cont'd*)

Key parameters		Open cut	Total 1998–99	Under-ground	Total 1999–2003
Electro-winning—maintenance	$/t Cu	14.87	659	15.32	766
Overheads	$/tore	5.08	3 474	5.21	3 215
Depreciation	$/tore	16.32	11 159	18.08	11 158
Total processing costs	US¢/lb Cu	31.59	46 028	27.66	44 017
Support		US¢/lb Cu	$000s	US¢/lb Cu	$000s
Operations		0.70	1 024	0.69	1 090
Accounting		0.31	448	0.31	488
Supply		0.25	363	0.22	352
Human resources		0.17	242	0.17	264
Safety		0.21	307	0.21	333
Environment		0.42	611	0.33	519
Infrastructure		0.24	350	0.24	377
Administration on cost		0.50	727	0.48	761
Depreciation		0.69	1 009	0.68	1 084
Head office		0.16	240	0.15	240
Royalty—state		1.01	1 469	1.05	1 679
Royalty—Esperanza ore		1.06	1 542	1.70	2 700
Total support costs		**5.72**	**8 332**	**6.21**	**9 887**
Total costs		**45.41**	**66 156**	**42.61**	**67 790**

Note: 1999/2003 costs are in escalated dollars. US dollar exchange rate: 1998–99 A$ = US$0.67; 1999–2003 A$ = US$0.6926.

Source: Aberfoyle Ltd Part B Statement, 6 July 1998.

By early 2003 production was running at 45 000 to 50 000 tonnes of copper metal. Development of the underground mine at Mammoth continued, with ore coming from the first stope (the Mammoth surface mine was placed on care and maintenance in 1999) with annualised production of 300 000 tonnes. Total operating costs were running at around US67¢ per pound (based on the same exchange rate as in table 8.29) compared with the forecast cost of US43¢ per pound. Some of the contributing reasons for this increased financial cost were lower specific gravities (3.15 versus 3.6), lower mined grades (7.8 per cent versus 8.2 per cent) and poorer recoveries (82 per cent versus 90 per cent). To counter these impacts a second stage plant expansion consisting of a 2.2 million tonne per year flotation plant was completed in March 2003. The underground decline was also widened to allow for larger, 55-tonne haulage trucks. The operation currently produces around 16 000 tonnes of contained copper in concentrate, while additional ore is now sourced from an underground mine at Esperanza South.

Clarksville zinc refinery — the cost of expansion

If mineral resources allow, it may at times be viable to expand an operation to reduce the unit cost and hence increase operating margins. However, this is only accomplished by further capital expenditure, which must be justified by the increased cash flow through higher sales. Obviously, a market must be available to allow for those increased sales. If the mineral resource is dependent on processing to a metal product, then expansion of the metallurgical operations will also be necessary. For example, in the late 1990s the Clarksville refinery in Tennessee processed zinc ore from its nearby mines. Additional ore reserves were available and it was determined that the US market could absorb additional production from the refinery, especially given the mine's lowest unit cost.

The plant had a location advantage in that it had a lower cost of delivery; it could acquire its acid more cheaply; and it was able to deliver to its customers on a just-in-time basis. Additionally, the plant had room to expand, which was cheaper than a greenfield site, and it had good transport infrastructure that would enable it to receive additional concentrates from outside the US as well as acid and metal delivery. Importantly, it had the necessary environmental approvals. In designing for expanded capacity the plant would be more sensitive to the iron content in the concentrate.

The existing production cost was US17.7¢ per pound of zinc metal. The proposed expansion was budgeted at US$400 million to increase production from 110000 to 310000 tonnes per year of zinc metal, with a resultant fall in operating costs to US13.2¢ per pound of metal, with primary costs allocated as shown in table 8.30.

Table 8.30: operating costs for expansion of the Clarkesville zinc refinery, 1998

Operating cost item	Cost (US$/t zinc)	Cost (US¢/lb)
Labour	44.2	2.0
Power	111.5	5.1
Supplies	104.5	4.7
Administration	31.1	1.4
Total	291.3	13.2

Source: Savage Resources Ltd response, December 1998.

If one assumes that the zinc price was US45¢ per pound at the time of the feasibility study, then the additional revenue obtained from the reduced cost would be US4.5¢ per pound for the first 110000 tonnes and US13.2¢ per pound for the extra 200000 tonnes, or US$70 million per year, for a pre-tax payback period of 5.7 years, which, given the nature of the operations, was a reasonable period.

Cloncurry copper project — working the assumptions

The Cloncurry project was a proposed open cut mine with an expected project life of nine years, as estimated in 1994. Working through the operating cost information listed in table 8.31, it is possible to estimate the operating cost per pound of copper at approximately US59¢, based on an exchange rate of 0.65 US$:A$.

The project mineralisation consisted of several deposits of supergene and oxide ore, which allowed for the addition of an SX-EW plant for the on-site production of copper metal. The prospectus provided the capital and operating figures, as shown in table 8.31.

Table 8.31: prospectus capital and operating figures for the Cloncurry copper project, 1994

Key parameters	Capital cost	Key parameters	Capital cost
Resource	3.2 mt @ 1.9% Cu	SX-EW plant	$5m
Mine recovery	95%	Site preparation	$1m
Mine dilution	10% @ 0.35% Cu	Water supply	$0.5m
Process recovery	80%	Power supply	$0.5m
Metal production	5500 tpy	Infrastructure	$1.5m
Waste ratio	4 to 7 (average of 5)	Working capital	$3.0m
Mining cost	$7.6/t of ore	Exploration and feasibility	$1.5m
Ore haulage	$1.7/t of ore	Replacement capital	$0.25m pa
Processing	$13.1/t of ore	Royalty	2% ad valorem
Administration	$1.8/t of ore	Other royalty	2% net smelter return
Project life	9 years	Tax rate	33%

Note: tpy = tonnes per year; ad valorem = percentage of net revenue.

Source: Murchison United Prospectus, 1994.

The prospectus did not show any cash-flow calculation, but it did say that the project would show an average annual after-tax cash flow of $4.8 million. Table 8.32 (overleaf) shows my initial estimate of the possible cash flows based on the operating and capital data provided in table 8.31. The important point is that the average operating conditions are met, but seeing that only average values were provided, there is scope to vary yearly inputs. However, ranges were supplied for the two important factors of production and waste.

The first assumption was that the tonnes mined started at the maximum of 450 000 and then eventually reduced to 250 000 tonnes at the end of the mine life, due to harder ore. There was no information to suggest this was likely and one could have chosen to have the minimum production at the beginning of the mine life due perhaps to initial production ramp-up. But it was a small project and the near-surface ore was oxide, which suggests it may have been softer.

The next variable to consider was the waste-to-ore ratio. As the project was an open cut, it would be logical to assume that the ratio would increase from 4 to 7 over the life of the mine. These two variables were adjusted so that the annual cash flow was met, but obviously there are many variations that could give a similar answer. All other parameters were checked to make sure that the prospective figures in table 8.31 were met. The reader should be aware that the working capital of $3 million was recovered at the end of the project. Readers might also like to build a model and see the degree of change that can be made within the range of possible values.

Another piece of information included in the prospectus was that the NPV at a discount rate of 10 per cent was $8.5 million. As can be seen in table 8.32 the NPV came out at $13.4 million. The reason for this difference is in the grade profile. We are told that the average grade is 1.9 per cent copper, but not how it might change over the nine-year mine life. If the grade profile shown in table 8.33 is used, then the NPV becomes $8.5 million while still maintaining all the other values and an annual average cash flow of $4.8 million.

Table 8.32: cash-flow estimates for the Cloncurry copper project based on 1994 prospectus figures

Key parameters		Year									
		1	2	3	4	5	6	7	8	9	10
Tonnes mined	000		0.45	0.40	0.40	0.40	0.35	0.35	0.34	0.30	0.26
Mine recovery	%		0.95	0.95	0.95	0.95	0.95	0.95	0.95	0.95	0.95
Dilution grade	%		0.35	0.35	0.35	0.35	0.35	0.35	0.35	0.35	0.35
Waste	000 t		1.8	1.7	1.8	1.8	1.6	1.8	2.0	1.8	1.8
Grade	% Cu		1.9	1.9	1.9	1.9	1.9	1.9	1.9	1.9	1.9
Metal recovery	%		0.8	0.8	0.8	0.8	0.8	0.8	0.8	0.8	0.8

Key parameters		Year									
		1	2	3	4	5	6	7	8	9	10
Cu metal	000 t		5.97	5.30	5.30	5.30	4.64	4.64	4.51	3.98	3.43
Price	$/t		1.45	1.45	1.45	1.45	1.45	1.45	1.45	1.45	1.45
Revenue	$m		19.1	17.0	17.0	17.0	14.9	14.9	14.4	12.7	11.0
Mining cost	$m		2.9	2.7	2.8	2.8	2.4	2.7	3.0	2.7	2.6
Processing cost	$m		7.5	6.6	6.6	6.6	5.8	5.8	5.6	5.0	4.3
Royalty	$m		0.4	0.3	0.3	0.3	0.3	0.3	0.3	0.3	0.2
Other royalty	$m		0.2	0.2	0.2	0.2	0.1	0.1	0.1	0.1	0.1
Replacement cap.	$m		0.25	0.25	0.25	0.25	0.25	0.25	0.25	0.25	0.25
Depreciation	$m		2.7	1.2	1.2	1.2	1.2	1.2	1.2	1.2	1.2
Pre-tax	$m		5.23	5.70	5.57	5.57	4.69	4.47	3.88	3.25	2.28
Tax	$m		1.73	1.88	1.84	1.84	1.55	1.48	1.28	1.07	0.75
Cash flow	$m	—13.3	6.24	5.05	4.96	4.96	4.37	4.23	3.83	3.40	5.76
NPV at 10%	$m	13.4									

Table 8.33: grade profile for the Cloncurry copper project based on 1994 prospectus figures

	Year									
	1	2	3	4	5	6	7	8	9	10
Grade	1.35	1.35	1.35	1.35	1.35	1.35	1.35	2.00	3.50	4.95

As the NPV is a time value concept it was necessary to reduce the up-front cash flows and increase the back-end cash flows to reduce the NPV, which was achieved by having lower grades at the beginning of the mine life and higher grades towards the end. The possibility of higher grades the deeper the mine goes is quite reasonable, but the distortion in the grade profile is quite severe. It is therefore likely that there are a number of other factors—especially given that there are several deposits that will be treated by the one plant—which are not provided in the prospectus, preventing an accurate determination of the project cash flow.

Tip

If NPV valuations are included in any prospectus or independent expert's report, the data provided to justify such a valuation should be sufficiently complete that an investor can model the project numbers and undertake their own valuation and sensitivity analysis.

Dairi zinc lead project—project gearing sensitivity

By mid 2003 a feasibility study had been completed by Herald Resources Ltd for the development of the Dairi underground mine located in Indonesia. Production of 1 million tonnes per annum of ore was planned, using drift mining and backfilling with waste from an initial reserve of 6.3 million tonnes at 16 per cent zinc and 9.9 per cent lead. Separate zinc and lead concentrates would be produced and trucked 190 kilometres to the coastal port of Medan for shipment to overseas smelters. Overall zinc recovery was expected to be 87 per cent, producing 230 000 tonnes per annum of concentrate grading 56 per cent zinc. Lead recovery was expected to be 79 per cent, producing 135 000 tonnes per annum of lead concentrate grading 61.5 per cent lead. No smelter penalties were expected (refer to chapter 7), with payment for 85 per cent of contained zinc and 95 per cent of lead. No credits were allowed for contained silver.

The company was planning to go to a bankable feasibility study that would take six to nine months, while discussions were under way with financiers and concentrate off-take groups. The forecast metal prices were based on a combination of 50 per cent of the future spot price and 50 per cent of forward London Metal Exchange (LME) prices. Given that first production was still some years away, consensus forecasts had to be used for the future spot price and the forward hedge curve applied to determine the future LME prices.

The zinc and lead prices were forecast at US$885 and US$520 per tonne respectively. The salient project parameters based on nominal (real) values are listed in table 8.34.

Table 8.34: Dairi project parameters, 2003

Key parameter	Cost (US$m)
Mining pre-production	16.9m
Plant and infrastructure	60.8m
Owner costs	$5.6m
Total capital cost	83.2m
Gross metal value	904.4m
Less	
On-site operating costs	271.1m
Government fees and charges	20.7m
Metal realisation costs	384.1m
Total costs	676.2m
Net operating cash flow	228.2m
Cost per pound zinc equivalent	0.30
Taxation	42.5m
Post-tax net cash flow	102.8m
NPV @ 10% ungeared	36.0m
IRR	23.2%
Payback period	3.3 years

Source: Herald Resources quarterly report, June 2003.

On a geared basis assuming 70 per cent debt and 30 per cent equity the NPV increased to US$38.7 million with the internal rate of return (IRR) at 38.6 per cent and the payback period for equity of 2.9 years (the debt was forecast to be paid back over 3.5 years). Assuming a two-year construction period, I have calculated the possible cash-flow profile for the geared and ungeared project as shown in figure 8.11. The geared return does not increase dramatically as a large part of the after-tax cash flows are used to pay off the debt in the early years of the project, due to the short mine life. Towards the end of 2009 the company was awaiting forestry approvals before developing the mine.

Figure 8.11: Dairi project cash-flow profile

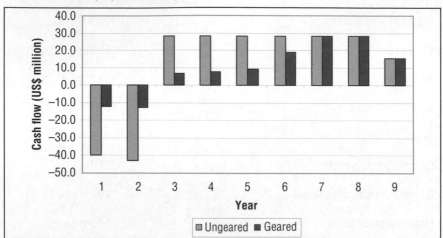

Offshore mining

The mining of offshore deposits is not uncommon these days, particularly for industrial sands and gravels, and diamonds. In most instances a dredge is used, which either scrapes or more commonly sucks up loose materials from the sea floor. There are many different forms of mechanical implementation that ultimately allow for the lifting of the product on board a ship or barge, and then transporting to onshore treatment facilities. The number of pre-feasibility studies has increased significantly as technology has improved and commodity prices have risen, with plans to develop offshore projects such as mining for iron ore, copper and phosphate.

Sandpiper phosphate project—wave height

One example of an offshore project is UCL Resources' Sandpiper phosphate (P_2O_5) deposit, located 50 kilometres off the coast of Namibia in water depths of between 180 and 300 metres. The resource is some 2 billion wet tonnes

(1.5b tonnes dry) of phosphate rock grading around 18.7 per cent P_2O_5 made up of unconsolidated fine sand–sized ooliths[2] and pellets mostly 150 to 200 microns in diameter. It is this small unconsolidated size that should allow for dredging of the material, which once onshore will be treated primarily through screening to increase the P_2O_5 grade to commercial levels of around 28 per cent for sale to manufacturers of phosphate fertilisers. The price received is very sensitive to the grade of P_2O_5.

Given the specialist nature of dredging it is more common to contract and modify the dredging equipment. In this case it is planned to be a 78 000 tonne ship capable of recovering about 50 000 tonnes of equivalent dry material, from an initial maximum depth of 225 metres, each cycle between mining and depositing product onshore. To determine the annual production rate it is therefore necessary to forecast the time it takes to complete each cycle and the number of cycles per year. While the production rate is expected to average 2.43 cycles per week, it is the number of weeks per year that is more critical and is a function of how rough the seas will be. It therefore becomes necessary to analyse sea conditions as shown in figure 8.12, which shows the monthly percentage of wave heights less than 3 metres.

Figure 8.12: percentage wave heights greater than 3 metres off the coast of Namibia

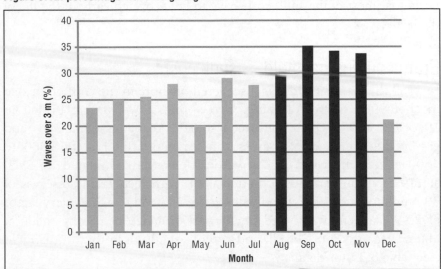

December to July would appear to be the best period for dredging, which would equate to around 3 million tonnes per year. Once on shore the

2 Tiny spherical grains of sedimentary rock where concentric layers have formed over a nucleus, such as a shell fragment.

ore can be dewatered and treated over a full year, thus requiring smaller onshore facilities and saving on capital costs. The dredging costs were estimated at US$22.51 per tonne plus a further US$0.55 per tonne from the onshore dredge storage pond to the treatment site. The capital cost for the dredge pond and transfer slurry pipeline were estimated at US$41.5 million. The treatment plant capital costs were estimated at US$64.6 million, and if it was decided to add a calciner[3] to increase the grade of the final product by 2.8 to 3.5 per cent P_2O_5, an additional capital cost of US$93.7 million would be required. Operating cost for the treatment plant was estimated at US$4.36 per tonne or US$33.36 per tonne if the calciner was included.

Oil and gas

The emphasis on costs associated with oil and gas fields is slightly different from that of hard rock mining projects. Exploration and capital costs play a more important part than operating costs, which are generally much lower than the product price (that is not to say that operating costs are not still important). Natural decline rates in production, particularly for oil, also mean that most of the sunk costs have to be recovered early in the life of the field.

Brutus oil and gas field — sunk costs

In 1989 the Brutus Field was discovered offshore in the Gulf of Mexico in about 900 metres of water. Two appraisal wells were drilled in 1995 and 1997, which confirmed some 100 metres of net oil- and gas-bearing sands over a gross sub-sea depth interval of 4000 to 5500 metres. Initial in-place hydrocarbons were estimated by Shell at 1192 million barrels of oil equivalent, with recoverable reserves of 309 million barrels of oil equivalent. The relatively low recovery factor of 25.9 per cent was based on the performance of nearby fields at Mars, Ursa and Ram Powell, and complex faulting in the Brutus Field (see table 8.35 for details).

---

3 High temperature kiln.

Table 8.35: Brutus Field oil and gas reserves, 1998

Resource	Units	Proved	Proved and unproved	Upside case
Oil	mmbbl	80.5	212.1	242.5
Gas	bcf	117.1	563.1	625.5
Oil equivalent	mmboe	100.7	309.2	350.4

Note: mmbbl = million barrels; bcf = billion cubic feet; mmboe = million barrels oil equivalent.

A further review of the reserves was undertaken in November 2000 by GCA on behalf of Shell, with the results shown in table 8.36. The 'most likely' case was analogous to proved and probable reserves and the 'high' case analogous to proved, probable and possible reserves.

Table 8.36: Brutus Field oil and gas reserves, 2000 review

	Unit	Low	Most likely	High
Oil	mmbbl	130.3	200.5	230.9
Gas	bcf	283.9	532.2	594.8
Oil equivalent	mmboe	170.2	292.3	333.5

In mid 1999 Shell approved the development of the field using a topsides processing facility that was capable of processing 130 000 barrels of oil and 300 million cubic feet of gas per day. The first stage development included all infrastructure and eight production wells (which would deplete the field in seven to eight years) and a second phase development commencing in 2009, which would side-track six of the existing wells plus two new wells to access additional reserves. The projected capital costs for pre–phase 1 and phase 1 development are shown in table 8.37 (overleaf).

Table 8.37: Brutus Field projected costs for pre–phase 1 and phase 1, 1999–2001

Key parameters	Costs (US$ million)			
	Pre-1999	1999	2000	2001
Fabrication	62.9	121.4	196.2	—
Leasehold	45.0	0.0	0.0	—
Seismic	6.1	0.1	5.1	—
Drilling	0.0	33.6	43.8	—
Other	41.1	0.0	0.0	—
Total	154.2	155.1	245.1	188.2

The cost for phase 2 was estimated at US$155 million, plus a further US$69.9 million for non-direct platform maintenance. The forecast operating costs and production profiles for the most likely case are as shown in table 8.38.

Table 8.38: Brutus Field most likely production and operating costs in phases 1 and 2, 2002–14

Year	Oil production (000s barrels/ day)	Gas production (millions cubic feet/day)	Operating costs (US$ millions)
Pre-2001			18.3
2002	17.4	22.5	13.0
2003	100.0	135.3	26.7
2004	100.0	146.3	34.2
2005	96.4	154.5	26.0
2006	66.8	147.5	28.8

Year	Oil production (000s barrels/ day)	Gas production (millions cubic feet/day)	Operating costs (US$ millions)
2007	44.1	150.9	23.1
2008	16.9	76.2	26.2
2009	10.9	49.3	21.0
2010	13.7	66.4	19.6
2011	28.0	151.8	18.5
2012	23.5	138.6	22.5
2013	21.6	144.1	17.3
2014	9.8	73.6	9.0

Revenues were subject to a 12.5 per cent federal royalty based on the well-head oil price less the quality differential and transportation cost of US$2.45 per barrel, while gas was based on the Henry Hub price (local Louisiana domestic price) less transportation costs of US39¢ per thousand cubic feet of gas (mcf). Federal taxes were 35 per cent plus an additional Louisiana state tax of 2.6 per cent. Costs and prices were expected to inflate by 2.5 per cent.

Using this information, which was provided in Shell's bidder's statement for the acquisition of Woodside Petroleum in December 2000, the after-tax US$ cash flow can be approximated as shown in table 8.39.

Table 8.39: Brutus Field approximate after-tax cash flow, 1998–2014

Year	Cash flow (US$m)
1998	−154.2
1999	−155.1
2000	−245.0

(continued)

Table 8.39: Brutus Field approximate after-tax cash flow, 1998–2014 (*cont'd*)

Year	Cash flow (US$m)
2001	−206.5
2002	93.3
2003	609.7
2004	629.7
2005	638.7
2006	484.4
2007	377.0
2008	2.8
2009	101.9
2010	140.5
2011	315.8
2012	278.2
2013	282.8
2014	135.0

The independent valuation of Brutus was US$1900 million based on a 2000 oil price of US$22 per barrel, an estimated Henry Hub price of US$3.10 per mcf, and a real discount rate of 6.5 per cent or, after adjusting for inflation of 2.5 per cent, a 9.16 per cent nominal (1.025 × 1.065) discount rate. Discounting the cash-flow stream results in a much lower figure of US$1200 million. However, the independent valuation was undertaken at the end of 2000, when half of the capital expenditures had already been spent. Adjusting the cash flow accordingly, and discounting to November 2000, results in a similar valuation.

The higher value is simply a function of not including the sunk costs in the development of the field. These costs still have an impact on future cash flows by reducing the future tax to pay through depreciation, but the project value has increased, as less capital is required to get the project off the ground. This does not take into account any risk adjustment that might be applied to the likelihood of a successful outcome.

For offshore Australian floating production facilities—as with most oil and gas projects—most operating costs are fixed. Figure 8.13 shows the allocation of operating costs for a medium-size operation of between 5000 and 15 000 barrels per day.

Figure 8.13: Australian floating production facility operating costs

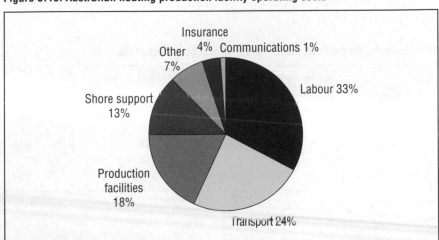

Diamonds

Valuations for diamonds are different from those for other commodities. As well as the grade of the deposit (carats of diamonds per tonne of ore) the value per carat of diamond can also change quite dramatically between and within deposits. So the quantity and quality of diamonds must be assessed (further information is provided in chapter 20).

Open cut or underground—Argyle mine

The Argyle mine in Australia is the largest diamond mine in the world, producing an average of 30 million carats per year by open cut mining from the AK1 pipe. The lamproite pipe is 2 kilometres long, varies in width from 500 metres to 150 metres, and has been tested to a depth of 1100 metres. At 31 March 2000, the reserve stood at 60.1 million tonnes at a grade of 3 carats per tonne (c/t) while the mineral resource was 168 million tonnes at 2.8 c/t. The reserve refers to the open cut portion of the resource. It was estimated that there was an additional 66 million tonnes at 3.1 c/t of the resource below the planned open cut that could be exploited by underground block-caving methods, which would allow the mine life to be extended to 2018. A number of major cutbacks (pushing the open cut walls back to allow access to deeper portions of the orebody) were planned beyond 2000 before it was considered that the overburden ratio would became too high beyond 2007, and it was then planned to go underground.

Table 8.40 shows the planned open cut production schedule in 2001, up to 2007.

Table 8.40: Argyle diamond mine — planned production schedule, 2001

Year	2001*	2002	2003	2004	2005	2006	2007	Total
Ore (million t)	7.3	10	10	10	10	10	2.8	60.1
Grade (c/t)	3.06	3.65	4.06	3.54	3.72	3.41	3.09	3.57
Waste (million t)	57.3	73.6	79.9	36.5	5.79	0.6	—	254

Note: * Nine months from 1 April 2001.

Source: Western Australian Diamond Trust (WADT) compulsory acquisition, May 2001.

From the numbers given in table 8.40, the average strip ratio was a little over four times, but peaked at nearly eight times in 2003. The average cost per tonne of material moved was forecast at $1.29 per tonne, plus a further $12.69 per tonne processing for an average cost of $19.43 and a peak cost for 2003 of $24.29 per tonne. This compares with average revenue of $58.55 per tonne of ore based on the average grade of 3.57, a recovery of 82 per cent and a long-term real price of $20.00 per carat. At first glance these figures might suggest that there was scope to extend the life of the open cut by further cutbacks before going underground. A rough estimate of the forecast average stripping ratio beyond 2007 was around nine times, which implied a cost of $25.59 per tonne for an operating margin of $32.96 per tonne. (From this gross operating margin, royalty, taxes, off-site costs and marketing have to be paid, with an estimated after-tax cash flow of around $20 per tonne, or $200 million per year.) However, if the pit went deeper beyond 2007, the average cost of $1.29 would increase substantially due to the increased haulage distances involved in moving the waste and ore. A more realistic long-term cost for moving material might have been $1.68 per tonne, which equates to a mining cost of $16.80 per tonne over the life of the open cut.

Although the operating margins of an open cut operation beyond 2007 might have been sufficient, it was a question of whether the higher economic returns from an underground operation outweighed the added risk of undertaking a more complex and unproven (within the context of the Argyle mine) mining method. The long-term underground operating cost was forecast at $5.88 per tonne based on an annual mine production of 6.5 million tonnes, compared with the estimated open cut cost of $16.80 per tonne. This saving of $10.92 had to offset the risk and the additional capital cost to undertake the underground development. The additional net underground costs were estimated at some $320 million, of which a little under half was ongoing annual sustaining capital. The IRR based on these simplified numbers was approximately 35.5 per cent on a pre-tax basis, which given the risks was probably the type of return required.

By early 2003 the open cut operation was scheduled to close in 2007. A $100 million decline was constructed and a final decision on an underground development was announced in 2006 from data gained from the decline's development, which was still in progress. Rio Tinto had decided to spend a further $150 million on an open pit cutback to allow for production from the open cut until 2008, while the underground reached maximum production. The block cave development was to cost US$760 million.

After slowing underground development in 2009 due to the GFC, in September 2010 it was announced that US$803m would be committed to ramp up production from the underground mine, which would be fully operational by 2013. Production of 9 million tonnes per year is expected with a mine life until at lease 2019. Current diamond production is about 8 to 9 million carats per year.

Open cut expansion to underground — Nimary goldmine

Another example of open cut to underground mining was the Nimary open cut goldmine, which in 1997–98 was one of Australia's lowest cost open cut producers, treating 800 000 tonnes per year, with an average grade of 4.8 grams per tonne (g/t). The installation of a ball mill was allowed for a planned increase in capacity to 1.25 million tonnes in 1998–99. Due to the high-grade nature of deeper underground reserves, it was also decided to start underground mining as well as open cut mining in 1999–2000. To accommodate the additional tonnage a further mill expansion was planned to 2 million tonnes. The capital costs, production profiles and operating costs are shown in table 8.41. Open cut ore was sourced from three pits with plans to go to a maximum depth of 290 metres.

Table 8.41: capital costs, production profiles and operating costs for Nimary goldmine, 1997

Key parameters	Capital costs ($ million)		
	1997–98	1998–99	1999–2000
Plant upgrade to 1.25 mtpa	6.0	—	—
Ancillary facilities	3.0	—	—
Plant upgrade to 2.0 mtpa	—	20.0	—
Underground development	—	15.5	—
Replacement capital	2.0	2.0	3.0
Mine exploration	4.0	4.0	4.0
Total	15.0	21.5	7.0

Production profiles	1997–98	1998–99	2000– 2004	Total/average
Open cut				
Mined (mtpa)	1.1	1.2	1.6	8.5
Grade (g/t Au)	4.33	4.88	4.88	4.81
Waste (mbcm pa)	10.8	12.2	9.2	86.0
Underground				
Mined (mtpa)	—	—	0.4	2.0

Indicative capital and operating costs

Key parameters	Capital costs ($ million)			
	1997–98	1998–99	1999–2000	
Processing				
Mill (mtpa)	1.03	1.25	2.00	11.30
Grade (g/t Au)	4.60	4.74	5.32	5.04
Recovery (%)	92	92	92	92
Gold produced (oz)	140 000	175 000	315 000	1 688 000
Costs	**1997–98**	**1998–99**	**1999–2000**	
Mining operation	31.2	31.3	54.8	
Milling and maintenance	12.0	14,5	22.2	
Administration and overheads	3.1	3.2	3.2	
Total ($m)	**46.3**	**49.0**	**80.2**	
Total ($/t)	**45.0**	**39.2**	**40.1**	
Total ($/oz)	**331**	**280**	**255**	

Note: mbcm – million bench cubic metres.

Source: Eagle Mining Part D Response, September 1997.

The Nimary valuation was $157.4 million based on a discount rate of 8 per cent and a gold price of US$350, and with an US$:A$ exchange rate at the time of 0.75. A critical assumption by the independent expert was that the known reserves would double. The open cut reserves at a 0.8 g/t cutoff were 5.055 million tonnes at an average grade of 4.87 g/t, with a resource of 7.683 million tonnes at 4.59 g/t. No underground reserves were estimated. From the table it is clear that additional open pittable reserves of 3.5 million tonnes would need to be delineated as well as a further 2.0 million tonnes at depth for the underground mine. High-grade materialisation had been intercepted at depths below 290 metres.

The operations eventually became part of the Normandy Group and were consolidated with the nearby Jundee mine. By late 2001 the high-grade open cut reserves had been mined out and operations were predominately from underground at rates of close to 700 000 tonnes per year and at higher grades of around 8.3 g/t. Potential to further increase underground reserves was considered good and plans were for the expansion of underground production to 1 million tonnes per annum.

Tip

It is not unusual, given the high cost of drill defining underground reserves, that only sufficient amounts for several years of production are categorised as being in the proved category, with drilling to proceed in advance of production to maintain a forward rolling proven reserve base. Obviously there must be sufficient geological information in the form of resources to give the company and shareholders comfort that further reserves can be defined over the longer term.

Mineral sands

Mineral sands are often a mixture of heavy minerals primarily used as a source for titanium. The metallurgy of producing products of titanium is often too complex to be undertaken on site (see chapter 20), but after recovering the heavy minerals there is an intermediate step of separating the individual minerals that can be processed at a separation plant if adequate and cheap power is available.

Ginkgo project—where to treat?

The Ginkgo mineral sands deposit is located in the Murray Basin of New South Wales, with a resource of 250 million tonnes containing 2.8 per cent heavy minerals. In late 2000 a pre-feasibility study suggested a mining rate of 12 million tonnes per year, with a stripping ratio of 1:1 based on a mineable tonnage of 125 million tonnes containing 3.74 per cent heavy minerals. The capital and operating costs are listed in table 8.42.

Table 8.42: Ginko mineral sands capital and operating costs, 2000

Capital cost item	Cost ($m)
Mine site	
Overburden removal—dragline, conveyors, hopper, etc.	24.0
Ore mining—dredge, barge, loaders, pontoons, etc.	16.6
Wet plant—plant, conveyor pre-treatment, power, etc.	28.5
Infrastructure—land acquisition, power lines, road upgrades, water, etc.	18.3
Administration—office, workshop, telecom, etc.	4.6
Off oito	
Dry plant—dry mill, limestone roaster, train loading, spares, etc.	47.?
Infrastructure—site acquisition, power, rail line upgrade, etc.	1.3
Administration—office, etc.	1.0
Port facility—conoontrate storage, etc.	1.0
Total	**142.5**

Operating cost item	Unit	Cost
Mine site		
Dragline	$/t moved	0.56
Dredge	$/t moved	0.19
Wet plant	$/t moved	0.30
Concentrate haulage	$/t trucked	17.00
Administration, maintenance	$m pa	3.20

(*continued*)

Table 8.42: Ginko mineral sands capital and operating costs, 2000 (*cont'd*)

Capital cost item		Cost ($m)
Off-site		
Dry mill plus ilmenite roaster	$/t concentrate	4.5
Labour	$m pa	4.2
Administration, maintenance	$m pa	3.4
Rail freight	$/t railed	11.0
Shipping and port charges	$/t railed	6.6

Source: Bemax Target statement, October 2000, included with permission of Bemax Resources NL and Resource Equity Consultants.

The major constituents of the mineral sands and assumed commodity prices at the time were:

» rutile — 12 per cent (US$450/t)

» leucoxene — 9 per cent (US$280/t)

» zircon — 10 per cent (US$320/t)

» monazite — 0.6 per cent (not given)

» ilmenite — 49 per cent (US$80/t)

» pseudorutile (last stage of alteration of ilmenite to leucoxene).

Based on an exchange rate of US$:A$0.60 and first production in 2003, the NPV for the project at a discount rate of 10.5 per cent was determined by an independent expert at $42 million. It is possible from the information provided to construct a financial cash-flow model that, using real dollars, can produce a similar NPV assuming a corporate tax rate of 30 per cent and a state royalty of 4 per cent.

In early 2001 further refinements to the feasibility study showed that total capital costs might be $166.9 million and that the total operating cost would be some $126.2 per tonne of concentrate. Further consideration was also given to the size and location of the mineral separation plant (MSP), which would treat 450 000 wet tonnes per year.

Four scenarios were considered:

» mine production 12 million tonnes per annum and MSP at Broken Hill

» mine production 12 million tonnes per annum and MSP at Mildura

» mine production 12 million tonnes per annum and MSP at Port Pirie

» lower capital cost for 6 million tonnes per year, using contractors for overburden stripping and MSP at Broken Hill.

The results of the analysis are shown in table 8.43. Note that the costs for the Broken Hill option with contract overburden mining result in a higher mining cost per tonne, but much lower capital costs. The differences in operating costs from the other alternatives are primarily the transportation costs from the mine to plant.

Table 8.43· Ginko mineral sands feasibility study, 2001

Key parameters	Broken Hill	Mildura	Port Pirie	Broken Hill 6 (mtpa)
Ilmenite sales (t)	558 734	558 734	558 734	558 734
Rutile sales (t)	470 513	470 513	470 513	470 513
Zircon sales (t)	349 209	349 209	349 209	349 209
Altered rutile sales (t)	845 453	845 453	845 453	845 453
Roasted ilmenite sales (t)	670 481	670 481	670 481	670 481
Total revenue ($m)	959	959	959	959
Operating costs ($m)	461	472	466	596
Mining costs ($/t)	3.80	3.88	3.83	4.83
Concentrate cost ($/t)	126	129	127	162
Operating surplus ($m)	498	487	494	364
Start-up capital costs ($m)	167	170	170	98

(*continued*)

Table 8.43: Ginko mineral sands feasibility study, 2001 (*cont'd*)

Key parameters	Broken Hill	Mildura	Port Pirie	Broken Hill 6 (mtpa)
Depreciation ($m)	193	197	197	125
Government charges ($m)	29	29	29	20
EBIT ($m)	275	262	267	218
Tax ($m)	83	79	80	66
Profit ($m)	193	183	187	153
NPV at 10% ($m)	55	48	50	99

Source: Bemax Announcement, March 2001, included with permission of Bemax Resources NL.

By late 2001 additional infill drilling had further defined the resource, with the resulting grade tonnage curve shown in figure 8.14. The results show that the deposit reduced in size with a total resource based on a 1 per cent cutoff of 205 million tonnes averaging 3.23 per cent, while the measured resource was 162 million tonnes at 3.56 per cent heavy minerals.

Figure 8.14: Argyle mineral sands grade tonnage curve

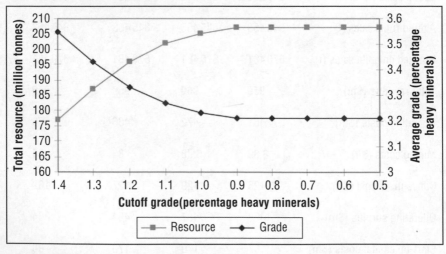

Data derived from Bemax announcement, October 2001.

By early 2002 a total of 585 holes had been drilled into the deposit and proven reserves of 133 million tonnes at 3.9 per cent had been defined, with an overburden ratio of 1.3 to 1.0. Production for the first seven years was expected to be 480 000 tonnes per year of concentrate for a capital cost of $180 million with wet concentrates shipped to MSP at Broken Hill. First shipments commenced in December 2005.

Iron ore

For most iron ore mines, no processing of the ore is required on-site, the mine product being shipped off to the blast furnaces. The grade of the ore is important with regard to the iron content and the level of other associated metals that may affect the quality of the iron produced (further information is provided in chapter 20). Blast furnace operators also prefer lumpy-sized pieces of ore that allow for a more efficient flow of oxygen in the blast furnace and so will pay a premium for the product in this form.

West Angelas project—indirect and contingency costs

The West Angelas iron ore project located in Western Australia was regarded as a 'new generation' lump ore producer for direct feed blast furnaces. In March 2000 approval was given for the mine to be developed as an incremental expansion on the existing Robe River mine, with initial production of 8 million tonnes in 2003 expanding to 20 million tonnes within eight years. The iron ore would be sent by rail to Robe River's existing rail line and then on to Cape Lambert, which would require expansion of the existing port and ship-loading facilities. Conventional open cut mining and ore processing methods were proposed to produce a mixture of lump (33 to 36 per cent), with over 62 per cent iron content, and sinter fines (64 to 67 per cent) with iron content of 62 per cent. The key parameters and capital costs are as shown in table 8.44.

Table 8.44: West Angelas iron ore project—key parameters and capital costs, 2000

Key parameters	
Ore reserves	441 million tonnes @ 62.1% Fe
Reserve life	25 years

(continued)

Table 8.44: West Angelas iron ore project—key parameters and capital costs, 2000 (*cont'd*)

Key parameters			
Additional mineral resource	469 million tonnes @ 61.9% Fe		
Cash operating cost (1999 dollars)	$7.65 per tonne of ore life average, excluding Cape Lambert operations		

	Direct cost ($m)	Indirect and contingency cost ($m)	Total cost ($m)
Mine	58	2	61
Plant and infrastructure	148	37	185
Railway (340 km)	394	61	456
Cape Lambert plant and infrastructure	156	38	194
Cape Lambert marine and rail yard	37	4	41
Owner costs	—	39	39
Capital spares and contingency	11	63	74
Total capital cost ($m)	805	244	1050

Source: North Limited (NBH) July 2000 target statement.

Near-term operating figures are shown in table 8.45. The NPV was estimated at between $660 million and $850 million, with an ungeared after-tax IRR of 15 to 16 per cent.

Table 8.45: West Angelas near-term operating figures, 2000

Year ending June	2001	2002	2003	2004	2005	2006
Sales volume (million tonnes)	—	—	7.5	9.2	12.4	16.7
Average price ($/wet tonnes)	—	—	28.0	28.2	28.8	29.1
Average cash cost ($/wet tonnes)	—	—	12.1	11.1	10.8	10.3
Capital expenditure ($m)	466.0	532.5	27.4	21.3	44.1	18.7

From table 8.45, it is apparent that the annual operating margin would increase from $119 million in 2003 to $314 million in 2006, as price and volume increased and, more importantly, the unit cost per tonne decreased. In June 2008, Rio Tinto provided the breakdown of Western Australian Pilbara iron ore operating costs as follows: employees, 30 per cent; contractors, 34 per cent; fuel and energy, 13 per cent; and materials and others, 23 per cent.

CHAPTER 9
Hedging commodities and exchange rates

The uncertainty arising from the volatility in commodity prices and exchange rates is of concern to management because of the possible negative impact on revenue, and hence profitability, for a company and its projects. The revenue is the product of the realised price times the volume of the commodity sold. As most commodities are sold in US dollars, the exchange rate for countries such as Australia at the time the commodities are sold is very important.

Commodity prices are also beyond the control of mining companies and, as budgets and plans are based on future commodity prices, the uncertainty adds to the difficulty of future planning.

Exchange-traded futures

Futures markets for commodities were originally established in London to provide an opportunity for buyers and sellers to establish a price for a commodity into the future, and contract to supply and take delivery at that price and at that future date. It is therefore possible for resource companies to sell certain commodities into the future at a fixed price.

The prices are set daily on the exchanges, and companies can buy or sell contracts through brokers. There are several major exchanges, including the Chicago Mercantile Exchange (COMEX), now merged with the New York Mercantile Exchange (NYMEX), and the London Metal Exchange (LME). Examples of the commonly traded base metal commodities on the LME are shown in table 9.1. Some of the important issues to note include:

» Forward markets are not available for all mineral commodities. It is important that commodities can be produced to a set standard so that they are readily exchangeable and that terminal markets exist where spot prices can be easily obtained. For example, although unsuccessful attempts have been made in the past, forward markets for coal do not formally exist due to the variety of coal qualities.

» Liquidity is important, so that forward prices can be established. As shown in table 9.1, a price for tin was not available for delivery in 27 months' time, as there were probably insufficient buyers or sellers to make a market. Additionally, exchanges will only trade contracts at certain time periods: that is, three, 15 and 27 months forward in the case of the LME.

» Forward prices are said to be in contango when the future price is higher than the current or spot price, or in backwardation when the future price is at a discount to the spot price. For cobalt, the three-month price is in backwardation while the three-month price for aluminium is in contango.

Table 9.1: commonly traded commodities on the LME, 19 January 2011

Commodity	Pricing Seller	Spot	3 month	15 month	27 month
Aluminium	US$/tonne	2181	2218	2335	2448
Copper	US$/tonne	8350	8370	8375	8300
Cobalt	US$/tonne	34500	33500	32625	—
Lead	US$/tonne	2131	2162	2233	2278
Molybdenum	US$/tonne	30500	30500	31675	—
Nickel	US$/tonne	19680	19740	19875	19860
Tin	US$/tonne	22000	22005	22065	—
Zinc	US$/tonne	2012	2032	2095	2123

Source: LME, 19 January 2011.

The premium or discount is a function of the perceived level of future demand and supply or, in the case of gold, interest rate differentials, which are discussed in the following section.

As discussed in chapter 4, futures markets are not very reliable predictors of future commodity prices.

A fully hedged position may also increase a company's risk profile if the commodity price moves against it and it is required to meet margin calls. For valuation purposes it is best to remove any existing hedge and treat the market-to-market value as an asset or liability, and then discount the unhedged cash flows at the company's cost of capital.

Over-the-counter futures

Over-the-counter futures transactions are contracts written between the client and a financial institution. The advantage of such contracts is often the ability of the financial institution to structure the contracts to meet the client's needs. Very complex structures are therefore possible and, most importantly, the duration of the contract can be much longer.

The ability of the financial institution to contract well into the future will depend on the availability of exchange-traded futures and of counterparties that might take the other side of the transaction (that is, buyers of the physical metal) and, importantly, the creditworthiness of the client. Table 9.2 sets out the possible maximum duration for contracts, although it must be stressed that the net pricing after costs might be quite prohibitive if the institution is unable to lay off some or all of the risk to third parties.

Table 9.2: possible maximum contract duration

Commodity	Maximum term (years)	Commodity	Maximum term (years)
Aluminium	7	Gold	15
Copper	7	Silver	10
Lead	3	Platinum and palladium	5
Nickel	5	Oil	10
Tin	3	Natural gas	12
Zinc	5	Foreign exchange	7

Gold futures

Gold markets are a special case, given the financial nature of the commodity. Forward sales can be up to 15 years into the future, but are more commonly for shorter periods. Companies can also forward sell all their future production up to their current reserves.

Goldmining companies can also use synthetic instruments, such as put and call options, to secure the future delivery price. The available methods can be very sophisticated and can allow producers to roll forward their position, so that they can maintain it into the future depending on the movement in the price of gold.

The financial nature of the commodity means that the critical aspect of gold futures is that the future gold price is always in contango, which reflects forward interest rates. In simple terms, banks have very large stores of gold bullion in their vaults that earn no income. The banks are therefore willing to lend the gold at low interest rates, or at what is more commonly referred to as a leasing rate. It is therefore possible for an investor to borrow the gold, sell it and invest the proceeds in the money market. If the interest rate provided by the money market is greater than the cost of leasing the gold, the investor will make a profit; however, the investor is exposed to variations in the gold price as the gold has to be returned to the bank at some time in the future. If the investor can also buy a futures contract that guarantees delivery of the gold at that future date, then the investor can lock in a margin at little or no risk.

The market will not allow such easy returns, so the future price that the investor is required to pay for the gold for delivery to the bank will be equal to the spot price plus the difference between the money market rate and the leasing rate. For example, if the spot price is US$1700, the leasing rate is 1 per cent per year and the money market rate is 3 per cent, then:

$$\text{Forward price in one year} = \text{US}\$1700 \times (1 + 0.03 - 0.01)$$
$$= \text{US}\$1734 \text{ per ounce}[1]$$

The structure by which a gold producer can forward sell its production and thus receive a price in one year's time is illustrated in figure 9.1.

---

1 Due to the compounding effects of interest the equation is a close approximation where the time period is greater than one year.

Figure 9.1: 12-month forward sale

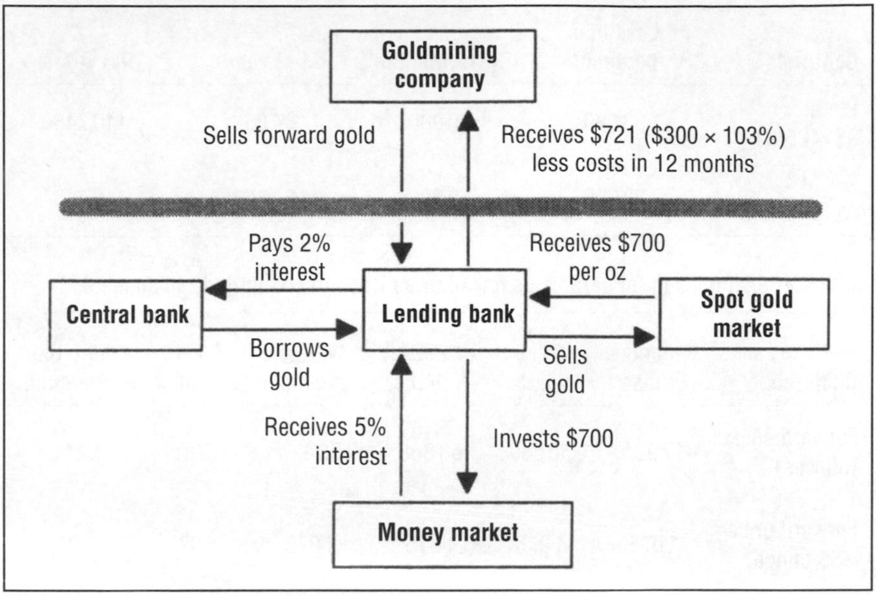

Producers, particularly in Australia, were attracted to the concept of selling part of their future production (usually enough to cover operating costs), or sometimes the majority of their production, at a premium to the current market. The recent strength in the gold price and world economic uncertainty, which suggests further gold price upside, has resulted in most operating gold companies remaining unhedged.

Tip

Forward sales are an insurance policy, in that they guarantee a future price. However, there is a modest cost, as with any insurance policy, and just as forward sales protect the downside movement in the price of a commodity, they also limit the upside in any price movement in excess of the forward sale.

Examples of hedging by St Barbara Limited and Adamus Resources Limited are shown in tables 9.3 and 9.4 (overleaf). The put option gives St Barbara the right, but not the obligation to deliver gold at a specific price at a certain date.

Table 9.3: examples of forward sales for St Barbara Limited, 30 June 2011

Contracts	Less than 6 months	6–12 months	1–2 years	1–5 years
Put at A$1425/oz	33 000	30 000	64 252	110 748
Call at A$1615/oz	33 000	30 000	64 252	110 748

Table 9.4: examples of forward sales for Adamas Resources Limited, 30 June 2011

Contracts	3 months or less	3–12 months	12–24 months	24–36 months	36–48 months	More than 48 months
Forward sold (ounces)	17 904	50 680	53 898	58 427	42 811	52 167
Forward price US$/ounce	1 075	1 075	1 075	1 075	1 075	1 075
Market value (US$m)	(3.6)	(10.1)	(10.4)	(11.2)	(8.4)	(11.2)

If the spot price is higher at that time, then the company would not make delivery. The trade-off for this implied benefit is a fee that must be paid by the company to obtain the option. The call options sold by the company give the owner of the option the right, but not the obligation to make delivery of gold at the set price. The company receives payment for agreeing to sell the call option, but if the future price is higher than the delivery price then the owner of the option will call on delivery and the company loses out on the higher gold price. Selling call options can offset the cost of buying put options.

In the case of Adamus, the company had forward sales contracts for gold where it was committed to deliver varying amounts of gold at different periods in the future at a fixed price (the prices could have varied for each of the periods). The US gold price as at 30 June 2011 was US$1242.40 and so all of the futures contracts were out of the money, as the future price was US$1075, or a loss of US$167.40 per ounce, which meant that for Adamas to cancel the contracts it would have to pay a total of $55 million. If the spot price were to drop below US$1075, then the contracts would be in the money.

Forward sales are not a panacea

At first sight, the concept of covering a project's production by forward cover looks attractive. Management often argues that in a falling commodity price environment the use of hedging can help protect the viability of mining operations, and that investors should not unduly penalise their stock. Yet even the share prices of mining companies that are heavily forward sold will fall during a time of declining commodity prices.

Simply put, if some shareholders invest, for example, in goldmining companies to benefit from an increasing gold price, then they will be sellers (irrespective of the level of hedging) when the gold price falls and thus the share price will fall. In a rising gold price market, a highly hedged goldmining company may not fully benefit from the higher gold price and therefore may not perform as well as an unhedged gold company.

As the spot gold price falls below the price of any forward contracts, the value of those existing forward contracts will increase. It is therefore possible for companies to sell their forward contracts and realise the profit (forward price less spot price less costs). Obviously, the company could no longer deliver the gold at the contract price and would have to accept the spot price at the time of delivery. If the current spot price is also below the cost of producing the gold, then the operation is no longer profitable. The company's preference may be to keep the operation going by utilising the forward sales rather than to close them out. However, this may not maximise the NPV to the shareholder. The optimum position may well be to close the mining operation and to close the forward sales. Obviously, this action is difficult to take given the dislocation of the workforce, the possible sterilisation of the existing ore reserves and the possible write-off of the mine's book value.

Exchange rates

As with commodity forward sales, mining companies outside the US can acquire forward cover for their exchange rate exposure: for example, with respect to the US$:A$ exchange rate (see table 9.5).

Table 9.5: forward exchange rates

Period	Spot	1 mth	3 mth	6 mth	9 mth	1 yr
A$:US$	1.040	1.036	1.030	1.021	1.012	1.004

Resource companies often choose to forward cover for several years, generally with a larger proportion of coverage for near-term sales. Clearly, the valuation of a company can be affected by the level of forward cover and the relative movement in exchange rates over time. As mentioned previously, in regard to commodity price cover, forward exchange rate cover is an insurance policy. In a rising exchange rate environment, the company will benefit but, on the reverse side, if the exchange rate falls below the cover rate, the company will not gain all the benefits of increased Australian dollar revenue.

See appendix F for the quarterly exchange rates for the Australian dollar against the US dollar and UK pound. Readers can use these figures to convert quoted commodity prices, operating costs and capital costs into another currency. The Australian Consumer Price Index (CPI) is also provided so that indicative current costs can be computed. For example, if the June 2008 operating cost was A$20 per tonne, then the September 2011 US dollar price would be: A$20/164.6 × 174.9 × 0.9781 = US$20.79 per tonne.[2]

The risks

For most forward contracts established by a resource company there is an obligation to supply the commodity or the currency at a future point in time at an agreed price. The counterparty, or the agent, broker or clearing house, will be concerned that, should the price of the commodity or the exchange rate move against the resource company and it fails to make delivery, there is the possibility of an unacceptable exposure. To counter this, the resource company may be required to meet margin calls (pay additional funds or increase debt) to cover the potential shortfall. If things go the wrong way it is possible for the company to become insolvent.

A major example of this was the Australian mining company Pasminco, which had undertaken an aggressive acquisition and development program, including the purchase and development of the Century zinc mine in September 1997 and the takeover of Savage Resources in March 1999 for a total cost of $1.6 billion. By July 2001 the financiers of Pasminco undertook a review of the company: the share price had fallen from around $1.50 to $0.05 between January 1998 and September 2001, and the zinc price had fallen from US$1074 to US$801 per tonne. Each US$100 fall in

---

2 164.6 is the June 2008 CPI; 174.9 is the September 2011 CPI; 0.9781 is the September 2011 US$:A$ exchange rate.

the zinc price reduced the company's $2 billion revenue by $150 million. By June 2001 Pasminco's debt had increased to $1891 million, primarily as a result of its acquisition program.

This might have been manageable, but there was an additional hedge exposure at the time of another $850 million! Given the declining revenue and the failure to arrange a standstill agreement with its financiers, an administrator was appointed in September 2001. The hedging the company had undertaken was not against a falling zinc price, which could have made all the difference, but against a strengthening Australian dollar. The weighted average hedging had been set at US$0.6599, but the exchange rate had fallen to US$0.50, resulting in the unrealised hedge loss.

For small companies that don't have the balance sheet resources to fund their own project developments, project finance, which is described in more detail in chapter 3, is often used. As the debt funding is recourse to the project, the banks will often insist that the forward sales are hedged where possible to ensure revenue. If there are problems delivering mine product to fulfil the forward contracts, and ironically if the commodity price increases, the mine may have to provide additional guarantees or funding to meet margin calls. If those financial facilities are not available then the project and the company may be at risk.

This two-edged sword was demonstrated by Lafayette's Ramu Ramu polymetallic mine in the Philippines where 65 per cent of production over the first 41 months of production, which commenced in late 2006, was hedged to fund a project debt facility of US$42 million. Heavy rains in November 2006 and discharge from an inadequately designed tailings dam resulted in the temporary closure of the mine and failure to deliver into the contracts. With rising commodity prices, the out-of-the-money hedge positions peaked within 16 months of initial mine start-up at US$192 million, which the company could not fund, ultimately resulting in the appointment of an administrator a little over a year later.

Hedging plays an important part in the financial management of mining projects in that it can provide some level of security against volatile commodity prices and exchange rates, but as shown, it can backfire and potentially ruin a company. One area of greater certainty, although it is fraught with complexity, is tax. This is dealt with in the next chapter.

CHAPTER 10
Taxation, depreciation, royalties and accounting standards

It's a fact of life that taxes must be paid on profits derived from mining. As well as a company being able to claim operating costs as a tax deduction, capital costs may also be claimed, but on a depreciated basis (discussed later). As resources are non-renewable, state and federal governments often also charge a royalty payment as a fee for a company's right to exploit the resource. The complexity of how all of these issues and other financial information should be presented to shareholders is governed by a maze of accounting standards.

Taxation

It is not possible, nor is it the intention of this book, to fully describe all the issues and procedures for determining the amount and timing of tax payable by a resource company or an individual project. However, it is worthwhile to make some general comments with specific reference to the resources industry.

Income (or revenue) derived from the mining and processing of minerals is generally assessable income for tax purposes. Table 10.1 (overleaf) provides details of corporate tax rates for a number of countries, but readers should be aware that taxes set by governments can change quickly and they should therefore make their own enquiries. In most jurisdictions 'losses and outgoings necessarily incurred in carrying on a business for the purposes of gaining or producing such income' are generally deductible from revenues and will therefore reduce the amount of tax ultimately payable. Costs of a non-capital nature are expensed in the tax year and include such items as:

» wages

» energy (fuel costs in generating power or the purchase of power from a grid)

» materials (such as chemicals or explosives)

» contract mining

» repairs (as long as there is no capital improvement beyond its original application).

The expenditure incurred in borrowing money (interest) used for the purposes of producing assessable income is also generally an allowable deduction.

Table 10.1: comparative tax rates for a number of mining countries

Country	Corporate tax	Value-added tax on imports	Dividend withholding tax
Argentina	35%	21%	0% or 35% if they exceed taxable profits
Bolivia	25%, plus 12.5% for mining under favourable mineral price conditions	13%	25%
Brazil	34%	20%	0%
Chile	17% income, plus progressive tax to 40%	19%	35%
China	25%	17%	10%
DRC	40%	13%	20%
Indonesia	25%; companies listed on Indonesian Stock Exchange may be eligible for 5% reduction	10%	20%
Kazakhstan	20% reducing to 15% in 2014; 3% to 32% resource rent tax on oil and gas condensates	12%	15%
Mexico	30%	16%	0%

Country	Corporate tax	Value-added tax on imports	Dividend withholding tax
Namibia	Diamonds 55%; petroleum 35%; others 37.5%	15%	10%
Papua New Guinea	Non-resident: mining 40%; gas 0%; new petroleum 45%	10%	17%
Philippines	30%	12%	30%, but may be lowered to 15%
Peru	30%	19%	4.1%
Russia	2% to the central government and 13.5% to 18% payable to the regional governments	18%	15%
Zambia	35%	16%	15%
Zimbabwe	25%	15%	15%

Sources: Deloitte, World Tax Rates, Ernst & Young Worldwide Corporate Tax Guide and PWC.

A problem arises with expenses of a capital nature, which have to be depreciated over a period greater than one year. The first issue is that of defining expenditure of a capital nature, and the second, to a lesser extent, is the specific provisions available to the resources industry.

The definitions or tests to determine expenses of a capital nature versus those of a revenue nature (which can still be ambiguous) can be divided into the following:

» *Fixed or circulating capital.* Expenditure that produces fixed assets (such as a processing plant) with a useful life of more than one year is of a capital nature, while expenditure that produces circulating capital is of a revenue nature.

» *Recurring or once-and-for-all expenditure.* A payment made once and for all is of a capital nature, while recurring expenditure is of a revenue nature.

» *Enduring benefit.* If the expenditure is not only made once and for all, but also brings about an enduring benefit, then it is of a capital nature.

Expenditure of a capital nature such as mining plant and equipment can be depreciated over the useful life of the asset. The depreciation is allowable as a deduction for tax purposes. The life of the asset and hence the rates of depreciation for tax purposes may be different from accounting depreciation rates. Also, in some cases, there may be accelerated rates of depreciation for tax purposes to encourage investment (more rapid depreciation will increase short-term cash flows, as less tax is paid, which will increase the NPV).

Depreciation methodology

There are two different methods of depreciation, one of which may be available to resource companies:

» *prime cost (straight line)*—an equal deduction for each year over the life of the asset

» *diminishing value (reducing balance)*—a set percentage of the written-down value of the asset in that year.

For example, assume that an asset such as a truck is acquired for $100 000. For tax purposes the prime cost rate is set at 20 per cent and the diminishing value rate at 30 per cent. The effective life of the asset is estimated at seven years. Figure 10.1 shows the level of depreciation for each method. In the case of the prime cost method, 20 per cent, or $20 000, is depreciated each year for five years.

Figure 10.1: depreciation of capital cost using the diminishing value and prime cost methods

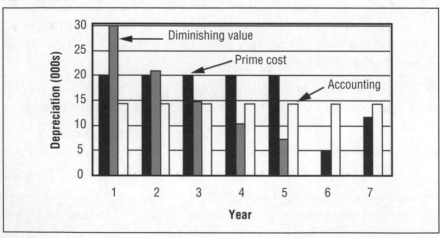

248

For the diminishing value method, 30 per cent, or $30 000, is claimed in the first year. The written-down value is then $70 000 so that in year 2, $21 000 is claimed ($70 000 × 30 per cent). In year 5, $7203 is claimed; however, there is still $16 807 of written-down value that can be claimed over the remainder of the asset's life. In year 7 the remaining written-down value of $11 765 would be claimed. For accounting purposes (as opposed to determining the tax payable), the level of depreciation each year could be $14 286 ($100 000/7 years). Note that the larger the allowable depreciation, the lower the tax and hence the larger the cash flow.

As the depreciation is a non-cash item it is simply a book entry to determine the correct level of tax to pay. The advantage of the diminishing value method is that it allows for increased cash flow in the early years and can therefore increase the project's net present value (NPV). In the previous example, the NPV of the prime cost discounted at 10 per cent is $75 816, while for the diminishing value method it is $76 057, or a 0.3 per cent advantage. Had the economic life been five years, then the advantage would have been 2.3 per cent, while for a 10-year life the diminishing value method would have resulted in a 0.7 per cent disadvantage.

The selection of prime cost or diminishing value depreciation may also be governed by the level of taxable income in the early period of the asset's life. If there were insufficient taxable income to make full use of the diminishing value method, then prime cost could be adopted.

Australian federal mining tax

The federal corporate tax rate in Australia is 30 per cent (reducing to 29 per cent in June 2013), and there is also a 10 per cent goods and services tax (GST). There is a 30 per cent withholding tax on dividends unless they are franked (corporate tax has been paid before dividend distribution), which falls to nil if full corprate tax has been paid. Both prime cost and diminishing value methods of depreciation are allowed, and once a method is selected for a particular asset it can't be changed for the remainder of that asset's life. The method selected in any one year is applicable to all new capital items for that year, but the method for new capital items can be changed from year to year.

Since mining operations have a finite life, there are special natural resource provisions for capital expenditure deductions. The main provisions are for the depreciation of capital items over the remaining life of the operation and the deduction of exploration expenditure during the year of expenditure, plus carry forward provisions, so long as the taxpayer carried on or proposed to carry on prescribed mining operations.

Table 10.2 lists some of the items for which the Australian Taxation Office (ATO) has set the effective lives and annual discounts allowed after 26 February 1992.

Table 10.2: examples of effective lives and annual depreciation (ATO) after 26 February 1992

Item	Effective life (years)	Prime cost (%)	Diminishing value (%)
Drill rigs	10	10.00	15.00
Bulldozers	9	11.11	22.22
Dragline	30	3.33	6.66
Continuous miner	10	10.00	15.00
Crushers	25	4.00	8.00
Filtration	15	6.67	13.33
SX-EW	17	5.88	11.76
Tailing dam	20	5.00	10.00
Pipelines	30	3.33	6.66
Offshore platform	30	3.33	6.66
LNG plant	30	3.33	6.66

Minerals resource rent tax

From June 2012 a minerals resource rent tax (MRRT)[1] will be introduced for iron ore mines and coalmines, similar to the petroleum resource rent tax (PRRT). The MRRT is a profit-based cash-flow tax where negative cash

1 For more information see Commonwealth of Australia, Exposure Draft Minerals Resource Rent Tax, 2011.

flows are carried forward and uplifted by an interest rate defined as the long-term bond rate (LTBR) plus 7 per cent. The MRRT applies only to profits upstream of the taxing point, which has been defined as at the run of mine stockpile. Upstream operating and capital expenditure are immediately deductible, as are state royalty payments grossed up by the MRRT tax rate. The effective MRRT tax rate is 22.5 per cent and is deductible for corporate tax purposes.

If a mining company's operations were in existence at 1 May 2010, then they are entitled to a starting base allowance based on their existing investments, which further reduces their mining profit. Companies can use one of two methods to calculate the starting base: one method uses the audited book value in fixed percentages over five years and can be uplifted at LTBR plus 7 per cent; the second method uses the market value depreciated over its remaining life with uplift in line with the Consumer Price Index. One area of potential contention will be the estimate of what constitutes market value of the assets at the taxing point and the implied commodity price at that point.

An example is shown in tables 10.3 and 10.4 (overleaf) for a hypothetical 10 million tonne per year iron ore operation. The book value model (table 10.3) assumes a value for the upstream assets of $600 million. Given the relatively large operating margins all of the state royalty and MRRT allowances are used each year with no resultant uplift. Due to the decreasing proportion of allowable MRRT allowance (36 per cent in year 1 and 15 per cent in year 4), the amount payable under MRRT increases.

For the market value case (table 10.4), it has been assumed that an adequate return is provided for a hypothetical third-party provider of the downstream services. This results in only 18 per cent of the iron ore sale price payable to the downstream services while the remaining 82 per cent of the price and hence market value of the operations based on the project's NPV is allocated to the upstream operations (in this case $4706 million for upstream). Under this scenario, assuming it could be justified, then the amount payable under MRRT is significantly reduced for the mining company. If a larger valuation is used for the downstream operations and hence a lower price at the taxing point, then the amount payable under the MRRT reduces. As mentioned before, the assumption on the appropriate price at the taxing point may become an area of debate amongst valuers.

Table 10.3: calculation of the MRRT using the book value model ($m)

Components	Year			
	1	2	3	4
Revenue	1500	1500	1500	1500
Operating	315	315	315	315
Royalty (divided by 22.5%)	500	500	500	500
Royalty utilised	500	500	500	500
Royalty uplift	0	0	0	0
MRRT allowance	216	144	90	90
MRRT unutilised	0	0	0	0
MRRT profit/loss	469	541	595	595
MRRT @ 22.5%	**106**	**122**	**134**	**134**

Table 10.4: calculation of the MRRT using the market value model ($m)

Components	Year			
	1	2	3	4
Revenue	1500	1500	1500	1500
Operating	315	315	315	315
Mining loss uplift	0	0	0	0
Royalty (divided by 22.5%)	500	500	500	500
Royalty utilised	500	500	500	500
Royalty uplift	0	0	0	0
MRRT allowance	4706	4235	3765	3294
MRRT unutilised	471	471	471	471
MRRT profit/loss	214	214	214	214
MRRT @ 22.5%	**48**	**48**	**48**	**48**

The petroleum resource rent tax (PRRT) is also a profits-based tax levied on an offshore petroleum project and is deductible for corporate tax purposes. The rate is 40 per cent of the project's taxable profit after all project capital and operating expenses and exploration expenditures have been deducted. Where deductions are greater than revenue, then exploration expenditures can be carried forward and uplifted by LTBR plus 15 per cent and other expenditures by LTBR plus 5 per cent. A simple example is shown in table 10.5, where construction of the oil field is during years 1 and 2 and first production in year 2, peaking in year 3 and then declining. The LTBR was set at 4 per cent and expenditures were carried forward with the appropriate uplift when expenditures exceeded taxable income. It is not until year 4 that the first PRRT is payable. Note also that exploration expenditures not directly related to the field can also be used to reduce PRRT, but obviously they can only be used once.

Table 10.5: calculation of the petroleum resource rent tax (PRRT) ($m)

Components	Year			
	1	2	3	4
Revenue	0	100	500	300
Operating and development costs	75	90	10	5
Operating and development costs carried forward	0	02	78	0
Total deductible operating and development costs	75	172	88	5
Notional taxable profit	−75	−72	412	295
Field exploration	50	50	20	10
Field exploration carried forward	0	60	130	0
Total deductible field exploration expenditure	50	110	150	10
Other exploration	100	70	50	50
Other exploration expenditure carried forward	0	119	225	16
Total deductible other exploration expenditure	100	189	275	66
Notional taxable profits less field exploration expenditures	−125	−181	261	285
Notional taxable profit less other exploration expenditure	−225	−370	−13	219
PRRT taxable receipts	0	0	0	219
PRRT @ 40%	**0**	**0**	**0**	**88**

US federal mining tax[2]

The US federal tax rate is applied on a sliding scale from 15 to 35 per cent, the maximum rate applying to profits above US$18.33 million. State and local governments may also impose income taxes from less than 1 per cent to 12 per cent, which are deductible against federal taxable income. The modified accelerated cost recovery system (MACRS) is the current method of accelerated asset depreciation allowing for faster depreciation of capital assets similar to double declining balance. Assets are placed into property classes and then a depreciation schedule (see table 10.6), which is used to determine the amount allowable for depreciation.

Table 10.6: US MACRS property class

Property class	Personal property (all property except real estate)
3-year property	Property with asset depreciating range (ADR) class life of four years or less
5-year property	Aircraft (of non-air transport companies); computers; petroleum drilling equipment; property with ADR class life of more than four years and less than 10 years
7-year property	All other property not assigned to another class
	Office furniture, fixtures and equipment; property with ADR class life of more than 10 years and less than 16 years; natural gas gathering lines
10-year property	Assets used in petroleum refining and certain food products
	Property with ADR class life of 16 years or more and less than 20 years

Recovery year	3-year property (%)	5-year property (%)	7-year property (%)	10-year property (%)
1	33.33	20.00	14.29	10.00
2	44.45	32.00	24.49	18.00
3	14.81	19.20	17.49	14.40
4	7.41	11.52	12.49	11.52
5		5.76	8.93	9.22
6			8.92	7.37

2 For more information see <www.irs.gov/publications/p946/ch04.html#en_US_2010_publink1000107509>.

Recovery year	3-year property (%)	5-year property (%)	7-year property (%)	10-year property (%)
7			8.93	6.55
8			4.46	6.55
9				6.56

In the US, recognition is also given to non-renewable resources that will deplete over time, and therefore an additional federal tax deduction (depletion allowance) is allowed. Two methods for calculating the depletion allowance are available (statutory depletion allowance and percentage method): the entity can claim whichever provides the larger tax deduction, and the methods can be changed from year to year.

The first method, the statutory depletion allowance method, allows for the smaller of 50 per cent of net income, which is defined as revenues less operating costs, royalties, state taxes, treatment charges, marketing costs and transportation costs, or a prescribed percentage of net revenue (revenue less royalties). Some of the prescribed percentages include:

» *22 per cent* — sulphur, uranium and, if from deposits in the US, other base metals

» *15 per cent* — gold, silver, copper, iron ore and oil shale, if from deposits in the US

» *14 per cent* — borax, granite, limestone, marble, mollusk shells, potash, slate and soapstone

» *10 per cent* — coal, lignite and sodium chloride.

The second method for calculating the depletion allowance method is the percentage method, where the mine's undepleted cost base at the beginning of the year plus un-expensed exploration expenditure is expensed on a per unit basis of production over the remaining reserves. For example, if the cost base is US$20 million, the remaining reserve base is 10 million tonnes (mt) and annual production is 2 mt, then the depletion is US$20m/10 mt × 2 mt = US$4 million.

There is no value-added tax in the US, although individual states may levy sales tax at different rates, while a withholding tax of 30 per cent may be applicable to dividends.

Canadian federal mining tax[3]

Since 1 January 2007, mining taxes and royalties are also payable to a province or a territory (varying from 10 per cent to 18 per cent), plus the federal income tax rate of 18 per cent in 2010, decreasing to 16.5 per cent in 2011 and 15 per cent by 2012. A 5 per cent GST that is not tax deductible is payable on imported equipment, while import duties may also be payable. Most capital assets under the capital cost allowance (CCA) acquired by mining and oil and gas companies qualify for a depreciation rate of 25 per cent on a declining balance basis.

Accelerated capital cost allowance (ACCA) can provide for an additional depreciation allowance of up to 100 per cent of asset cost, in addition to the normal 25 per cent rate of depreciation. To be eligible for that accelerated depreciation, assets must have been acquired before the beginning of commercial production, or for major expansions, or (since 1996) for the portion of investment expenditures in excess of 5 per cent of gross income from the mine. The amount of ACCA claimed in a year cannot exceed the income of the mine. In the calculation of taxable income, the ACCA deduction is taken after the normal CCA, but before Canadian exploration expenses (CEEs) and Canadian development expenses (CDEs).

CEEs are incurred by the taxpayer for the purpose of determining the existence, location, extent or quality of a mineral resource, or petroleum or natural gas in Canada, and pre-production development expenses incurred for the purpose of bringing a new mine into production, including clearing, removing overburden and stripping, and sinking a mineshaft. There is an optional 100 per cent deduction available in respect of CEEs in the year that the expenditure is incurred, and the unused balance in a particular year can be carried forward indefinitely.

CDEs consist of expenses incurred in drilling, converting and completing an oil well, or sinking or excavating a mineshaft, main haulage or similar underground work for a mine built or excavated after the mine came into production, and the cost of any mineral property. CDEs are accumulated in a pool where the taxpayer can deduct up to 30 per cent of the unclaimed balance in that pool at the end of each year. Unclaimed balances may be carried forward indefinitely.

Canadian Oil and Gas Property Expense (COGPE) is the cost of acquiring an oil or gas well; an interest or right to explore, drill or extract

---

3 For more information see <www.nrcan.gc.ca/minerals-metals/business-market/mining-taxation-regime/4212>.

petroleum or natural gas; or a qualifying interest or right in oil or gas production (excluding Crown royalties). An optional deduction is allowed for up to 10 per cent per year on a declining balance basis.

There is a 25 per cent withholding tax on dividends while provincial and territory goods and services tax can vary from 5 per cent to 13 per cent.

South African mining tax[4]

The corporate tax in South Africa is 28 per cent plus a value-added tax of 14 per cent on imported equipment except in the case of exports. There is no import duty on complete units of plant, but it may be applicable to spares and components. Dividend withholding tax is 10 per cent.

A mining company may derive income from mining for gold, mining operations other than mining for gold and from non-mining operations. Capital expenditure is deductible immediately from income derived by a taxpayer from mining operations, but may only be claimed once production has commenced. Capital expenditure includes expenditure (other than interest or finance charges) on mine development, general administration and management prior to the commencement of production or during any period of non-production. The deduction of capital expenditure in relation to any one mine is restricted to the taxable income from mining on that mine (ring fenced) However, Canada's minister of finance may rule that these costs may be set off against the income of another mine.

A capital allowance is calculated as a percentage per annum of capital expenditure for new mine developments and is a deduction against income. It is calculated at the rate of 10 per cent per annum for a 'post-1973 goldmine' or 'any other deep level goldmine', or 12 per cent per annum for any 'post-1990 goldmine' or any natural oil mine. The gold tax rate (percentage) is equal to $45 - (225 \div x)$ if a company has elected to be exempt from the secondary tax on companies; 'x' is the ratio of mining taxable income to the mining revenue. For example, if the ratio of taxable income to revenue is 50 per cent, then the gold tax rate $(y) = 45\% - 2.25\% \div 0.5 = 40.5\%$. The secondary tax on companies is calculated at the rate of 12.5 per cent of any dividend declared by any company on or after 14 March 1996. Companies mining for gold were entitled to exercise an irrevocable election to be exempt from payment of secondary tax on companies. The formula for a goldmining company that has not chosen to be exempt from the secondary tax on companies is $y = 35 - (175 \div x)$.

---

4 See <www.bullion.org.za/MediaReleases/Downloads/Taxation02.06.08.htm>.

Mining companies earning taxable income derived from mining for diamonds and other minerals and base metals are taxed on a flat rate of 29 per cent, but such companies are also liable to the secondary tax at the rate of 12.5 per cent.

Government and state/territory royalties

For many states and national governments, royalties are payable by mining companies on the resources they extract. The reason that royalties are often payable for minerals and not other commodities is that minerals are not renewable. For example, in Australia mineral resources are vested in the Crown, and so state governments charge royalties for the right to use them. The federal government has jurisdiction over most of offshore Australia and charges royalties on oil and gas production.

Royalties generally take the form of either unit royalties, which are a fixed cost-per-unit of production, or ad valorem royalties, which are charges based on the value of the commodity. Profit-based royalties are rarer, such as the Australian federal government's resource rent tax for newer offshore oil and gas discoveries, discussed before, where additional taxes are paid once the project has delivered a specific rate of return to the developer. Brief summaries of the royalty rates for the major mineral-producing countries/states are listed in appendix C.

Accounting standards for exploration

Accounting standards set the parameters by which companies report their annual accounts and financial results. This in itself is a complex area and varies from one jurisdiction to another. However, the introduction of the International Financial Reporting Standards (IFRS)[5] has resulted in most countries—including Australia, South Africa and the European Union (EU)—adopting this universal standard. The US, which operates under US GAAP (Generally Accepted Accounting Principles), is moving towards 'no significant differences' between the standards, although it is possible that the US will eventually adopt IFRS.

---

5 For more information see IFRS and US GAAP similarities and differences October 2011.

The area of interest and most concern is the unique nature of the resources industry and the need to provide methodologies for covering such areas as:

» treatment of costs arising from exploration, evaluation, development and construction

» restoration costs for an area of interest

» inventories

» sales revenue

» disclosures in the accounts and group accounts.

The crux of the problem is the treatment of exploration and other costs prior to the discovery or development, or both, of a project.

However, the two key IFRS standards (IAS 16—Property, Plant and Equipment, and IAS 38—Intangible Assets) currently exclude exploration activity. The earlier IFRS 6—Exploration for and Evaluation of Mineral Resources allows, as an interim measure, the capitalisation of exploration costs until commercial viability has been evaluated. Work is proceeding on a single IFRS for mining, oil and gas that will include a standard definition of reserves and resources. In early 2011 IFRS 13 *Fair Value Measurement* (effective January 2013) provided guidance on the more complex issue of 'fair value' of an asset (designed more for non-mineral resources that don't include all the uncertainties of future commodity prices and reserves).

Some of the important issues under the standard (excluding financial instruments and liabilities) include the following:

» Fair value is the price that would be received to sell an asset or paid to transfer a liability in an orderly transaction between market participants at the measurement date.

» Highest and best use is the use of an asset by market participants that maximises the value of the asset (often the current use).

» Maximum value is in combination with other assets and liabilities (but not funding liabilities) or standalone basis.

» The exit transaction takes place in the principal market or the most advantageous market if no principal market.

» Fair value does not include transaction costs but includes transportation costs from current location to principal market.

» Market participants are independent, knowledgeable, able and willing to enter into a transaction.

The hierarchy of determining fair value starts with the question: Is there a quoted price for an identical asset? If so it must be used without adjustment (Level 1). For a mineral resource it is unlikely that there is a quoted price for an identical asset, but in my experience a value may be determined if the asset belongs to a listed entity which has a market value. If a value can't be determined directly, then observable inputs other than quoted prices for an identical asset should be used (Level 2). If there is no observable identical asset, which is often the case, then unobservable inputs need to be used (Level 3).

The valuation techniques include market, income and cost approaches with market participant assumptions, which are discussed more fully in chapter 11. Level 3 fair value measurements require disclosure of the unobservable inputs and assumptions used, a description of the valuation process and a sensitivity analysis to changes in the unobservable inputs. If a multiple valuation approach is adopted the reasonableness of the range of values should be evaluated with a point in the range as the most representative of fair value.

The standard also makes specific mention of fair value measurement using present value techniques and the need to include a risk premium to reflect the amount of compensation the market would demand for taking on the uncertainty inherent in future cash flows. Three different approaches for risk adjustment are:

» adjusting the discount rate to observed rates of return for comparable assets traded in the market and applying to the most likely cash flows

» risk adjusting the expected cash flows (probability weighted average of all outcomes) and applying a risk-free discount rate

» risk adjusting the discount rate that market participants require and applying it to the expected cash flows.

There are further difficulties, as inventory and revenue recognition under IFRS specifically excludes minerals, and there are numerous specific guidance principles that are difficult to apply to mining, such as functional currency, mine commissioning costs, joint ventures, hedging programs, embedded derivatives and impairment rules.

An important part of the accounting standards is the treatment of exploration and other costs prior to the discovery and development of a project. One approach is to expense or write off all the costs as they are incurred, which would reduce the company's profit for that year.[6] The alternative approach, IFRS 6 *Exploration for and Evaluation of Mineral Resources*, allows companies to elect to partially or fully carry forward the costs (not treat them as costs for that year's profit calculation, although they may be for tax purposes) and recognise them as exploration and evaluation assets provided that rights to tenure of the area of interest (an individual, favourable geological area) are current and provided one of the following conditions is met:

1   such costs are expected to be recouped through successful development and exploitation of the area of interest or, alternatively, by its sale

2   exploration and evaluation activities in the area of interest have not at balance date reached a stage that permits a reasonable assessment of the existence or otherwise of economically recoverable reserves, and active and significant operations in, or in relation to, the area of interest are continuing.

Once the area of interest comes into production, the carry forward costs are amortised (depreciated) over the life of the project. The amortisation is often based on the unit of production, so that each unit of saleable product carries an equal amount of carry forward costs. Therefore, if the amount of saleable product varies from year to year, or if the total recoverable quantity of saleable product varies, then so will that year's level of amortisation.

These provisions give wide discretion to resource companies in treating their exploration expenditure. This can result in two very similar resource companies reporting quite different profits, depending on how they elect to treat their exploration expenditure. Analysts will often adjust reported earnings to bring resource companies on to a similar footing, and thus attempt to ensure that they all have the same quality of earnings.

The danger is in point 2, where companies choose to continue to carry forward exploration expenditure in the hope of an economic discovery. The

---

6 This is the approach that would be taken for tax whereby the exploration expenditure can be expensed as soon as income becomes available.

area of interest can be quite broad: for example, oil and gas companies may choose to consider a number of exploration permits within a sedimentary basin as one area. Even though the drilling of one exploration well may prove a particular structure in the basin as not containing any economic reserves, the costs are carried forward in the hope that nearby structures will prove successful. The argument given is that the annual profits derived from outside the current producing areas will be adversely affected by exploration expenditure and that future discoveries should pay for the current exploration expenditure.

In practical terms, previous unsuccessful exploration costs are sunk costs: that is, they may have little value. Some geological data may have been derived, but it is unlikely that the exploration data can be sold for any meaningful value, and the sale of the permit interest will generally realise a sum far less than the previous expenditure.

To include these relatively valueless sunk costs on the balance sheet as assets that at some future date may have to be written off in a more dramatic way is not appropriate. IFRS 6 requires that exploration and evaluation assets should be assessed for impairment, and if the carrying value exceeds the recoverable amount the asset should be written down. The market is sophisticated enough to appreciate the impact on company profits of writing off exploration expenditure as it occurs. However, company accounts do not always make clear to the market the likelihood of future exploration success and the likely impact of possible lumpy write-offs on future profits. It is the sudden and unexpected write-off of exploration expenditure that concerns the market. Another concern is that the previous profit results may have been artificially high due to low exploration write-offs. Companies should make their policies clear and show, if applicable, the regional levels of accumulated expenditure.

Tip

It is important to remember that IFRS 6 (as an accounting item) affects the reporting of company profits, but may not have an effect on tax paid or the annual cash flow of the company. Investors should ensure that the company has a conservative policy and that only relatively modest levels of accumulated exploration expenditure appear on the accounts when measured against shareholders' funds. This will mitigate the impact of any major write-downs in the future.

Costs that are expected to be incurred for the restoration of the permit area after the cessation of operations should be provided for as part of the cost of the exploration, evaluation, development, construction or production phases.

Inventories (stockpiles) should be brought to the accounts as soon as those materials that can be converted to saleable product can be adequately measured: for example, broken ore ready to be crushed, or stockpiles of concentrate or hydrocarbons. Due to the difficulty of accurately determining the ultimate saleable value of mineral inventories, it is common practice to value only those inventories that are in a saleable form.[7]

Sales revenue can only be brought to account when the product is in a saleable form and the product has passed to the purchaser or has left the physical control of the vendor. If the final realisable price is still subject to quality tests, the most reliable estimates should be used. It is therefore possible that the profit results for a given period can be distorted due to timing differences between the shipment of product and the cost of production for that period.

The following disclosures should be made in the accounts:

» any aggregate amounts of exploration, evaluation or development expenditure written off in the period other than by way of normal amortisation

» amounts for amortisation of exploration, evaluation and development for the period

» government royalties paid and payable on sales or production for the period

» if material, the costs carried forward for areas of interest still in the exploration, evaluation or development stage, where production has not commenced

» where production has commenced, costs carried forward in respect of an area of interest, which should be shown as a separate deduction.

It is not only carry forward exploration expenditure that sometimes needs to be written off when there is little chance of economic success. The capital costs of a project that are shown in the annual accounts may also have to

---

7 Investors should be wary when companies report significant profit increases, as these may be the result of additional sales from stockpiles, the exhaustion of which may result in a fall in profits, even though trading conditions may be strong.

be written off when the project is no longer deemed to be economically viable. For example, in November 1997 the US mining company Pegasus Gold Inc. wrote off US$353.5 million of shareholders' funds after it placed the Mt Todd goldmine on care and maintenance. This write-down—made up of US$122.6 million for acquisition costs, US$49.4 million for deferred pre-production and development costs, and US$181.3 million for property and equipment—was the result of calculating the project's NPV, which proved to be significantly less than its book value. (For more detail on Pegasus and Mt Todd, see chapter 3.)

Historically, the company had over a 5- and 10-year time frame achieved a premium of US$39 and US$31 per ounce over the spot gold price through the use of forward hedges (see chapter 9). The company therefore used a long-term realisable price of US$385 per ounce based on a forecast spot price of US$335 in 1998 and US$375 in 1999. Even this long-term forecast was somewhat optimistic, based on the then spot price of less than US$300.[8] The operating costs, at the time of closure, were over US$300 per ounce and potential cost-cutting measures were unable to reduce the cost of operations to a profitable level.

Once the liability for taxation has been determined, we are usually in a position to finally estimate the returns that a project might deliver to its investors. In the next chapter we will look at the different methodologies that are often applied to gain an insight into the actual or relative values of mining projects and the companies that own them.

---

8 Vista Gold is currently undertaking valuation work to determine if the mine can be restarted.

CHAPTER 11
Valuation methodologies

Valuation techniques can be divided into two broad categories:

» *Fundamental*—where the underlying 'fair' or 'intrinsic' value is derived by such methods as discounting future cash flows to the present time.

» *Technical/statistical/graphical*—where most commonly historical charts are used to predict a potential change in value or share price, or both.

A resource company's primary asset is the opportunity to extract its ore reserves and mineral resources. The most representative way to calculate this value is by using a discounted cash flow (DCF) methodology, which measures the net present value (NPV) of future cash flow streams under specific commodity-pricing and operating cost assumptions.[1] The net present value(s) (NPV) of the project(s) is added to the company's other net assets to derive its net asset value (NAV). In the current cycle, valuation methodology has evolved to place greater emphasis on near-term earnings and cash flows.

Until recently this has resulted in most resource companies trading at a premium to the fundamental value derived from discounted cash flow

---

1 Hoskold proposed in 1877 one of the first valuation methods employing discount rates to value mining properties that incorporated a risk-free rate and a speculative rate with the following formula:
$P = A \div (rf/((1 + rf)^n - 1) + rs)$
where:
P = sinking fund present value
A = annual annuity
rf = risk-free rate
rs = speculative rate
n = number of years.
The formula assumes that cash flow from the project would be employed in two ways: one as a sinking fund invested at a safe interest rate that would be used to replace the property once its resources were depleted and the other to provide investors a return in excess of the risk-free rate. The application of the formula is impractical in modern-day valuation.

(DCF), based on long-term commodity price assumptions. This can be attributed to investors' willingness to factor a takeover premium, reward companies for current strong cash flows and hold a view that commodity price assumptions may prove conservative. However, the GFC and the more recent European credit crisis have resulted in many stocks trading at a discount to their fundamental value as the market comes to grips with the potential medium-term impact on commodity prices.

Intuitively, the fundamental approach is the more appealing, in that an attempt is made to determine the true value of a project or company. For the decision process for a resource company or an investor, fundamental analysis fits in best with economic and market theory. By discounting future cash flows available to the investor by the appropriate discount rate, the current value of the asset can be determined and an investment decision can be made based on the intrinsic return generated by the asset or share. The difficulty arises in predicting the future cash flows and the appropriate discount rate to apply. A valuation methodology based on a blend of NAV and traditional multiples also reduces the inherent NPV sensitivity to commodity price and discount rate assumptions.

For listed mining companies, there is a clear link between the value of their resource assets and their market share price. Relative pricing techniques, such as the share price to earnings (net profit after tax) ratio (PE), are generally applied to companies as a whole, while specific business or enterprise values (market capitalisation less net cash) are more often estimated on a pre-tax basis, such as price to earnings before interest and tax (EBIT). Comparisons of multiples are made taking the view that a multiple significantly different from the pack suggests an anomaly and therefore a potential price change. Alternatively, by applying an appropriate market or sector multiple, it is possible to estimate what is a fair price. These techniques assume that the average or sector multiples are the appropriate multiples to apply; however, there are often factors that warrant a divergence from the norm. The art of valuation is the ability to identify and quantify what differences, if any, are present.

Charting techniques rely on some identifiable pattern in the past movements of a share or commodity price. The technique does not lend itself to valuing projects as such. Empirical studies (and some would say common sense) suggest that the future movement in a share or commodity price is not governed by its past movements. However, herd mentality is a powerful force and, if enough investors or traders believe that the charts have indicated that some support or resistance level has been breached, they may act in unison and the prediction may become self-fulfilling.

Share price performance for resource companies is affected primarily, among other things, by commodity prices, exchange rates and production. In the past I have constructed nomograms, which are charts that show, for relative movements in the above parameters, whether a listed share is a buy or a sell at that time. I achieved only limited success (as with charting) due to the non-stationarity variation in the underlying relationship of the environment. Things change over time and therefore any one sure-fire scheme is often valid only for a very short period of time, if at all.

These approaches are more fully discussed in the following pages.

Fundamental value

IFRS 13 *Fair Value Measurement* refers to three methods that can be applied to determining the fundamental value of an asset:

» *Income approach* — converts future amounts into a single current value such as the NPV of future cash flows or option pricing

» *Market approach* — prices and other relevant information are generated by market transactions involving comparable assets

» *Cost base approach* — often referred to as the current replacement cost, which is the amount that would be required to replace the service capacity of the asset adjusted for obsolescence: that is, depreciated, optimised, replacement cost (DORC).

Value is often in the eye of the beholder, so, perhaps more important than any other approach, determining the fundamental value of a resource company and its share price is the best way to determine if that company is a buy or a sell. Clearly, if the fundamental value of a share in a given company is determined to be greater than its share price (market value), then it should be a buy and, conversely, if the fundamental value is below its share price then it is a sell. Alternatively, the exercise can come down to determining the fair market value (FMV) of an asset, which is often defined as the price that a willing seller sells an asset at arm's length to a willing buyer.

It is not uncommon for the share price to be different from the fundamental value. This would initially suggest that equity markets are inefficient, which goes against most academic theory. In my experience markets are quite efficient once they become aware of, and factor in, all available information. However, there can be a lag before the market is fully informed. This lag has decreased over time as technology has improved the flow of information. Any further difficulty or problem arises not so much with the lag in obtaining the information, but rather in analysing the information correctly and determining what it means to the company going into the future.

Thus the release of a significant exploration result will be reflected in the share price quite quickly, and indeed the market may even pre-empt the forthcoming results (see chapter 16). The greater inefficiencies relate to forecasting into the future. If a company has a positive growth profile for its fundamental value over the next few years, then, all other things being equal, the share price will grow as those results are achieved. If, through careful analysis, it can be shown that the growth impact may be greater than the market expects, then the stock can be re-rated in a positive way, as the more thorough evaluation is widely dispersed over a longer period of time. The trick is to determine the true current fundamental value or NAV and how it might change over time. The basic components of the valuation are shown in table 11.1.

Table 11.1: valuation components

Asset	Description	Valuation methodology
Resource project(s)	Currently producing profits and cash flow	Discounted cash flow, market comparisons, market multiples
Resource prospects	Deposits under current evaluation	Geologically defined, but require economic evaluation and justification for development
Exploration acreage	Areas that may provide prospects	Expenditure commitments, recent sale transactions, expected monetary value, other companies in same area
Other assets	Investments	Market or inferred valuation
Cash		Annual and quarterly accounts
Less debt		Annual and quarterly accounts
Net asset value (NAV)	Sum of the above values	

The NAV can then be divided by the equivalent number of shares on issue to determine the value backing per share, which can then be compared with the share price. The NAV can also be forecast for future years to determine if there is fundamental growth, and hence whether the shares represent a good medium- to long-term investment.

A crucial part is determining the fundamental value of existing or likely future projects. These projects will require some capital expenditure and hopefully will return cash flow to the company over the life of the project. All of these cash flows need to be brought to one point in time (now, next year, or whatever time period the investor is interested in) to provide an estimate of the fundamental value at that time.

Income approach

Under this general heading are the methodologies that consider the earning capacity of the project or company. Although these are generally the preferred methodologies, they do require sufficient information to derive future cash flows.

Discounted cash flow and net present value

The most valuable tool that analysts, companies and investors have in determining the fundamental value of a project or a company is to discount future cash flows and determine the NPV. This is the time value of money. Consider the example of a special interest-bearing account where, if you deposit $1000 in that account, you will be paid $315.47 at the end of each of the next four years. At the end of that period there will be no further payments owed to you. The cash-flow stream to you is shown in table 11.2.

Table 11.2: cash-flow stream example

Now	Year 1	Year 2	Year 3	Year 4
−$1000	$315.47	$315.47	$315.47	$315.47

For your $1000 investment (negative flow) you will receive a total of $1261.88 (positive flow), which is the sum of the four $315.47 payments. Clearly, interest has been paid on your deposit (investment). From trial and error, and a pocket calculator, you could determine that the interest paid to you is 10 per cent. In more detail the ledger for the account could be as shown in table 11.3 (overleaf).

Table 11.3: cash flow stream example

	Now	Year 1	Year 2	Year 3	Year 4
Deposit	$1000				
Interest		$100.00	$78.45	$54.75	$28.68
Payment		$315.47	$315.47	$315.47	$315.47
Balance	$1000	$784.53	$547.51	$286.79	$0.00

Table 11.3 shows that $1000 is deposited; a payment of $315.47 is paid each year; and at the end of the period there are no funds left. The amount paid in excess of the $1000 is the interest that accumulates each year on the remaining balance. The account has provided a 10 per cent internal rate of return (IRR) on your investment. This is quite different from providing a compounding 10 per cent rate of return, where the $1000 and accumulated interest is left in the account for the four years, and the whole amount is withdrawn at the end. The withdrawal at the end in this case would be $1464.10.

The higher figure is due to the accumulation of interest on the interest, which does not occur in the example in tables 11.2 (on p. 269) and 11.3. The example shown in tables 11.2 and 11.3 is not all that different from the case of a mining project. For a mining project there is an initial capital expenditure to develop the project and net cash flows each year from the sale of a commodity. It is therefore possible to determine the IRR provided by the project by solving the following equation:

$$\text{IRR} = i \text{ when } \sum^{0 \text{ to } n} CF_n \div (1 + i)^n = 0$$

In our example, using the above equation and 10 per cent (or 0.1) for i we get the following:

$$-\$1000 \div (1 + 1.1)^0 + \$315.47 \div (1.1)^1 + \$315.47 \div (1.1)^2$$

$$+ \$315.47 \div (1.1)^3 + \$315.47 \div (1.1)^4$$

which equals:

$$-\$1000 + \$286.79 + \$260.72 + \$237.02 + \$215.47$$

which equals zero.

Therefore, as we already know, the IRR is 10 per cent. There is no direct method of solving for i, only trial and error in selecting different interest rates for it, and calculating the resulting value (which is the NPV we discuss in the following section), until the NPV equals zero.

What if a company or an investor considered an 8 per cent return to be adequate? We know the previous example generates a return of 10 per cent, therefore it would meet the required hurdle. But if we don't know what return the example generated, then the previous equation could be used to calculate the NPV at an 8 per cent discount rate.

$$-\$1000 \div (1 + 0.08)^0 + \$315.47 \div (1.08)^1 + \$315.47 \div (1.08)^2$$

$$+ \$315.47 \div (1.08)^3 + \$315.47 \div (1.08)^4$$

which equals:

$$-\$1000 + \$292.10 + \$270.46 + \$250.43 + \$231.88$$

which in turn equals an NPV of $44.87.

The above procedure for determining the NPV at 8 per cent of $44.87 can be expressed mathematically as:

$$NPV = \Sigma^{0 \text{ to } n} \, CF_n \div (1 + i)^n$$

Trial and error is obviously not required, as long as we know the appropriate discount rate to apply (see chapter 17). The NPV is a positive dollar value, as we know the cash flow is capable of providing 10 per cent and therefore the positive value is indicating that the internal rate of return is greater than 8 per cent. If the same exercise is carried out at 12 per cent, the NPV is:

$$-\$1000 \div (1 + 0.12)^0 + \$315.47 \div (1.12)^1 + \$315.47 \div (1.12)^2$$

$$+ \$315.47 \div (1.12)^3 + \$315.47 \div (1.12)^4$$

which equals:

$$-\$1000 + \$281.67 + \$251.49 + \$224.55 + \$200.49$$

which in turn equals $41.80.

The negative NPV of $41.80 tells us that the cash-flow stream is providing a return of less than 12 per cent. In figure 11.1 (overleaf) the NPV is plotted at different discount rates. Note how the curve cuts the x axis at 10 per cent where the NPV is zero, and hence 10 per cent is by definition the IRR.

Figure 11.1: NPV at different discount rates

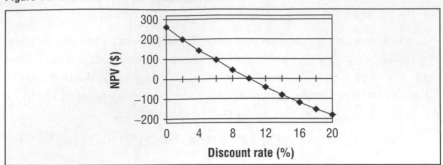

If, for a project, the future cash flow can be estimated and an appropriate discount rate is applied, then the NPV of the project can be determined. It is important that the future cash flow is discretionary, whereby all the cash flow can be distributed to the owner or shareholders. An investor or company should be willing to pay up to the NPV to gain access to that cash flow over time. For example, if a project's NPV is zero dollars then investors should be indifferent to another similar class (risk) investment as they both provide the same return; however, if our investment has a positive NPV and is therefore providing a higher return, then investors should be willing to pay a premium to participate in that opportunity. *Therefore the NPV, shown in figure 11.1, is the value we can use for resource projects and prospects.* (For further information on continuous discounting and annuities, see appendix G.)

Real option analysis might also be applied that incorporates NPV analysis. The topic is more fully explained in chapter 15.

Salvage and terminal value

The cash flows for a majority of resource projects can be modelled over the life of the project. At the end of the project life, the economic ore reserves will have been exploited; however, working plant and equipment will probably still belong to the project. The salvage value of the remaining equipment at the end of the mine life may be significant, but generally, given the secondhand value of mining and processing equipment and the large future cash flow discount factor, more often than not it is likely to be insignificant. It should also be remembered that there may be an additional cost of environmental remedial work at the end of the project's life that may mitigate the salvage value.

In some cases, such as coalmines, the mine life may be much longer than the financial model, which at most might go out 20 to 25 years. Clearly, there is some terminal value applicable to the operation beyond the financial model period (this is particularly relevant to industrial operations, which can have very long operating lives).

The terminal value of the remaining life of the project can be estimated as a multiple of the average remaining cash flows. The multiple can be the inverse of the discount rate, as will be discussed. The terminal value will then be discounted back from the last year of the financial model. More conservative multiples are often applied to the average cash flow, given the difficulty in forecasting so far into the future and the approximations that are often applied in calculating the average cash flow. However, the terminal value can still be significant. In figure 11.2 the terminal value is shown as a percentage of the total NPV, where the number of years for the terminal value period equals the number of years included in the cash-flow model. For discount rates around 10 per cent the terminal value could represent 15 per cent of the total value.

Figure 11.2: Terminal value as percentage of project NPV

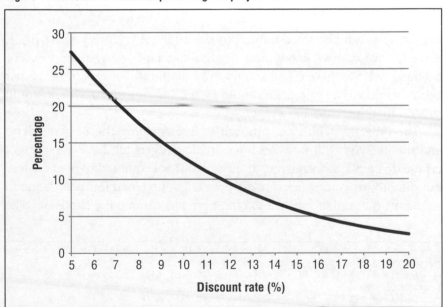

Dividend valuation model

As discussed later in this chapter, the dividend yield (Yd) is equal to the dividend (D) a company may pay to its shareholders divided by the share price (P), expressed as a percentage. It can also be shown that the present value of an infinitely long stream of equal cash flows or dividends is equal to the cash flow or dividend divided by the discount rate.[2]

If we assume for the moment that the current share price of a company is equal to the present value of all future dividends and that those dividends are expected to remain constant over a long period, then:

$$P = D \div i$$

where i is the appropriate discount rate for the company. Further, if the dividends are expected to grow annually by a percentage rate of g, then:

$$P = D \div (i - g)$$

Obviously, we know the current share price of a resource stock, and if we can accurately estimate next year's dividend and the likely growth rate in the dividend, we can estimate the discount rate applied by the market. For example, if the share price is $1.50 and the dividend is expected to be 10 cents and the growth rate 5 per cent per year, then:

$$i = 10 \div 150 + 5\% = 11.7\%$$

The analysis can be turned around to determine the 'correct' share price, if we believe that we know the true discount rate (see chapter 17). For example, we may have calculated that the discount rate should be 10 per cent, therefore the share price should be $2 and not $1.50, which would suggest that the shares are a buy.

The difficulty with this approach is in estimating the next dividend and the likely growth rate. Resource stocks, in general, have a history of erratic dividend payments due to the volatility of commodity prices. More importantly, resource stocks are not generally purchased for their dividend payments but, rather for their exploration and commodity exposure. The

---

2 If we assume the price (P) is equal to the present value (PV) of the infinite (n) stream of dividends (D) where the discount rate is i, then:

$PV = D \div (1 + i)^1 + D \div (1 + i)^2 + D \div (1 + i)^3 + \ldots + D \div (1 + i)^n$ **(1)**

Rearranging:

$PV = D \div (1 + i)^1 \times (1 + 1 \div (1 + i)^1 + 1 \div (1 + i)^2 + \ldots + 1 \div (1 + i)^{n-1})$

Multiplying both sides by $1 \div (1 + i)^1$:

$PV \times (1 \div (1 + i)^1) = D \div (1 + i)^1 \times (1 \div (1 + i)^1 + 1 \div (1 + i)^2 + 1 \div (1 + i)^3 + \ldots + 1 \div (1 + i)^n)$ **(2)**

Subtracting (2) from (1):

$PV \times (1 - 1 \div (1 + i)^1) = D \div (1 + i)^1$

Simplifying: $PV = D/i$.

For the case where D is expected to grow by g per cent per annum, the equation becomes:

$PV = D \div (i - g)$

dividend valuation model therefore has little application in the valuation of resource stocks.

From this analysis, if we have an infinite series of income or dividends (D) and our discount rate is i, then the present value PV = D ÷ i.

For companies whose stay-in-business expenditure is similar to annual depreciation, the discretionary cash flow will be similar to the company's profit or earnings. If we assume that the earnings (E) of a company are for all intents and purposes indefinite and are expected to grow at g, then the share price P = E ÷ (i − g) or the earnings multiple PE = 1 ÷ (r − g). Unfortunately for resource companies, finite reserves and volatile commodity prices and exchange rates make this simple approach difficult to apply.

It is possible to derive a number of financial ratios based on a company's share price, cash flows and profits. If these ratios are computed for different companies they can be ranked accordingly and in theory determine the relative values. Comparisons can be further expanded to look at other criteria such as reserves, but things are never so simple and often there are good reasons why differences may exist between companies within and between sectors.

Earnings per share and price to earnings ratio

Earnings per share (EPS) is most simply defined as the net reported profit after tax divided by the number of shares on issue. The resulting value is usually stated as cents per share. For example, if the expected earnings for the first year of operation are $10 million and the number of shares on issue is 100 million, then the forecast EPS is estimated at 10¢ per share. This is a forecast EPS; however, historical and current year values can also be determined if meaningful data are available.

For valuation purposes it is the current and future years that are important. The EPS on its own is somewhat meaningless unless it is compared with the current share price. Clearly, if two companies are each forecast to generate an EPS of 10¢ for the current year, then they would be viewed differently if one had a share price of $1 and the other $5. The next step is to divide the share price by the EPS to obtain a ratio or multiple for more easy comparison. This is the price to earnings ratio or PE (sometimes also referred to as the PER ratio) that indicates the number of years to recover the current share price. In the case of the two companies discussed, one would have a PE of 10 times (100¢/10¢) and the other of 50 times

(500¢/10¢). All other factors being equal, the lower the PE the better, as you are paying a lower price for the earnings generated.

The PE can be, and often is, used as a relative gauge of a company's share price against other similar companies. The same approach can be adopted for whole sectors, where the average, or more correctly, the weighted average PE for all the stocks that make up the sector, is calculated.[3] The weighted average is calculated by summing the product of each company's PE by its market capitalisation and then dividing by the total market capitalisation of the stocks included in the sector. Table 11.4 lists indicative sector PEs on the ASX for the current financial year, next year and the year after.

Table 11.4: indicative ASX sector PEs, 2011–14

Sector	2011–12	2012–13	2013–14
All Ordinaries	11.3	10.3	10.1
Resources	10.8	9.6	10.2
Metals and mining	9.5	8.9	9.7
Energy	16.0	13.8	14.2
Gold	15.2	9.9	10.4

PEs must be compared for the same time period. If a company has a lower PE than the sector average, this would initially suggest that the stock is underpriced. However, equity markets are never that simple, except perhaps for short-term aberrations, when the stock price could well be too low when compared with the sector average. There are often mitigating circumstances that justify variation from the weighted mean.

The PE is only one snapshot in time, albeit with a current share price and a future EPS. Other factors may well influence a company's PE. For example, the market may be concerned about the quality of management and their ability to achieve the forecast earnings. Perhaps the company has a poor balance sheet or the projects generating the earnings are low quality and, therefore, the risk of generating the earnings is higher than average. A common factor influencing the PE is the project's life. As mentioned, mining projects have finite lives and if the project is towards the end of its

---

3 The S&P/ASX provides indices for different sectors that are made up of similar types of listed securities; for example, oil and gas stocks. The index is then adjusted for changes in the market capitalisation of the companies that make up the index.

operating life or is a short-term project, then the ability to maintain the earnings would be in question. This issue will be further expanded upon in the following section.

The reverse situation can exist, where a stock's PE may be higher than the sector average. Again, there are often specific issues that warrant or justify the market's willingness to pay a premium. Management may be held in high regard; existing projects may have above-average lives; or the company's balance sheet may be very sound.

A stock can have high or infinitely high current-year PEs if it is expected to generate little or no profits for the current year. Therefore, market analysts tend to forecast earnings over several years to show the trend in earnings and PE. If the earnings trend is declining over time, then the current PE may be below average to reflect the negative trend, while if the earnings are expected to increase, then a higher price (premium) could be justified and hence a higher-than-average short-term PE.

In table 11.5 the prospects for Company A look good, with the PE expected to fall as earnings increase over the next few years. It should be stressed that the PEs are calculated on the basis of the current share price and that share price might and should increase over time as those higher earnings are achieved and maintained into the future. For Company B the outlook is not so good, with earnings expected to disappear the year after next, and so the current share price has been discounted and the current PE looks attractive for the wrong reason: that is, declining earnings. The trick is to find those stocks that are trading at a lower PE for the right reasons. In other words, although the current PE of Company A, at first sight, looks far too high there may still be worthwhile reasons for investing in that company.

Table 11.5: hypothetical example of PE comparisons

	PEs		
	Current year	Next year	Year after next
Sector average	15	13	11
Company A (growth)	30	14	10
Company B (decline)	8	20	—

The market, or sector, PEs, as with company PEs, are set by the equities market in terms of the prices quoted for shares on a stock exchange.

However, the actual PEs can only be determined by looking at consensus earnings forecasts, as published by, say, broker analysts or, on rare occasions, by a company itself.[4] These forecasts may or may not be correct and so PEs are only an estimate of the underlying value implied by the market.

If you look at the forecast multiples for the sectors that make up the resources index, you can see the variations between sectors over time. These variations are often the result of the market's view on such issues as the outlook for movements in commodity prices, to which the equities provide exposure, and the potential for exploration success. For the gold sector the outlook is for the gold price to perhaps increase in the medium term due to the current credit crisis, so investors are willing to pay a premium for the sector. On the other hand, the outlook for base metals is less certain so the sector is trading at a relative discount (lower PE) to the other sectors.

Cash flow and price to cash flow ratios

Many commentators argue that cash flow multiples are more meaningful than earnings multiples, as earnings can vary due to the vagaries of accounting approaches undertaken from company to company. Profit is an opinion, while cash flow is a fact. The simple approach that is often used to estimate the cash flow is to add back all non-cash items, such as depreciation and amortisation, to the after-tax earnings. The theory is that the cash flow is more representative of the return generated to shareholders. This is an important issue, but the approach of adding back non-cash items is only an approximate method.

As table 11.6 shows, the price to cash flow ratio (PCFR) is lower than the PE due to the higher value obtained when calculating the cash flow. All of the previous discussion on comparing an individual company's PCFR with its peers and the market applies with the previous caveat that individual stocks can be priced quite differently on the back of other information that may not be directly impacting on the current multiple. A low PCFR may therefore be indicative of a company that is cheap, and hence a buy, while a high PCFR may suggest a sell.

---

4 It should be remembered that the forecast PEs are also a function of earnings that are dependent on the commodity price assumptions made by analysts and the market. Therefore different market participants may have different PE forecasts for individual companies.

Table 11.6: price to cash flow ratio for ASX sectors, 2011–14

ASX sector	2011–12	2012–13	2013–14
All Ordinaries	10.7	9.7	9.6
Resources	10.4	9.2	9.9
Metals and mining	8.7	8.1	9.0
Energy	13.0	10.8	11.2
Gold	12.1	7.1	7.3

More often than not, a company PE is the preferred method of relative comparison even though initially the PCFR may seem more robust. One explanation for this relates to discretionary cash flow; that is, the amount of cash that is available to shareholders that the board of the company will either pay in dividends or reinvest in the capital growth of the company. This is often better defined by the PE than by the PCFR.

We mentioned the importance of discretionary cash flow, but as an initial estimate, after-tax earnings are a reasonable proxy. For established companies (more commonly industrials and major resource companies) the level of depreciation is not very different from stay-in-business capital expenditure, which is the expenditure necessary each year to keep the business going and which is not discretionary. If depreciation is subtracted from the cash flow estimate you are back to the company earnings, so the PE is a quick estimate of the discretionary cash-flow ratio.

EV and EBITDA

The enterprise value (EV) of a company can be defined as its market capitalisation (share price multiplied by number of issued shares) less any net cash or, more often, plus any net debt.[5] For example, if the company has 100 million shares on issue with a share price of $1 per share, then the market capitalisation is $100 million. If the company's net debt (debt less cash) is $50 million, the project's market-inferred EV is $100 million plus $50 million, or $150 million. The resulting figure therefore reflects more accurately the market view of the business's value.

---

5 Some practitioners will not include cash in the calculation of EV unless it is surplus to working capital requirements.

EBITDA is the company's earnings before interest, tax, depreciation and amortisation. This figure is an estimate of the ungeared cash flow. The EV/EBITDA ratio (see table 11.7) is therefore effectively an ungeared price to cash flow ratio. When comparing companies from a similar sector, the variability of this ratio between companies is often a lot less than for other ratios and so it can be more meaningful when trying to identify expensive or cheap stocks. As with other ratios, the EV/EBITDA ratio should not be used on its own in deciding on the relative value of a resources stock.

Table 11.7: EV/EBITDA ratios for ASX sectors, 2011–14

ASX sector	2011–12	2012–13	2013–14
All Ordinaries	6.9	6.1	5.8
Resources	6.3	5.2	5.2
Metals and mining	5.8	4.9	4.9
Energy	9.1	7.7	7.6
Gold	8.4	5.6	5.7

Dividend yield

Many investors are interested in receiving a dividend from stocks they hold. The yield is simply the dividend divided by the price, quoted as a percentage. Obviously, the higher the yield the more attractive the stock. There is a trade-off for a company between providing the dividend or reinvesting that cash flow into exploration or new projects with the aim of increasing the capital growth. Some resource companies make it clear that they are in business not to provide dividends, but to invest surplus cash flow in growth.

Due to the high requirements of cash by resource companies for exploration and development, the yields tend to be lower than for industrial companies. Under current tax laws in Australia, shareholders can receive a tax credit on their dividends. The proportion of franking (imputation) is a function of the tax paid by the company and the amount of dividends paid. Table 11.8 compares 2012 estimates of the dividend yield.

Table 11.8: estimated dividend yield for ASX sectors, 2011–14

	2011–12 (%)	2012–13 (%)	2013–14 (%)
All Ordinaries	4.7	5.0	5.3
Resources	2.6	2.9	2.9
Metals and mining	2.7	3.0	3.0
Energy	2.8	3.0	3.0
Gold	1.2	1.5	1.5

Comparisons

Table 11.9 shows a comparison of the ratios for two of the largest mining companies in the world: BHP Billiton and Rio Tinto. Towards the end of 2011 BHP had the higher PE, PCFR, EV/EBITDA and dividend yield, which would suggest that it was the more expensive of the two companies. However, at the time iron ore prices were in decline, and Rio Tinto was seen as the more exposed to the commodity, and so it might be more appropriate to say that the premium for BHP was justified on its more defensive earnings stream.

Table 11.9: comparison of company ratios for BHP Billiton and Rio Tinto, 2011–14

Ratio	Company	2011–12	2012–13	2013–14
PE	BHP Billiton	10.2	10.4	11.2
	Rio Tinto	8.4	7.7	8.7
PCFR	BHP Billiton	9.4	9.5	10.3
	Rio Tinto	7.7	7.2	8.3
Dividend yield (%)	BHP Billiton	3.0	3.2	3.4
EV/EBITDA	Rio Tinto	2.0	2.3	2.6
	BHP Billiton	5.8	5.1	5.2
	Rio Tinto	5.2	4.5	4.4

Multiples are not stationary and will change over time as a function of share price and earnings. At any point in time, dependent on the circumstances, the relativities between BHP and Rio Tinto can be quite different, as shown in figures 11.3 and 11.4 (overleaf).

Figure 11.3: historical EV/EBITDA ratios for Rio Tinto

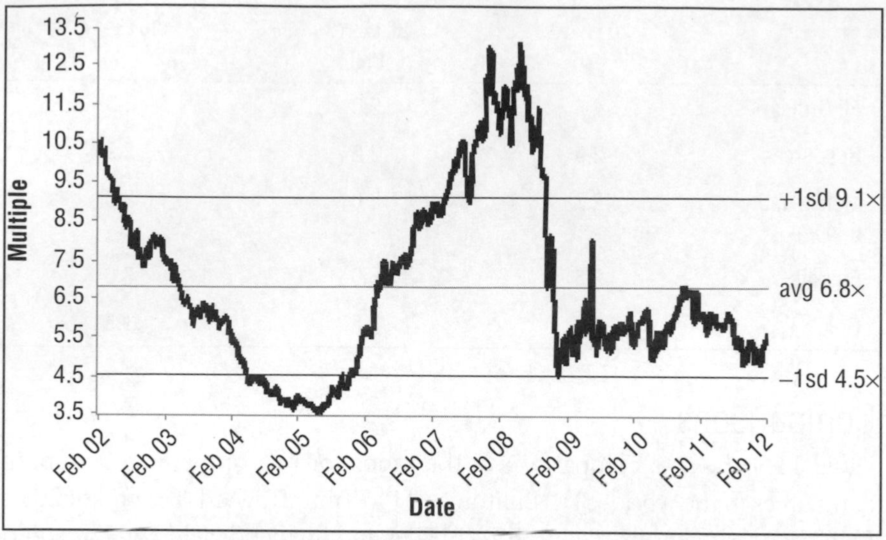

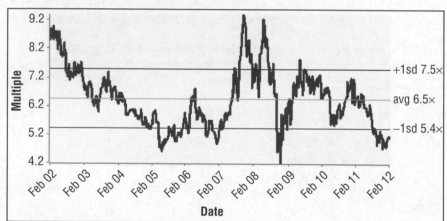

Source: CLSA Eval@tor.

Figure 11.4: historical EV/EBITDA ratios for BHP Billiton

Source: CSA Eval@tor.

Economic value added

Economic value added (EVA) can be defined as the adjusted net operating profit after tax less the return on capital expected by investors. If the figure is positive then the company is adding value. The difficulty is in the definition of the values used in determining the EVA. For example, in its simplest form the net profit after tax is equal to the earnings before interest and tax (EBIT) plus goodwill and amortisation less tax. However, hundreds of adjustments can be made to the income statement to derive the 'true' adjusted net operating profit after tax, which represents operational profit and should only include cash flows from the ongoing operations and ignores abnormals, extraordinary items and goodwill. Balance sheet adjustments are also undertaken to define the invested capital, which in its simplest form is working capital plus non-current assets, or alternatively equity plus debt (enterprise value).

For example, assume that the invested capital is $100 million and that the weighted average cost of capital (WACC) is 12 per cent (a detailed explanation of WACC is provided in chapter 17). The expected return on capital is $100 million × 12% = $12 million. If the adjusted net profit is estimated to be greater than $12 million, the company is adding value to that required by shareholders. EVA therefore measures surplus value created, and in some ways is not too dissimilar to the NPV approach described earlier. The present value of all future year EVAs should approach the NPV of the cash flows. EVA is an annual figure and therefore the year on-year change is the incremental EVA. The EVA efficiency can also be measured as the ratio of the EVA to a constant level of investment. Given the nature of resource companies with finite projects, EVA has not been embraced to the same extent it has for long life industrial companies, and so NPV is still the preferred valuation technique for resource companies and their projects.

Residual income valuation method

This method is increasing in popularity and is similar to EVA, except that it looks at the present value of the surplus return on the book value of the company's net operating assets. For example, if the book value at the beginning of year 1 is BV_0 and the net income for the year is NI_1 then the surplus return value for year 1 is:

$$(NI_1 - WACC \times BV_0) \div (1 + WACC)^1$$

This calculation can then be done for each subsequent year n, $(NI_n - WACC \times BV_{n-1}) \div (1 + WACC)^n$, summed and added to BV_0 to derive the discounted residual income valuation. The formula implies that investors should only be willing to pay more than the book value if the firm or project can generate earnings above its WACC. An advantage of the model is that it should not be affected by the accounting methodology chosen and there is no need to determine discretionary cash flows. If the depreciation used for both NPV and the residual income is the same and working capital is ignored, then equivalent valuations would be obtained.

Market approach

These approaches can be used with projects at all stages of development, albeit with different levels of confidence. They generally rely on some form of comparison to market known measures when future cash flows are considered too unreliable to predict or perhaps as a cross-check when the NPV can be calculated.

Previous transactions

Previous market transactions for planned projects[6] can provide a guide to value, but the variability in project metrics may result in considerable variation, as shown in table 11.10. This is due to the uncertainty surrounding such issues as the likely development of a project, future capital and operating costs, and in the case of coal the availability of markets and perhaps the quality and amount of coal ultimately recoverable. However, prices paid generally reflect the underlying asset value and are a good indicator of FMV. The average price paid was $1.57/t, but this was over a considerable length of time, during which the price of coal changed dramatically. This is one of the major disadvantages of the method: it is not always possible to find a number of like transactions to the asset being valued and at the date of the valuation.

Table 11.10: Market purchase price for coal projects

Date	Tenement	Coal type	Mine type*	Production (mtpa)	Resources (mt)	Price ($/t)
Jul 11	Woori	Thermal	o/c	6.0	84	0.90
May 11	Cordrilla	PCI	o/c	4.0	79	6.85
Jul 10	Sutton Forest	Coking	u/g	n.a.	115	0.62
Feb 10	Broughton	Coking	o/c	n.a.	30	0.31
Nov 09	Maules Creek	Thermal coking	u/g, o/c	12	407	1.18

6 The methodology can also be used for operating mines, but the NPV should be used in preference whenever possible.

Date	Tenement	Coal type	Mine type	Production (mtpa)	Resources (mt)	Price ($/t)
Oct 09	Vickery	Thermal	o/c	n.a.	300	0.12
Aug 09	Narrabri	Thermal	u/g	0.7 to 6.0	474	3.38
Aug 08	Narrabri	Thermal	u/g	0.7 to 6.0	474	3.52
Jul 08	New Saraji	Coking	u/g	10.0	690	3.55
Feb 08	Narrabri	Thermal	u/g	0.7 to 6.0	474	1.90
Jan 08	Moolarben	Thermal	u/g, o/c	13.0	705	1.28
Dec 07	Middlemont	Coking/ PCI	o/c	n.a.	100	3.92
Sep 07	Anvil Hill	Thermal	o/c	10.5	500	0.85
Nov 06	Avondale	Coking	u/g	0.2	137	0.19
Jul 05	Belvedere	Coking	u/g	13 to 14	2745	0.005
Jul 05	Monto	Thermal	o/c	10	2745	0.005
Jun 05	Kingaroy	Thermal	o/c	n.a.	315	0.02
Jun 05	Broughton	Coking	o/c	n.a.	25	1.60
Apr 05	Millennium	Coking	o/c	1.5 to 3	374	0.61
Mar 05	Millennium	Coking	o/c	1.5 to 3	361	0.66
Average						1.57

Notes: o/c = open cut mine; u/g = underground mine; PCI = pulverised coal injection.

In some cases there are financial transactions for similar tenements that hold no compliant resources. In this case it is possible to define a value per area such as square kilometre or square mile and, in some cases, if strike lengths of potential mineralisation are known, a $ value per kilometre or mile.

In the May 2011 Independent Expert Report for the takeover of Abra Mining, Xstract Mining provided a list of 22 base metal exploration transactions (discounted for the time of the transaction and a Kilburn rating), ranging from $400 per square kilometre to $401 600 per square kilometre. The wide range is a reflection of the perceived exploration potential of the individual tenements and highlights that the methodology needs to be used with care and is best as a cross-check for other more robust methods.

Production, reserve and resource exposure

Analysts will often use a rule of thumb or yardstick to compare stocks in terms of the exposure to a particular commodity based on the level of production and the share price. For example, consider two profitable gold stocks as detailed in table 11.11.

Table 11.11: example of a comparison of commodity and reserve exposure for two profitable gold stocks

Company	Share price	Market capitalisation ($ million)	Annual production (000 oz)	Cash cost (US$/oz)	Reserves (million oz)
Company A	1.5	150	100	240	0.6
Company B	1.0	600	340	220	3.0

Company A is the smaller company by market capitalisation, which is a reflection of lower production and reserves (operating life), and a slightly higher cost of production than Company B. An investor's exposure to the gold price can be determined by dividing the annual production by the market capitalisation or, better still, EV. For Company A the exposure is 0.67 ounces per $1000 investment while for Company B the exposure is 0.57 ounces.

One might be tempted to argue that the exposure should be calculated with regard to the amount of profitable gold produced. However, both companies are making profits and therefore any increase in the gold price will impact on all of the gold produced. Company A therefore represents the better investment for exposure to the gold price. Comparative tables or rankings can be produced for all the stocks within a sector to show the more sensitive stock for any given commodity.[7] It is not uncommon for stocks with a smaller market capitalisation to exhibit higher sensitivity to commodity prices as, generally, higher premiums are paid by the market for the larger companies, which consequently results in lower sensitivity.

Another approach is to compare the reserves of the companies. Clearly, larger reserves are an advantage as they represent the inventory of the company. Company B has the larger reserves and longer potential mine life. The reserves per market capitalisation are also higher at 5 ounces per $1000, while for Company A the value is 4 ounces. Again it is not uncommon for larger market-capitalised gold companies to have larger reserves and larger reserves per market capitalisation.

---

7 Obviously, the level of price hedging undertaken by companies needs to be included in the analysis.

This is somewhat at odds with the previous case of annual production, but it should be remembered that it will take many years to extract the reserves. Therefore, it might be more meaningful to discount the future reserves to get a present value for comparison purposes.

Many other factors will upset the rankings, such as hedging, the cash cost of production, earnings, quality of management and the exploration potential of the company. Although rankings can be a useful guide, they are not a straightforward solution to determining which stocks are fundamentally the best buy or sell. Obviously since the companies are in production it should be possible and preferable to determine estimates of future cash flows and hence each company's NPV to get a more robust comparison of valuations.

When projects are not in production and NPV is not deemed suitable, but compliant resources have been defined, then a comparative approach can be applied. A value per unit of resource, usually enterprise value (EV), for similar listed companies and projects is calculated, as shown in table 11.12 for a number of gold companies.

Table 11.12: commodity resource exposure for a number of gold companies

Company	EV ($M)	Resources			EV/ Resource (US$/oz)
		Tonnes (MT)	Grade (g/t)	Ounces (Moz)	
Republic Gold	14.5	46.0	1.23	1.8	8.0
Millennium Minerals	9.9	28.9	1.24	1.2	8.6
Atlantic Gold	12.7	23.3	1.61	1.2	10.6
Minotaur Exploration	4.5	7.9	1.61	0.4	10.9
Aragon	27.0	11.5	4.04	1.5	18.1
Dragon Mountain	37.6	24.6	1.54	1.2	31.0
Excalibur Mining	6.3	1.6	4.00	0.2	31.3
Midas Resources	22.6	4.9	2.27	0.4	63.6
Azumah	78.2	17.0	2.01	1.1	71.0
Chalice	62.2	5.0	5.22	0.8	74.0
Cortona Resources	26.1	1.4	6.20	0.3	91.1
Weighted average		**15.6**	**1.8**	**0.9**	**29.9**

The weighted average EV per ounce of resource is US$29.9 in table 11.12. The range of values is from US$8.0 to US$91.1 per ounce, with the majority at the lower end. The variance in the EV per ounce is ultimately a reflection of the implied operating margins (grade), the size and location of the resource, and the timing and likelihood of development. The proportion of resources defined as measured, indicated or inferred will also vary between the companies and often no cutoff grade is provided or applied to the resources. The companies may also have other tenements, and in some cases resources for other commodities, which can unduly effect the result. The location of projects with respect to country risk, or in some cases countries with enhanced exploration appeal such as Ghana, also complicates the analysis.

The valuations are for listed resource companies and it can be argued that a control premium should also be applied for a 100 per cent interest to determine fair market value per ounce. If the project or company under consideration has a compliant resource, then the appropriate EV/ounce can be applied. An advantage of the method is that often a number of listed companies can be used for comparison and the EV can be selected as at the valuation date, but the obvious difficulty is in deciding what is the appropriate value to choose.

The performance of the stocks listed in table 11.12 was compared over a nine-month period and the results are shown in figure 11.5. Over this period the companies with the lower EV/oz outperformed those with higher values, which could be attributed to a number of factors, including a re-rating of the stocks through a greater certainty over the viability of their resources. Investors should be cautious in applying this form of stock selection.

Figure 11.5: relative time performance

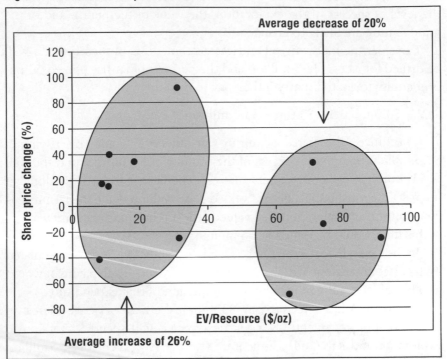

Joint venture or earn-in

It is not uncommon for mining and energy companies to defray some of their exploration risk by having outside parties pay for some or all of the exploration expenditure for an interest in their exploration tenements. If details of the joint venture or earn-in are available, then it may be possible to determine an implied valuation for the tenement. However, this can be difficult to value given the possibility of exit clauses and their potential effect on the value.

If a willing buyer acquires an interest (x per cent) in a permit for a price ($y), the implied value (V) for the permit is:

(1) $V = \$y \div x\%$ if the $y is retained by the seller

(2) $V = \$y \div x\% - \$y$ if the $y is to be spent on the permit

In the case of equation (2), the value of the joint venture between the two parties would be V + $y; that is, the implied value of the permit plus the cash that would be spent on the permit. Obviously over time, subject to the level of success of the exploration, the value of the permit and of the joint venture are likely to change.

Consider the following oil and gas example. It is proposed that a well be drilled for a cost of $3 million and the permit holder has offered 50 per cent equity to another party if they pay to drill the well:

$$V = \$3.0m \div 0.5 - \$3.0m = \$3.0 \text{ million}$$

The farminee (the party acquiring an interest) would be paying a $1.5 million premium in excess of the pro rata obligation to fund the well of $1.5 million for a 50 per cent interest. The farmor (the party selling an interest) is contributing a permit valued at $3 million while the farminee is contributing an exploration well valued at $3 million, and the joint venture at this time would be valued at $6 million.

In the case where the earn-in is staged, the valuation could be calculated as the discounted sum of each of the future payments. Each payment would also be subject to the probability of completion of that expenditure.

Company A has agreed to pay $3 million for a 30 per cent interest in an exploration tenement. Over the next year it will spend $1 million in exploration and at the end it can acquire a further 10 per cent for $1.5 million and another 10 per cent if it spends a further $2 million on exploration the following year. At the end of the second year it can pay a further $2 million for 10 per cent, and if it spends $3 million in exploration during the third year it will earn another 20 per cent. Company A can withdraw from the project when it wishes. Table 11.13 lists the annual payments, the implied valuations using the formulas given and the probabilities that it will complete the next exploration phase. Note that at the end of year 1 Company A has to have spent the $1 million on exploration to acquire the additional 10 per cent for $1.5 million so 5 per cent equity has been allocated to each expenditure.

Table 11.13: annual payments, implied valuations and the probability of completing the next exploration phase for Company A in a joint venture

	Initial	Year 1	Year 2	Year 3
Exploration expenditure ($m)	—	1.0	2.0	3.0
Percentage interest	—	5.0	10.0	20.0
Acquisition expenditure ($m)	3.0	1.5	2.0	—

	Initial	Year 1	Year 2	Year 3
Interest (%)	30.0	5.0	10.0	—
Implied value ($m)	10.0	49.0	38.0	12.0
Probability (%)	100.0	70.0	50.0	10.0
Discount 10%	1.00	0.91	0.83	0.75
Adjusted value ($m)	10.0	31.2	15.7	0.9

The maximum implied value of the joint venture agreement on a probability-adjusted basis is $31.2 million. Obviously as each stage is completed the probabilities and values will change. A difficulty with any earn-in approach, as mentioned, could be the potential effect of any unknown special termination or performance clauses that might muddy the implied value.

Cost base approach

This approach is best suited for early stage development or exploration, and relies on previous expenditures or commitments, or both, which are either decreased or increased to reflect current market conditions and prospectivity of the tenement.

Past expenditure multiple

One of the most used valuation methods applied to exploration properties is previous exploration expenditure. This is a very raw evaluation as sunk costs are sunk and the implication that the current value is related to the level of previous expenditure is often tenuous. The method can be enhanced by multiplying the value by a multiplier that can range from 0 to 5 to reflect the future potential of the permit, sometimes called the multiple of exploration expenditure method, but again this is somewhat subjective, as shown here:

» 0.5 to 1.0—work to date justifies next stage of exploration

» 1.0 to 2.0—strong indications of potential for economic mineralisation

» 2.0 to 3.0—ore grade intersections or exposures indicative of economic resource.

Needless to say, any past exploration expenditure that doesn't add to the knowledge base of the property should be excluded from the assessment. In other words, if all previous expenditure had shown no exploration potential, there is little or no value applicable to that permit with regard to previous exploration expenditure.

Prospectivity rating

An enhancement of the method is the Kilburn geoscience rating method, which is a way of applying multiplying factors.[8] The method starts with the base acquisition cost (BAC), which is the average cost to acquire a unit area of a tenement or permit and to meet all statutory expenditure commitments for a period of 12 months. For example, in the 2001 Pacmin Mining target statement, Snowden Corporate Services provided their BAC estimates for the following Western Australian unit areas: exploration licence—$335/square kilometre; prospecting licence—$42/hectare; mining lease—$111/hectare. The appropriate BAC was multiplied by the accumulated appropriate weighting factors, which are listed in table 11.14.

Table 11.14: Kilburn geoscience rating method criteria

Rating	Off-property factor	On-property factor	Anomaly factor	Geological factor
0.1				Unfavourable lithology
0.2				Unfavourable with structures
0.3				Generally favourable
0.4				Lithology (10%–20%)
0.5			Extensive previous exploration with poor results	Alluvium covered, generally favourable lithology (50%)
0.6				

8 Kilburn L.C. 1990, 'Valuation of mineral properties which do not contain exploitable properties', CIM Bulletin, vol. 83, no. 940.

Rating	Off-property factor	On-property factor	Anomaly factor	Geological factor
0.7				
0.8				
0.9				Generally favourable lithology (50%)
1	No known mineralisation	No known mineralisation	No targets outlined	Generally favourable lithology (70%)
1.5	Minor workings	Minor workings	Several well-defined targets	
2	Several old workings	Several old workings		Generally favourable lithology
2.5				
3	Abundant workings	Abundant workings	Several significant sub-economic intersections	Generally favourable lithology with structures Generally favourable lithology with structures along strike of a major mine
3.5	Abundant workings/ mines historical production >200 000 oz	Abundant workings/ mines Historical production >100 000 oz		
4				
4.5				
5	Along strike significant mine(s) with production reserves > 1 m oz	Historical production 500 000 oz	Several significant ore-grade correlatable intersections	
10	Along strike significant mine(s) with production reserves > 1 m oz			

Source: Pacmin Mining Corporation Target Statement, 14/09/01, p. 28 © Snowden Mining
Industry Consultants and KPMG Corporate Finance (Aust.) Pty Ltd

Charting, technical analysis and nomograms

There are some differences, although at times these are somewhat blurred, between the analysis undertaken in charting and what might be defined as technical analysis. Basically, they both rely on some identifiable pattern in the past movements of a share or commodity price so that the likely direction can be predicted into the immediate future.

Although the techniques do not lend themselves to valuing projects as such, they are in common use in the prediction of share price and commodity price movements. Charting generally refers to the analysis of trends and patterns in the raw data, while technical analysis goes a step further and modifies the data by such devices as moving averages, and then also analyses the filtered patterns. For the purposes of this brief discussion, I will use the term charting to include both disciplines.

There are a number of aspects of charting that investors do find intuitively acceptable. For example, share and commodity prices do follow trends rather than totally random and volatile movements (random numbers, however, can also show visual trends, as discussed later). The trick is not to show that a commodity or stock price is in an increasing or declining trend, but rather to predict when that trend will change.

The theoretical difficulty is that if the change in trend or direction can be accurately predicted—for example, a fall in the price of a commodity—investors and traders would sell the commodity in anticipation of the decline and hence the fall would occur prior to the predicted fall.

If charting could make successful predictions, then the market would be inefficient and investors could get something for nothing. Empirical studies such as filter rules, and some would say common sense, suggest that future movements in a share or commodity price are not governed by its past movements.

Consider figure 11.6. It shows the movements in the copper price over several years, with some simple trends drawn in that show points of trend breakthrough. However, included in the same chart is another series pattern, but this has been generated using random numbers with a similar mean and standard deviation to the copper price. Can you guess which is the copper and which is the random number series?

Figure 11.6: trends in copper prices and in random numbers

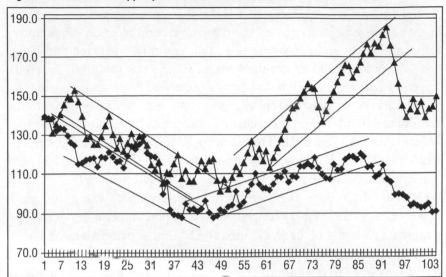

The results show an important point. The random numbers (or a random walk) that are not related can produce patterns not dissimilar to those seen in the market. Randomness does not mean that each succeeding value has to move in an opposite direction. Clearly, patterns or trends can be generated randomly. Therefore, what is described as a change in sentiment, and hence a change in trend, can also occur in a set of random numbers.

However, herd mentality is a powerful force, and if enough investors or traders believe that the charts have indicated that some support or resistance level has been breached, they may act in unison and the prediction may become self-fulfilling in the short term. The danger is that the signal may be false, as so often is the case, and the investor gets caught out in the longer term.

Numerous approaches have been developed in an attempt to predict the future from past events, or, to put it another way, to get a free lunch. Not all approaches adopt a charting technique. Some can be more sophisticated, such as the nomogram 1 developed some years ago. The concept was used for two major resource companies, BHP and Mt Isa Mines, on the basis that their share price performance was a function of a number of specific parameters, primarily exchange rates and commodity prices.

By analysing historical share price performance and the relative movements in the share price to exogenous variables, it was possible to construct a relationship between each of the factors. A nomogram, as shown in figure 11.7, was constructed so that as each of the variables changed it was possible to predict if the share price was out of line with historical patterns. Conceptually, for any given combination of parameter values there was an appropriate price that could be predicted and hence the nomograms could inform the investor if the stock was a buy or a sell.

The procedure for BHP was to draw a horizontal line from the share price to an intercept with the current exchange rate, then vertically down to the appropriate oil price, then horizontally to the left to the All Ordinaries Index and then vertically down. The final intercept at the bottom left would indicate, relative to the tested exogenous variables, whether an investor should increase or decrease his or her exposure to the relevant shares (buy or sell).

In the short term the nomogram's performance was quite good; however, if circumstances changed, such as a new mineral discovery, that required a re-rating of the stock, then the historical pattern was no longer valid (non-stationary) and the performance of the nomogram deteriorated. It was necessary to re-compute the data to generate a new nomogram. An extended time frame was again required to get a new set of data, which greatly reduced the effectiveness of the methodology.

Figure 11.7: BHP share price nomogram

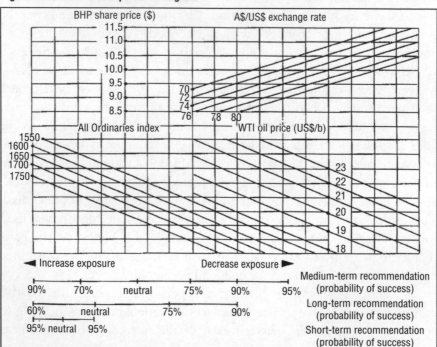

The simple conclusion is that you don't get something for nothing. Detailed fundamental analysis, with a small amount of charting and some luck, is required to achieve above-average returns from the market.

Valuations not only are required to determine the relative value of a company, but sometimes also have to be allocated between the company's different assets and may need to be considered during takeovers, which are discussed in the following chapter.

CHAPTER 12
Takeovers and fair value allocation

A considerable amount of effort may be put into determining what we believe, based on the available information, is the correct valuation for a mining company and on that basis decide whether a stock is a buy or a sell. Valuations are also often critical in takeovers and mergers, where experts are required to give an opinion on the relative merits of such proposals. In general they will also use a bottom-up approach by valuing different components and combining them to come up with a net asset value. Control premium may also have to be added to reflect the additional benefits an acquirer might get with 100 per cent control.

However, if we assume that the bid price from an acquirer is a good indicator of a company's value (or the market value adjusted for control) then sometimes it is necessary to allocate that valuation to the different components that make up the company.

Takeovers and mergers

Resource companies can increase their asset base through a takeover of a listed resource company or by way of a scheme of arrangement where the shareholders agree to a merger. In most cases, an 'expert' report and opinion will be sought to help shareholders make an informed decision on whether to accept the offer price or scheme put in front of them. These reports are a major source of information on resource companies and their mining operations, as discussed in chapter 8. The techniques employed by the expert in determining the fair market value (FMV) of the company or assets, or both, are the same as those outlined in the previous chapters of this book. The FMV should be at arm's length at a price that a willing buyer will pay and a willing seller will sell. In most cases the valuation, which is undertaken by the expert, will be very subjective, depending on the individual's expertise and experience.

Expert's report

The difficulty encountered by the expert is in determining the 'correct' value. As the previous chapters highlight, there are numerous ways to arrive at a value—from sector multiples to net present values—and even these values can vary considerably depending on the assumptions made. The expert is therefore likely to provide a range of values for a number of the components that make up the company's asset base. For example, in the case of the 1996 takeover bid for Gasgoyne Gold Mines by Sons of Gwalia, both of which were Australian companies listed on the ASX, the independent expert in the Part B response by the board of Gasgoyne provided the range of valuations given in table 12.1 for Gasgoyne. To highlight the impact that different approaches and varying assumptions can have on the range of values, three methods were applied to arrive at the values for the Yilgarn Star goldmine. The first consisted of a fundamental analysis of the project's NPV, as shown in table 12.2.

Table 12.1: valuations for Gasgoyne Gold Mines, 1996

Asset	Low ($m)	Most likely ($m)	High ($m)
Yilgarn Star (50%)	90	100	110
Awak Mas (45%)	50	60	70
Exploration	8	11	12
Other liabilities	(8)	(8)	(8)
Total	140	163	184
Value per share	$2.50	$2.89	$3.26

Source: Part B Statement by Gasgoyne Gold Mines N.L., March 1996, included with permission of the Sons of Gwalia Administrator.

Four different operating scenarios were considered in calculating the NPV. Scenarios 1 and 2 assumed two different milling rates of 750 000 tonnes and 1 million tonnes per annum respectively. Note how the mine life, capital and operating cost vary accordingly. For scenarios 3 and 4, again the two different milling rates were assumed, but the recoverable ore reserve was increased by 3.2 million tonnes at an average grade of 5.8 g/t.

The additional reserves would be accessed by underground mining after the development of a shaft and ore-hoisting facilities for an additional capital cost of $42 million. The Yilgarn mine had an NPV range of between $67 million and $109 million.

Table 12.2: Yilgarn Star goldmine fundamental analysis of NPV, 1996

Operating parameter	Scenario 1	Scenario 2	Scenario 3	Scenario 4
Mill throughput (000s tpa)	750	1000	750	1000
Mine life (years)	9	8	13	11
Total ore milled (000s t)	6622	6622	9838	9838
Head grade (g/t)	4.76	4.76	5.1	5.1
Total capital expenditure ($m)	32.6	39.9	81.3	87.3
Gold production (000s oz)	963.6	963.6	1531.2	1531.2
Average total unit cost ($/t)	45.23	44.57	46.28	45.59
Average cash operating cost ($/oz)	311	306	297	293
Project NPV ($m)	139	135	219	210
Gasgoyne's 50% interest ($m)	70	67	109	105

Note: tpa = tonnes per annum.

Assumptions: discount rate 6 per cent per annum; interest rate 4 per cent per annum; exchange rate US$0.765:A$1.00; gold price US$395 increasing at real interest rate.

Source: Part B Statement by Gasgoyne Gold Mines N.L, March 1996, included with permission of the Sons of Gwalia Administrator.

The second method of valuation was an implied market value based on the market capitalisation of Orion Resources NL, a listed company that held a 45 per cent interest in Yilgarn Star. If Orion's only asset had been this interest, it would have been a relatively easy matter to imply a value for Gasgoyne's 50 per cent share. However, Orion had a number of other assets, including a 45 per cent interest in the Salsigne goldmine. It was therefore necessary to value the goldmine and other assets, and then determine that proportion of Orion's market capitalisation that could be apportioned to its interest in the Gasgoyne goldmine, as shown in table 12.3 (overleaf).

Table 12.3: Orion's market capitalisation, 1996

Key parameters	Low ($m)	High ($m)
Market capitalisation of Orion	114.2	114.2
less estimated value of Salsigne	35.0	25.0
less estimated value of exploration portfolio	10.0	5.0
less estimated value of investments	3.6	3.6
less working capital	(4.7)	(4.7)
less estimated value of hedge positions	2.0	2.0
Implied value of Orion's 45% interest in Yilgarn Star	68.3	83.3
Implied value of Gasgoyne's 50% interest in Yilgarn Star	75.9	92.6

Source: Part B Statement by Gasgoyne Gold Mines N.L., March 1996, included with permission of the Sons of Gwalia Administrator.

The third method of valuation of Yilgarn Star was an implied value based on industry rules of thumb. In this case the market value per ounce of reserve or resource was compared with the cash operating costs. In other words, a linear relationship was computed for 28 listed gold-producing companies so that, based on Yilgarn's cash operating cost of $300 per ounce, the implied value was $150 per ounce of resource and $340 per ounce of reserve. Based on Yilgarn's resource and reserves, the implied value for 50 per cent of the mine was estimated at between $108 and $118 million. Table 12.4 summarises the range of valuations for Yilgarn Star.

Table 12.4: Yilgarn Star goldmine: summary of range of valuations

Valuation method	$m
Net present valuation	67 to 100
Implied market value (Orion share price)	76 to 93
Implied market value (rule of thumb)	108 to 118

From this range of valuations the expert chose a most likely value of $100 million with a low of $90 million and a high of $110 million. The example clearly shows the inexact science involved in the valuation process. Indeed, additional methods such as cash-flow multiples or operating margins could have been applied to provide further values. Ultimately a 'fair' valuation had to be chosen, and in this case it was $100 million.

This value is at the upper end of the NPV, although, as the previous data show, it could be exceeded. The $100 million valuation is higher than the implied value from Orion, but the reliability of the valuation range is subject to correctly estimating the values of Orion's other assets. Rule of thumb suggests that a higher value could be justified, although the robustness of the relationships between market capitalisation, reserves and operating costs is not high, and the equity markets are known to apply a premium to the fundamental value. A similar process was also undertaken to arrive at a valuation for Gasgoyne's other assets in determining the final most likely fair value of $2.89 per share.

Valuing exploration acreage

Invariably with any resource company there will be exploration areas (permits) within its portfolio where most likely little or no resource has been defined, but the potential exists. An implied value may therefore need to be quantified. Indeed, for some companies the only value may be its exploration plays and, for some, the value may be quite significant if the likelihood of a discovery is thought to be high.

The expert responsible for the valuation should use all information available to determine the appropriate value. The factors that would be considered include the geological setting of the permit, previous exploration activity in the area and surrounding areas, any existing mineral resource in the adjacent area, and existing infrastructure and its impact of the economic viability of the permit. The valuation methodologies have been discussed in the previous chapter.

Market and control premium

In some cases, particularly for gold producers, listed companies may trade on a stock market at a premium to their assessed NPV. The NPV can be seen as the consensus value of analysts in the market. The market premium is a reflection of the market's expectation that the companies might make new discoveries, or in other words provide 'blue sky', by increasing their known reserves base and provide an option value for commodity price volatility (see chapter 4).

An important issue in the analyst's determination of the NPV is that the correct discount rate has been applied and that the forecast commodity prices are in line with the market's expectation. The market premium is most pronounced for the gold sector, although this has decreased over recent times. One argument for the disparity is that analysts use too high a discount rate. It can be argued that due to the theoretical, and at times practical, ability of producers to hedge all of their future gold production, the elimination of price risk results in a lower discount rate (although in 2011 fewer producers hedge due to the recent increases in the gold price). For other sectors where hedging of commodity prices is not so prevalent, it is not uncommon for the NPV to be at a premium to the share price. This is sometimes caused by an overly optimistic view by analysts on commodity prices and operational improvements in the company. However, it is often a sign that the stock could be re-rated by the market as it becomes fully aware of the issues enunciated by the analyst.

Although the shareholders of a listed company are the owners of the company, they have no direct say in operations. If a third party acquires a controlling interest, it will gain the benefits of management control over such matters as dividends, operational and strategic direction, company information and financing decisions. If the third party gains 100 per cent of the company, then it will have control of its cash flow and perhaps gain group tax benefits. For these benefits, the market expects a premium for control. This premium is often defined as the difference between the bid price and the share price prior to the takeover (although on some occasions the price may increase prior to the bid in anticipation). The premium paid for takeovers in the resources sector is generally in the range of 20 to 35 per cent, with an average of around 30 per cent.[1]

Table 12.5 summarises most of the mining and energy takeovers and schemes of arrangement over the last five years in Australia. In all but a few cases the bid price is at a premium to the last traded price prior to the takeover announcement (takeover premium). In the table, the boards of the companies also undertook an independent valuation of their company so that shareholders could make an informed decision on whether they should accept the bid.

---

1 For example, KPMG (2008) analysed 528 takeovers for an adjusted average 20 day premium of 23.1 per cent (median of 18.1 per cent); and RSM Bird Cameron (2010) calculated a premium for resource companies of 26.4 per cent, 29.9 per cent and 33.9 per cent for two, five and 20 days prior to the bid or scheme of arrangement announcement respectively.

Table 12.5: mining and energy takeovers and schemes, 2007–11

Target	Offeror	Takeover date	Offer price	Offer price premium* (%)	Valuation premium (%)
Gawler	Elixir	23 Mar 07	$0.23	2.3	−15.0
Elkedra	Vaaldiam	4 Jul 07	$0.36	21.6	−0.3
Mavuzi	Mantra	27 Sep 07	$0.40	21.2	−19.7
Perseverance	Northgate	29 Oct 07	$0.20	37.9	17.2
RSP	Xstrata	5 Dec 07	$3.30	35.8	58.4
Olympia Resources	Territory Mineral	11 Mar 08	$0.10	53.8	253.8
Equigold	Lihir	20 Mar 08	$5.33	24.0	−8.1
Great Artesian	Drillsearch	18 Apr 08	$0.20	85.7	38.1
Bemax	Cristal	26 May 08	$0.32	45.5	28.2
Sapex	Linc	12 Jun 08	$0.72	3.6	−26.6
Anzon	Roc	16 Jun 08	$1.69	29.5	10.3
Sunshine Gas	Queensland Gas	20 Aug 08	$2.70	22.7	11.4
Indophil	Stanhill	25 Aug 08	$1.30	7.8	22.7
Portman	Cliffs	11 Sep 08	$21.50	21.5	−23.2
Incremental Petroleum	TransAtlantic	27 Oct 08	$1.05	12.9	160.2

(continued)

Table 12.5: mining and energy takeovers and schemes, 2007–11 (*cont'd*)

Target	Offeror	Takeover date	Offer price	Offer price premium* (%)	Valuation premium (%)
Queensland Ores	Outback Metals	18 Feb 09	$0.01	16.0	255.6
Gloucester	Noble Group	27 Feb 09	$4.85	24.4	143.6
Terrain Minerals	Iron Mountain	10 Mar 09	$0.07	90.5	237.8
Target Energy	Blaze	8 Apr 09	$0.06	76.4	230.6
Dioro Exploration NL	Avoca Resources	14 Apr 09	$0.53	−68.8	10.6
Bonaparte Diamond	Minemakers/Union	5 Mar 09	$0.06	34.9	20.9
Consolidated Rutile	Unimin	17 Apr 09	$0.45	40.6	32.8
North Australian Diamonds	Legend	12 May 09	$0.01	9.1	32.3
Adelphi	AWE	17 May 10	$0.40	42.9	117.9
Bowen Energy	Bhushan	10 Jul 09	$0.14	12.0	−63.8
RMA Energy	CREC Resources	10 Aug 09	$0.07	38.3	42.6
Felix Resources	Yanzhou	13 Aug 09	$18.05	6.8	4.7
Herald Resources Ltd	PT Burni	21 Aug 09	$0.70	75.0	212.5
Sino Gold	Eldorado	26 Aug 09	$6.95	17.4	7.6
Vulcan Resources	Universal Resources	3 Sep 09	$0.38	245.5	204.5
United Minerals	BHP	16 Oct 09	$1.30	42.9	−25.8
Energy Developments	Pacific Equity	19 Oct 09	$2.75	14.1	50.6

Target	Offeror	Takeover date	Offer price	Offer price premium* (%)	Valuation premium (%)
Pacmag	Entrée	30 Nov 09	$0.31	34.8	69.6
Gloucester	Macarthur Coal	22 Dec 09	$8.00	22.1	26.0
Aurox	Atlas	10 Mar 10	$0.74	174.1	46.3
CBH Resources	Toho	16 Mar 10	$0.24	41.2	27.6
Arrow Energy	Shell	8 Mar 10	$4.70	35.1	20.7
DMC Mining	Cape Lambert	23 Mar 10	$0.40	33.3	66.7
Gloucester	Noble	8 Apr 10	$12.60	35.3	24.0
Adelphi	AWE	17 May 10	$0.40	42.9	117.9
Centennial	Banpu Pcl	5 Jul 10	$6.20	40.0	45.6
North Queensland Metals	Heemskirk	5 Jul 10	$0.36	33.3	55.6
Mosaic	AGL Energy	1 Jul 10	$0.15	92.3	109.0
Andean	Goldcorp	3 Sep 10	$6.50	32.9	30.3
Northern Energy	New Hope	8 Oct 10	$1.50	34.5	269.5
Copper Strike	Karara	12 Oct 10	$0.11	15.8	268.5
Dominion Mining	Kingsgate	20 Oct 10	$3.31	21.2	10.8
Mantra	JSC	15 Dec 10	$8.00	6.7	−10.9
Giralia	Atlas	21 Dec 10	$4.57	52.8	0.0
BC Iron	Regent Pacific	21 Jan 11	$3.30	3.8	24.7
Aragon Resources	Westgold Resources	7 Feb 11	$0.32	31.7	22.9

(continued)

Table 12.5: mining and energy takeovers and schemes, 2007–11 (*cont'd*)

Target	Offeror	Takeover date	Offer price	Offer price premium* (%)	Valuation premium (%)
White Canyon	Denison Mines	23 Feb 11	$0.24	20.0	−4.0
Auzex Resources	GGG Resources PLC	14 Mar 11	$0.53	−15.2	20.0
Abra Mining	HNC	1 Apr 11	$0.40	33.3	28.0
Territory Resources	Exxaro/Noble Group	23 May 11	$0.50	78.6	64.3
Conquest	Catalpa	15 Jun 11	$0.52	14.5	42.2
FerrAus	Atlas	27 Jun 11	$0.88	37.1	31.1
Eastern Star Gas	Santos	18 Jul 11	$0.90	51.3	50.4
Meridian	Northwest	19 Jul 11	$0.14	21.7	10.9
Coal & Allied	Rit Tinto	5 Aug 11	$125.00	37.4	31.6
Adamus	Endeavour	22 Aug 11	$0.68	4.0	3.1
Minara	Glencore	24 Aug 11	$0.87	35.9	30.5
Bow Energy BOW	Arrow	22 Aug 11	$1.52	7.4	−5.7
Geothermal	Havilah	26 Aug 11	$0.33	140.7	−11.1
Brockman — BRM	Wah Nam	12 Dec 11	$2.83	25.0	27.2
Average				**37.2**	**54.9**
Median				**33.3**	**28.0**
Adjusted average				**32.4**	**30.0**
Adjusted median				**33.1**	**27.8**

*On previous day

The independent expert gets access to all the company's information and in all cases provided a valuation per share, as was discussed in the previous example for Gasgoyne (see table 12.1 on p. 300). Interestingly, the expert reports show a valuation premium on average of nearly 55 per cent, but when the outliers are removed (plus or minus 100 per cent premiums) the adjusted averages and medians are similar and are in line with the offer price premiums.

The question as to why the unadjusted independent values is so much higher than the last share price is partially a function of the independent expert's adding the entire control premium to the share price by way of, in most cases, a fundamental valuation of the company. It is important that the expert does not add any synergistic benefits or similar benefits that might accrue to the bidder, as these are not available to the current shareholders. One could argue that the bidder's price will be less than the expert's value, as the bidder will not be in possession of all of the information (only what is in the public domain), and will bid a lower figure in the hope of getting the company at a good price and allow some flexibility to increase the price if necessary to win the bid. A cynic might also suggest that the independent expert (who is paid by the offeree) may come up with the best valuation possible in the best interests of the shareholders, as long as the shareholders don't lose an opportunity to sell their shares at the bid price that subsequently proves to be a high point for the company (which has certainly happened in some cases in the past).

Fair and reasonable

There are no set definitions of what is fair or reasonable with regard to the valuation of resource companies for the purposes of a takeover or merger. However, the Australian Securities and Investments Commission (ASIC) Regulatory Guide 111 provides views on the meaning of a fair and reasonable offer for the shares of a target company. These views are:

» *Fair.* An offer is considered fair if the value of the offer price or consideration is equal to, or greater than, the value of the securities that are the subject of the offer (assuming 100 per cent ownership and therefore control of the company). In the Gasgoyne example (see table 12.1 on p. 300), the assessed, or most likely, value was $2.89; therefore, a bid price equal to or greater than this value could be assessed as fair.

» *Reasonable.* An offer is considered reasonable if it is fair, but if an offer is not fair it may still be considered reasonable if an expert believes that there are sufficient reasons for shareholders to accept the offer in the absence of any higher bid before the close of that offer. The types of special circumstances that the expert might consider are: the pre-existing holding by the offeror; liquidity in the shares of the target company; any significant shareholder blocks; the likelihood of another offer; benefits of achieving 100 per cent ownership; special value to the offeror; and value to an alternate offeror.

The Valmin Code

The Valmin Code and guidelines were adopted in 1995 and are applicable in Australia to all relevant independent expert's reports subject to the jurisdiction of the Australian Securities and Investments Commission (ASIC) and the *Corporations Act 2007*. The Code sets the standards for those suitably qualified and experienced in preparing the reports. The Code doesn't, however, give guidance as to how to value. Types of reports covered by the Code include technical reports, valuation reports, and fairness and reasonableness reports. Some of the more important requirements are:

» The expert must aim for maximum rather than minimum disclosure, and ensure that the report is not false or misleading and does not omit material matters.

» The valuation process must be objective and rigorous, and any assumptions must be reasonable and disclosed.

» The expert is independent and perceived and acknowledged as independent by the commissioning entity, with no material present or contingent interest in or association with the commissioning entity.

» The valuation methodology(ies) is (are) solely the responsibility of the expert, who must not be influenced by the commissioning entity, and the expert must state the reasons for selecting the methodology.

» Full disclosure of all material information must be made by the commissioning entity to the expert.

» Where the ASX and corporations law permits, information that the commissioning entity considers to be confidential and is provided to the expert may not appear in the public version of the report; however, the expert must indicate in the report the extent to which this confidential information has been relied upon by the expert.

» The report must state the source of all material information and data used in preparing the report.

» A range of values must be determined, reflecting the uncertainties in the data and interaction of assumptions made, and a sensitivity analysis provided showing the effects of changes in the most significant assumptions.

» If it is impossible or impracticable to obtain sufficient data to provide a valuation the expert is to be under no obligation to do so, and if the valuation is zero or negative this must be stated.

National Instrument 43-101

The Canadian National Instrument 43-101 (NI 43-101) requires substantially more technical disclosure to the Canadian market, as it is a code for securities disclosure, whereas the JORC Code is primarily for reporting the status of a mineral resource. Information that is required includes the following:

» name of qualified person and relationship to issuer

» whether data verified, how, any limitation and why not verified

» if mineral resource or reserve is disclosed, the issuer must provide:

 – effective date

 – quantity and grade or quality

 – key assumptions and methods used

 – discussion of environmental, permitting, legal, title, taxation, socio-political, marketing and other issues

 – statement that mineral resources that are not mineral reserves are not economically viable, if economic analysis of mineral resources is included

 – in most cases must lodge technical report 43-101F1, which is very prescriptive.

The technical report required under NI 43-101 provides a summary of material information and the requirements for the preparation and content of the report is summarised in table 12.6 (overleaf).

Table 12.6: contents of NI 43-101 technical report

Title page	Mineral processing and metallurgical testing
Data and signature page	Mineral resource estimates
Table of contents	Mineral reserve estimates
Summary	Mining methods
Introduction	Recovery methods
Reliance on other experts	Project infrastructure
Property description and location	Market studies and contracts
Accessibility, climate, local resources, infrastructure and physiography	Environmental studies, permitting and social impact
History	Capital and operating costs
Geological setting	Economic analysis
Deposit types	Adjacent properties
Exploration	Other relevant data and information
Drilling	Interpretation and conclusions
Sample preparation, analysis and security	Recommendations
Data verification	References

Source:<www.osc.gov.on.ca/en/SecuritiesLaw_ni_20110624_43-101_mineral-projects.htm>.

Fair market value and its components

Fair market value (FMV) is generally defined as the price an asset will trade between a knowledgeable and willing seller and a knowledgeable and willing buyer. Let's assume that the market capitalisation of a company is $2 billion based on its share price and issued capital as at the date of valuation. If we add a control premium of, say, 30 per cent (see previous section on takeovers and mergers) we arrive at an FMV of $2.6 billion. Adjusting for cash and debt held by the company for a net debt of $100 million, the EV of the assets is $2.5 billion.

It is not uncommon for both accounting and tax purposes to have to allocate the EV ($2.5 billion) to different components that make up the assets of the company. A company's assets and liabilities are normally detailed in its balance sheet, but balance sheet entries are historical in nature and therefore may not add up the market's view of the value of the current total assets as defined by the EV.

A resource company can be viewed as made up of a number of components, most of which can be valued independently of each other. These include:

» *Property, plant and equipment (PPE)*. The plant is normally valued at its book value as shown in the balance sheet, which is the depreciated value of the historical acquisition price. If the plant had a 20-year operating life and was 10 years old, then the historical value would have been depreciated to 50 per cent (10 years divided by 20 years). Alternatively the plant could be valued at its salvage value: that is, the value that could be received by closing the plant down and selling it for parts and scrap. Finally, the plant could be valued at the cost of replacing it optimally (with current technology) and then depreciated in the same manner as the book value, in other words depreciated optimised replacement cost (DORC).

» *Mine development*. Permanent mine openings, such as shafts and declines in underground mines or haul roads in open cut operations, provide a benefit that can extend for more than a year and are therefore also depreciated over their operating lives for the purposes of a balance sheet. While it is highly unlikely that mine development would have a salvage value, a DORC could be calculated as well as an opportunity cost.

» *Mining information*. For balance sheet purposes, once mining operations commenced or are intended to commence, expenses generally related to drill-hole data used to obtain information about the orebody can be capitalised and then can be depreciated over the life of the orebody.[2] Again, the DORC could be determined as if the data were lost, but not all of the data might need to be replaced to continue and complete mining (optimised), while it might take some time to replicate so there could be an opportunity cost.

» *Exploration information*. Exploration information is generally capitalised (not expensed in the profit and loss of the company) and not depreciated with respect to the balance sheet, but accumulated until an economic discovery is made and then developed, whence

---

2 Drilling for grade control would generally be expensed as an operating cost.

it becomes mining information and depreciated. If no discovery is made and it is determined that the tenement is unlikely to result in a discovery in the future, then the exploration information would be written off with respect to the profit and loss, and the balance sheet. As with mining information, the exploration information could be determine using DORC as if the data were lost, but again not all of the data might need to be replaced to continue and complete mining (optimised), while it might take some time to replicate so there could be an opportunity cost.

» *Mining right.* This is the right to exploit all known reserves and resources and as yet undiscovered mineralisation on the mining and exploration tenements held by the company. Mining right is a critical component of valuation and the most difficult to value independently of all other assets. The right may be in the form of ownership of the mineral within the tenement or the right to exploit any mineral found within the tenement. The mining right value can be determined by calculating the difference between the EV and sum of the other assets such as PPE, mine development, mining and exploration information. However, undeveloped resources and other exploration tenements also have to be valued and included within the total valuation process. The analysis might look like the one shown in table 12.7.

Table 12.7: example of valuation of a company's mining right

	Value ($ billion)
EV	2.5
Less	
PPE	0.8
Mining information	$0.1
Exploration information	$0.2
Mining right	**$1.4**

Impairment or opportunity cost

For valuation purposes 'best use' should be the guiding factor and, in most cases, best use is to keep the plant in operation and value it in current terms, such as DORC (if it can be determined). One additional consideration is the inclusion of any opportunity cost or impairment cost. That is, if the plant were replaced optimally it would take time to construct and under those conditions the mine would have to stop operating. There would be a loss of cash flow, which when discounted provides an impairment or opportunity cost as a net present value that could be added to the DORC. The opportunity cost could be relatively significant depending on the time impact on operations.

This approach can be used for all asset classes, such as exploration information, development information, mine development and transport infrastructure, as well as property, plant and equipment. If the methodology were applied to one asset, then logic would suggest it should be applied to all asset classes. The problem is that the sum of opportunity cost for all assets could exceed the total NPV, which would suggest that the mining right is negative! One solution might be to assume all of the assets are replaced concurrently and therefore the opportunity cost only goes to the asset with the longest time to replace. However, why should that asset, which might not be the most important asset, get what might be a significant increase in value compared with all the other assets, which play an equal part in generating future cash flows? Further, what happens if two asset classes are expected to take the same length of time to replace? Does that mean the NPV value has to be shared equally?

The problem is that while the DORC may be based on historical or current costs, the opportunity cost is based on future cash flows that, other than for tax calculations, are unrelated to the historical or current values. More importantly, the NPV is usually based on the most likely parameter outcomes with zero probability of a catastrophic loss of an asset that results in the termination of operations for possibly several years, let alone the possibility of losing all assets simultaneously. The classic NPV is therefore not appropriate for the calculation of opportunity cost.

Goodwill

When there is an observable price for a mining project or company, perhaps through a takeover or listed share price (EV), and the implied value exceeds the sum of the individual asset values, including the mining right, then the difference is sometimes attributed to goodwill, or perhaps, in the case of an industrial company, to the brand name. A common example is Coca-Cola, where the EV exceeds the sum of the assets many times over. The goodwill is often seen as the ability to acquire customers. In my opinion there is little if any attributable goodwill in mining, as a homogeneous product is generally produced that can't be differentiated and therefore there is no attractive force to generate custom.

Another area where goodwill may be attributable is a company's ability to generate additional cash flow above the norm due to its in-house expertise. Again there is generally little to differentiate the in-house ability of mining companies, although the management of some companies may be seen as better than average. Quantifying goodwill that the market may be willing to pay to get access to better management is a difficult task and may not be a material amount.

It is not uncommon when we calculate the NPV of future cash flows generated from mining operations (particularly in the case of gold assets) that the NPV will be less than, say, the EV or FMV. It would be easy to just assume the difference is goodwill, and although there may be cases, particularly in a takeover, where the buyer may be willing to pay a premium that could be termed goodwill, it would be wrong to assume so. There are a number of contributing factors that can explain the difference, which have already been alluded to.

The primary reason is that often the NPV may be based on the life of mine (LOM) plans that only include reserves. Most companies will also have resources, some or all of which may become reserves and extend or expand the LOM plans and thus increase NPV. The company may hold significant exploration tenements that has to be valued and added to the overall valuation. Even then the valuation may still be less than the EV or FMV. The area of difference may then come down to simply the assumptions used, particularly commodity prices and the discount rate applied.

There is always uncertainty about the assumptions that have been made in any of the foregoing analysis. In the next chapter we look at some ways in which we can incorporate uncertainty in our valuations.

CHAPTER 13

Quantifying the risk

Given the relative complexity of a mining financial model and the uncertainty over many of the input assumptions, several methods can be used to help determine where the greatest risk might lie and how that might impact on a mining project's valuation, and these are described in this chapter. Sensitivity analysis looks at the relative sensitivity of input parameters, while probability analysis incorporates the inputs simultaneously. Finally, the payback period lets us know how long our greatest risk exposure might be.

Sensitivity analysis

Sensitivity analysis is commonly used to show how the valuation might change if outcomes prove to be different from what has been assumed. The simplest way is to look at the critical parameters, one at a time, and model the change in the base case valuation, such as the NPV, for plus and minus variation in the parameter assumption to determine its relative sensitivity.

Consider a very simple hypothetical mining project that has a purchase price of $50 million and is expected to provide the pre-tax cash-flow profile shown in table 13.1.

Table 13.1: hypothetical mining project pre-tax cash flow projection over four years

Key parameters	Year 1	Year 2	Year 3	Year 4
Revenue ($m)	50.0	52	54.1	56.2
Mining cost ($m)	10.0	10.4	10.8	11.2

(continued)

317

Table 13.1: hypothetical mining project pre-tax cash flow projection over four years (*cont'd*)

Key parameters	Year 1	Year 2	Year 3	Year 4
Milling cost ($m)	24.5	25.5	26.5	27.5
Pre-tax ($m)	15.5	16.1	16.8	17.4

Assuming for the moment that the pre-tax cash flows are meaningful for our valuation purposes (there may be sufficient tax losses so that tax is not payable), and our discount rate is 10 per cent, then the following NPV would be obtained:

$$NPV_{10\%} = -\$50m + \$15.5m \div (1 + 0.12)^1 + \$16.1m \div (1.12)^2$$

$$+ \$16.8m \div (1.12)^3 + \$17.4m \div (1.12)^4$$

$$= \$1.9m$$

As figure 13.1 shows, the internal rate of return (IRR) is 11.7 per cent. In theory, we should be willing to pay up to $51.9 million ($50 million + $1.9 million) for the project's positive cash flow. However, the cash-flow projection is based on a large number of assumptions, the major ones being the expected revenue, and mining and milling costs. Although the best estimates may have been made of these future values, there is always a risk that these assumptions may prove to be incorrect.

Figure 13.1: hypothetical mining project—NPV

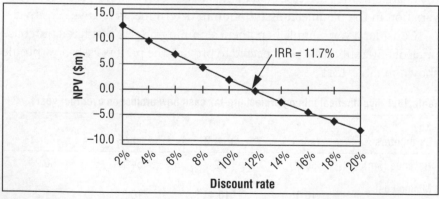

Figure 13.2 shows the relative sensitivity of the project's NPV to changes in revenue, mining cost and milling cost. The base case for our project is

an NPV of $1.9 million. Each of the three parameters has been changed by plus and minus 20 per cent.

As would be expected, the NPV increases in the case of increasing revenue, and decreases as the mining and milling costs increase. Conversely, the NPV falls as the revenue decreases and rises as the costs decrease. The slope of the lines clearly shows the sensitivity of the NPV to changes in the parameter assumptions. For example, the revenue is the most sensitive with a 20 per cent increase in revenue resulting in an increase in the NPV to $35.4 million, while a reduction in milling costs of 20 per cent results in an increase in the NPV to $18.3 million, while for mining costs the improvement in the NPV is only to $8.6 million.

Figure 13.2: hypothetical mining project parameter sensitivity

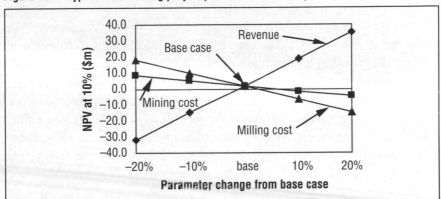

What the figure clearly shows is that for a small change in the revenue assumption—which is generally made up of product sales multiplied by the expected price—the NPV is very sensitive. In an evaluation of a project or company these parameters would have to be carefully considered prior to investment and carefully monitored during the life of the project. As revenue is the largest single cash item for a project or company, it is usually the most sensitive. However, it is possible to mitigate the potential impact through contracts, forward sales or hedging. What the analysis doesn't indicate is the likelihood or probability of a change in the base case NPV. This can be allowed for using probability analysis, which is discussed in the following section.

As well as applying sensitivity analysis to a project, the technique can also be used to analyse parameters such as earnings and earnings per share that might affect the value of a company or its share price.

Probability analysis

In the previous example on sensitivity analysis, three operating parameters were forecast to determine the project's cash flow: these were revenue, mining cost and milling cost. The values were the best estimates that could be made on available information, but only time would tell if the best estimates were correct. If the experts making the prediction had been asked if the final outcome could be different from their best estimate, the answer would most likely have been 'yes'. The experts could then have been asked to give an estimate of the probability that the ultimate value(s) would be different from their best estimate.

For example, the revenue value for year 1 is estimated at $50 million, the value being based on the expected production level and commodity price. After some analysis the experts might state that the base case estimate of $50 million is the most likely, but that it is conservative. The experts consider that the maximum possible value for year 1 is $56.4 million or 13 per cent higher than the most likely value. The worst case is estimated at $47.6 million or 5 per cent lower than the base case. It is within this range of $47.6 million to $56.4 million that the 'true' outcome is expected to occur, with the most likely case still $50 million. A number of intermediate values could then be selected and the expert's prediction used to define a probability distribution for that parameter, as shown in figure 13.3.

Figure 13.3: hypothetical mining project—probability distribution for revenue

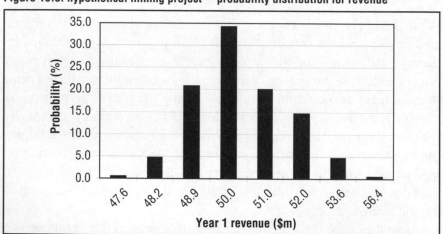

Note that the highest probability is assigned to the base case of $50 million, as it is still the most likely outcome. The range of possible outcomes is between the lowest and highest estimate, and the total probability of the discrete outcomes must add up to 100 per cent. The average value (mean) of the distribution is $51.4 million, which is different from the mode or most likely value of $50 million.

The discrete probability chart can be drawn as a cumulative probability chart (the probabilities are added together) where the possible outcomes are shown as a probability of the actual result being greater or less than that value. For example, as shown in figure 13.4, there is a 60 per cent chance that the true value will be less than or equal to the base case and a 40 per cent chance that the true value will be greater than the base case. Again there is a zero probability of a true value less than $47.6 million (100 per cent chance greater than) and a zero probability of a value greater than $56.4 million (100 per cent chance less than).

Figure 13.4: hypothetical mining project—cumulative probability for revenue

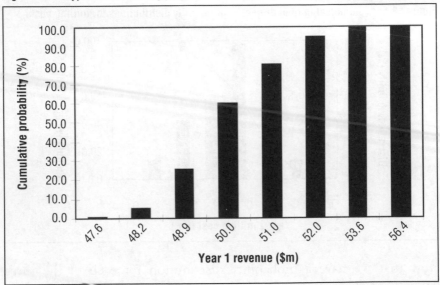

Similar discrete and cumulative probability distributions have also been determined for the mining costs and milling costs (see figures 13.5 and 13.6, overleaf). Again, due to the conservative nature of the experts, the probability of a true value less than the base case is higher than for a true value greater than the base case (the reverse of the revenue, as in the sensitivity analysis).

Figure 13.5: hypothetical mining project—probability distributions for mining costs

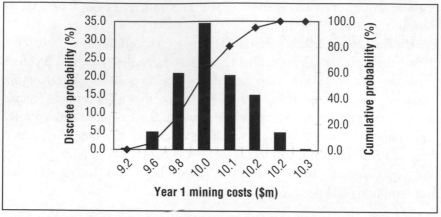

Figure 13.6: hypothetical mining project—probability distributions for milling costs

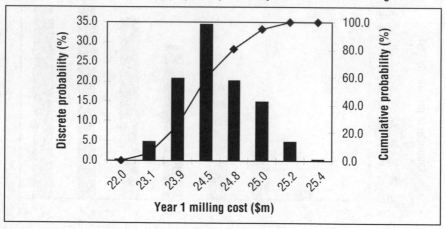

Now that we have a probability distribution for each of the three parameters that make up our financial model, the next step is to convert them into a probability distribution for the project's NPV. If the three base case parameter values were selected and applied to the financial model then, clearly, the base case NPV of $1.9 million would be derived. If another three discrete parameter values were randomly selected within each parameter's minimum and maximum range, a new NPV value could be calculated. This process could be repeated hundreds of times with a new NPV calculated each time. The NPVs can then be plotted to produce a discrete and cumulative probability of the likely outcomes (assuming that the three distributions are not correlated: that is, they are independent of each other). This process of random generation of the possible outcomes is referred to as Monte Carlo simulation.

However, just taking some random values for each parameter within its possible range of outcomes is not enough. The random values selected must mimic the probability distribution of each parameter. Take, for example, the probability distribution for revenue shown in figure 13.7. If 11 random values equally (uniformly) distributed from 0 to 100 per cent probability are selected along the right-hand scale and the corresponding revenue value determined from the x axis, then the following values would be obtained (see table 13.2).

Figure 13.7: hypothetical mining project—cumulative probability distributions for revenue

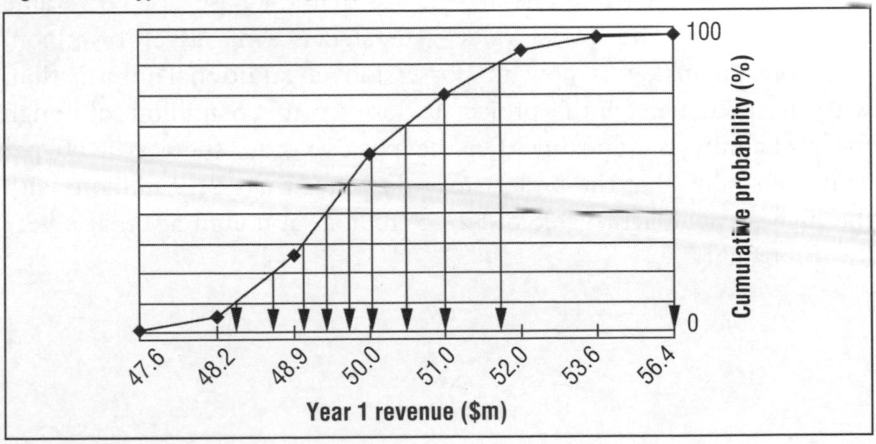

Table 13.2: probability distribution

Probability (%)	0	10	20	30	40	50	60	70	80	90	100
Value ($m)	47.6	48.4	48.7	49.0	49.3	49.6	50.0	50.5	51.0	51.7	56.4

The important point to note with regard to table 13.2 is that, although the random numbers selected are uniform (that is, the percentage intervals from 0 to 100 per cent), the values for revenue are not linear but mimic the probability distribution. That is, there are more values clustered around the base case value of $50 million, as opposed to the minimum and maximum values. If a sufficiently large number of random numbers were selected, then a revenue histogram would be generated very similar to the original one.[1]

We now have the procedure that enables us to determine the distribution of the NPV. Three uniformly distributed random numbers are generated and the three parameter values are determined from their cumulative probability distributions and an NPV is calculated. The process is repeated many times and a histogram of the NPV is generated. The results of 300 such simulations of the NPV for the example project are shown in figure 13.8.

The first observation to be made, with respect to the simulation of the example project's NPV distribution, is that there is a 40 per cent probability that the true value may be less than the base case NPV value of $1.9 million. The lowest value generated is a negative $6 million. The decision maker is now in possession of additional information, with the potential for the project to lose up to $6 million, although the probability is quite low. On the positive side, there is a 60 per cent probability that the project may do better than $1.9 million, with the highest value achievable of $24.6 million, although again at a very low probability.

---

1 To convert the random number to the parameter value, an equation of the probability distribution for that parameter is required. This is not always possible and, therefore, two approaches can be adopted. First, the cumulative probability histogram can be partitioned into a number of discrete intervals so that when a random number is generated the computer program will determine which interval the random number falls into and the corresponding parameter value. The larger the number of intervals that the distribution is partitioned into, the closer the fit to the curve. Second, many parameter distributions are similar to the normal distribution and therefore normally distributed random numbers can be used and adjusted by the distribution's mean and standard deviation. Computer programs and spreadsheets provide functions that generate uniformly distributed random numbers. Excel provides the function RAND( ), which generates a uniform random number between 0 and 1, while the ToolPak allows various distributions. To convert uniform distributed numbers to normally distributed numbers with a mean of 0 and a standard deviation of 1, the following function can be used: generate two uniform random numbers r1 and r2. Let s = r1 squared + r2 squared, then if s is equal to or greater than 1, set normal distribution number n to 0, otherwise, n = r1 × ((–2 × LN(s) ÷ (s)) to the power 0.5).

Figure 13.8: hypothetical mining project—probability distributions for simulated project NPV

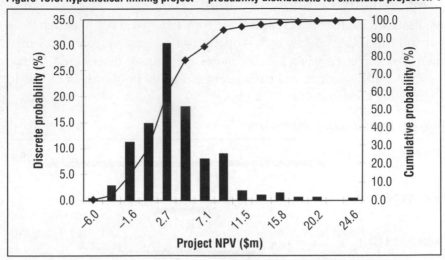

However, an investor might ask what NPV can be expected with an 80 per cent chance of success. From the analysis the answer is a negative $1 million (the NPV value is read off from the 20 per cent cumulative probability, as there is an 80 per cent chance of a greater value). This could place the investor in a difficult position, with the project unable to meet the required hurdle rate (10 per cent discount rate) at an acceptable probability of success. However, on a risk-to-reward basis the skew of the distribution to high values could still encourage the investor to proceed.

The distribution shown does exhibit some volatility at the high NPV end. This can be partially explained by the level of efficiency in generating random numbers. The larger the number of simulations the better the uniform spread of the random numbers and hence the quality of the resultant distribution.

After its initial heyday some 30 years ago, Monte Carlo simulation lost favour due to the high cost of computing power and the added difficulty of producing meaningful probability distributions for the individual project parameters. Application in the resources industry and, particularly, in oil and gas projects has increased over recent years in line with the increasing power of personal computers and the availability of commercial add-on packages. The methodology does aid in the decision-making process, avoids point estimates and provides a feel for the robustness of the project.

Does sensitivity reflect probability?

As discussed in chapter 12, experts are sometimes required to determine a fair and reasonable value, which is often described as a range within which there is a preferred value. These figures are usually determined from a sensitivity analysis of critical parameters and might be shown as a tornado chart of the previous example in figure 13.9.

Figure 13.9: expert tornado chart of NPV

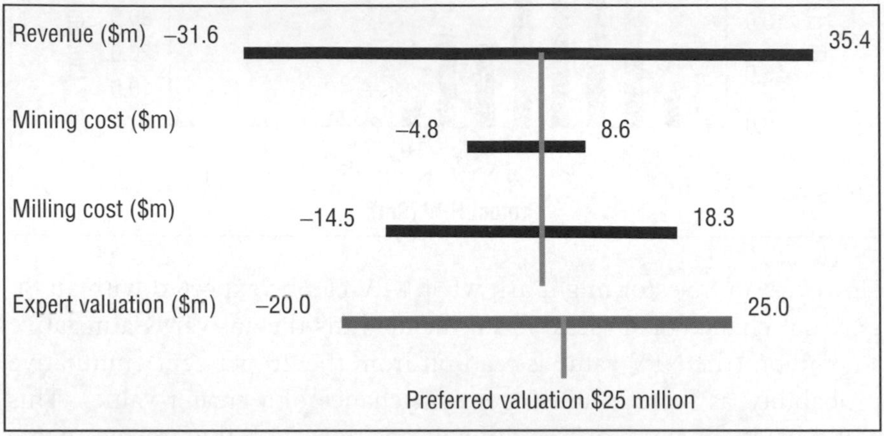

The expert has effectively amalgamated each of the possible outcomes into a preferred range of −$20 million to $25 million. Clearly, the expert feels that the tail ends of each of the sensitivities are much less likely to occur, so there is an implied non-linear distribution of the likely outcomes for each parameter—the same as we did before with probability analysis. The expert is also saying that when combining the sensitivities to get a range it is less likely that the preferred value will be towards either end and again we have an implied probability distribution, although in this case it is intuitive rather than mathematically computed.

Payback period

Another method that can provide some measure of an investment's riskiness is the payback period. This is generally defined as the time it takes to recover the original investment. For example, if a million-dollar capital investment is expected to generate an after-tax cash flow of $250 000 a year, then the payback period is four years (that is, $1 million by $250 000).

For investments in shares, the payback period can be considered the time it takes to recover the initial investment through dividends, but this ignores the capital gain or loss that might be achieved during this period. Obviously, the shorter the payback period, the better. Although this approach is simple to calculate, it doesn't take into account the time value of money as described in chapter 11.

The riskiness of an investment can be gauged by the payback period itself, and its relativity to the life of the investment or project. Take, for example, two resource projects, each with a three-year payback period. If project A has an operating life of five years and project B has a life of 15 years, all other factors being equal, project B should be less risky. As mentioned, the shorter the payback period the better, as we would like to get our investment back as quickly as possible. But things can go wrong. For example, if commodity prices prove to be lower than anticipated, project B's life gives us a better chance of recovering our investment. For project A, the two remaining operating years after the first three years may not be long enough for commodity prices to recover and return our original investment, let alone an adequate return.

CHAPTER 14
Cutoff grade theory

An important concept with regard to most mineral deposits is the cutoff grade and its impact on the economics of a project. Consider, for the moment, a block of ore that is estimated to weigh 1 tonne and contain 3 grams of gold. At a gold price of, say, US$1500 per ounce the value of the gold in the block of ore is approximately US$145. Clearly, if it cost more than US$145 to mine, treat and extract the gold from that tonne of ore, it would be uneconomic to mine. Conversely, if the cost were less than US$145, it could be economic to mine the ore.

When companies quote mining reserves, under the JORC definition, the ore has to be economically recoverable. If all the tonnes of ore in a deposit contained the same grade of gold, it would be a simple case (once the cost to recover the gold had been calculated) to determine whether the orebody was economic to mine.

The difficulty is not that all the tonnes of ore that make an orebody contain the same grade of gold. If all tonnes could be measured and a histogram plotted of the results, one might get the spread shown in figure 14.1 (overleaf). The chart shows that 30 per cent of the total tonnage has an average grade of 3 grams per tonne, 20 per cent of the tonnage has a grade of 2.5 grams per tonne, 8 per cent of the tonnage has a grade of 4 grams per tonne, and so on. Each bar represents an interval rather than a discrete point, so the 3 grams per tonne bar with a reading of 30 per cent would include tonnes of ore with grades ranging from 2.75 to 3.25 grams per tonne.

The mean (average) grade of the distribution shown in the figure is 3.2 grams per tonne, the mode (the most frequent observation) is 3 grams per tonne and the median value (that value where 50 per cent of the tonnage is above and 50 per cent below) is 2.75 grams per tonne.

Statistically, the most common distribution is the normal distribution, which is bell shaped and where the mean, mode and median are the same value. In this example, all three parameters are different due to the skewed nature of the data towards the higher grade end. This is typical of a log normal distribution that is common for mineral deposits, particularly nuggety deposits such as gold.

Figure 14.1: gold ore grades—hypothetical distribution

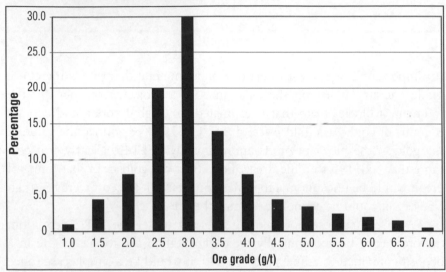

Initial estimate

Let's assume that a preliminary feasibility study provides the costs, as shown in table 14.1, for recovering gold from this deposit.

Table 14.1: hypothetical cost of gold recovery

Cost	US$/tonne of ore treated
Overburden removal	31.0
Mining cost	6.0
Treatment charge	40.0
Administration and refining	15.0
Total cost	**92.0**

Metallurgical tests also show that only 95 per cent of the gold in the ore will be recovered. The question is this: what is the minimum amount of gold the project needs in 1 tonne of ore to make it economically recoverable? Clearly, from this table there has to be enough gold recovered to provide US$92 of revenue to cover costs. The grade that provides US$92 is the cutoff grade. Assume that the gold price is US$1500 per ounce, which is equivalent to US$48.23 per gram (US$1500/31.1 grams per ounce).

Cutoff grade = total cost (tc)/recovery (rf)/price per unit of metal (pr)

= US$92/tonne/0.95/US$48.23/gram

= 2 grams per tonne

Reversing the logic, we require 2 grams per tonne of ore since we will only recover 95 per cent or 1.91 grams, for which we will be paid US$48.23 per gram or US$92 per tonne, which is equal to our total cost.

Returning to the original tonnage grade distribution (see figure 14.1) we can see (in simple terms) that approximately 14 per cent of our orebody has a grade of less than or equal to 2 grams per tonne. Obviously, in mining the orebody, we would attempt not to mine and certainly would not treat the 14 per cent of tonnage below cutoff grade. The size of our economic ore reserve for reporting purposes has been reduced to 86 per cent of our original tonnage. At the same time as reducing the tonnage above cutoff, by discarding the low-grade blocks, the remaining average grade must increase, as lower grade ore is no longer included. Table 14.2 clearly shows the impact of increasing the cutoff grade on the remaining tonnage and grade.

Table 14.2: effect of increasing the cutoff grade for gold ore

Cutoff grade (g/t)	1.0	1.5	2.0	2.5	3.0	3.5	4.0
Tonnage (%)	99.0	94.5	86.5	66.5	36.5	22.5	14.5
Average grade (g/t)	3.24	3.32	3.44	3.73	4.32	4.83	5.29

Increasing the cutoff grade reduces economic tonnage, but increases the grade. The full grade/tonnage curve is shown in figure 14.2 (overleaf).

Figure 14.2: gold ore grade/tonnage curve

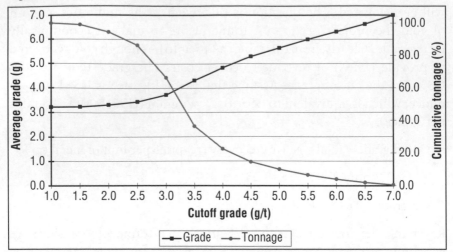

Impact on fundamental value

Let us further assume in our example that the annual treatment capacity is 10 per cent of the original total reserve. With a zero cutoff grade, the original life would be 10 years (100 per cent/10 per cent). However, as the cutoff grade increases, the mine life would decrease due to diminishing reserves, but the annual gold production would increase due to the higher grade. It is, therefore, possible to estimate the NPV for each cutoff grade, assuming the capital cost would be relatively fixed, since we know the operating cost, the mine life, the gold price and hence the revenue generated.

As table 14.3 clearly shows, the relative NPV increases initially as the cutoff grade increases. This is due to the greater benefit of a higher annual cash flow due to a higher annual average grade outweighing the shorter mine life. However, eventually the shorter mine life becomes too significant and the NPV declines. It is quite probable that the actual NPV (after taking into account the capital cost) would become negative as the mine life and the total recovered metal becomes too small.

Table 14.3: estimating NPV for each gold ore cutoff grade

Cutoff grade (g/t)	1.0	1.5	2.0	2.5	3.0	3.5	4.0
Mine life (yrs)	9.9	9.5	8.7	6.7	3.7	2.3	1.5
Relative NPV	1.0	1.04	1.07	1.08	0.9	0.7	0.6

Another point to note in table 14.3 is the slightly higher NPV, with a cutoff grade of 2.5 grams per tonne, compared with the cutoff grade of 2.0 grams per tonne. A higher project NPV may be achieved by selecting a cutoff somewhere between 2.0 grams and 2.5 grams per tonne, or perhaps slightly higher than 2.5 grams per tonne. The advent of cheap and powerful computer time has allowed the simulation of the optimum economic recovery of an ore deposit. The optimum cutoff grade with regard to maximising the project's NPV is therefore not necessarily the simple equation shown previously.

In the example, a larger NPV was achieved through a higher cutoff, as a consequence of increased annual revenue outweighing the reduced mine life. This is a function of the grade/tonnage curve for the ore reserve. KF Lane (1988) was at the forefront in developing cutoff grade theory that takes into account the optimisation of the cutoff and hence the NPV. Additionally, the cutoff grade will vary depending on whether the limiting factor for a project is the mine's capacity, the mill capacity or the market for the commodity. It is beyond the scope of this book to provide all of the relevant detail.[1] The conflicting objectives that impact on the NPV are summarised in table 14.4.

Table 14.4: impact of conflicting factors on NPV

Key parameter		Conflicting objectives
Capital cost	Increases with increasing annual production	Keep to a minimum for a given production rate
Annual mine production	Increases for economies of scale and higher revenue	Subject to available ore reserves, but must be adequate to justify the capital expenditure
Mine life	Subject to reserves and annual production	Maximise for NPV and the benefits of the community as a whole

---

1 The optimum cutoff grade for mill constrained operation (the most common case) can be determined from Lane's equation where:

cutoff grade = (tr + ΔNPV)/rf/pr

where tr equals the treatment charge and ΔNPV equals the change in the project NPV per unit, from the current year to the next.

In the above example, the original cutoff grade was estimated at 2 g/t. If the NPV was determined to be $47.5 per tonne of ore treated, based on the initial cutoff grade of 2 g/t and a discount rate of 10 per cent, then ΔNPV = $4.75 per tonne ($47.5 × 10%). The new optimum cutoff grade therefore is: (18 + 4.75)/0.95/10 = 2.39 g/t, which suggests the optimum is slightly below 2.5 g/t as derived via the grade tonnage curve previously. A new NPV can then be recalculated based on the new cutoff grade and the process repeated until the cutoff grade stabilises at the optimum level.

Life of mine

Another important factor to note is that orebodies are not homogeneous when it comes to grades. In the preceding section we have been discussing the tonnages and grades for the whole deposit without regard to how the grade might change with location and, in particular, with depth.

An example is shown in figure 14.3 of the grade tonnage curve for Hot Chili's Productora project in Chile. The company's JORC resource of 85.15 million tonnes (mt) is based on a cutoff grade of 0.3 per cent copper for an average grade of 0.57 per cent copper or a copper equivalent (CU Eq) of 0.8 per cent, if the gold (0.1 g/t) and the molybdenum (Mo) (146 g/t) are included.[2] Figure 14.4 shows the change in the tonnage and grade for indicated and inferred resources as well as the total grade with depth. The variability in mineralised zones is also shown in a typical cross-section.

Figure 14.3: Productora gold project—grade tonnage curves

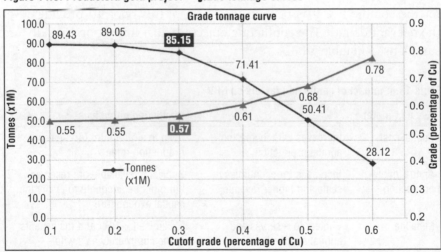

Source: Hot Chili Quarterly Report, Period End September 30, 2011, p. 4. Reproduced with permission from Hot Chili.

---

2 Based on the following prices: copper, US$1.80/lb; gold, US$850/oz; and Mo, US$15/lb.

Figure 14.4: Productora gold project—resources versus depth

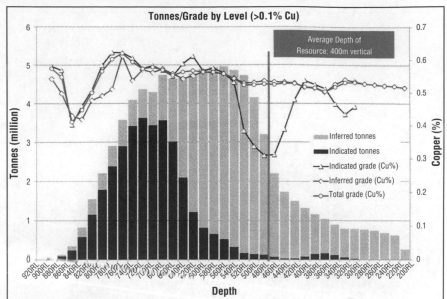

Source: Hot Chili Quarterly Report, Period End September 30, 2011, p. 4. Reproduced with permission from Hot Chili.

What is abundantly clear is that the grade and tonnage change with depth (increasing depth as the reduced level (RL) decreases) and therefore this has to be taken into account when modelling the tonnage and in particular the grade over the operating life of this mine.

Finally, figure 14.5 (overleaf) shows the variability in the mineralisation for a cross-section of the orebody. All of these factors of grade and tonnage variation with cutoff grade, and changes over depth and structural variability impact on the long-term planning of mine production.

Figure 14.5: Productora gold project—mineralisation in cross-section

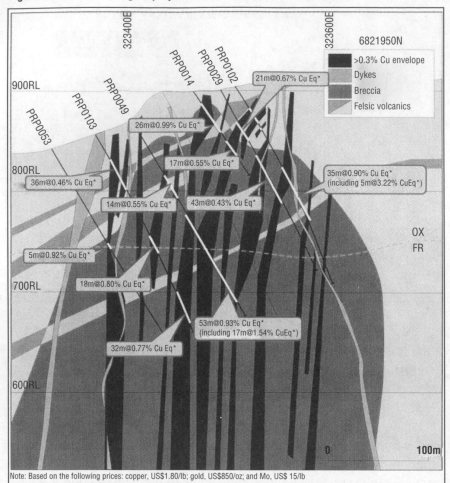

Note: Based on the following prices: copper, US$1.80/lb; gold, US$850/oz; and Mo, US$ 15/lb

Source: From p. 8 of the Hot Chili Red Copper Chilean Projects Annual General Meeting, November 2011. Reproduced with permission from Hot Chili.

CHAPTER 15

Share price performance and real options

Future movements in the share price for a resources company will be the result of the influence of many financial and operating parameters, both real and perceived. The time frame considered is important. For example, issues such as commodity prices and exploration announcements will influence price movements on a day-to-day basis. In the longer term, the change in fundamental value will dictate the overall direction of the share price. The fundamental value, in turn, will be influenced by longer term trends in commodity prices and management's ability to find and develop economic deposits.

On a macro scale the most important of these issues are evident in the following forms:

» *Earnings growth*. This is perhaps the most important single parameter that influences the future share price. If the price to earnings ratio (PE) is maintained, and the earnings increase over time, then so will the share price. Often the market will anticipate the likely earnings growth and increase the share price well in advance of the actual increase in earnings.

» *Increasing cash flow*. As well as earnings one can also consider growth in the future cash flow, which usually goes hand in hand with earnings growth. It is often argued that cash flow is the more important parameter, and from a fundamental point of view, as mentioned previously, the earnings or net profit are often a good surrogate for discretionary cash flow. Operating cash-flow growth is obviously also important in ensuring a positive outlook for the share price. Although resource companies have a good understanding of their future operating cash flows, it is sometimes surprising, given its relative importance to the marketplace, that some companies have little knowledge of their future earnings profile.

» *Exploration success.* This is the lifeblood of any resources company. Success can be achieved directly through the application of the company's funds in the ground, or indirectly through acquisition. The acquisition of exploration acreage, with known discoveries, obviously allows for a greater level of success, but at a price. The increased purchase price is obviously the premium that has to be paid to acquire the acreage, but this can still often lead to a re-rating of the company's share price, as long as the market believes that there is still further value in the prospect. The greatest reward, however, comes from the original discovery of a new mineral deposit. Any increase in the share price is not so much a reflection of the additional reserves as of management's ability to convert them into future earnings. It doesn't matter how large the discovery is, if it proves to be uneconomic, the share price will react accordingly. An active and well-managed exploration program is therefore essential. There are no easy rules that allow for predicting the likely future outcome of any program; however, a few simple observations are:

    — exploration acreage should be located in known areas of mineral occurrences; that is, at a good address

    — an exploration budget should be in keeping with the company's size and the level of cash flow generated from existing operations

    — management should have a track record of exploration success.

Value in the ground

The fundamental value of a resource stock can be defined by the NPV of the future cash flows generated by the company's mineral project(s). Consider the simple case of a company with only one known mineral resource and cash for exploration. In the early phase, after initial discovery, drilling and later infill drilling will be undertaken to define the resource. Pre-feasibility studies will be conducted, initially to determine whether the resource can be economically exploited.

Bankable feasibility studies will then be conducted with the aim of obtaining the required debt funding and, if necessary, additional equity funds will be raised to develop the project. The mine will then be constructed and, once complete, mining and processing of the mineral will commence. A typical profile of the end-of-year cash flows and the NPVs for the life of a hypothetical mine is shown in figure 15.1.

Figure 15.1: hypothetical mine—end-of-year cash flow and NPV

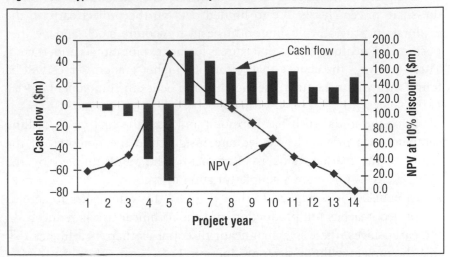

The first point to note in figure 15.1 is the initial low negative cash flow that represents the exploration expenditure, followed by engineering studies, infill drilling and feasibility studies in the second and third years. Years 4 and 5 are the construction years in which the major capital expenditure is undertaken, followed by the first year of positive cash flow in year 6. Cash flows are expected to decline after the first two years, as the grade of ore declines, and by year 14, the mine comes to an end, with some salvage value for equipment expected.

After the initial discovery in year 1, the project's NPV (with perfect forward vision) is estimated to be $26.4 million. As each year passes, the NPV increases as the negative cash flows become sunk costs and no longer play any direct part in the forward cash-flow stream, except the impact on future tax payable. The NPV peaks at $182.4 million, at the end of year 5, after all the negative yearly cash flows have been passed. The NPV then decreases over time as the future cash flows diminish in value and, more importantly, diminish in number.

The NPV profile could represent, all other things being equal, the future share price profile for the company (subject to other exploration expenditure and dividends paid as cash; reserves could also accumulate over the project life). The share price would jump on discovery to reflect the initial value of $26.4 million for the project, plus other assets, which, in this case, is the remaining cash. Over time, the share price should increase as the value of the project increases. However, the market is never that simple. The initial reaction to a discovery is often an overreaction by the share price. This is due to limited data on the project early in the exploration program plus an enthusiasm to acquire stock and be in a position for any further windfall gain as further exploration is undertaken. There is always the chance that additional higher grade reserves will be found that will further increase the NPV and hence the fundamental price of the shares.

Once the initial rush has subsided and, say, the first year's drilling campaign has provided an adequate insight into the potential of the resource, the market value is often below the value implied by the NPV. The reason is often a simple function of risk. In figure 15.2 a risk-adjustment factor is applied to the NPV, and this diminishes to zero as the project reaches full production and the technical risk is reduced. In the early stages, there is a significant discount as there is a higher risk that the project will not reach production. Even during the construction phase, when funds have been committed, there will still be some discount applied due to the risk of completion and the successful implementation of technology and mining techniques to produce a saleable commodity at an economic price.

Figure 15.2: hypothetical project risk-adjusted value

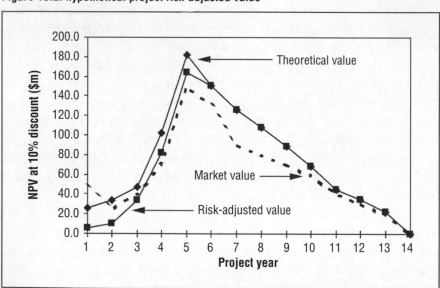

A further difficulty arises when one looks at the figure and the valuation at the end of year 5. From that point on, the value of the company will decline over the life of the project. So why would an investor pay the year 5 price for the company? If the company has other projects, continuing exploration success and a high dividend yield, these might all be mitigating factors to encourage continued investment.

The market value curve represents a possible scenario for the trajectory of the company's share price. There is an initial overreaction until the market becomes more fully informed, and then pricing falls into line with the risk-adjusted values. Once the project is in production, the share price will often fall below the theoretical NPV, unless there is further upside in the project or other company activity, as investors seek out other opportunities.

Figure 15.2 demonstrates the possible impact of a finite life on the value of a resource project and of the company. The value will decline over time once the project is in full production, unless further reserves are found or commodity prices increase significantly. It is important that resource companies have a portfolio of projects from grassroots exploration to discoveries, and new projects thus replacing the older declining operations.

Zero or one?

One approach to valuing an exploration play, particularly in the oil and gas industry, is to estimate the likely or expected value (EV). This is a 'risked' approach to value, as the possible outcomes are weighted by their likely probability of success. In some ways this is not too dissimilar to probability analysis (see chapter 13).

Consider an example where management has assessed a geological structure, which is to be tested by the drilling of an exploration well, as having recoverable reserves of 40 million barrels of oil. From the available information, management believes that this structure has a one-in-five chance of exploration success (compared with a more common industry standard of 1 in 10). However, success will be known with certainty only once the well is drilled. On an NPV basis, the value per barrel is estimated at US$5.

The value of the potential discovery to the company is, therefore, the recoverable reserve multiplied by the value per barrel multiplied by the probability of success:

Value of discovery = 40 million barrels × US$5 × 0.2 (1 in 5)

= US$40 million

Until completion of the well, the market may actually value the project at US$40 million, if it agrees with management's assessment. (More often than not, the market tends to be more conservative than management.)

Once the well is drilled, either a commercial discovery (probability of one) is made or it is not (probability of zero). A 20 per cent chance is not a possible outcome. Additionally, if a discovery is made the size of the oil field could vary from the initial estimate (which might have been the largest size possible based on the seismic interpretation). Management could also quantify a range of outcomes, as shown in table 15.1, where the value of the prospect is the product of size, probability and value per barrel.

Table 15.1: hypothetical oil project range of outcomes post discovery

Size (million barrels recoverable)%	Value per barrel (US$)	Value of prospect (US$m)	Probability of size	Expected value of prospect (US$m)
10	5	50	40	20
20	5	100	30	30
30	5	150	20	30
40	5	200	10	20
Total			100	100

The expected value, which is the sum of all of the risk-adjusted outcomes for value from table 15.1, is US$100 million. With a 20 per cent chance of a successful outcome, the probability-adjusted outcome is US$20 million (US$100 million times 20 per cent), compared with the original forecast of US$40 million. But again, the drilling will go a long way to confirming either a zero dollar value or an expected value of US$100 million or any value of up to US$200 million.

It is this wide difference in value that is often reflected in the share price performance. For example, in the first instance the share price performance might match the lower value of between zero and US$20 million, rather than management's expectation of US$40 million. Once the drilling starts the share price may rise in anticipation as a result of the demand for stock by investors who see the risk–reward ratio as attractive. If the well fails to encounter any economic hydrocarbons, the value of the well will fall back to zero. However, if the results are positive, the perceived value may initially approach US$100 million, until more detailed information becomes available as to the true size of the field.

Diversification

As well as earnings growth and exploration success, other issues, such as diversification, often arise in the debate over which resource stocks offer the best investment.

Management sometimes argues that diversification in mineral production is a means of protecting the interests of shareholders. The argument is that by producing a suite of mineral products the earnings are partially protected if one commodity price is weak, as it might be compensated by the stronger price of another commodity. However, efficient portfolio theory would suggest that investors are best positioned to decide the mixture of risk and reward of their portfolios themselves. Investors should therefore be able to decide on the mixture of the commodity exposure by investing in listed resource companies that have a direct and relatively pure exposure to a single commodity price. Diversification by a company will only provide one specific mix of exposure and increase the difficulty for investors to make efficient investment decisions.

Another important aspect arises from the implied 'option value' (which will be described in more detail) that a listed equity provides through its commodity exposure.[1] In other words, investors may be willing to pay a premium to gain exposure to the commodity price volatility provided by the company's shares. Owning shares is often an easier means of gaining commodity exposure at a lower holding cost than purchasing the commodity itself. If the commodity price is seen to be highly volatile, then the premium that might be paid will be a reflection of that volatility over

---

1 The concept of an implied option value from commodity price variation in a share price is different from the physical market for stock options. Nevertheless, there is sufficient market evidence to argue that one exists. For example, in the 1990s when the gold price was relatively volatile, gold shares traded well above their fundamental value. This premium reflected not only the exploration potential and the low barriers to entry, but also the ability to gain exposure to a commodity price that could increase significantly. In more recent times, as the volatility of the gold price has decreased, so has the premium paid for gold shares. The volatility does not mean that the share price only goes up, but rather that higher volatility is defined by the standard deviation in the price changes (both positive and negative) over a given period.

the investor's investment time frame. If a company diversifies, the premium is obviously diminished.

Diversification and hedging, as discussed in chapter 9, reduce the impact of price volatility and hence theoretical value. However, the concern for management is on the downside, when prices fall and pressure is placed on the share price. For the diversification to be truly successful, it has to be widespread over many commodities or classes of commodities. For example, commodities such as base metals move over the longer term in the same direction, primarily in line with world industrial production. The diversification, therefore, needs to be between classes of commodities such as base metals, precious metals, industrial minerals, oil and gas, coal and iron ore. There is still no guarantee that the benefits of diversification will outweigh the negatives, or that the company's share price performance won't be adversely affected by negative commodity price movements.

Options value

Throughout this book mention has been made of financial options, particularly company options listed on the stock exchange that are issued by the company. Termed call options, they give the holder the right, but not the obligation, to convert the option into ordinary shares in the company some time in the future at a pre-set exercise price. There are also exchange-traded stock options, both call options, which are similar to the company options, and futures, exchange-traded company options, which although similar to listed call options are issued by traders and not by the company. These exchanges also allow the trading of put options, where the buyer has the right, but not the obligation, to sell stock in the future at a predetermined price.

In valuing options the principal parameters to consider are:

» S ($) — the strike or exercise price to be paid to buy the share

» T (years) — the time to expiry of the option after which the right to buy the share is lost

» P ($) — the current share price or current value

» V (%) — the volatility in the share price (or more correctly in the value of the underlying asset), which is generally computed from historical data as the annualised standard deviation of returns expressed as a percentage

» *r (%)* — the prevailing risk-free interest rates,[2] preferably for the time period t.

The most common method of valuing an option is by using the Black & Scholes option model, where the call option price (OP) is defined as:

$$OP = P \times N(X) - S \exp(-rT) \times N(X - V \times \sqrt{T})$$

where:

$$X = (\ln(P/S) + (r + V \times V/2) \times T))/(V \times \sqrt{T}) \text{ and}$$

$N(X)$ = the normal distribution function, which in Excel is written as NORMSDIST (x) and ln is the natural logarithmic function written in Excel as LN(x).

The first part of the equation, $P \times N(X)$, calculates the expected benefit from purchasing the stock by multiplying the share price by the change in the call premium with respect to the change in the underlying share price. The second part of the model, S exp(–rT) multiplied by N(X – V $\sqrt{(T)}$), calculates the present value of the exercise price payment on the day of expiry and the probability that at maturity the share price is greater than the exercise price. Thus the fair market value of the call option is determined by the difference between these two parts.

The model assumes that no dividends are paid during the life of the option. If future dividend payments are expected to be paid, common practice is to subtract the present value of future dividends from the stock price.[3]

The model also assumes the options are European, which can only be exercised at the expiry date. By comparison American options allow for exercise any time during the life of the option. This increased flexibility makes them more valuable. Despite this, most options are only exercised

---

2 Binomial and Black & Scholes models use continuous discount rates so the discrete annual risk-free rate r_d has to be converted to the continuous discount rate r where $r = \ln(1 + r_d)$.

3 On the basis that the share price might fall after a dividend payment, the option holder would be negatively impacted as the value of the option would decrease. The model can therefore be modified for dividends forgone (d) as follows:

$$OP = P \times \exp(-d \times T) \times N(X) - S \exp(-r \times T) \times N(X - V \sqrt{(T)})$$
and
$$X = (\ln(P/S) + (r - d + V \times V/2) \times (T)) \div (V \times \sqrt{T})$$

towards the end of their life because early exercise could be suboptimal (in the absence of dividends), resulting in a loss of value. Towards expiry the difference in time value between an American and European call option becomes so small that the advantages gained in using the model for American options is only minor.

Other assumptions of the Black & Scholes model include that the market is efficient and that the underlying stock follows a continuous Ito process.[4] Further, it assumes that no commissions are charged on the buying or selling of options and that the risk-free rate is constant and known, although obviously it may in reality alter over the life of the option. Finally, it also assumes that the expected returns on the underlying stock are normally distributed, which generally is not unreasonable. Consider the following example:

$S = \$1.25$

$T = 4$ years to expiry

$P = \$1.00$

$V = 0.50$ (equivalent to 50%)

$r = 0.05$ (5%)

Then:

$$X = (LN(1 \div 1.25) + (0.05 + 0.5 \times 0.5 \div 2)) \div (0.5 \times SQRT(4))$$
$$= 0.4769$$

and

$$OP = 1.00 \times NORMSDIST(0.4769) - 1.25 \times EXP(-0.05 \times 4)$$
$$\times NORMSDIST(0.4769 - 0.5 \times SQRT(4)) = \$0.376$$

In other words, the options have an implied price of 38¢ based on the Black & Scholes model. It should be noted that increasing the volatility or the exercise period increases the option value.

The only value not fully described is the volatility (V) of the shares, shown as 0.50 (50 per cent). The value is calculated from the share's return based on historical prices and can be defined as the standard deviation

---

4 An Ito process in continuous time is where an observation in time depends on the preceding observation, only so that the market cannot consistently predict the direction of the market or a stock and is *continuous* if it can be 'drawn without picking up a pen from paper'.

of the log differences multiplied by the square root of the time interval. Therefore:

$$V = \sqrt{(\Sigma^{1 \text{ to } n}(u_i - u_a)^2 /(n - 1))} \div \sqrt{(\text{time interval})}$$

where:

n = the number of past price observations less 1

u_i = the log difference at time t

u_a = average of log differences.

For example, assume that you have 50 (n = 50) price observations with the first two prices being $0.98 and $1.00. The log difference for the second observation i = 1 is: LN(1.00 ÷ 0.98) = 0.0202 (there is no value for the observation $0.98 as there is no preceding value). This value is calculated in the same way for each observation and then averaged to get u_a.

The 'time interval' value depends on the frequency of price observations, so, for example, if you use monthly price data then you multiply by $\sqrt{12}$, or weekly $\sqrt{52}$ and daily $\sqrt{253}$ (assuming there are 253 trading days) to get the annual volatility. The above is basically the standard deviation of the log price differences that can be shortened in Excel by using STDEVA equation for the series of log price differences and then multiplying by the square root of the appropriate time interval.

It is possible to determine the market-implied volatility for traded options. For example, BHP Billiton June 2012 call options with an exercise price of $40 were being traded on ASX at $1.32. The time to exercise was seven months and the BHP share price at the time was $36.65. Using the above equations the market-implied volatility was 21.7 per cent.

Binomial model

The advantage of the Black & Scholes model is that it is easy to use due to some simplifying assumptions—a black box. Another approach to valuing options, which is more transparent, is the binomial model, which creates a tree of possible future share price movements by working forward from the present to option expiry, and then 'induces' the option's price. At each step it is assumed that the stock price will move up or down by an amount calculated using volatility and the length of the time step.

Consider the simple tree in figure 15.3, with only one node and two branches (the time step is equal to, say, one year). Assume that after one year there is a 50 per cent risk-neutral probability that the initial $1 share price will increase to $1.63 or a 50 per cent chance it will decrease to $0.61. Assuming the exercise price is $1.25, then the value of the option can be estimated for each of these cases—$0.38 ($1.63 less $1.25, that being the exercise price) and $0 ($0.61 less $1.25)—and then discounted back to a present value using a risk-free rate of, say, 5 per cent.[5] The resultant value is 50 per cent times $0.38 × exp(−0.05 × 1) where exp(−0.05 × 1) is continuously discounted for one year at 5 per cent (see appendix G) for equations for continuous discounting plus 50 per cent times $0, which equals $0.18.

Figure 15.3: one-year binomial tree for option valuation

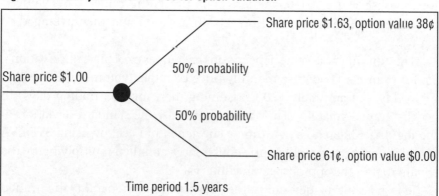

Share price $1.00

50% probability

Share price $1.63, option value 38¢

50% probability

Share price 61¢, option value $0.00

Time period 1.5 years

Therefore, if we know the probability that a share price will increase or decrease, and we have an estimate of the likely change in the share price, we can produce a binomial tree to equate all of the possible outcomes and then work back, estimating the expected discounted values for each time period.

Using the original example, where the time to option exercise was four years, and using yearly time periods (tp) for the analysis, we end up with a binomial tree as shown in figure 15.4 (see p. 350). The value by which the share value will increase (Up) is given by the equation $\exp(V \times tp^2)$ and decrease (Dp) by $1 \div \exp(V \times tp^2)$. The bold numbers in figure 15.4

5 Ideally, we should use real-world probabilities of the up and down movements and a real-world discount rate appropriate for the risk of the option, but this is computationally very difficult, so risk-free discount rates are commonly applied.

can therefore be calculated by starting at the current price of $1 and going forward one year where the price increase is:

$1 \times \exp(0.5 \times 1^2) = \$1 \times 1.65 = \$1.65$

and the price decrease is:

$1 \div \exp(0.5 \times 1^2) = \$1 \times 0.61 = \$0.61$

Moving from left to right in figure 15.4, each of the subsequent bold values is calculated in the same way as an increase or decrease of the previous period value. The probability for an increasing value (Pu) is given by the equation Pu = (exp(r × tp) – Dp) ÷ (Du – Dp), while the probability of a decreasing value (Pd) is (1 – Pu). Substituting the values are Pu = 0.43 and Pd = 0.57. The next step, starting at the right of figure 15.4 and working your way left, is to determine the greater of the expected value or option exercise value as shown at each of the bold values.

For example, the value of $6.14 below $7.39 in year 4 is estimated by subtracting the exercise price of $1.25 from $7.39 as exercising the option at that time is the only alternative and it would be attractive to do so given that the share price is considerably higher than the exercise price of $1.25. Looking at the bottom right-hand corner, the share price of 14¢ is less than the exercise price of $1.25, therefore the option would not be exercised and has $0 value. The value determined in year 3 below $4.48 is the expected value of the two previous values that is $6.14 × 0.43 + $1.47 × 0.57 = $3.48, which is then discounted one year $3.48 × exp(–.05) = $3.29. The $3.29 has to be compared with the alternative of exercising the option ($4.48 – $1.25 = $3.23) and, as it is greater, the option would not be exercised, so the value remains at $3.48. If it is more valuable to exercise the option than the expected value, then the exercise value of the option is used.

The procedure is repeated moving back to the left in figure 15.4 (overleaf) until the final valuation of 38.1¢ is derived for the current period, which compares favourably with the Black & Scholes value of 37.6¢. The greater the number of time periods in the binomial tree, the closer the value derived from the binomial method will converge to the Black & Scholes value.

Figure 15.4: four-year binomial tree for option valuation

Current	Year 1	Year 2	Year 3	Year 4
				$7.39
				$6.14
			$4.48	
			$3.29	
		$2.72		**$2.72**
		$1.66		$1.47
	$1.65		**$1.65**	
	$0.81		$0.60	
$1.00		**$1.00**		**$1.00**
$0.38		$0.24		$0.00
	$0.61		**$0.61**	
	$0.10		$0.00	
		$0.37		**$0.37**
		$0.00		$0.00
			$0.22	
			$0.00	
				$0.14
				$0.00

Monte Carlo model

Since, by using a the binomial tree, we are dealing with a potentially large number of possible outcomes with associated probabilities, a Monte Carlo approach can be employed to value an option by computer-modelling possible share price movements from the present until option expiry. The following equation is used to simulate the price movement:

$$P_t = P_{t-1} + P_{t-1} \times (r \times tp + Rand^6 \times V \times tp)$$

where Rand is a random number from a normal distribution with a mean of zero and a variance of 1.

---

6 Obtained from Excel by NormalValue (0,1)

Using the same assumptions as our previous Black & Scholes example and a one-year time period (tp):

$$P_t = P_{t-1} + P_{t-1} \times (.05 + \text{Rand} \times .5)$$

The price is determined from P_0 ($1) to P_4; if P_4 is less than $1.25 the option is valued at $0 and if P_4 is greater than $1.25 it is valued at the difference between the two.

A total of 15 000 price path simulations were generated to determine the theoretical share price for each simulation at the time of exercise, after which the value of each simulation was discounted to a present value using the risk-free rate. The expected value was then determined from the probability distribution of outcomes with an average of 38.5¢, which is close to the Black & Scholes value of 37.6¢. Again, as per the binomial method, as the number of time intervals (tp) increases, the Monte Carlo valuation converges towards the Black & Scholes valuation.

Figure 15.5 plots a histogram of the results from 15 000 simulations (note the y axis is a logarithmic scale), with nearly two-thirds of the simulations resulting in a zero valuation for the option and nearly another third less than $2. Two simulations were in excess of $13.

Figure 15.5: Monte Carlo simulation of option values

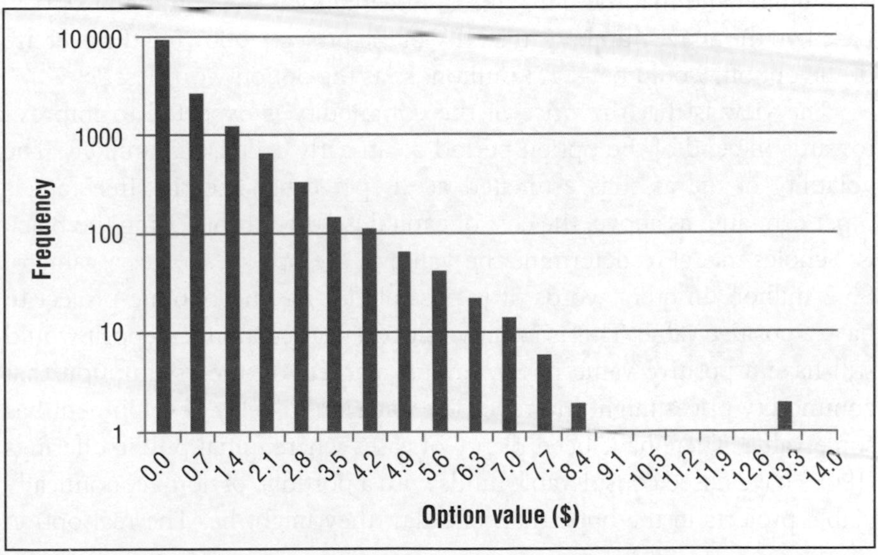

Real options[7]

In the previous analysis it was shown that the Black & Scholes, binomial and Monte Carlo methods could be used to determine the value of financial options. The key word is financial, as each method relies on the Black & Scholes assumption that the price of a share can never be negative and has a tendency to exhibit a lognormal distribution of outcomes. That is, prices will tend to increase over time. The other critical feature is the ability to make a decision in the future subject to the economic condition at the time, which can be quantified as a present-day value.

In real option analysis, we want to use financial option methods to quantify the value of having the opportunity to make a future decision with respect to a resource project or a real asset, which may not necessarily have the same characteristics as a financial asset. In some instances we may be able to see a project as the equivalent to a financial instrument, but, more often than not, a resource project will possess different attributes, such as a negative return, which will require a more detailed analysis using the commonly applied binomial model.

In the first instance, consider a mining project where the owner is offering an option to purchase the property within the next three years for a payment of $35 million, which discounted to today's value at 10 per cent is $26.3 million. Analysis of the project shows that it has an NPV today of $25 million and that the only area of uncertainty is the commodity price. Based on the above numbers, the NPV of the project, following the exercise of the option, would be −$1.3 million, so is the option worthless?

The view is that the price of the commodity is expected to improve towards the end of the option period so an early exercise is unlikely. The volatility of the asset is estimated at 40 per cent. The risk-free rate is 5 per cent and, as above, the cost of capital is 10 per cent. Using the Black & Scholes model to determine the value of the option, we get a value of $5.2 million. In other words, it is possible for an uneconomic project to have a positive value. This is intuitive since a near-economic deposit would still have a positive value in the capital markets on the assumption that commodity prices might improve. The decision to delay development has some value. There have been plenty of cases where initial public offerings (IPOs) have raised considerable funds with a portfolio of non-economically viable projects in the hope that, one day, they might be. The real option

---

7 For more detail see Kodukula (2006).

value is thus $6.5 million, the difference between the base case value of –$1.3 million and the Black & Scholes value of $5.2 million.

In the previous example, the volatility of the asset was estimated at 40 per cent without any explanation. To simplify matters it was assumed that the only area of uncertainty was the commodity price; therefore an obvious method of determining the volatility of the project in this case would be to estimate the volatility of the commodity price. However, real projects are more complex than this. So how might one go about estimating the volatility of a real project?

Perhaps the best way, once a project's future cash flow has been determined, is to run a Monte Carlo analysis of the possible cash-flow outcomes incorporating all of the parameters that would contribute to project volatility. For each simulation the volatility can be calculated in the same way as described previously for share price volatility. The average of the simulated volatilities can then be taken as the expected value of the likely project volatility. There are some limitations to this methodology such as negative cash flows where the log differences can't be calculated. Alternatively, you could use similar projects or securities to provide a proxy for your own project, or interrogate management to determine their opinion of likely changes in the project's outcomes.

In another example, the NPV of a large, long-life undeveloped magnetite mine was found to be marginal at $18 million for an investment of $250 million, which was available to the company. Even though this return was a low value, it did meet the company's cost of capital and there was strong shareholder interest in a commitment to commence mining. A Monte Carlo simulation of the yearly cash flows resulting from changes in the expected iron ore price, and possible annual variations in the average iron ore grade mined, generated an average volatility in NPV of a surprisingly high 35 per cent. Management was concerned about the possible near-term cyclical weakness in the iron ore price, which in particular could impact on the first five years of production, just after completion of mine construction. Management also determined that if the mine was abandoned it should be possible to salvage some $60 million from existing mine plant and equipment, which would subsequently decline in value at a rate of 10 per cent per year.

The binomial valuation was therefore undertaken, as shown in figure 15.6 (overleaf). Rather than comparing the exercise price with the yearly value (bold), the comparator becomes the plant salvage value for each year. The salvage value is used when it is greater than the NPV value. For example, in year 5 the salvage value is $60 million $\times 0.9^5 = \$35.43$ million. In the bottom right-hand corner of figure 15.6, the NPV of $3.13 million is less than the salvage value, so the mine would be closed and the salvage value obtained.

Figure 15.6: five-year binomial tree for mine abandonment ($m)

Current	Year 1	Year 2	Year 3	Year 4	Year 5
					$103.58
					$103.58
				$72.99	
				$72.99	
			$51.44		$51.44
			$53.81		$51.44
		$36.25		$36.25	
		$48.60		$41.09	
	$25.54		$25.54		$25.54
	$54.00		$43.74		$35.43
$18.00		$18.00		$18.00	
$51.37		$48.60		$39.37	
	$12.68		$12.68		$12.68
	$54.00		$43.74		$35.43
		$8.94		$8.94	
		$48.60		$39.37	
			$6.30		$6.30
			$43.74		$35.43
				$4.44	
				$39.37	
					$3.13
					$35.43

The real option value to abandon the operation and salvage plant and equipment is therefore $33.4 million calculated as the difference between the NPV of $18 million and the option value of $51.4 million.

Decision trees

The binomial model is very similar to a decision tree, in which management can map out a number of points in the future where a decision may have to be made, and determine the outcome of making that decision and its probability of success. Consider the following simplified example.

Example

A mineral discovery has been made from an initial drilling program that has defined a deposit as uneconomic due to inadequate tonnage. Analysis of existing data suggests that the deposit may extend along strike and that sufficient tonnage might be defined from a $1.5 million drilling program. If this drilling is successful, a $3 million infill drilling program would then be undertaken to confirm the grade and continuity of the deposit. If this were to prove successful, a trial pit would be dug to provide bulk samples for metallurgical testing, and a bankable feasibility study would be completed for $5 million. Bank debt plus additional equity funding would then be raised to construct the mine that is estimated to have an NPV at that time of $50 million.

There is a one-year time period between each decision and one year to complete the bank funding and commence project development. The decision tree is shown in figure 15.7 (overleaf). At each node (decision point) there is a possibility that the expenditure will be unsuccessful and the venture will have no value (in reality the project would still have some value as discussed in the previous example, but for simplicity let's assume no value). The probabilities of success or failure are also estimated at each decision point.

Working backwards (as in a binomial model) from the $50 million, discounting at 10 per cent per year (the cost of capital) and applying the probabilities of success, then:

At node d we get a value of:
$50 m $\div$ (1 + 0.1) $\times$ 0.9 + $0 $\times$ 0.1 − $2 m = $38.9 m

At node c:
$38.9 $\div$ (1 + 0.1) $\times$ 0.7 + $0 $\times$ 0.3 − $5 m = $19.8 m

At node b:
$19.8 $\div$ (1 + 0.1) $\times$ 0.5 + $0 $\times$ 0.5 − $3 m = $6 m

At node a:
$6.0 $\div$ (1 + 0.1) $\times$ 0.8 + $0 $\times$ 0.2 − $1.5 m = $2.9 m

So although the project may be too small to be economic and may therefore have a zero NPV value, the more flexible approach of real options, or in this case a decision tree, where management has the ability to make alternative decisions, provides a value of $2.9 million. Note that this value doesn't explicitly incorporate any commodity price volatility; implicitly price would probably impact on the decision making of management and on the results of the feasibility study. Again, Monte Carlo analysis can be employed to further enhance the methodology. The advantage of the decision tree is its greater flexibility in real-life situations when it is possible to map out alternatives. This can sometimes be a limiting factor in the ability to design an appropriate decision tree, but it is not constrained by the economic constraints of classical financial option analysis.

Figure 15.7: decision tree

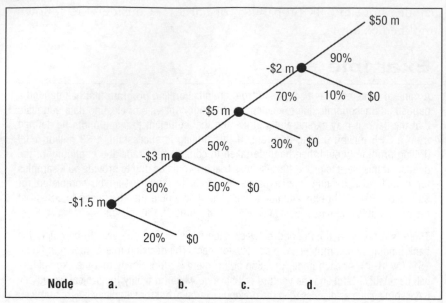

The value-add for real options is therefore greatest where a project is marginal and the volatility is high. If the project economics are robust, then it is likely that the project will go ahead and any real option value will be deemed as relatively unimportant. If the project is marginal, then economic decisions will be critical and perhaps difficult, so any additional value that might be determined could greatly enhance decision making.

The use of real options is still at a relatively early stage, but this type of analysis has been employed in practice to value alternatives, in preference to a purely deterministic approach, although its more widespread adoption in the industry is yet to be seen. The real option value concept shows that new discoveries can add value long before a full evaluation has been completed. The opportunity for management to make alternative decisions can also have an implied value. In the next chapter a number of examples will show how discoveries and decisions to expand existing operations can have a positive value, as long as the decisions are the correct ones.

CHAPTER 16

Impact of exploration, development and expansion

The listed resources sector provides investors with a unique opportunity to participate in exploration successes and a significant increase in the value of their shares that can be achieved over a relatively short time frame. The value of a company can increase many times overnight, if the initial drilling results indicate the potential for a major find. However, it takes time — with further drilling, feasibility studies and capital funding — before the discovery can be brought into production and the true value of the deposit realised.

The risk (after the initial scramble by investors wanting to get set in the stock for the ride-up in value) is that the share price may fall as the true value of the exploration success becomes more apparent. The two factors most commonly clarified in the early part of the exploration program are the tonnage, or volume, and the grade, or quality, of the deposit.

Once a discovery is confirmed as having reasonable potential for development, there is a lengthy period of evaluation, design, funding and construction before a project can be brought into production. This chapter discusses five examples that highlight the issues to consider when determining a project's value, and hence the movement in the share price as the market comes to grips with exploration results — and the risks of getting it wrong.

Just as exploration success can result in a positive revaluation of a listed resource company, so can significant expansion of an existing project with the likelihood of increased future earnings. It is not uncommon for companies to expand their operations when further exploration defines additional reserves that can justify the higher production rates.

Although additional capital will generally be required to allow for the expansion, the increased throughput should provide for additional cash flow to more than justify the expansion. The risk that a company and its shareholders face is in the translation of those additional reserves into a finished saleable product at an economic cost, which is highlighted in the examples on Cultus Petroleum and Selwyn Mines.

Valuing an initial discovery

The first case involves the discovery of the Ernest Henry copper/gold deposit in Queensland, which was announced on 12 December 1991. In April 1992, a drilling program commenced to test the size of the deposit. Exploration holes were drilled on an 80- by 160-metre grid. By June of that year, a total of 16 diamond core holes had been completed, and an ASX release stated that a zone of copper/gold primary mineralisation, about 200 metres wide, 150 metres thick and 600 metres in length (strike) to a maximum vertical depth of 400 metres, had been defined. Further, the release stated that the mineralisation lay some 40 metres below younger sedimentary rock, that a secondary copper mineralisation averaging 35 metres was above the primary mineralisation, and that typical drill intersections averaged 1.6 per cent copper and 0.8 g/t gold. Geophysical data also suggested that the primary mineralisation might extend a further 400 metres along the strike.

Some additional assay results were released on several drill holes, which are summarised in graphical form in figure 16.1. Further, it was stated that the average specific gravity (SG) of the primary zone was estimated at 3.28 and that good metallurgical recoveries were achievable.

The question facing analysts (such as the author) who at the time were covering the companies that had interests in the discovery (this was further complicated by litigation over who was the actual owner of the lease) was this: what was the value of this discovery?

The first step was to use the available data to value the estimated resource. The section shown in figure 16.1 was only a simple interpretation (as time would prove) of a much more complex geological structure. An overall resource could be estimated as follows:

Primary zone = 1000 m × 150 m × 200 m × 3.28 SG
= 98.4 million tonnes at 1.6 per cent copper and 0.8 g/t gold

Secondary zone = 400 m × 35 m × 200 m × 2 SG
= 5.6 million tonnes at 2.3 per cent copper and 0.8 g/t gold

Figure 16.1: Ernest Henry long section

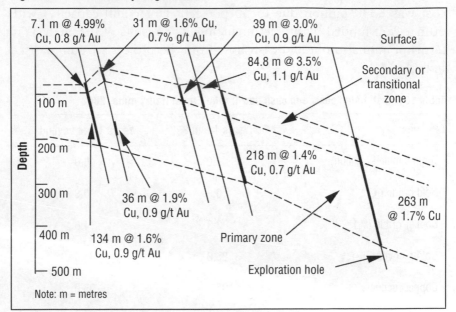

A lower SG was applied to the secondary zone due to the effects of oxidation. Given that the orebody was trending deeper, the secondary zone was expected not to extend for the same length of the orebody, so it was calculated for only 400 metres.

Having estimated the possible resource, the next step was to place a value on its economic recovery. First, an estimate of the likely mining rates was made based on the total resource. It was decided by the author that the secondary resource would be mined initially at 3 million tonnes per annum over two years and then the primary resource at 6 million tonnes per annum to give a maximum operating mine life of 19 years. However, no cutoff grade was applied so that the likely mine life would be less, and the average mined grade higher than the average grade indicated by the ASX release.

For modelling purposes only 12 years were used. Average annual production was estimated to be 120 000 ounces of gold and 87 000 tonnes of copper. At the time, further assumptions were made on the likely recoveries based on industry standards, the then current metal price and exchange rates, smelter charges (TC/RC), operating costs (including average overburden rates), freight rates and government royalties. The capital cost was estimated at some $230 million (actual cost was $330 million due to 50 per cent larger mill capacity) with 60 per cent funded by project financing. The results of the analysis in terms of annual profit and cash flow from the project are summarised in table 16.1.

Table 16.1: estimated costs and cash flow for the Ernest Henry mine, 2002

Per year	Years 1 and 2	Years 3 and beyond
Tonnes milled (million)	3.0	6.0
Gold grade (g/t)	0.8	0.8
Copper grade (%)	2.3	1.6
Gold recovery (%)	85.0	85.0
Copper recovery (%)	95.0	95.0
Gold production (000s oz)	65.8	131.6
Copper production ('000s t)	65.6	91.2
US$:A$ exchange rate	0.72	0.72
Gold price (US$/oz)	425.0	425.0
Copper price (US¢/lb)	84.9	103.6
Gross revenue ($m)	209.3	367.0
TC/RC charges ($m)	50.2	69.8
Marketing/freight ($m)	3.3	4.6
Cost per tonne treated ($)	41.9	34.6
Net revenue ($m)	155.9	292.6
Operating costs ($m)	63.9	120.0
Transport cost ($m)	5.2	7.3

Per year	Years 1 and 2	Years 3 and beyond
Depreciation ($m)	10.5	21.0
Royalties ($m)	3.1	5.9
Interest cost ($m)	10.0	10.0
Taxable income ($m)	63.1	128.4
Tax at 33% ($m)	20.8	42.4
Net profit ($m)	42.8	86.1
Cash flow ($m)	52.8	107.1

From this analysis it was possible to estimate the potential impact on the company's earnings, and then by applying the appropriate earnings multiple the theoretical share price movement. The cash flows were also used to estimate the NPV for the project of around $350 million.

An additional difficulty for valuation was a legal dispute over ownership of the resource, which Savage Resources ultimately won. The movement in the share price when Savage won the court action resulted in an increase in the company's market capitalisation of some $175 million, which was in line with the previous NPV adjusted for the then existing development risk. The reserves/resources for Ernest Henry (from December 2002) are shown in table 16.2.

Table 16.2: reserves and resources of the Ernest Henry mine, December 2002

Category	Cutoff grade (% Cu)	Tonnes (million)	Copper (%)	Gold (g/t)
Open cut resource	0.27	121.0	0.93	0.46
Open cut reserve	0.30	88.7	1.03	0.51
Underground resource	2.00	5.0	1.70	0.85

Following the takeover of MIM by Xstrata (a joint venturer in the mine) the forecast operating statistics in table 16.3 (overleaf) became available in 2003.

Table 16.3: forecast operating statistics for the Ernest Henry mine, 2003

Category	Year to June 2004	Life of mine
Tonnes treated (mt)	10.4	124.5
Copper grade (%)	0.95	0.93
Gold grade (g/t)	0.52	0.47
Copper recovery (%)	89.3	89.2
Gold recovery (%)	69.1	68.9
Copper concentrate grade (%)	28.0	27.9
Concentrate production (000 t)	316.0	3698.0
Payable copper (000 t)	85.4	997.0
Payable gold (000 oz)	114.5	1239.0
Operating costs ($m)		
Mining (inc. mine tech services)	92.4	973.0
Concentrating	39.0	444.0
Treatment and refining charges	59.6	680.0
Transport and handling	29.6	255.0
Site overheads (admin. and infrastructure)	27.1	329.0
Environmental	4.5	15.0
Total	247.5	**2656.0**
Per tonne treated ($)	24.18	21.66
Sustaining capital (mine, mill, etc.)	9.2	54.3
Capital, rehabilitation and closure ($m)		29.0

Source: MIM information memorandum, May 2003.

The treatment cost per tonne of ore milled to June 2004 forecast by the independent expert's report, in MIM's defence against the takeover bid by Xstrata, was $24.18. This compares with my original forecast in 1991 of $34.60. The difference can be attributed primarily to the economies of scale of a 10.4 million tonne per year plant compared with the original forecast of 6 million tonnes per year. In December 2009 Xstrata approved the conversion of the mine from open cut to underground for an investment of $589 million. Production is now by way of a decline at 3 mtpa producing 25 000 tonnes of copper and 35 000 ounces of gold. With the commissioning of a shaft in 2013, production is expected to increase to 6 mtpa until at least 2024.

High grade is best

In September 1997 Jubilee Gold Mines announced that an initial exploration hole at the West Australian Cosmos prospect had intersected massive sulphides, over 9.15 metres at a depth of 125 metres, with significant nickel grades. This first hole included 3.02 metres with 7.54 per cent nickel, 1.2 metres with 12.1 per cent nickel, and 1.2 metres with 10.5 per cent nickel. The share price increased significantly, as you can see in figure 16.2.

Figure 16.2: share price, July–December 2007

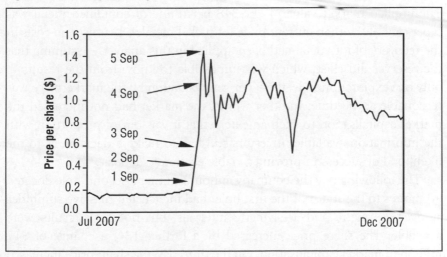

On the first day after the release of the drilling result, the share price jumped by 14.5¢ (an increase of 130 per cent) and the company's market capitalisation increased by $14 million. The only other information generally known to the market at the time was that the mineralisation surfaced as a gossan, with the sulphides starting 50 metres below the surface and dipping at 75 degrees. The mineralisation also occurred within a strong 400-metre-long coincident geochemical and electromagnetic anomaly.

The risk associated with valuing a deposit on the results of only one exploration hole is obviously very high. Nevertheless, the market placed an initial value on it of $14 million. The obvious question at the time was whether this value was at all consistent with the information available. Similar discoveries had previously been made in the area and they were, more often than not, small in tonnage but high in grade. Making some basic assumptions at the time, such as the true width of the orebody at, say, 2 5 metres and a specific gravity of 3, then the following could have been assumed:

Estimated in situ tonnage = 2.5 m × 100 m × 350 m × 3 SG = 262 500 tonnes

Estimated in situ metal content = 262 500 × 7.5% = 19 688 tonnes of nickel

Implied market value = $14 million/19 688 = $711 or US$348 per tonne of metal

The implied market value of US$348 per tonne of contained metal was 5 per cent of the then current price for nickel metal. Obviously no costs in the recovery of the metal had been applied in this analysis. Assuming that the reserves did exist, which was impossible to know from the results of only one exploration hole, the 5 per cent valuation by the marketplace was reasonable at the time. In other words, the market had not increased the market capitalisation to such an extent that it was out of proportion with the information available. Investors still had to make a decision as to the likelihood of success in proving a viable economic deposit.

The following day the company announced that a second hole, located 40 metres to the south of the first hole, had intersected massive sulphides at over 2.4-metre and 19.1-metre intervals, but no assay results were available. The share price increased by a further 18¢, a change of $17 million in market capitalisation. On the third day, the share price increased by a further 16¢ as the story became more widely known to the market.

On the fourth day after the discovery, the company announced that the grades of the second hole were 3 metres with 8.85 per cent nickel, 22.3 metres with 9.29 per cent nickel, and 18.1 metres with 10.67 per cent nickel. On the back of these very high nickel grades the share price increased by a further 59¢. The following (fifth) day the share price increased a further 14¢. Over a five-day period, based on the results of two exploration holes, the share price had increased a staggering seven and a half times, from 19¢ to $1.44! (This is what makes the resources sector so exciting and rewarding, as long as one is aware of the risks.) The market capitalisation had increased by $119 million, or the equivalent of US$4230 per tonne of contained metal or 64 per cent of the then current metal price.

A reality check at the time would have suggested that this was too high a price to pay for metal in the ground. Industry costs would suggest that the cash operating margin for nickel production from sulphide ores was in the order of less than 20 per cent of the then metal price, let alone the need for capital costs to develop the project. Of course, there was always the potential for a larger ultimate resource—this then becomes the trade-off between the risk of additional resources and reward of a higher share price, which at the time did not seem justified.

The next business day, the company announced that the third exploration hole had intersected no massive sulphides as a dolerite dyke had cut off the mineralisation to the south. The share price fell by 40¢ as the potential ore reserves could now be lower. Ten days later the company announced the results of its fourth and fifth exploration holes. The best intersections were 2.65 metres with 5.88 per cent nickel and 2.1 metres with 1.81 per cent nickel. The lower grades and thickness resulted in a further fall in the share price.

However, continued drilling resulted in an ore resource open in depth to the north that could potentially be 500 000 tonnes at 9.5 per cent nickel, larger and richer than the previous estimate. The share price had reached a steady level that placed a value of around US$850 per contained tonne of nickel or approximately 14 per cent of the current nickel price. Given that the exploration risk had been greatly reduced and there was always potential for further discoveries this valuation seemed reasonable.

Cosmos was ultimately to prove to be a success story, with mining operations starting in late 1999, initially by open cut and from mid 2003 by underground development. Ore is processed at 150 000 tonnes per year to produce about 10 000 tonnes of nickel in concentrate. The project was initially developed for a modest $38 million and had a forecast life of mine cash operating cost of US57¢ per pound of nickel and a total cost after treating and refining of US$1.35 per pound. This made Cosmos towards the turn of the twentieth century one of the world's lowest-cost producers thanks to its high-grade ore. Jubilee Mines was ultimately taken over by Xstrata in April 2008 for a price of $23 per share!

Development time frame

On 6 June 2006 Cudeco Limited (CDU) announced the discovery of high-grade copper zones at its Rocklands project in Queensland. On 15 June, CDU announced three copper zones with a combined strike length of 2075 metres, widths of 40 to 200 metres and depths of 90 metres, but no drill-hole locations. The company's share price increased from $0.49 to $0.75. On 29 June, the company announced inferred resource of 59 million tonnes at 2.04 per cent of copper and by 6 July the share price had increased to $7.11 for a market capitalisation of US$600 million. Cudeco's share trading was suspended from 6 July to 17 July as the exchange sought an independent geologist report on whether Cudeco's announcement was JORC-compliant. On 17 July the company announced a revised inferred resource figure of 25 million tonnes at 1.57 per cent of copper and a target of 34 million tonnes. Cudeco's share price fell to $3.56.

As at 6 June there was no indication of tonnage, but the weighted average grade from the drilling was 1.86 per cent copper. On 15 June the weighted average of all drilling was 1.7 per cent and if one assumed an orebody with a 2000-metre strike length, a width of 120 metres and a depth of 90 metres, then that would equate to a volume of 21.6 million cubic metres. Assuming a specific gravity of 2.5 that would have suggested an orebody of possibly 54 million tonnes and, at a copper price at the time of US$3.2 per pound, an in situ value of US$6.5 billion. However, assuming a long-term copper price of US$2 per pound, operation costs of US$0.5 to US$1 per pound, a three-year construction period, 10-year operating life, 30 per cent tax, and 20 per cent discount rate, the NPV of the deposit would have been US$550 million to US$825 million.

So the market valuation before the suspension of trading was in line with realistic assumptions based on the then available information. Indeed, if you had done the calculation as at 15 June, when the market capitalisation was US$64 million, it would have been a reasonable decision to buy the shares and benefit from the re-rating of the stock prior to its suspension.

Over the last five years Cudeco's share price has been volatile, but has continued to trade around $3.50 (see figure 16.3). Large amounts of capital have been raised over this period to fund exploration, so the market capitalisation has increased to more than US$650 million. The JORC resource estimates as at May 2011 were:

» measured and indicated resource — 30.3 million tonnes (mt) @1.70 per cent copper equivalent (0.8 per cent Cu, Co, Au cutoff)[1]

» measured, indicated and inferred — 272.9 mt @ 0.62 per cent copper equivalent (0.2 per cent Cu, Co, Au cutoff).

Figure 16.3: Cudeco Limited share price, January 2006–November 2011

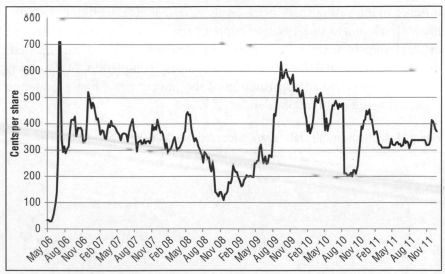

So why hasn't the share price performed? First, it should be noted that, although resources have increased significantly over the years, albeit at a relatively low cutoff grade, the measured and indicated resources, at what would appear an economic cutoff, have not increased significantly in tonnage and grade since 2006. Obviously, with all the drilling that has occurred, certainty over the resource has improved markedly.

---

1 A cutoff grade of 0.8 per cent Cu equivalent was applied where each of the commodities were converted into equivalent copper grades using the following price assumptions: Cu US$2/lb with 95 per cent recovery, Co US$25/lb with 90 per cent recovery, Au US$900/oz with 75 per cent recovery.

Second, while the exploration potential remains significant and discoveries continue to be made, to date the only information about development is the company's plans for a 10-year, 3 mtpa open cut operation, which is subject to completion of a definitive feasibility study, the company receiving a mining licence and securing funding for the $200 million capital cost. If all of these hurdles are cleared, then first production could commence in 2013. So the development risks still remain and until these are removed a re-rating of the share price is likely to remain impeded.

When the development hurdles mentioned previously are cleared, and mining projects move into the development stage, further share price appreciation can be expected. Figure 16.4 shows the share price of Discovery Minerals (DML) adjusted for changes in the copper price since it first announced an inferred copper resource in 2006. Over that time a number of increasing share price levels were met, as uncertainty over the likely development of its Boseto copper project was reduced. By the end of 2011 the share price had more than doubled to $1.30 (unadjusted) due to the potential for increased resources, completion of financing and commencement of construction of the project, with first production expected in the first half of calendar 2012.

Figure 16.4: Discovery Minerals' share price, January 2006–November 2011

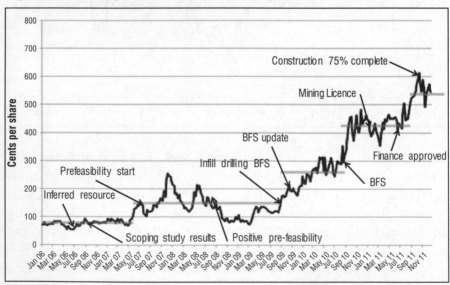

Disappearing resource

This case study concerns Cultus Petroleum, an oil and gas company that announced an offshore West Australian oil discovery called Cornea in 1997. Within seven months the company's share price tripled. Subsequently, over a two-month period, the share price halved (and later it fell further, until the company was taken over by OMV in 1999) as it became more apparent that the volume of oil and prospectivity was potentially a lot less. The share price performance is shown in figure 16.5 (on p. 371), with the approximate announcement dates of critical information annotated.

1 After drilling two exploration wells on the Cornea prospect, the company announced that formation pressure tests had been made and that one sample of oil and two samples of water were recovered. The company stated that it believed the information to date 'was positive with respect to an oil/gas discovery; however, it had drawn no conclusions as to the extent of the accumulation'. (Note: with the $1 increase in price over the next few days, the market had inferred a possible recoverable reserve of 150 million barrels, based on the increase in the market capitalisation of the company, its percentage interest in the project and a $5 NPV per barrel of oil. In hindsight, this was to infer a significant reserve given the relatively limited information available.)

2 The testing of a side-track well provided inconclusive results.

3 The three-well program to date had proven a gross oil column of a minimum 20 metres to a maximum of 50 metres with oil samples of 28° American Petroleum Institute (API) gravity. (Note: to translate the gross oil column to reserves would have required additional data on such factors as net oil column, area of closure and porosity, as detailed in chapter 6, which was not generally available to the public. The API was also low by regional standards.)

4 A small onshore oil discovery was announced.

5 The company's financial results were released.

6 Another onshore exploration well proved uneconomic.

7 Another small onshore gas discovery was announced.

8 Further detail provided about the offshore Cornea gas and oil discovery indicated a 26-metre gas cap and a 22- to 55-metre oil column with a total of 40 litres of oil recovered at 28° API.

9 The company announced a placement of stock to raise funds to investigate the offshore discovery. Comments by representatives of the company suggested potential recoverable reserves of 180–800 million barrels of oil. The major unknown issues were the likely recovery factor and the size of the field. No production tests had been undertaken to maintain confidentiality, while Cultus and its partner bid for two next-door exploration permits. The joint venturers were successful in their bid for the additional permits with planned expenditure of $180 million on exploration over a three-year period including 46 wells and 1600 kilometres squared of 3D seismic.[2]

10 After a request from the ASX the company announced that some of the reservoir sands could have recoveries of 15 per cent to 20 per cent, while the best sands would have up to 40 per cent. The operator of the permit had previously indicated a range of 5 to 35 per cent.

11 A separate smaller offshore oil discovery was announced.

12 The first results of the next step-out well (5 kilometres to the south) on the original offshore discovery were released, indicating that the hydrocarbons were recovered over the target intervals, but the quality of the hydrocarbons and sandstones was variable. (Note: the step-out is a critical test of the size and continuity of the oil-bearing structure; however, the initial release was not very encouraging and the share price started its decline.)

13 Drilling was completed and electric logs were run, but no further information was provided.

14 Initial results of a second step-out well were released. Only 5.3 litres of oil were recovered; however, a production test was to be undertaken.

15 A drill stem test of the step-out well produced 7.2 barrels of 15° API oil and 8500 cubic metres of gas per day. (Note: this result was very discouraging and thus greatly reduced the viability of the original discovery.)

2 Ultimately, after drilling five wells to demonstrate the lack of commercial structures in the permits, the joint venturers asked to be released from further obligations.

Figure 16.5: Cultus Petroleum share price, January–October 1997

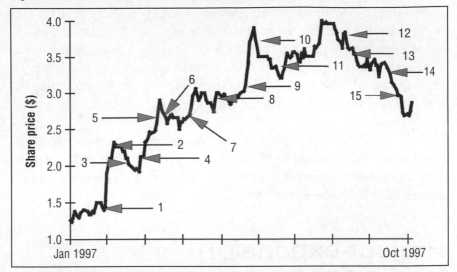

With hindsight, it is easy to say that the market overreacted to the original exploration release (Shell Development, Cultus's joint venture partner, had advised it in June 1997 that the Cornea field held between 0.6 billion and 2.7 billion barrels of oil in place). However, had further drilling proved that the large structure held significant volumes of recoverable oil, then the story would have turned out quite differently.

There was a simple check after the initial re-rating of the stock that should have warned investors. As mentioned before, based on the initial increase in the market capitalisation of the company, the market was inferring a recoverable reserve of 150 million barrels. By the time the company's share price reached a peak, the value had risen to nearly 400 million barrels based on very limited drilling of the structure, and only limited data from the drilling undertaken to that point in time. Exploration success in offshore oil exploration is low and when discoveries are made, the recoverable reserves often prove to be below initial expectations.

So what do these three exploration case studies teach us with the benefit of hindsight? First, over time, as more exploration is carried out, the resource base and the economics of a discovery are likely to change.

The trick is to quantify the risk in choosing whether to participate in the future success, once the discovery is announced to the market.

Once invested (you may have been fortunate enough to have been a shareholder before the discovery), when should you sell, if at all? It may be impossible to predict the final outcome of the exploration campaign, but at each critical point in time, an estimate of the fundamental value or at least the implied market value should be assessed. If the market has 'run away' with its valuation, then one should be cautious, but always watchful, as the resource could expand to meet the market's expectation.

One conservative approach, if the market is significantly above the fundamental value, would be to sell some of your shares to lock in a profit early. Ultimately the market will reach fair value once the discovery is fully delineated, as we have seen in the previous examples.

Project expansion

Significant valuation increases can also occur through mining expansions, which allow for increased profits and NPVs for mining companies—but things can go wrong. In June 2000 Selwyn Mines Limited was floated with the aim of funding the then recently restarted mining operations at the Mt Elliot underground gold and copper mine. Several previous operators had spent approximately $45 million on these operations since 1982, and a modest $2.5 million was raised to enable processing of 515 000 tonnes per year at the Selwyn plant to recover 13 000 tpa of copper and 19 000 ounces of gold in concentrate. Table 16.4 summarises the company's forecasts at the time.

Table 16.4: Selwyn Mines forecasts, 2002–02

Year to June	2001	2002
Ore treated (000 t)	518	519
Copper grade (%)	2.91	3.42
Gold grade (g/t)	1.49	1.65
Concentrate produced (t)	46 871	58 208
Copper in concentrate (mlb)*	28.9	35.9

Year to June	2001	2002
Exchange rate (US$:A$)		
Revenue ($ million)	47.5	58.4
EBIT ($ million)	2.69	9.09
NPAT[†] ($ million)	2.13	9.02

Notes: * mlb = million pounds; † NPAT = net profit after tax.

The first production report came out in July 2000 for the quarter ended June 2000, which showed cash costs of US$0.56 per pound copper compared with the forecast of US$0.59 per pound. Although grade and ore milled was below budget, these were more than offset by higher recoveries. Additional information was provided on cash reserves ($4.4 million), drawn debt facilities ($6.7 million), hedging of gold and copper in place, and foreign exchange cover of US$45.6 million at an exchange rate of 0.6073.

The September 2000 quarterly report showed that plant throughput and concentrate shipments were above budget and operating costs were now down to US$0.55/lb. Revised reserve and resource estimation was also under way. At the November annual general meeting the chairman informed shareholders that plant throughput was running at an annualised rate of 700 000 tonnes, and that the return on equity for 2000–01 had been an impressive 49 per cent. The December 2000 quarterly production report confirmed the annualised production rate of 700 000 tonnes with concentrate production up 4 per cent with an increase in contained gold and copper, while the March 2001 production report showed continued increased production of copper, although gold production was down 11 per cent.

In May 2001, on the back of the preceding favourable operating statistics, the company announced plans to undertake a bankable feasibility study to expand the plant to 2 million tonnes per year with a 15-year mine life, 29 per cent IRR on a $42 million investment and a 3.5 year payback period. In July the company announced that a more modest expansion to 1.7 million tonnes per year for a capital cost of $13 million over two years was being evaluated, but with resources increased to 30 million tonnes at 1.62 g/t gold and 1.5 per cent copper the mine could ultimately be expanded to 3 million tonnes per year. By the end of August the financial results for the year to June 2001 were announced with a profit of $5.2 million, 143 per cent higher than the prospectus forecast.

The company announced in October 2001 that production was in line with budgets and that the now 2 million tonne per year sulphide expansion project (SEP) was on schedule to be completed by March 2002. In November 2001, at the annual general meeting, the chairman informed shareholders that, after the mine expansion, profits for 2002 would be considerably greater than those in the prospectus and that operating costs would fall to slightly above US$0.40 per pound of copper. It was at this point that the market began to re-rate the company and the share price increased on the basis of the potential for increased profits.

The company took advantage of the increased share price to raise $5.85 million for exploration and working capital purposes, and the plant expansion was ahead of schedule. By late February the company announced that commissioning of the plant was under way and scheduled to be completed by the end of March. On 20 March 2002 the managing director commented that the SEP would have a 10-year life based on higher reserves, and, due to the lower cutoff grade, lower grades would be treated (not always a good sign), but higher tonnage would result in a 50 per cent increase in metal output. The sensitivity of resource tonnage to different gold (Au) and copper (Cu) cutoff grades is shown in figure 16.6

Figure 16.6: copper and gold grade tonnage curves for Mt Elliot mine

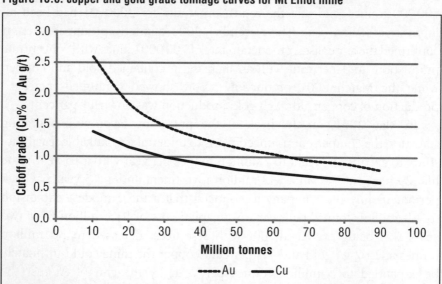

The NPV was estimated at $75 million at 10 per cent discount at a copper price of US$0.70 per pound, gold at US$275 per ounce, an exchange rate of 0.51 to the US$ and a minimum operating life of eight years. Operating costs were forecast to be mid US$0.40 per pound and the expansion would cost $15 million. After-tax earnings would be some $12 million and ongoing capital expenditure for the SEP $2.5 million.

Earnings for the 2002 financial year were not expected to meet the prospectus forecast due the lower grade and implementation of the SEP. The total market-to-market value (if all of the hedges were closed out at that point in time) of the hedging at the end of December 2001 was a negative $4.2 million. The company's loan facility was increased to $15 million plus a $5 million overrun for which the banks required the company to take out a further 240 000 ounce hedge at $562 an ounce and another US$63.4 million currency hedge at US$0.5115. The first signs of financial stress were now beginning to show, but this was not necessarily a problem so long as the increased metal output could be achieved. The March 2002 quarterly report confirmed that the plant expansion and commissioning was now scheduled for completion in the June quarter, that there were no major problems and that the Lady Ella open cut was being developed as an additional source of ore. Half of the capital was being spent on reopening additional areas 251 and 222 in the Starra underground mines.

On 9 May 2002 the managing director reported that a US$0.05 per pound increase in the copper price would increase earnings by $3.5 million after tax and that a US$0.05 exchange rate drop would increase after-tax earnings by $5 million. Hence, 240 000 ounces, representing 70 per cent of gold production to 2006, was hedged at $562 per ounce. More importantly, the managing director mentioned that as at March the mines had moved over to owner-operator rather than contract mining, and that the new underground fleet, costing $15 million, was financed through a combination of operating leases, hire purchase and a finance lease.

On 25 July the June quarterly report showed that only 309 100 tonnes had been treated, which was well below the new increased plant's quarterly capacity of 500 000 tonnes. The reason for the fall was the shortage of soft ore, which was being mined from the new underground developments 251 and 222 (work index 10) to be blended at 2:1 with the harder Mt Elliot ore (work index 17). Recoveries were also lower due to the influence of surface stockpile ores that were used to help with the lower tonnage. Cash operating costs were now US$0.65 per pound of copper. The cost of the

SEP had also increased from $15 million to $20 million. The share price had been falling since April as the market became less comfortable with the company's ability to meet its production targets, and by the time the June report was released much of the previous share price gains had been lost (see figure 16.7).

Figure 16.7: Selwyn Mines, June 2000–December 2002

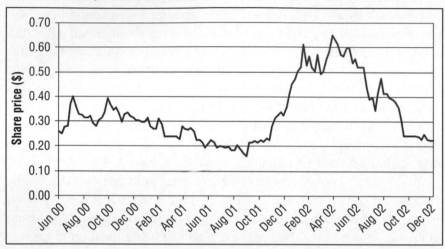

In September a preliminary profit of $1.164 million for the year ended June 2002 was announced, substantially down on expectations due to higher costs and lower production. It is interesting to note that, although mill throughput was up, production of copper in concentrate was down 28 per cent due to lower grades, but revenue of $63 million was above prospectus due to better metal prices. The major negative was the much lower grades of copper (2.15 per cent versus 3.42 per cent) and gold (1.15 g/t versus 1.65 g/t). A new off-take agreement for concentrates until 2005 was entered into with Glencore, which provided the company with a facility of US$8 million to be paid back out of the exports of concentrate, a further sign of corporate stress.

The September 2002 production report released in mid October showed that plant throughput remained at a low quarterly rate of 368 078 tonnes, with copper in concentrate at 3306 tonnes and gold at 11 749 ounces, well below budget due to a lack of underground ore and problems in optimising the crushing and grinding circuits. The cost of production had increased to US$0.94 per pound of copper at a time when the copper price was US$0.67 per pound. An additional crusher and screen was planned to handle course material and the operating cost for the 2003 financial year was now expected to be US$0.57 per pound. Due to the commissioning problems, costs of $1.765 million were capitalised.

Bank facilities of $18.4 million were varied, and fully drawn during the quarter. Due to the increased funding, additional hedging for gold and exchange rates was required: US$70 million of currency cover was in place, with a further 230 000 ounces of gold. The marked-to-market value was now a loss of $21.4 million! On 16 October the company asked for a voluntary suspension of trading until 4 November as it negotiated for a new equity capital raising. By 14 November an unwritten rights issue to raise $12.7 million was confirmed together with the announcement that the company would report a loss for the six months to 31 December. At the annual general meeting later that month the chairman announced that the company hoped to make a small profit for the financial year to June 2003, but that the loss for the first quarter was $5.2 million. In December the managing director stated that the current debt was $31 million and cash assets, including the rights issue, were some $13 million. Total costs for the SEP were now expected to be $25.5 million due to the delays and added requirements to meet production forecasts. On 24 December 2002 the company announced that it would not be able to meet its previously revised forecast of US$0.57 per pound of copper, or production of 20 500 tonnes of copper and 74 000 ounces of gold for the 2003 financial year. The board therefore decided that the cutoff grade would be increased and mill throughput rates lowered to 1.7 million tonnes per year and that a cost-cutting exercise would be undertaken. Due to the change the underwriter withdrew its support for the rights issue, which in turn was withdrawn, and funds were returned to investors. The company's bank then refused to release any funds and the board sought to appoint an administrator, after which its bank appointed a receiver. At the time the bank had a loan exposure of $11.5 million, but also a 220 000 ounce gold marked-to-market hedge exposure of a further $25 million.

It is easy with hindsight, even allowing for the limitations of public information, to be critical of the events that overtook Selwyn as it rose from a market capitalisation of $20 million, peaked at $60 million and then ended with little or no value for its shareholders. The revival of the operations started well, and the company was profitable and exceeded its forecasts. There is always pressure on the management and the board of a company to grow in value, and one way for most mines to do this is to expand production.

Exploration had been successful and by applying a lower cutoff grade the tonnage was greatly increased, allowing for a larger mining operation with a mine life of more than eight years. As I have mentioned elsewhere in this book, grade is king, and therefore lowering the cutoff grade did increase the tonnage, but it also reduced the mined grade. Reducing grades need not be a problem if the economies of scale — through increased ore tonnage — outweigh the lower grade, so that in Selwyn's case the cost per pound of copper could be reduced.

The critical issue was the ability of management to increase mined tonnage and expand the plant to successfully accommodate the increased throughput. What became evident was not only the difficulty that is often encountered in getting planned tonnage when opening new underground production stopes, but also that sufficient soft ore had to be mined to be blended with the harder ore so that the plant could crush and grind the ore. This suggests that the front end of the plant — which is often the most expensive both in terms of capital and operating costs — was under-designed to keep costs down, but became captive to the soft ore that didn't eventuate.

As well as the plant costs that increased as attempts were made to rectify the problems, the company's debt expanded, because the company not only funded the plant and underground development, but also chose to buy a mining fleet to become its own operator. In principle, mining companies should run their own fleet, as it is in their capacity as miners that they can add the greater value. However, Selwyn was a young and small mining company and, without knowing all the issues at the time, it might have been wiser to have waited and built up more expertise. With a modest balance sheet the increasing debt requirements were funded, effectively, by the reserves in the ground, which required further hedging of the commodity prices and exchange rate.

While price and exchange rate movements were in the company's favour the debt was not a major issue for the lenders, but when they moved against Selwyn and the likelihood of meeting its commitment for delivery of the commodities lessened, the pressure would have built up enormously. The failure of the additional equity raising was the proverbial straw that broke the company's back and, coupled with a marked-to-market exposure of $25 million, by December 2002 the end had come.[3]

Once the market became convinced that the expansion was under way in late 2001, the share price had risen rapidly to reflect the increased earnings potential of the company. Watching out for mining companies that plan to expand production can often position shareholders for significant share price appreciation. On the flipside, shareholders have to be vigilant for the first signs of operations going awry, such as those announced in the June quarterly report in late July 2001. Another sign once the market is informed is the actions of the directors: some in Selwyn's case were sellers of their stock in July 2001 and most of them had sold their stock by December 2002.

Rapid expansion and the inability to meet a growing debt are not limited to small mining companies, but can also have dire consequences for large companies, such as in the case of Pasminco, which is discussed in chapter 9. Working out fundamental value (including the future impacts of debt, reserves, commodity prices and costs) is critical in the ultimate valuation of an asset. However, in determining the absolute value it is necessary to discount to the present, and to this end we need to decide on the appropriate discount rate, which is discussed in the next chapter.

---

3 In 2003 Ivanhoe Australia acquired the leases and towards the end of 2011 resources were 570 mt at 0.44 per cent copper and 0.26g/t gold.

CHAPTER 17

Determining the appropriate discount rate

Fundamental analysis plays a key role in determining such issues as the 'correct' value of a share price, the 'correct' purchase price for a mineral resource, or making the 'correct' decision on whether to develop a new project or not. The fundamental value is determined by discounting future cash flows. The cash flows need to be those cash flows that can be put back into the pockets of the investors. The portion of the cash flow, if any, that is required to keep the project going is not included, therefore it is the discretionary cash flow that is important. Once the discretionary cash flows have been determined, both negative (investment) and positive (return), then they are discounted to one point in time (commonly the present) to give the NPV.

The cash flows need to be discounted by an appropriate discount rate. This does not preclude the analyst from discounting at a number of different discount rates, but in determining the 'fair' value, it is important to choose the appropriate discount rate. The capital markets theory, discussed later, is the most common approach to determining the appropriate discount. The discount rate can be seen as a hurdle rate that needs to be achieved to meet the market's minimum expectation for listed equities. If a positive NPV is achieved at that discount rate, then additional value is being added to the company.

Some companies take the approach of selecting a higher discount rate on the basis that if the prospect achieves that higher rate, then more value is being generated, which is positive for the company's share price. In one way, this is no different from seeking a higher positive NPV at the correct discount rate, but the disadvantage of using a higher discount rate is that it is difficult to estimate how this will translate to the share price. For example, a project's NPV at the market's company discount rate may be $20 million, which translates to say 50¢ per share, while the NPV at 15 per cent (management's preferred discount rate) is $0. Obviously, management can calculate both, but the risk is that a project that is acceptable to shareholders and adds value at a 12 per cent discount rate may be unacceptable to management at the 15 per cent discount rate, and therefore not be developed or purchased by the company.

Another often quoted reason for selecting an artificially high discount rate is to take into account the riskiness of the project or perhaps location (country risk). The market discount rate already takes into account the risk class of projects that the company normally undertakes by way of the beta. If a riskier class of project is contemplated (which implies a higher beta and thus a higher discount rate), then it may be better to test the critical parameters and ensure that the market's required return is met under the most testing of project conditions, rather than to take an arbitrary discount rate that does not relate individually to riskier projects. Using a higher discount rate than the company's cost of capital for some projects implies that a lower discount rate should be used for other less risky projects. If a project is contemplated that is not the norm for the company, then it may be appropriate to adjust the discount rate accordingly although my preference is to look at the project parameters rather than increase the hurdle rate.

Resource company betas

A resource company's beta (β) is a numerical way of describing how that stock's share price, on average, will behave compared with the world's financial equity markets. Because there is no easy way of calculating how world markets in total behave on a day-to-day basis, it is more common to compare, say, a listed company with the appropriate listed market as defined by an Accumulation Index. The index is a measure of the change in the value of the whole equity market including dividends. In calculating a company's beta, dividends paid by the company should also be included. One approach to calculating the beta is to determine the percentage change in the index and the percentage change in the share price for a given period of, say, one month. This calculation is repeated for a number of periods; for example, over two years, as shown in table 17.1.

Table 17.1: percentage change for calculation of beta

Monthly Accumulation Index	Change (%)	Hypothetical share price	Change (%)
8 399	—	1.50	—
8 203	−2.3	1.45	−3.0
8 566	4.4	1.53	5.5
8 783	2.5	1.58	3.2
9 129	3.9	1.67	5.4
9 164	0.4	1.68	0.5
8 955	−2.3	1.63	−3.0
9 347	4.4	1.73	6.0
9 173	−1.9	1.69	−2.4
9 119	−0.6	1.67	−0.8
8 869	−2.7	1.68	0.3
9 260	4.4	1.78	5.9
9 394	1.4	1.81	1.7
9 698	3.2	1.91	5.8
9 867	1.7	1.90	−0.5
10 065	2.0	1.96	2.8
10 069	0.0	1.96	0.0
10 217	1.5	2.00	2.0
10 151	−0.7	1.98	−0.9
10 455	3.0	2.06	4.0
10 993	5.1	2.19	6.7
11 541	5 0	2.36	7.5
11 583	0.4	2.37	0.5
11 016	−4.9	2.21	−6.7
11 239	2.0	2.27	2.6

For the first two-month period at the top of the table, the percentage change in the index is –2.3 per cent, as the index fell month on month. There is no value for the first month unless we extend the time series further back. Our share price fell by 3 per cent. Each set of monthly movements can then be plotted on a chart, with one point representing the intersection of an index value corresponding to the x axis (horizontal) and the share value corresponding to the y axis (vertical), as shown in figure 17.1. Any dividends paid by the company need to be included in the calculation of monthly returns.

As well as the 24 points on the chart, a line of best fit has been drawn. The slope of this line, that is the relative angle the line makes to the horizontal, is 1.26. This implies that the share price will move in most cases, but not always, in the same direction as the index (this is positive beta, although on two occasions the share price went in the opposite direction to the index), by 26 per cent more than the index. In other words, if the market as defined by the index increases by 10 per cent during one month, then on average the share price should move by 12.6 per cent; that is, 10 per cent multiplied by 1.26.

Statistically, the line of best fit in figure 17.1 has a 'goodness of fit' (R^2) equal to 0.92, which means that there is a strong correlation between the index movement and the share price. In practice, the goodness of fit is seldom this high (often from near zero to a little above 0.5) and further statistical adjustments may be applied to provide a more meaningful relationship. However, in determining an appropriate cost of equity capital it is the best indicator that is available. Table 17.2 lists geared betas (unadjusted for any company debt) for a number of mining companies.

Figure 17.1: plotting for beta

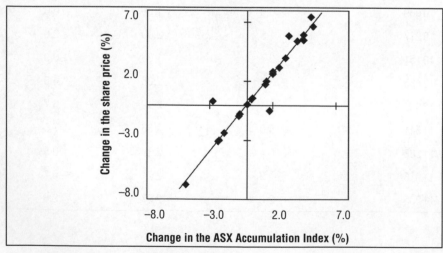

Table 17.2: beta and goodness of fit for selected resource companies

Company	Geared beta	Debt/Equity	Ungeared beta
BHP	1.60	0.08	1.52
Rio Tinto	1.70	0.18	1.51
Vale	1.50	0.22	1.30
Woodside	1.50	0.20	1.32
Newcrest	0.85	0.03	0.83
Fortescue	1.95	0.34	1.58
Average	**1.52**	**0.18**	**1.34**

The geared betas in table 17.2 are historical, as they have obviously been derived from historical observations. It would be more meaningful to use a forecast beta, but such a value can only be estimated given that future observations cannot be made. In theory, over time the historical beta should approach 1 and so a qualitative adjustment could be made. It is possible to modify the geared betas using this equation to arrive at the ungeared beta (βa):

$$\beta a = \beta/(1 + (D/E \times (1 - t)))$$

where:

D = company debt

E = company equity (market capitalisation)

t = corporate tax rate

If an appropriate beta is sought for a company or project, then ungeared betas can be determined for a number of similar companies or projects to derive an average and then, assuming an appropriate debt to equity ratio, the equation above can be reversed to get the geared beta.

Capital asset pricing model

The capital asset pricing model (CAPM) provides a methodology to determine the level of return expected by shareholders from their investment in a particular listed company. Investors generally expect a capital gain by way of share price appreciation, or a yield by way of dividends, or some combination of both. From the previous section, a company's beta is a quantification of the previous return experienced by shareholders, relative to the market as defined by an Accumulation Index.

If the past returns for the market can be determined, then the return for the share we hold (r_e) can be estimated by multiplying the market return by the beta. A leap of faith is now required, because the CAPM assumes that past values are a good estimate of future values. Further, it is also possible to estimate in the past what return the market (r_m) has provided compared to the risk-free return (r_f) of government bonds. Putting this all together the CAPM equation becomes:

$r_e = r_f + \beta$ times $(r_m - r_f)$

where:

r_e = the expected return by shareholders

r_f = the risk-free rate provided by government bonds

r_m = the market return

Historically, the premium provided by the equity markets over the risk-free rate is generally between 4 and 6 per cent, with 6 per cent the more common figure employed in valuations.[1] In our example, the beta of our stock was estimated at 1.26, and in January 2011 the Australian 10-year government bonds provided a return of 3.84 per cent per year. Therefore, return to equity can be estimated as:

$3.84\% + 1.26 \times (6\%) = 11.40\%$

If the same exercise were done for a US stock, where the 10-year rate is 2.64 per cent the r_e would be 10.20 per cent, reflecting the lower cost of capital in the US.

Effectively, what this equation means is that, to maintain the previous performance as defined by the beta of 1.26, the shareholders of our hypothetical company are expecting a return of 11.4 per cent on their investment in the form of capital appreciation or dividend yield or both. This assumes that the historical estimate of the beta, the market premium and the current risk-free rate are sound estimates for the future. Clearly, this may not be the case, but in the absence of any better approach, the CAPM is still the favoured method.

1 Hathaway (2005): historical average 4.5 per cent. Brailsford (2007): 6.2 per cent from 1883 to 2005, and 6.3 per cent from 1958 to 2005. Hancock (2006): most likely 5 per cent to 6 per cent, although one-year premium over last 30 years was 4.5 per cent to 5 per cent. Officer (2009), 1883 to 2008 was 7.1 per cent, and 1958 to 2008 was 5.7 per cent (could add a further 1 per cent for dividend imputation).

It is sometimes argued that any valuation and hence the CAPM should be based on the price-making or marginal investor. For a large resource company that investor is likely to be foreign and therefore the beta should be based on a well-diversified foreign portfolio, which is often represented by the Morgan Stanley Capital Index.

Weighted average cost of capital

If a mining company were able to source all its funding needs from the equity market, then its cost of capital would simply be its equity cost of capital estimated by the CAPM. However, mining companies can also source capital by way of the debt markets, hence we use a weighted average cost of capital (WACC). Debt can come in two forms: on–balance sheet corporate debt and off–balance sheet project finance. The former will be discussed in the following example.

The first step is to determine the likely future ratio of equity to debt for the company. Without any forward knowledge, an estimate can be made from the existing debt/equity ratio. By analysing the company's balance sheet, it is possible to determine the current level of bank debt and, from the interest cost in the notes to the profit and loss statement, the interest paid (r_d). Ideally, it would be best to estimate the expected level of debt in the immediate future. The equity component is determined by calculating the market equity; that is, the market capitalisation of the company, which is the share price multiplied by the number of issued securities. Again these estimates are somewhat subjective. The WACC[2] is defined as shown on the following page.

---

2 The WACC approach was designed for a tax system where interest costs are tax deductible for a company, but any dividends are not deductible, either for the company or the shareholders receiving the dividends. Thus gearing (debt) in the company would increase the return to shareholders. However, under current tax laws in Australia, shareholders receive a tax credit on their dividends (dividend imputation) for any tax paid by the company. There is some debate on whether any adjustment for imputation should be made to the WACC and what form this should take. The major issues of concern are that companies don't always distribute all of their franking credits and that not all shareholders can make full use of the credits that they do receive. A possible adjustment is as follows:

WACC = E/V × r_e × (1 – t) ÷ (1 – t x (1 – f)) + D/V × rd × (1 – t) where f = market value of franking credits

(continued)

$$WACC = E/V \times r_e + D/V \times r_d \times (1 - t)$$

where:

V = equity and debt

E/V = the proportion of equity

D/V = the proportion of debt

r_e = the cost of equity (CAPM)

r_d = the cost of debt

t = the corporate tax rate.

For example, in our hypothetical company the cost of equity (r_e) was calculated at 11.4 per cent and the last price quoted was $2.27. Assume that there are 100 million shares on issue, which means the market capitalisation would be $227 million (E). Also assume that the debt level is $50 million (D), that the interest payable is 8 per cent (r_d) and that the corporate tax rate is 30 per cent (t). Therefore:

V = $227 million + $50 million = $277 million

and:

$$WACC = 227 \div 277 \times 11.4\% + 50 \div 277 \times 8\% \times (1 - 0.30)$$

$$= 9.34\% + 1.01$$

$$= 10.35\%$$

It has been suggested that an average for the market value should be 50 per cent. In our example, if franked dividends were paid then:

WACC = 227 ÷ 277 × 11.4% × (1 − 0.30) ÷ (1 − 0.30 x (1 − 0.5)) + 50 ÷ 277 × 8% × (1 − 0.30)
= 7.69% + 1.01%
= 8.70%

Another, intuitively simpler, approach is not to change the discount rate, but to add the franking credits to the cash flow and reduce the company's tax payable. The difficulty of course is in knowing what, if any, future dividends will be paid by the company or, effectively, from the project to the company's shareholders.

As described, the WACC is an after-tax calculation with the assumption that the capital investment is a mix of debt and equity in proportion to the company's debt/equity ratio. In other words, there is no way to differentiate the dollars spent as debt or equity, except in the case of project finance that has recourse to the project cash flows and is not part of the company's balance sheet debt. However, it is still possible to model the cash flows after tax after allowing for the interest cost for the proportion of debt that would nominally be used in the capital expenditure. The discount rate would then become r_e, the cost of equity. This approach should result in the same valuation, although it is not common practice.

The WACC is an after-tax calculation; therefore, for discounting purposes it should be applied to after-tax cash flows. However, the tax shelter provided by the interest component from the company's balance sheet debt is accounted for in the WACC equation. Therefore, the after-tax calculation of cash flow excludes the interest cost component.

Adjustment for hedging

A major aspect of the theory on discount rates is the risk associated with uncertain future commodity prices. If a hedging program can be executed that fixes the future price of the commodity, then that risk is eliminated and it could be argued that the discount rate should be adjusted. Because of the unique nature of gold, which is more a financial instrument than a commodity, such hedging programs could in theory be undertaken, although in practice they would be difficult to implement and in a market environment where the gold price is increasing, gold producers are loath to hedge at all.

However, if the future risk of price variation can been removed, the gold price (and hence the revenue) should be discounted by the risk-free rate r_f. Further, the future gold price is in contango (as discussed in chapter 9), with the compounding premium to the spot price not too dissimilar from r_f (slightly lower at market rate less leasing rate less costs). Therefore, compounding the spot gold price by r_f and then discounting by r_f ends up with the spot price. This suggests that the revenue should be computed using the spot gold price and be discounted at a zero discount rate. The difficulty arises with the operating cost; discounting at a zero discount rate would overstate its present value. A separate discount rate can therefore be applied to the operating costs with a discount rate of, say, r_f, as variations are within control of management. Of greater concern is the impact on tax, as a spot price–based revenue will be lower than the actual revenue figures achieved. Thus, the tax will be underestimated and the present value will be much higher than normal practice.

Empirical evidence suggests that normal WACC methods underestimate the present value of gold producers. Therefore, the application of a zero discount rate for gold producer revenues may be a more meaningful approach to reconciling the difference between the producer's present value and its share price. For relative comparisons, consistency is important and thus either approach may be applicable. However, for an absolute valuation in determining whether a particular producer is a buy or a sell, the zero discount rate appears to fit better with market observation. It is not uncommon for analysts to take a middle road approach and discount unhedged future cash flows of gold stocks by r_f. This obviously increases the NPV of the gold company, helping to bring it more into line with the market's valuation.

As mentioned previously in this book, a number of issues need to be addressed in the valuation for investment decisions. One final aspect that is discussed in the next chapter is dealing with inflation.

CHAPTER 18

Dealing with inflation

As well as having to deal with the uncertainty of forecasting future parameter values that go into the determination of company or project valuation, the valuer is also faced with the likelihood of inflation (increasing parameter values over time). The rates of inflation can be different among parameters and may also change over time. Current or nominal values include the effect of inflation, while constant or real values exclude inflation. It is important that the correct methodologies are applied under an inflationary or non-inflationary environment.

After the appropriate discount rate has been determined, the company's future cash flows can be discounted by that discount rate to determine the NPV. The discount rate that has been calculated using the WACC is a current or nominal value; that is, it assumes inflation is present. The cash flows also have to be current or nominal, so that there is no mismatch between the discount rate and the cash flows. Some practitioners argue that it is more difficult, and subject to greater risk, to calculate what the future inflation rates will be for the purposes of determining the cash flows. They argue that constant or real future cash flows, which are not adjusted for any future inflation, should be used. The approach is therefore to adjust the discount rate to a constant or real discount rate.

Take, for example, a WACC of 14 per cent and assume the forecast inflation rate for a mining project is 4 per cent. The first approach to determine the real discount rate would be to subtract the inflation rate from the discount rate to come up with a real discount rate of 10 per cent. This is not correct because it does not take into account the compounding effect of interest rates.

The correct calculation is to use the Fisher equation, which is:

1 + real rate = (1 + nominal rate) ÷ (1 + inflation rate)

which for our example would be:

1 + real rate = (1 + 0.14) ÷ (1 + 0.04)

= 1.096

Therefore the real discount rate is:

1.096 − 1 = 0.096 = 9.6%

In table 18.1 the cash flows for a hypothetical case are shown both in inflated terms, where the revenue and operating costs increase by 4 per cent, and in non-inflated terms, in which revenue and costs remain constant.

Table 18.1: cash flows for a hypothetical company in inflated and non-inflated terms ($ million)

	Escalation	Year 1	Year 2	Year 3	Year 4
Inflated values (nominal)					
Revenue	4%	104.0	108.2	112.5	117.0
Operating cost	4%	52.0	54.1	56.2	58.5
Cash flow	—	52.0	54.1	56.2	58.5
NPV at 14%	$159.8	—	—	—	—
Non-inflated values (real)					
Revenue	0%	100.0	100.0	100.0	100.0
Operating cost	0%	50.0	50.0	50.0	50.0
Cash flow	—	50.0	50.0	50.0	50.0
NPV at 9.6%	$159.8	—	—	—	—

The nominal discount rate of 14 per cent is applied to the inflated cash flow for an NPV of $159.8 million. The real discount rate of 9.6 per cent is applied to the real cash flows and results in the same answer of $159.8 million. If the discount rate of 10 per cent had been applied, then the NPV of the real cash flows would have been $158.5 million. The Fisher equation has allowed for the correct discount rate and, importantly, the answer is the same whether real or nominal.

Table 18.2 uses the same assumptions as table 18.1; however, tax has been included. The NPV obviously decreases as the payment of tax reduces the cash flow to the equity holders. Importantly, the NPV of $111.9 million is the same for either case of real or nominal. The addition of tax does not impact on the effectiveness of the two discount rates, as the tax is in the same proportion for either the real or the nominal pre-tax cash flow.

Table 18.2: cash flows with tax ($ million)

	Escalation	Year 1	Year 2	Year 3	Year 4
Inflated values (nominal)					
Revenue	4%	104.0	108.2	112.5	117
Operating cost	4%	52.0	54.1	56.2	58.5
Pre-tax	—	52.0	54.1	56.2	58.5
Tax	30%	15.6	16.2	16.9	17.6
Cash flow	—	36.40	37.87	39.34	40.95
NPV at 14%	$111.9				
Non-inflated values (real)					
Revenue	0%	100.0	100.0	100.0	100.0
Operating cost	0%	50.0	50.0	50.0	50.0
Pre-tax	—	50.0	50.0	50.0	50.0
Tax	30%	15.0	15.0	15.0	15.0
Cash flow	—	35.0	35.0	35.0	35.0
NPV at 9.6%	$111.9	—	—	—	—

In the next example in table 18.3 (overleaf), depreciation has been included in the calculation of the NPV. As would be expected, this time the NPV increases, as the tax paid has decreased due to the allowable depreciation. However, on first sight the Fisher equation has not worked, as the NPV for the real discount rate suggests that it is higher at $131.0 million compared with the nominal discount rate NPV of $129.4 million. Some practitioners have erroneously suggested that higher valuations are achieved from real discount rates, therefore, so as not to penalise the project, real discount rates should be used in preference. This is not true as, correctly applied, the same value is achieved whether real or nominal.

Table 18.3: cash flows with depreciation ($ million)

	Escalation	Year 1	Year 2	Year 3	Year 4
Inflated values (nominal)					
Revenue	4%	104.0	108.2	112.5	117
Operating cost	4%	52.0	54.1	56.2	58.5
Depreciation	—	20.0	20.0	20.0	20.0
Pre-tax	—	32.0	34.1	36.2	38.5
Tax	30%	9.6	10.2	10.9	11.6
Cash flow	—	42.40	43.87	45.34	46.95
NPV at 14%	$129.4	—	—	—	—
No inflation (real)					
Revenue	0%	100.0	100.0	100.0	100.0
Operating cost	0%	50.0	50.0	50.0	50.0
Depreciation	—	20.0	20.0	20.0	20.0
Pre-tax	—	30.0	30.0	30.0	30.0
Tax	30%	9.0	9.0	9.0	9.0
Cash flow	—	41.0	41.0	41.0	41.0
NPV at 9.6%	$131.0	—	—	—	—

The reason for the difference lies in the treatment of depreciation for tax purposes. Depreciation is based on historical values and so no allowance is made for inflation. Therefore, the depreciation is in real terms in both a nominal and a real environment, and thus the depreciation has to be adjusted in one or other of the cases. In the real case, the depreciation has acted as a tax shield and increased the NPV.

Two approaches can be contemplated. One approach is to inflate the depreciation by 4 per cent annually in the inflated value case, which will reduce the pre-tax figure and hence the tax paid. This would increase the NPV to $131.0 million, so the Fisher equation would still hold. However, in the nominal or inflated case we can't increase the depreciation as the Tax Commissioner won't allow us to! The other approach, as shown in table 18.4, is to discount the depreciation by 4 per cent per year for the real case. This increases the pre-tax values and hence increases the tax paid and lowers the NPV for the real discount case to $129.4 million.

Table 18.4: cash flows with discounted depreciation ($ million)

	Escalation	Year 1	Year 2	Year 3	Year 4
Revenue	0%	100.0	100.0	100.0	100.0
Operating costs	0%	50.0	50.0	50.0	50.0
Depreciation	4%	19.2	18.5	17.8	17.1
Pre-tax	—	30.8	31.5	32.2	32.9
Tax	30%	9.24	9.5	9.7	9.9
Cash flow	—	40.77	40.55	40.33	40.13
NPV at 9.6%	$129.4	—	—	—	—

The important point to note is that the same answer should be derived whether the cash-flow analysis is done in real or nominal terms. The difficulty comes in the adjustments that have to be made with regard to depreciation and other tax-driven issues.

In constructing a project cash-flow model, it is common to forecast the internal values—such as production volumes, grades and recoveries—in current (nominal) terms rather than in constant (real) terms. In other words, there is an attempt to model or forecast how the project is likely to perform from a technical point of view. In everyday life we tend to think of issues in nominal terms, rather than to discount everything into real terms; one example would be home loan repayments. It is therefore advisable to also model the project financials in current (nominal) terms.

At first sight, it might still seem simpler to model in constant terms and adjust the discount rate and the depreciation. However, in the previous examples, the increases in revenue and costs were both 4 per cent. What happens if the inflation rates are different—say, 4 per cent for costs and 3 per cent for revenue—and what if the rate of inflation is expected to change during the life of the project? The necessary adjustments become increasingly complex and mitigate the added difficulty in attempting to forecast the future inflation rates and hence cash flows in current (nominal) terms.

The failure to properly account for inflation is still occasionally apparent in internal company valuations. Other issues such as the appropriate discount rate and the proper incorporation of risk are also at times mishandled. All the issues critical to completing a project valuation have now been addressed in the previous chapters. In the next chapter we put all these concepts together and look at a hypothetical case study.

CHAPTER 19

Agricola Mining — a hypothetical example

To help put into context many of the issues discussed in this book, a simple hypothetical study is presented in this chapter. The aim is to determine the fundamental value of a company, taking into account the impact of a recent mineral discovery.

Agricola Mining[1] is a hypothetical public company listed on a stock exchange. The pertinent information is as follows:

» issued capital: 70 million ordinary shares

» current share price: 50¢

» average daily turnover: $50 000

» shareholders' funds: $25 million

» cash: $10 million

» debt: nil

» company beta: 1.1.

---

1 In 1556, Georgius Agricola published *de re Metallica*, the first book on mining, which was based on field research and observation. The book provides numerous drawings of various mining and metallurgical techniques, and a history of mining from antiquity to his day. Written in Latin, it was not until 1912 that it was translated by former US President Herbert Hoover and his wife. Herbert Hoover was a mining engineer who spent the early part of his career in the goldfields of Western Australia.

Exploration discovery

The company has made an important discovery of the new commodity metallica. After the initial discovery, a large infill drilling program was undertaken to define the resource. An example of one cross-section of the orebody, from east to west, is shown in figure 19.1. Six exploration holes have intersected three mineralised zones lying one on top of the other. A total of 13 mineralised intercepts were made for this cross-section. The length of each intercept has been measured and the grade for each intercept has been determined from assaying. There are many more cross-sections not shown that define the orebody in the third dimension. The orebodies also deepen in a southerly direction.

Figure 19.1: cross-section of orebody

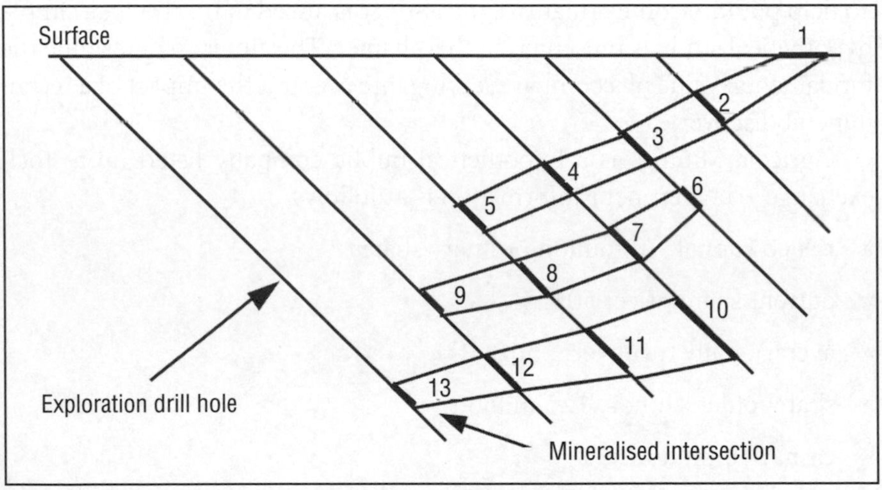

The top orebody is exposed on the surface and has been sampled at location 1. At intercepts 5, 6, 9, 10 and 13 the orebodies are likely to extend beyond the drill holes. Each intercept will be given a volume of influence (the volume of ore that will be assigned the same grade as the drill hole intercept), which for this example is defined by half the distance to the next drill hole and the true thickness.

Methods for more complex ore reserve calculations are detailed in chapter 5. Details of each of the 13 grade intercepts are listed in table 19.1.

Table 19.1: exploration result for one cross-section

Hole number	Grade (%)	Thickness (m)	Area of influence (m^2)	Tonnage (t)	Metal (t)
1	1.0	2.0	200	1 000	10
2	2.5	4.0	400	4 000	100
3	3.5	4.0	400	4 000	140
4	3.0	3.5	400	3 500	105
5	3.0	3.0	400	3 000	90
6	3.5	2.0	400	2 000	70
7	3.8	5.0	400	5 000	190
8	4.0	4.0	400	4 000	160
9	4.2	2.5	400	2 500	105
10	4.5	10.0	400	10 000	450
11	4.8	6.0	400	6 000	288
12	5.0	4.0	400	4 000	200
13	5.0	3.0	400	3 000	150
	Total	—	—	52 000	2058

The tonnage for each intercept is defined by the thickness multiplied by the area of influence and then multiplied by the specific gravity of the ore, in this case 2.5. The tonnage multiplied by the grade provides an estimate of the contained metal in the ore.

Ore reserves and waste

If the project proves economic to develop, the orebodies would probably be extracted by open cut methods due to the near-surface nature of the mineralisation. It will, therefore, be necessary to determine the waste to ore ratio. This will vary over time depending on the sequence in which the orebodies are mined. For example, in figure 19.2, possible open cut pit designs are shown. The upper orebody is removed first (open cut 1), followed by the middle (open cut 2) and then the deeper orebody (open cut 3).

Figure 19.2: possible open cut sequence

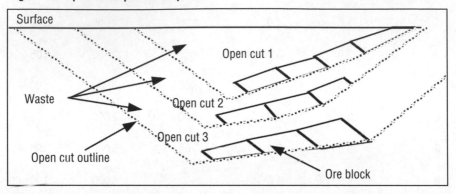

For each open cut sequence, it is possible to calculate the number of ore blocks to mine, the average grade mined and contained metal, and the amount of waste to be removed. The total ore for this cross-section is estimated at 52 000 tonnes with an average grade of 4 per cent and an average stripping ratio of 4.6 to 1.0 (see table 19.2).

Table 19.2: cross-section results

Open cut	Number of ore blocks	Tonnage (t)	Grade (%)	Metal (t)	Waste (t)	Strip ratio
1	5	15 500	2.9	445	49 600	3.2
2	4	13 500	3.9	525	58 050	4.3
3	4	23 000	4.7	1088	133 400	5.8
Total		52 000	4.0	2058	241 050	4.6

There are another 70 cross-sections with differing numbers of exploration drill holes and intercepts. However, the total number of blocks defined is

800 for a total resource of 5.46 million tonnes. The grade tonnage curve for the 800 blocks of ore is shown in figure 19.3.[2]

Figure 19.3: grade/tonnage curve

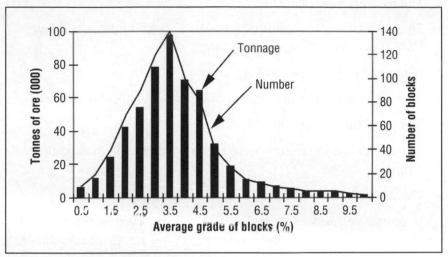

Cutoff grade

The weighted average grade of all 800 blocks is 3.7 per cent. It is possible that some of the lower grade blocks might be uneconomical to mine and treat, therefore an economical cutoff grade should be calculated using the following information:

» The spot price for metallica is US$3500 per tonne of processed metal. The long-term price growth rate is assumed to be 2 per cent per year.

» There is a tolling and refining charge of US$500 per tonne of metal, increasing in line with metal price increases. There are no credits or penalty charges.

» There is a marketing, insurance and transport charge of US$50 per tonne of concentrate. Concentrate grade is anticipated to be approximately 8 multiplied by the ore grade.

---

2 In practice, the ore reserve blocks may be considerably larger in number and smaller in size, so that the boundaries of the orebody can be adequately modelled. The size of blocks chosen to model the mining of the orebody should be equal to the selected mining unit; that is, the size of block that can be differentiated by the pit mining unit. This could amount to more than 100 000 blocks. Larger sized blocks can be chosen that may not result in a significant variation to the grade tonnage curve.

» There is a government royalty of 5 per cent of net mine gate revenue.

» There is a milling cost to produce a concentrate at the rate of US$25 per tonne of ore milled. Metallica ore is difficult to treat.

» Mill recovery is 90 per cent.

» There is a mining contracting cost of US$2.5 per tonne mined and US$1.5 per tonne of waste.

» Mining dilution is 5 per cent.

» There is an administration charge of US$3 per tonne of ore milled.

» The initial mill size is 500 000 tonnes per year.

» There is an average waste-to-ore ratio of 5 times with a maximum of 7 times.

» There is an interest charge of 7 per cent on debt.

An approximate break-even analysis shows that, even at the maximum waste-to-ore ratio of 7, it is still economic to mine by open cut methods.

$$\text{Break-even} = ((US\$3500 - US\$500) \times 3.7\% \times 90\% \times$$
$$(100\% - 5\%) - US\$25 - US\$2.50 - US\$3 - US\$50 \div 8) \div 1.5$$
$$= 38.8 \text{ times}$$

An initial economic cutoff grade has also been calculated as follows:

$$\text{Cutoff grade} = (US\$25 + US\$2.50 + US\$3 + US\$1.50 \times 5 + US\$50 \div 8) \div$$
$$((US\$3500 - US\$500) \times 90\% \times (100\% - 5\%) = 1.73\%$$

Based on a cutoff grade of, say, 2 per cent, the ore reserve above cutoff is 4.6 million tonnes with a weighted average grade of 4.1 per cent.

Mining schedule

The next step is to design a mine plan that will ensure adequate ore feed to the mill, while maximising cash flow as early as possible in the life of the operation to maximise the NPV. The results of the mine planning are detailed in table 19.3.

Table 19.3: mining schedule

Year	1	2	3	4	5	6	7	8	9	Total
Ore										
(000 t)	510	510	510	510	510	510	510	510	510	4590
Grade	4.5%	4.7%	4.3%	4.1%	4.0%	3.9%	3.9%	3.8%	3.5%	4.1%
Metal										
(000 t)	22.95	23.97	21.93	20.91	20.4	19.89	19.89	19.38	17.85	187.17
Waste										
(000 t)	2091	2142	1989	2295	2448	2652	2805	3060	3315	22 797

The milling rate of 510 000 tonnes per year has been chosen as a reasonable rate, given the size of the deposit and likely demand for the product. This equates to an hourly mill throughput of 64 tonnes based on 95 per cent availability and two weeks per annum of scheduled down time for preventative maintenance. The 5 per cent expected dilution (waste mined with the ore) has been included in the forecast mine grade.

Feasibility study

The mill cost has been estimated at $55 million as detailed in table 19.4, while ground works, tailings dam, power supply, water and mine accommodation will cost a further $25 million. Construction is expected to take two years. No costing has been provided for the mining fleet, as this will be provided by the contractor. Additionally, the company would have spent a total of $10 million on exploration and feasibility studies to reach the decision point to commence the mine construction.

Table 19.4: mill plant costs

Mill plant	Cost $m
Crushing	2.6
Recycled crushing	4.8
Stockpile feed	1.4
Stockpile reclaim	2.9
Grinding circuit	35.7

(continued)

Table 19.4: mill plant costs (*cont'd*)

Mill plant	Cost $m
Flotation circuit	4.5
Concentrate treatment	1.3
Tailings thickener	1.1
Reagent storage	0.2
Piping	0.5
Total	**55.0**

Agricola will also require $6 million in working capital, which represents approximately three months of operating costs before the first of the sales revenue will be received. It has also been estimated that a further $1 million of working capital would be required in year 8 due to increasing operating costs. This amount could come out of operating cash flow, but for calculating the NPV we need the discretionary cash flow; hence the $1 million will not be available to the equity holders and has to be accounted for in our project cash flow. The total of $7 million in working capital would be recovered after operations at the mine have finished, but for simplicity we will assume that it will be received in year 11 at the end of the mine life.

A simplified feasibility study is shown in table 19.5 (on pp. 408–10). Note that there are some rounding differences. The following notes explain each of the critical parameters, assumptions and calculations:

» The concentrate grade and tonnage has been calculated on the basis of an average 90 per cent recovery factor for the mill and the expected increase in concentrate grade that varies from 8.5 to 7.5 multiplied by the head grade into the mill. Variations in recovery and concentrate grade are dependent on the mine head grade.

» The waste has been determined with reference to the mine plans and the sequence of blocks mined each year. The waste-to-ore ratio increases over the life of the mine as the orebodies go deeper towards the south and the average grades decline.

» The price of metallica is expected to increase by 2 per cent per year from the spot price of US$3500. The smelter charge of US$500 is also expected to move in proportion to movements in the metal price. The inflation rate is forecast at 3 per cent per year and will affect all operating costs.

» The metal revenue is calculated by multiplying the annual contained metal in concentrate by the forecast price. Given the relatively low tonnage of concentrate shipped each year, delays in transportation are not expected and therefore for simplicity all sales and revenue are expected in the year of production.

» For year 3, metal revenue of $75.2 million is calculated by multiplying metal produced of 20 700 tonnes by US$3641/t. Strictly speaking, in the first year of operation there is a lag between the sale of the first product and payment, hence the need for working capital, but for simplification we will assume, as mentioned previously, that a full year's revenue and cash flow will be received in the first year.

» Net revenue to the mine is calculated by subtracting from the metal revenue the smelter and refining charge per tonne of metal and the costs of marketing, insurance and freight (based on a tonne per concentrate basis). For year 3, the smelting and refining charge of US$10.7 million is the product of multiplying 20 700 tonnes by a cost of US$520.

» The figure for earnings before interest, tax and depreciation (EBITDA) is calculated by subtracting all mine costs from the net revenue.

» The 5 per cent royalty charge is calculated on the net revenue to the mine, while the administration, mining and milling costs are calculated by multiplying the inflated cost(s) by the appropriate tonnes mined or milled. For year 3, the administration charge of US$1.6 million is the product of multiplying 510 000 tonnes by US$3.18 (the inflated cost of US$3 per tonne), the mining ore cost of US$1.4 million is the product of 510 000 tonnes at US$2.65 per tonne, mining waste cost of US$3.3 million is the product of 2.09 million tonnes at US$1.59 per tonne, and the milling cost of US$13.5 million is the product of 510 000 tonnes at US$26.52 per tonne. Total costs are $22.9 million, which, subtracted from net revenue of $61.3 million, leaves an EBITDA of $38.4 million (ignoring rounding errors).

» The next part of the model determines the cash flow that can be generated from the project ignoring project financing. The budget for developing the mine is US$80 million, while additional capital is expected to be spent in most years, to replace capital equipment such as pumps, and on minor plant alterations, as the grade of the ore changes through the mine life. Tax is payable on income at the rate of 30 per cent, which is calculated by subtracting the allowable tax deductions from the EBITDA. The allowable tax deductions are the capital expenditures, which are depreciated over the remaining life of the project, and the exploration and feasibility expenditures of US$10 million on the project and a further US$5 million in regional expenditure, which are deductible immediately. For year 3, the pre-tax income of US$14.5 million is calculated by subtracting from the EBITDA of US$38.4 million depreciation of US$8.9 million (US$80 million divided by 9 years) and exploration expenditure of US$15 million. The cash flow in year 3 ($26 million) is then the EBITDA ($38.4 million) less capital expenditure ($2 million), less tax ($4.4 million), less working capital ($6 million). The depreciation is not a cash-flow item, only a book entry to calculate the tax payable and no interest is applicable.

» Once the yearly cash flows have been calculated it is possible to determine the project's NPV. Year 1 and year 2 have negative capital expenditure cash flows of US$30 million and US$50 million respectively to construct the project. The NPV has been calculated for each year of the project at a 12 per cent discount based on the remaining cash flows. For the beginning of year 1, the project NPV of the cash flows is US$43.9 million, peaking in year 3 at $138.4 million after the major development expenditures have been sunk and then the NPV declines as the number of operating years remaining declines. If Agricola were able to fund the capital investment from its own balance sheet, then the NPV attributable would be $43.9 million.

» The next portion of the model is designed to calculate the interest payable on any project financing that might be used to fund the project. More details of the decision and impact are discussed later, but in the example, 62.5 per cent of the capital costs are funded through project debt. The US$50 million of debt is modelled to be paid back in equal instalments over the mine life, but in practice this may not be the case with payments tailored to the annual cash flow. The interest charge is 7 per cent of the outstanding debt at the end of the previous year. Therefore, in year 3 the interest cost is 7 per cent of US$50 million, or US$3.5 million. Subtracting the interest from the EBITDA and depreciation provides the figures for earnings before tax (EBT), from which the tax can be calculated as before.

» The cash flow attributable to equity, after project financing, is derived by subtracting from EBITDA ($38.4 million) capital expenditure ($2.0 million), debt repayment ($5.6 million), interest ($3.5 million), tax ($3.3 million) and working capital ($6 million) for a value in year 3 of $18.0 million. The capital expenditure in year 2 has also been reduced by $50 million, as this will be paid by debt and not equity. The NPV of equity for each year is also shown with a value in year 1 of $53.5 million. This is higher than the project NPV as the equity participants have benefited from the leverage effect of cheaper project financing, but the risks have increased as any adverse financial operating conditions will be felt first by the Agricola shareholders. In year 3 the equity NPV is lower than project NPV as the debt and interest have to be paid first before the equity holder get their share of cash flow, but in return they have only had to fund $30 million of the $80 million capital expenditure (ignoring exploration and ongoing capital expenditures).

» The final step shown in the table, which is not generally part of a financial feasibility study, is to estimate the likely reported earnings by Agricola. The major change is in the calculation of depreciation for reporting purposes. In the example shown, all capital and exploration expenditure has been depreciated on a per-tonne-of-metallica-produced basis over the life of the project. This procedure, to some extent, smoothes out the depreciation and hence the reported tax and profit (but not tax paid that remains as per the feasibility study). For year 3 the reported profit becomes $16.3 million compared with a geared project profit of $7.7 million (which is lower due to the exploration write-off allowable in the first year). The cash flow, as often derived by the equity markets, is simply the earnings plus the depreciation. Year 3 is thus $11.6 million depreciation, plus $16.3 million profit for a cash flow of $27.9 million.

Table 19.5: feasibility study for Agricola's metallica deposit (revenues and costs are $ million unless otherwise shown)

Year	1	2	3	4	5	6	7	8	9	10	11
Ore treated (000s t)	—	—	510	510	510	510	510	510	510	510	510
Ore treated grade	—	—	4.5%	4.7%	4.3%	4.1%	4.0%	3.9%	3.9%	3.8%	3.5%
Concentrate (000s t)	—	—	60.0	60.0	61.4	62.2	63.8	63.8	63.8	65.4	68.0
Concentrate grade	—	—	34%	36%	32%	30%	29%	28%	28%	27%	24%a
Metal (000s t)	—	—	20.7	21.6	19.7	18.8	18.4	17.9	17.9	17.4	16.1
Waste (000s t)	—	3570	2091	2142	1989	2295	2448	2652	2805	3060	3315
Metal price US$/tonne	3500	3570	3641	3714	3789	3864	3942	4020	4101	4183	4266
Inflation	3%	3%	3%	3%	3%	3%	3%	3%	3%	3%	3%
Smelter charge US$/t	500	510	520	531	541	552	563	574	586	598	609
Metal price A$/t	3500	3570	3641	3714	3789	3864	3942	4020	4101	4183	4266
Metal revenue	—	—	75.2	80.1	74.8	72.7	72.4	72.0	73.4	73.0	68.5
less TC/RC	—	—	10.7	11.4	10.7	10.4	10.3	10.3	10.5	10.4	9.8
Sales revenue	—	—	64.5	68.7	64.1	62.3	62.0	61.7	62.9	62.5	58.7
less Marketing	—	—	3.2	3.3	3.5	3.6	3.8	3.9	4.0	4.3	4.6
Net revenue	—	—	61.3	65.4	60.6	58.7	58.2	57.8	58.9	58.3	54.2
less	—	—	—	—	—	—	—	—	—	—	—
Royalty	—	—	3.1	3.3	3.0	2.9	2.9	2.9	2.9	2.9	2.7
Administration	—	—	1.6	1.7	1.7	1.8	1.8	1.9	1.9	2.0	2.1

Agricola Mining—a hypothetical example

Year	1	2	3	4	5	6	7	8	9	10	11
Mining ore	—	—	1.4	1.4	1.4	1.5	1.5	1.6	1.6	1.7	1.7
Mining waste	—	—	3.3	3.5	3.4	4.0	4.4	4.9	5.3	6.0	6.7
Milling	—	—	13.5	13.9	14.4	14.8	15.2	15.7	16.2	16.6	17.1
Total costs	—	—	**22.9**	**23.8**	**23.9**	**25.0**	**25.9**	**26.9**	**28.0**	**29.2**	**30.3**
EBITDA	—	—	38.4	41.6	36.7	33.8	32.4	30.9	30.9	29.1	23.9
Capital expenditure	30.0	50.0	2.0	1.0	1.5	1.5	0.5	0.5	1.0	0.5	0.0
Taxation depreciation	—	—	8.9	9.1	9.3	9.5	9.8	10.0	10.1	10.6	11.1
Depreciation carried fwd	—	80.0	73.1	65.0	57.2	49.2	39.8	30.4	21.2	11.1	0.0
Exploration carried fwd	—	15	—	—	—	—	—	—	—	—	—
Pre tax income (EBT)	—	—	14.5	32.5	27.5	24.2	22.5	20.9	20.8	18.4	12.8
Tax @ 30%	—	—	4.4	9.7	8.2	7.3	6.8	6.3	6.2	5.5	3.8
less Working capital	—	—	6.0	—	—	—	—	1.0	—	—	-7.0
Project cash flow	-30.0	-50.0	26.0	30.9	27.0	25.0	25.1	23.1	23.7	23.0	27.1
Project NPV @ 12%	43.9	79.2	138.7	129.3	113.9	100.6	87.7	73.1	58.8	42.1	24.2
Debt outstanding	—	50.0	44.4	38.9	33.3	27.8	22.2	16.7	11.1	5.6	0.0
less Debt repayment	—	—	5.6	5.6	5.6	5.6	5.6	5.6	5.6	5.6	5.6
less Interest cost @ 7%	—	—	3.5	3.1	2.7	2.3	1.9	1.6	1.2	0.8	0.4
Pre tax income (EBT)	—	—	11.0	29.4	24.7	21.9	20.6	19.3	19.6	17.7	12.4
Tax @ 30%	—	—	3.3	8.8	7.4	6.6	6.2	5.8	5.9	5.3	3.7
Project profit	—	—	7.7	20.6	17.3	15.3	14.4	13.5	13.7	12.4	8.7
less Working capital	—	—	6.0	—	—	—	—	1.0	—	—	-7.0

(continued)

Table 19.5: feasibility study for Agricola's metallica deposit (revenues and costs are $ million unless otherwise shown) (cont'd)

Year	1	2	3	4	5	6	7	8	9	10	11
Equity cash flow	-30.0	0.0	18.0	23.1	19.5	17.8	18.2	16.4	17.3	16.9	21.2
Equity NPV @ 12%	53.5	90.0	100.7	94.8	83.0	73.5	64.5	54.0	44.1	32.0	19.0
Profit Forecast	—	—	—	—	—	—	—	—	—	—	—
EBTDA	—	—	34.9	38.5	34.0	31.4	30.4	29.3	29.7	28.3	23.5
Depreciation	—	—	11.6	12.2	11.1	10.6	10.4	10.1	10.1	9.8	9.1
Pre tax	—	—	23.2	26.3	22.9	20.8	20.1	19.2	19.6	18.5	14.4
Tax @ 30%	—	—	7.0	7.9	6.9	6.2	6.0	5.8	5.9	5.5	4.3
Reported profit	—	—	16.3	18.4	16.0	14.6	14.0	13.4	13.8	12.9	10.1
Reported cash flow	—	—	27.9	30.6	27.1	25.2	24.4	23.5	23.8	22.8	19.2
Debt coverage ratio	—	—	3.25	4.17	3.52	3.21	3.27	2.96	3.11	3.05	3.82
Project NPV @ 9.3%	59.3	—	—	—	—	—	—	—	—	—	—

Fundamental value

Given the market size of Agricola, it will be necessary to fund a portion of the capital expenditure by way of debt. The balance sheet is probably not strong enough to arrange corporate debt, and thus 62.5 per cent project finance was incorporated in the previous worked example. The debt coverage ratio looks sound with average coverage at around two times (see chapter 3). Indeed, it may be possible to increase the debt funding, but given the project risks, a higher equity component will make it easier to raise the debt.

Agricola will therefore have to raise additional equity, as the current cash of $10 million is clearly insufficient to meet ongoing exploration costs, the feasibility study, the $30 million contribution to capital expenditure plus an additional $6 million in working capital. The capital raising will therefore have to be around $40 million, which will allow for the cost of the capital raising, working capital and some cost overruns. A rights issue, which entitles all existing shareholders to subscribe for additional shares in the company, is probably the best approach, markets permitting. The additional shares will be issued at a 10 per cent discount to the existing share price.

The questions to ask are: is the current share price a true reflection of the project's value? What will be the dilutionary impact of the rights issue on the company? What is the theoretical share price outlook for the company?

In terms of the current value, one approach is to look at the net asset value of the company as follows:

Cash: US$10 million

Project's NPV[3]: US$43.9 million

Other exploration assets: US$5 million

Less debt: US$0 million

Company valuation: US$58.9 million

Value per share: US$0.59.

---

3 The cash flow has been discounted by 12 per cent, which is the equity cost of capital (r_e) derived from the CAPM: $r_e = 5.4\% + 1.1 \times 6\% = 12\%$. The WACC has not been used, as the project debt will not be a recourse to the shareholders and the company has no corporate debt and is not planning to acquire any.

The project's NPV has been used as the market is unaware at this stage of what funding will be required. The share price premium would not be unusual, given the potential upside from the project via a commodity price movement and further exploration success. If the equity NPV (after the project financing) of US$53.5 million is used in calculating the fundamental value, then the value per share increases to 69¢ per share, reflecting the gearing effect of the debt. However, a rights issue will be required to raise the necessary funds. To raise $40 million at a 10 per cent discount, or at 45¢ per share, will require the issue of 88.9 million shares, which is a significant but not unmanageable dilution.

The theoretical ex-price (share price after the issue) is 47¢.[4] However, once the capital has been raised, and the project finance is in place, the probability of a successful development of the mine is greatly enhanced. The share price may therefore reflect this greater degree of certainty, although there still will be risks associated with the project's successful completion and the risk of adverse movements in the commodity price. As discussed in chapter 15, the medium-term price target will be towards the peak NPV of $100.7 million for the project and a theoretical share price of 63¢.

This relatively low value is a result of the dilutionary effect of the equity raising, which can sometimes be overlooked when considering the economic impact of a new project on a listed resource company. The market capitalisation of the company may well exceed the implied fundamental value of the company's assets. Subject to the perceived outlook for the sector and the overall market environment, it is not unusual to see companies at a premium to their fundamental value.

Relative sector comparisons is another approach to valuing the company. Appropriate future price multiples can be applied to the estimates of the future reported earnings and cash flow. The difficulty is that applicable multiples three years out are not readily available. The best approach is to use next year's sector multiples and discount the value to today. For example, next year's sector earnings and cash-flow multiples are estimated to be 12 and 5 respectively. Using the reported

---

4 ($0.50 × 70 million shares + $0.45 × 88.9 million shares)/(70 million shares + 88.9 million shares).

earnings and cash-flow estimates for year 3 of $16.3 million and $27.9 million respectively, we have a market valuation of $195.6 million and $139.5 million. If we take $150 million as a reasonable estimate and discount for two years at the sector equity discount rate of 10 per cent, the implied value is $124.0 million or $0.78 per share in today's terms. Again this figure may not be achieved given the risks associated with the project. The target share price over the next two years could be $0.86; year 3's earnings and cash flow would then be only one year away (assuming that the market multiples have not changed in the meantime).

In the example it was assumed that, given the market size of Agricola Mining, project financing would be used to help fund the project. If it is assumed that it had the balance sheet post the rights issue to fund the project through corporate debt and equity, then the WACC would be used to discount the project cash flow to derive a valuation.

If we assume a debt/equity ratio of 71 per cent ($50 million ÷ $70 million) and a corporate interest rate of 8 per cent, then the WACC would be:

$$70 \div 120 \times 12\% + 50 \div 120 \times (1 - 0.3) \times 8\% = 9.3\%$$

The cash flow to be discounted is the after-tax ungeared (no interest) project cash flow, with a resultant valuation of $59.3 million.

Sensitivity analysis

The validity of the project's valuation is only as good as the parameter inputs. Sensitivity analysis can be a valuable tool for providing some indication of the possible risk from a deleterious movement in certain parameters, and conversely the reward if things go in favour of the project. In figure 19.4 (overleaf), sensitivity analysis has been conducted on the base case equity NPV of $53.5 million. The expected increase in the metallica metal price (2 per cent per annum) has been varied from a negative growth of 1 per cent to a positive growth rate of 4 per cent, while the inflation rate (3 per cent per year) has been varied from 0 to 5 per cent.

Figure 19.4: sensitivity analysis

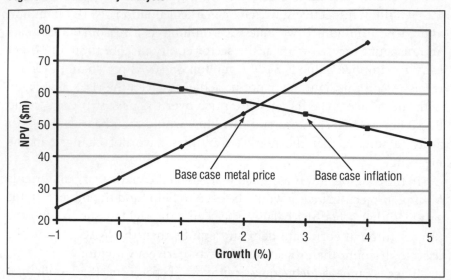

Clearly, the metal price is more sensitive. Even with a fall in metal price of 1 per cent per year, the project is still viable, although the project financing may be put at risk because of inadequate cover. Obviously, other parameters can also be tested, but in general they are less sensitive and known with more certainty.

Probability analysis

Only the two previous parameters of metal price increase and the inflation rate have been selected to generate a probability distribution of the year 1 equity NPV. The expected probability distributions of likely outcomes for the two parameters are shown in figure 19.5. Note that the base case values have the greatest probability of occurring.

The results of a Monte Carlo simulation are shown in figure 19.6. The first point to notice is that the outcome with the highest discrete probability is for an NPV of around $56 million, similar to the base case valuation of $53.5 million. The second point to note is that, if an 80 per cent probability of success is required by the Board of Agricola, then the likely NPV outcome is around $41.6 million and not the base case value of $53.5 million. Fortunately for this simulation, based on the probability constraints, no negative NPV is derived, indicating a relatively robust project.

Figure 19.5: probability distribution

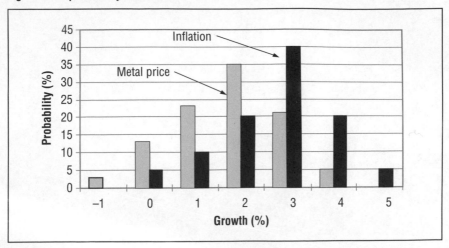

Figure 19.6: Monte Carlo simulation

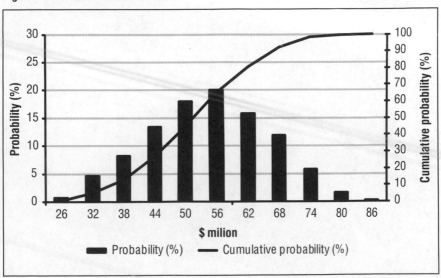

In this chapter we have looked at all of the generic issues that play a part in putting together a financial model to determine the viability of a project and then an assessment of the risks. But individual project valuations will vary in the first instance due to the type of commodity, the mining and metallurgical processes, and the markets. The next chapter provides a summary of the salient points for the major resource commodities to help provide an insight into some of the characteristics that investors should be familiar with.

CHAPTER 20
Commodity profiles

The discovery, mining and processing of mineral commodities is the lifeblood of the resources industry. There are dozens of economic elements that are mined in the form of hundreds of different minerals. It is not possible to cover all of the commodities and provide all of the relevant detail. However, it is important to appreciate some of the issues relating to the more common mineral resources. In the following pages I have attempted to distil a large number of source documents into easily read summaries, but by their very nature there will be some omissions. (For additional information, see appendix H for abbreviations, conversions and energy factors.)

The descriptions cover the following topics:

» *Commodity*. Includes chemical or elemental symbol, specific gravity and melting point.

» *Price*. In US$ terms, in most common form or value per tonne. Forward market premiums are included where applicable. These prices are only valid at the time of writing.

» *Supply/demand*. A brief description is given of the world market, with comments on end-use applications where appropriate. A major source of information was the US Geological Survey.

» *Geology*. Gives a brief description of the form in which the mineral or commodity is found.

» *Average grades*. For economic deposits, the range of mineable grades is provided. Each deposit has to be judged on its own particular merits and so the values provided are only a guide.

» *Costs.* In some cases indicative capital costs and, where meaningful, operating costs are provided on an annual tonne basis. Again, each deposit has to be judged on its own particular merits and thus the values provided are only a guide. Further details are provided in chapter 8.

» *Specific mineral processing and metallurgy issues.* Covers general metallurgical and mineral processing issues specific to that element. However, in the case of some commodities the discussion centres more on product specifications. The aim is to give a feel for some of the more important issues that the reader should be familiar with.

» *Refining charges.* Charges for mines that produce a concentrate that is then sent for further processing. The resultant net price received by the mine can vary greatly when compared with the quoted terminal price. For some products, particularly bulk commodities, this is not an issue. More detailed information can be found in *Cost Estimation Handbook* (1993).

Aluminium, Alumina and Bauxite

Commodity　　　　Symbol: Al, specific gravity of 2.58 and melting point of 658°C.

Price　　　　US$2240/t (alumina spot: US$300/t; bauxite: US$25 to US$40/t). LME forward markets are available for up to 27 months into the future.

Supply/demand　　World production in 2011 is estimated at approximately 44 million tonnes. The major producers are China (40 per cent), Russia (9 per cent), Canada (7 per cent), the US and Australia (each 5 per cent).

Total bauxite production for 2011 was approximately 220 million tonnes. The major producers are Australia (30 per cent), China (21 per cent), Brazil (14 per cent), Jamaica (9 per cent), Vietnam (9 per cent) and India (9 per cent).

World reserves of bauxite are around 29 billion tonnes; 26 per cent in Guinea, 21 per cent in Australia, 12 per cent in Brazil and 7 per cent in each of Jamaica and Vietnam.

Geology

Not found as a native metal, although it constitutes 8 per cent of the Earth's crust. Aluminium is associated with clay materials and some silicates. Major source is bauxite (hydrated oxides), generally found in tropical regions.

Average grades

Economic mine grades of bauxite have aluminium content of 25 to 35 per cent.

Capital and mining costs

Bauxite mining operations are low-cost open cut operations with long-term contracts to supply dedicated alumina refineries. The alumina refinery's major cost is the consumption of caustic soda, while for the aluminium smelter the greatest cost is the supply of electricity.

Metallurgy

Step 1: Refining—ground bauxite ore (to less than 7 mm) is digested in aqueous caustic soda.

The pregnant liquor is cooled and the alumina (Al_2O_3) is precipitated out and then calcined to anhydrous alumina.

Step 2: Smelting—electrolysis using carbon anodes is used to refine the alumina to aluminium.

Approximately 16 kWh/kg of aluminium production is required.

The reactive equation is $2Al_2O_3 + 3C = 4Al + 3CO_2$.

Pricing

Bauxite. Bonus/penalty systems with regard to price are determined by the content of alumina and silica. The higher the level of silica, the greater the amount of caustic soda lost in the recovery of alumina (1.0 t of silica reacts with 0.8 t of caustic soda). Typical proportions for Australian bauxite are Al_2O_3: 55 per cent; SiO_2: 4 per cent; Fe_2O_3: 12 per cent; TiO_2: 3 per cent; loss on ignition: 26 per cent.

Pricing is generally set at long-term contracts and is not made public. However, an indicative price for premium grade would be around 1.0 to 1.5 per cent of the aluminium price.

Alumina. Alumina is generally sold under medium-term contracts, with some small amounts sold on the spot market. Prices are not generally published, but contract can be linked to average three-month LME prices two months before sale. Contract prices are usually set at around 12 to 15 per cent of the aluminium price. The primary constituents and their costs, which define the price ratios of alumina and aluminium, are shown in table 20.1. Alumina prices were around US$420 per tonne in May 2011 when the aluminium price was US$2700 per tonne with alumina price falling to around US$300 by the end of 2011.

Table 20.1: costs of primary constituents of alumina and aluminium

Mineral	Quantities required (estimate)	Cost (US$/t)
Alumina	3.5 t bauxite	90
	60 kg of caustic soda	30
	Energy 1 MWh/t (steam)	60

Mineral	Quantities required (estimate)	Cost (US$/t)
Aluminium	Carbon anode (0.7 t carbon)	350
	2 t alumina	600
	Energy 16 MWh/t (grid)	650

Chromium

Commodity   Symbol: Cr. The only ore of chromium is mineral chromite (Fe, Mg) Cr_2O_4; specific gravity of 4.5 to 4.8.

Price   Ferrochrome (high carbon) US$2400/t, low carbon US$4800/t.

Supply/demand   About 50 per cent of chromite is produced in South Africa with a further 35 per cent coming from India and Kazakhstan. Production for 2011 was some 24 million tonnes (mt). Chromite is converted into ferrochrome (FeCr) of which 80 per cent is utilised in the production of stainless steel with an average content of 18 per cent. World reserves are some 480 mt.

Geology   Chromite is found in layered ultramafic rocks such as peridotite and metamorphic rocks such as serpentines.

Average grade   Grades are often quoted as the percentage of Cr_2O_3, usually averaging around 40 to 45 per cent and the Fe ratio of 1.5 to 3 times.

Capital and mining costs   The costs for mining chromite are similar to those for other base metal mining operations.

The ore is sorted into different size fractions by heavy media, while silica may be removed from finer fractions by gravity techniques.

Product range will therefore be from lump to fine with higher prices for lump. Fines will also be formed into pellets for better processing.

The cash cost of conversion of chromite to ferrochrome by International Ferro Metals Limited for 2011 was approximately $0.84 per pound, including cost of ore $0.24, coke $0.22 and power $0.21.

Metallurgy

Ferrochrome is produced by carbon reduction at high temperature by coal or coke to form an iron-chromium alloy.

Typically, an electric arc furnace is used with temperatures of around 2800^0C consuming some 3500 kWh per tonne of ferrochrome. Chemical grade ferrochrome (low in silica) is used by the chemical industry to produce sodium dichromate.

Foundry grade (low silica and specific size distribution) is used as moulding sand due to its low coefficient of thermal expansion and good heat transfer properties. Charge chrome is used as an additive in 170 different types of stainless steel for resistance to most types of wet and dry corrosion.

Charge chrome has a large proportion of free iron plus high silicon content that makes it preferable to high carbon chrome, as it reduces the need for steel manufacturers to charge their furnace with ferro-silicon.

Intermediate carbon ferrochrome is used for tool steels, and alloy steels for springs and valves. Low carbon ferrochrome with 59 to 61 per cent ferrochrome and 0.02 to 0.06 per cent carbon content is used in specialist applications.

Coal

Coal is a sedimentary fossil fuel composed of carbon (50 to 98 per cent), hydrogen (3 to 13 per cent) and other minor elements, primarily sulphur, as well as water and inorganic matter, which is referred to as ash. Coals are altered remains of old land vegetation, forest growth, and so on, that have been transformed by chemical microbial action, heat and pressure resulting in the removal of hydrogen and oxygen from the wood tissue into a material richer in carbon. The different types of coal, their relative abundance and uses are shown in figure 20.1, while coal characteristics are listed in table 20.2 (overleaf). The harder coals, such as anthracite, are formed through later exposure to elevated temperature and pressure. The coal market can be divided into two broad categories: steaming or thermal coal, used for the generation of heat in the production of electrical power; and metallurgical or coking coal, used in the production of iron and steel.

Figure 20.1: coal types and their uses

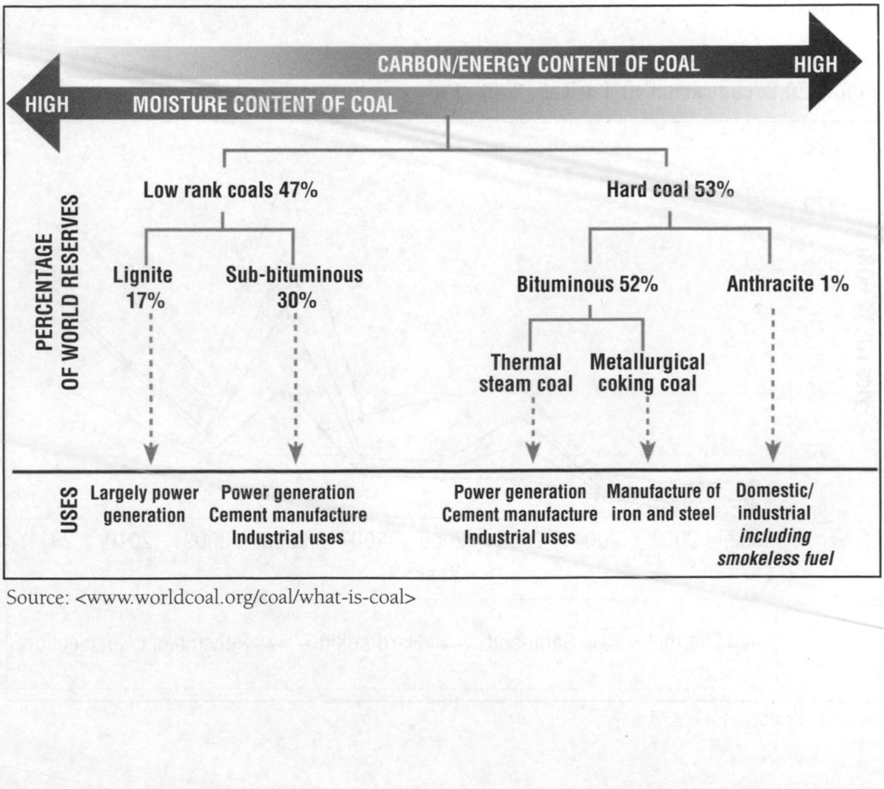

Source: <www.worldcoal.org/coal/what-is-coal>

Table 20.2: basic characteristics of each coal type

Rank	Moisture (%)	Calories (Kcal/kg)	Carbon (%)
Lignite	> 20	3850 to 6000	45 to 65
Semi-bituminous		5500 to 7150	60 to 75
Bituminous		7700 to 8800	75 to 90
Semi-anthracite		8250 to 8525	90 to 93
Anthracite		8000 to 8250	93 to 95

The prices for coal saw a significant increase from 2007 due to increased steel production and higher energy prices (see figure 20.2). The GFC and European credit crisis have put some recent downward pressure on prices particularly for hard coking coals as the demand for steel appears to be weakening.

Figure 20.2: contracted coal prices, 2002–11

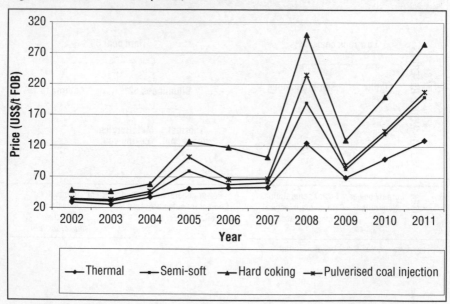

Note: FOB = free on board ship.

World reserves are 860 billion tonnes, of which the US accounts for 28 per cent, Russian Federation 18 per cent, China 13 per cent, Australia 9 per cent and India 7 per cent. Global coal production for 2010 was 7.3 billion tonnes; China produced 48 per cent; US, 15 per cent; Europe, 11.5 per cent; Australia and India, 5 per cent each.

Coking coal

Commodity Symbol: C, specific gravity of 1.0 to 1.8. Can be classified as hard coking, pulverised coal injection (PCI) or semi-soft coking coals.

Price Hard coking coal around US$285; PCI around $208; and semi-soft coking around US$200/t. Previously sold on evergreen contracts, with volumes and prices set for one year beginning in April of each year, but more recently contacts have gone over to quarterly price setting and in some cases monthly.

Supply/demand Metallurgical coals can be divided into hard coking coals for the production of hard coke to go into blast furnaces, and cheaper semi-soft or soft coking coals, which have weaker coking properties, that are blended with hard coking coals to reduce costs.

Blast furnaces require specific blends of coals that meet both technical specifications and economic imperatives.

The most sought-after and highest priced coals are the hard coking coals. Another type of metallurgical coal is PCI coal, which falls into two categories: high volatile low rank bituminous and low volatile semi-anthracite coals.

The PCI coals are injected into the raceway of the blast furnace as a means of reducing production costs through lower consumption of coking coal and oil in the production of pig iron. PCI coals don't require any coke-making or other process stage other than grinding before injection.

Characteristics Suitable for the production of coke for blast furnaces. The coal therefore needs to have good coking and caking properties, such as fluidity, crucible swelling number and appropriate rank.

Ash and moisture should be low, as should sulphur and phosphorus, which have a negative impact on pig iron production. The primary coal parameters are listed in table 20.3.

Capital costs Subject to size, location and type of mining operation. Capital costs are sometimes quoted as a dollar amount per annual tonne sold.

Open cut: $35 to $140 per annual tonne.

Underground: $45 to $175 per annual tonne.

Operating costs Variable and subject to location and project type.

Open cut: waste removal $2 to $3 per cubic metre; ore removal $1.5 to $3 per tonne of run of mine (ROM) coal.

Underground: $20 to $70 per tonne of ROM coal.

Other costs: washing $5 to $11 per tonne ROM coal; transport $4 to $15 per tonne of coal; ship loading $3 to $8 per tonne of coal.

Table 20.3: coking coal quality parameters

Standard	Description	Value	Preference
Ash	Inorganic residue	Lower the better	7 to 14.5%
Coke strength (CSR)	Strength in blast furnace	Higher the better	—
Crucible swelling number (CSN)	Amount coal swells on heating	0: low; 9: superior	3 to 9
Fixed carbon	—	Higher the better	51 to 70.6%
Fluidity	As coal melts its plastic range is measured	Higher the better	10 to 10 000
Gross calorific value	Amount of heat liberated	Higher the better	6600 to 7900 Kcal*/kg
Moisture	In the coal as measured	Lower the better	1 to 3%
Phosphorus	—	Lower the better	0.011 to 0.09%
Sulphur	—	Lower the better	0.3 to 1.29%
Volatile matter	Material distilled off on heating	Lower the better	16 to 38%

*Kcal = kilocalories.

Mill recovery or yield

Coal washing is the process by which ash or waste is removed from the ROM coal to increase its value and meet specifications. Fine coal particles of less than 0.5 mm are also removed. The most common method of separation of coal from waste utilises specific gravity through heavy media separation.

Common yields range between 70 and 85 per cent.

Steaming coal

Commodity   Symbol: C, specific gravity of 1.14 to 1.40. Often referred to as thermal coal.

Price   All coals contain energy and produce heat, and the selection of a coal for power generation is primarily one of cost, subject to the coal's particular qualities, such as ash and sulphur content.

Thermal coals are usually the cheapest in price. Price relates to the energy level that the coal can provide. The base price is set for an energy level of 6700 Kcal/kg and then adjusted pro rata.

The current base contract prices approximately US$130/t. Previously sold on evergreen contracts, with volumes and prices renegotiated around April of each year. However, pricing now determined quarterly and in some cases monthly. Spot markets are more prevalent than for coking coals.

Supply/demand   World mine production is approximately 5300 million tonnes per year, including brown coal, although world trade is 800 million tonnes per annum. Steaming coals are used for the production of cement and primarily in the production of heat for the generation of steam and hence electricity. Major exporters include Indonesia (30 per cent), Australia (16 per cent) and Russia (12 per cent).

Characteristics   Suitable for the production of heat for power generation. The coal therefore needs to have good energy attributes. Ash and moisture should be low.

Ash fusion temperature, sulphur and volatile matter are also of concern to buyers. The primary coal quality parameters are listed in table 20.4.

Table 20.4: steaming coal quality parameters

Standard	Description	Value	Preference
Ash	Inorganic residue	Lower the better	11 to 25%
Ash fusion	Softening temperature	Higher the better	+1560°C
Crucible swelling number (CSN)	Amount coal swells on heating	0: low (1 to 3); 9: superior	—
Fixed carbon	—	Higher the better	51.5 to 56.5%
Gross calorific value	Amount of heat liberated	Higher the better	6200 to 7200 Kcal/kg
Inherent moisture	In the coal as measured	Lower the better	1.5 to 3%
Total moisture	Moisture content	Lower the better	7 to 9%
Phosphorus	—	Lower the better	0.01 to 0.2%
Sulphur	—	Lower the better	0.4 to 0.8%
Volatile matter	Material distilled off on heating	Lower the better	22 to 33%

Capital cost Subject to size, location and type of mining operation. Capital costs are sometimes quoted as dollar per annual tonne sold.

Open cut: $35 to $140 per annual tonne.

Underground: $45 to $135 per annual tonne

Operating costs Variable and subject to location and project type.

Open cut: waste removal $2 to $3 per cubic metre; ore removal $1.5 to $3 per tonne of run of mine (ROM) coal

Underground: $20 to $70 per tonne of ROM coal.

Other costs: washing $5 to $11 per tonne ROM coal; transport $4 to $15 per tonne of coal; ship loading $3 to $8 per tonne of coal.

Mill recovery   Coal washing is the process by which ash or waste is removed from the ROM coal to increase its value and meet specifications.

Fine coal particles of less than 0.5 mm are also removed. The most common method of separation of coal from waste utilises specific gravity through heavy media separation. Common yields fall between the range of 70 and 85 per cent.

Coal seam methane

Commodity   Symbol: CH_4, methane gas associated with coal deposits that is similar although purer than natural gas found in conventional sedimentary reservoirs (see later section on natural gas, p. 462).

Price   Is dependent on local market prices for natural gas (methane). Sales will generally be made under long-term contracts for the supply of annual volumes.

Supply/demand   The potential for coal bed methane is enormous given the large coal reserves existing in many countries, particularly Australia and the US.

The difficulty is finding suitable coal seams that allow for cost-effective recovery of the methane.

Geology   Natural gas formed during the coalification process where the gas is trapped by absorption onto the coal grain surface or micro pores, and is held in place by the reservoir pressure (water). The coal seam therefore acts as a source, reservoir and seal for the methane.

As the micro pore surface area is very large, coal seams can hold more cubic metres of methane per tonne of coal than most sandstone reservoirs (up to three times).

The permeability of the coal is a function of the cleat or natural fracture system of the coal, as well as of other fractures and joints.

Best coals in general are low volatile (R_0 1.0 to R_0 2.0 per cent), high vitrinite, low-ash coals, but permeability may be offset by in situ stresses and secondary mineral infilling.

Capital cost

Due to the relatively low production rates of gas from coal bed methane wells relative to conventional reservoirs, it is necessary to drill a significant number of closely spaced wells. These wells are generally shallow and therefore have low drilling costs of some $100 000 to $200 000 each. To complete the well, including fracturing, a further $200 000 to $300 000 each may be required.

Gas recovery

The gas saturation is the actual gas held in the coal seam relative to the maximum gas that could be held at that pressure.

If the measured methane content is less than full saturation ($10 m^3/t$) then when a well is drilled, initially only water will be produced until the pressure drops sufficiently to the critical desorption pressure (2.7 megapascals, or mPa) to allow desorption and hence production of gas, as shown in figure 20.3 (overleaf). If this critical pressure is low then it will take longer for the well to produce gas and the amount recovered will be much less.

It is often necessary to stimulate the coals to help production by hydraulic fracturing or cavitation. Production rates can be quite variable, with initial gas production rising as pressure drops, then tailing off over time. Individual well rates can vary anywhere between 10 mcf per day to 1000 mcf per day.

Figure 20.3: methane desorption isotherm

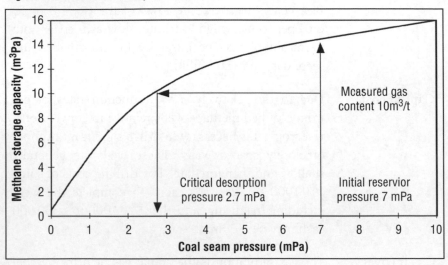

Cobalt

Commodity Symbol: Co, specific gravity of 8.9 and melting point of 1500°C.

Price US$32 000/t LME forward markets are available for up to 15 months into the future.

Sales generally based on contracts such as the two-year renewable contract for the Western Australian Murrin Murrin nickel mine with Glencore.

Supply/demand　World mine production in 2011 was approximately 98 000 tonnes, with the major source of supply being the Congo (50 per cent) and approximately another 7 per cent from each of Zambia, Russia, Canada and China.

World reserves are some 7.5 million tonnes with most (75 per cent) located in the Congo, Cuba and Australia.

Consumption is primarily for superalloys and speciality steels, as well as for magnetic alloys, catalysts, cutting materials and paint driers.

There are few substitutes for cobalt, but rather a trend towards replacement by materials such as ceramics. Australian annual production is 4000 tonnes of contained cobalt.

Geology　Cobalt production comes chiefly as a by-product from copper smelting in Zaire and Zambia. It is often associated with copper, arsenic, nickel and silver. Economic deposits occur as veins of smaltite $(Co,Ni)As_{3-n}$ and cobaltite $(CoAsS)$, as cobaltiferous pyrrhotite or as asbolite (oxide of manganese sometimes containing up to 40 per cent cobalt).

Average grades　As a by-product, grades are not a meaningful parameter; however, the grades of cobalt associated with the Australian nickel projects are around 0.1 per cent.

Metallurgy　In the recovery of cobalt from a lateritic nickel operation, the first stage will generally consist of the production of a mixed sulphide containing principally nickel and sulphur with some 3 to 5 per cent cobalt.

The mixed sulphide is produced by the pressure acid leach of the mine ore, to produce a leach liquor, followed by neutralisation and precipitation of the mixed sulphides using hydrogen sulphide. Solvent extraction is used to recover the cobalt from solution where it can be formed into briquettes after hydrogen reduction and sintering or electro-won to produce purer cobalt cathode. At QNI's Yabula treatment plant in Queensland, cobalt remains in the leach liquor after preferential separation of the nickel. The cobalt is then precipitated as cobalt sulphide, thickened, dried and drummed for sale. The cobalt sulphide contains 43 per cent cobalt, 1 per cent nickel and 35 per cent sulphur plus moisture.

Copper

Commodity   Symbol: Cu, specific gravity of 8.9 and melting point of 1100°C.

Price   US$8050/t. Forward copper markets are quoted on the LME, and COMEX up to 27 months ahead. It is possible to obtain forward cover up to seven years.

Supply/demand   World mine production for 2011 was approximately 16.1 million tonnes: 34 per cent from Chile, 7 per cent each from China, Peru and the US, and 6 per cent from Australia.

World reserves are some 690 million tonnes with Chile accounting for 28 per cent. Consumption is primarily in the electrical, automotive and chemical industries. Australian annual refined production is approximately 0.8 million tonnes.

Geology   Found as native copper and primarily in sulphide minerals of chalcopyrite and chalcocite. Gold and silver can be found associated with copper ores.

Average grades	Economic mine grades can vary from a low of 0.25 per cent for open cut mines to 2 per cent and upwards for underground mines, depending on the level of associated metals such as gold.
Capital cost	Subject to size, location and type of mining operation. Cost can be quoted as dollars per annual tonne treated through the mill. See chapter 8 for more details.
	SX-EW: approx. $3000 per annual tonne of copper metal.
Mill recovery	Dependent on the type of ore and the process, with typical recoveries of between 85 and 95 per cent.
Metallurgy	First stage of recovery at the mine site is production of a concentrate by froth flotation (see chapter 7). The concentrate grade (20 to 40 per cent), which is sent to a smelter for recovery, can be some 10 to 30 times greater than the grade of the ore. Copper may also be leached from ore on site by the application of acid to dissolve the copper (solvent extraction). The copper metal is then generally recovered on site by electro-winning, hence the name SX-EW.
Refining charges	For the sale of concentrates to a smelter the typical terms include reduction in the metal payable and a treatment and refining charge (TC/RC).
	A price participation (PP) formula may be included to increase the TC/RC if the metal price is above a set level and to decrease it if the metal price is below a fixed level.
	Continued shortages of concentrates have meant that the PP has been excluded from many contracts. Refining charges may also be applicable for any precious metals and penalties applicable for undesirable elements such as lead.

Payable metal: 96.5 per cent of copper content (min. deduction 1.1 per cent), gold content less 1 g/t, 90 per cent of silver content (min. deduction 30 g/t).

TC/RC: TC of US60/t of concentrate and an RC of US$0.06/lb of copper metal. Although charges have increased in recent times compared with previous lows, they are still substantially below the previous high of US$170/US$0.17 in early 2005.

Diamonds

Commodity Symbol: C, pure carbon in cubic crystal structure, specific gravity of 3.52. (Note: 1 carat equals approximately 0.2 grams.)

Price Price relates to size and quality of the diamond.

Diamonds sold from the mines are rough. They then go on to polishing centres for retail sales or, if low quality, directly for industrial applications. Some 20 per cent of gem production accounts for 50 per cent of market value, while the top 2 per cent accounts for 15 per cent of market value.

Marketing The vast majority of rough diamond sales (approximately 40 per cent) are to the Diamond Trading Company (DTC), formerly the Central Selling Organisation, which regulates the sales to gem-cutters. The DTC charges a 10 per cent commission fee based on gross value. However, the majority of sales (75 per cent) are by long-term contracts.

Supply/demand The world diamond market is shown in figure 20.4.

Figure 20.4: world diamond market

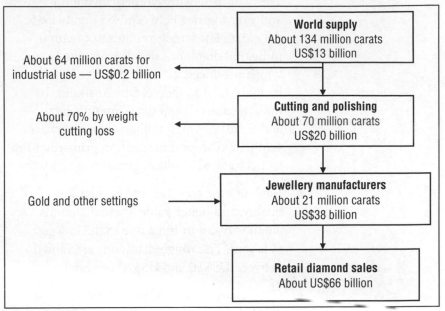

Geology	Primary deposits occur in igneous rocks of ultrabasic composition, often in the form of breccia pipes. The diamonds are formed 200 kilometres below the Earth's surface and are brought up via the pipes. Secondary deposits can also be found as alluvials, sourced from the primary deposits. Alluvial deposits can have very high-quality diamonds.
Average grades	The economic significance of a deposit is a function not only of the grade in terms of carats per tonne, but also of the quality distribution of the diamonds. Economic mine grades can vary from 0.05 to 2.00 carats per tonne.
Diamond factors	Diamonds can be classified into the following:

» *Industrial or boart*. These low-grade diamonds are used in industrial applications, for instance as abrasives, due to their hardness.

They compete with synthetic diamonds and vary in price between US$1 and US$5 per carat. The largest producer of natural industrial diamonds in 2011 was the Congo, which produced 22 million carats: followed by Russia, 15 million carats; Australia, 10 million carats; Botswana, 7 million carats; and South Africa, 5 million carats. However, synthetic diamond production primarily from China totalled 4 billion carats!

» *Semi- or near gem*. Because of their low quality, and hence value, these diamonds are mostly cut in India due to the low cost of labour. The rough diamonds are valued between US$10 and US$20 per carat.

» *Gem quality*. The DTC sorts diamonds into 2500 classifications and they are offered to major cutting centres throughout the world at monthly sightings. The three factors that are the primary determinants of value are colour, clarity and cut.

» *Colour*. Colour has the most impact on the eye and therefore is very important. The colour occurs due to absorption of light associated with trace elements; for example, manganese produces the rare pink diamonds from Argyle. The most valuable is the white or colourless stone, although the rarest colour is red, followed by green, blue, purple and brown.

» *Cut*. A rough diamond is coated in a yellow or brown transparent skin. By cutting the diamond the unique optical properties of the high refractive index and colour dispersion are released.

There are numerous shapes such as navettes, baguettes, pears, square or emerald cut, but the most popular and effective is the brilliant cut devised in the first century BC (see table 20.5). De Beers, Alrosa, BHP Billiton and Rio Tinto are responsible for some 70 per cent of global production currently at 134 million carats, valued at around US$13 billion.

For gem quality the approximate value increases in each step to polished goods in jewellery is 15 per cent for sorting, 15 per cent for polishing, 5 per cent for dealing, 35 per cent jewellery manufacture and finally a 150 to 200 per cent mark-up for retail.

Table 20.5: cut diamond characteristics

Colour	Clarity	Cut
Exceptional white + (D)	Flawless (FL)	Proportion
Exceptional white (E)	Internally flawless (IF)	American ideal cut
Rare white + (F)	Very, very slightly included (VVS)	(Tolkowsky brilliant)
Rare white (G)	Very slightly included (VS)	Finish, symmetry
White (H)	Slightly included (SI)	Polish: very good, good, medium, poor
Slightly tinted white (I–J)	Imperfect (I1–I3)	—
Tinted white (K–L)	—	—
Tinted colour (M–Z)	—	—
Fancy diamonds	—	—

Gold

Commodity

Symbol: Au, specific gravity of 19.3 and melting point of 1060°C. Pure gold is described as 24 carat.

Price

US$1650/oz, 99.99 per cent pure. (Note: 1 oz = 31.1 g.) Forward gold markets are quoted on the LME and NYMEX up to 54 months ahead.

Current premium is about US$15 per year, therefore one ounce can be sold for US$1675 in 12 months' time. Gold can be sold up to 10 years into the future at increasing prices.

Supply/demand

World mine production is approximately 2700 tonnes per year. Consumption is primarily for jewellery and electronics. World reserves of finished product are 40 000 tonnes in financial institutions and another 40 000 tonnes in private hands. Major producing countries include China (355 tonnes), Australia (270 tonnes), US (240 tonnes) and Russia (200 tonnes). World mineable reserves are 51 million tonnes with 15 per cent in Australia; 12 per cent located in South Africa; 10 per cent in Russia; and 6 per cent in each of Indonesia, Chile and the US.

Geology

Generally found in a free state throughout nature, but often alloyed with silver or copper and with some other minerals. Native gold ranges from 85 to 95 per cent gold, with the remainder generally silver. Gold ore can be found as either free milling (non-refractory) or as sulphides (refractory).

Average grades

Economic mine grades can vary from a low of 0.2 g/t for a heap leach operation to 1 g/t for open cut. Underground mines vary from around 4 g/t to 25 g/t.

Metallurgy	Free gold can be separated by gravity. Non-refractory gold is most often recovered using cyanide as the leach agent either in tanks or heap leach pads. Refractory ores generally undergo a combination of flotation to recover the sulphide minerals and then roasting to remove the sulphur. Cyanide leaching is then used to recover the gold.
Mill recovery	Dependent on the type of ore and the process. For most non-refractory ores using CIP or carbon-in-leach (CIL), the recoveries vary from a low of 85 per cent to a high of 98 per cent. Refractory ores, after removal of sulphides, have recoveries of 60 to 85 per cent. These stages and performance of CIP are summarised in table 20.6.

Table 20.6: carbon-in-pulp (CIP) gold recovery

Stages	Performance
Fine grind to about 75 microns	Average grade, say, 3 g/t
Mix in tanks with water and cyanide	Grade increases to 100 g/t
Add carbon to absorb gold from cyanide	2000 to 6000 g/t carbon
Gold stripped from carbon into solution	Grade increases to 300 g/t
Use electrolysis to plate gold on steel	Dore production (gold–silver mix)
Carbon consumption	8 to 40 g/t
Cyanide consumption	0.1 to 1.5 kg/t ore

Refining charges Gold is refined to 99.99 per cent and stamped for a charge of approximately $2 to $6 per ounce.

The refinery will pay for between 99.80 and 99.95 per cent of the gold content. Gold dore delivered to the refinery generally needs to be 70 per cent plus gold content, and penalty rates apply for deleterious elements such as iron, lead, tellurium and nickel. The refinery will pay for between 95 and 99 per cent of the silver content.

Heavy mineral sands

The heavy mineral sands include titanium (rutile, ilmenite and leucoxene), zirconium and monazite.

Commodity Heavy mineral sands can be separated into the following constituents

Titanium: symbol Ti, not found naturally but as oxides of:

» *Rutile*: approximately 95 per cent TiO_2, specific gravity of 4.2

» *Ilmenite*: $FeOTiO_2$, minimum TiO_2 content 47 per cent, with ratio of iron varying due to the level of intergrowth of magnetite or hematite, specific gravity of 4.5 to 5.0

» *Leucoxene*: approximately 85 to 92 per cent TiO_2, due to natural leaching of iron from ilmenite.

» *Zirconium*: symbol Zr, specific gravity of 4.08 and melting point of 1300°C found as complex silicates mainly as Zircon ($ZrSiO_4$) with specific gravity of 4.7

> » *Monazite*: phosphate of rare earth metals
> $(Ce,La,Yt)PO_4$ plus thoria ThO_2 and silica SiO_2
> with specific gravity of 5.3

Price   See table 20.7.

Table 20.7: heavy mineral pricing

Mineral	Specification	Price (US$/tonne)
Rutile	min. 95% TiO_2	2340
Ilmenite	min. 50% TiO_2	250–300
Leucoxene	say, 85% TiO_2	800
Titanium dioxide pigment	—	3200
Monazite	55% to 60% rare earths	55000
Zircon	min. 66% ZrO_2	2400

Marketing   Generally all sold on evergreen contracts with
                                volumes and prices renegotiated each year. The
                                prices will vary from those shown in table 20.7,
                                depending on the quality of the product provided.

                                Titanium. End product and processing route will
                                define the prices payable for the various titanium
                                feed stocks. Grain size and the level of ZrO_2 and
                                Fe_2O_3 can be important.

                                Zirconium. Quality grade zircon is preferred with
                                over 65 per cent ZrO_2 and minimum quantities of
                                Fe_2O_3 and TiO_2 at around 0.04 to 0.05 per cent.

Monazite. Generally sold to processors as a concentrate with some 55 to 60 per cent rare earths (the major source of rare earths is bastnasite (Ce, La) CO_3F or (La, Ce)CO_3F or (Y, Ce)CO_3F).

Supply/demand
World production of ilmenite in 2011 was around 6 million tonnes, primarily from Australia (15 per cent), South Africa (17 per cent), Canada (12 per cent), India (9 per cent) and China (8 per cent). World reserves of 650 million tonnes are located in China (31 per cent), Australia (15 per cent), India (13 per cent) and South Africa (10 per cent). Production of rutile was 700 000 tonnes from Australia (57 per cent), South Africa (19 per cent), Sierra Leone (9 per cent) and Ukraine (8 per cent). World reserves are 42 million tonnes, predominantly in Australia (43 per cent), South Africa (20 per cent), India (18 per cent), Sierra Leone (9 per cent) and Ukraine (6 per cent).

Titanium. Some 94 per cent of the world's titanium is consumed as titanium dioxide pigment, predominantly for the manufacture of paint and fillers for paper and plastics. World pigment capacity in 2011 was 6.55 million tonnes, predominantly in China (31 per cent), the US (22 per cent), Germany (5 per cent), Japan (5 per cent), the UK (5 per cent) and Australia (4 per cent). Titanium can also be used as a metal, given its high strength and resistance to heat, and for welding rods and ceramics.

World production of titanium sponge for 2011 was about 186 000 tonnes from China (32 per cent), Japan (30 per cent), Russia (22 per cent), Kazakhstan (10 per cent) and Ukraine (5 per cent). The spot prices of rutile and ilmenite can be quite volatile, depending on the world demand for paint; as, for example, shown by US housing starts, although most sales are by way of contracts that are adjusted for inflation.

Zircon. Production for 2011 was 1.41 million tonnes coming from Australia (50 per cent), South Africa (25 per cent) and China (7 per cent).

World reserves were 52 million tonnes, primarily in Australia (40 per cent), South Africa (27 per cent), Ukraine (8 per cent) and India (7 per cent). Zircon has excellent high temperature and insulation properties. It is used in such applications as refractory blocks in furnaces containing molten metal, foundry sands, nuclear reactors, zirconium metal, ceramics and abrasives.

Monazite. The process of separating the rare earths is costly, and their prices are dependent on markets such as television screens for europium and yttrium, and incandescent mantles for thorium.

Total world production of monazite and bastnasite in 2007 was around 124 000 tonnes while reserves are some 88 million tonnes.

Geology

Heavy mineral sands are formed through the weathering process of the land surface and the accumulation of economic concentrations of the valuable commodities. The most common form of sorting and deposition occurs in old beach placers, which are formed by wave action where the coarser grained minerals (more valuable due to their resistance to weathering) are deposited towards the old shorelines.

Average grades

Typical grades of heavy minerals in beach sands vary from 3 to 25 per cent. The composition or suit of economic minerals can vary greatly within the percentage. An example of the mix of economic minerals within the heavy minerals is shown in table 20.8 (overleaf).

Table 20.8: mineral assemblage, Cooljarloo Deposit in Western Australia

Mineral	Grade (%)	Mineral	Grade (%)
Ilmenite	62	Zircon	12.0
Rutile	4	Monazite	0.2
Leucoxene	6	Other	15.8

Mining methods

Given the relative ease of mining beach sands, dry sand mining can be employed where conventional front-end loaders and trucks are used to deliver the sands to the wet plant. More commonly, wet sand mining is utilised with a dredge floating in an artificially made pond. The dredge excavates the sand ahead of it, removes the heavy mineral sands and uses the waste to fill the pond behind it.

Wet plant recovery

The first stage is to recover the heavy minerals from the sand. Gravity can be employed — due to the high specific gravity of the economic minerals (4.2 to 5.3) — to separate them mostly from quartz, which has a specific gravity of 2.65. Spiral classifiers and tables are predominantly used with overall recoveries of some 80 to 95 per cent.

Dry plant recovery

The heavy mineral sands are dried and then separated by magnetics and electrostatics.

Table 20.9 shows how each of the four primary minerals has a unique combination of the two characteristics that allows for their relatively easy separation.

Table 20.9: unique characteristics among heavy metals

Mineral	Susceptible to	
	Magnetism	Electrostatics
Rutile	Low	Conductor
Ilmenite	High	Conductor
Zircon	Low	Non-conductor
Monazite	High	Non-conductor

Recovery

Typical final recoveries of the minerals are as follows: rutile: 70 per cent; ilmenite: 85 per cent; zircon: 60 per cent.

Synthetic rutile

Most ilmenite producers value add by upgrading some portion of their ilmenite to synthetic rutile. This is a two-stage process whereby the iron content in the ilmenite is first metallised in a high temperature (1000°C) rotating kiln. The reduced ilmenite is then treated with ammonia chloride to remove the iron with a resulting grade of TiO_2 of around 93 per cent.

Metallurgy

It is worthwhile to briefly discuss some of the issues surrounding the processing of the titanium minerals, given the impact it can have on the economics of a project. The major application is in the production of titanium pigment for the paint industry (6.6 million tonnes of TiO_2 in 2011), due to the high refractive index (2.7). Two processes are used: the sulphate route and the dominant chlorine route.

The sulphate route uses sulphuric acid to treat ilmenite and produce sulphates that are purified to $Ti(OH)_4$ by hydrolysis and then calcined at 800–1000°C to form TiO_2.

Rutile and synthetic rutile are not used in this process as they are not readily soluble in sulphuric acid, rather ilmenite grading 44 to 58 per cent TiO_2. Rutile and synthetic rutile (ilmenite can also be used) are processed by the chlorine route, where titanium tetrachloride (tickle) is formed when gaseous chloride at 800°C is passed through rutile in the presence of a strong reducing agent.

This is then hydrolysed with steam or oxidised with air to form TiO_2. The chloride route is the preferred method in the production of higher quality pigment. Tickle is also used in the manufacture of titanium metal. Approximately 39 per cent of final product is sulphate pigment; 51 per cent, chloride pigment; and 10 per cent, titanium sponge.

Iron ore

Commodity

Iron: symbol Fe, specific gravity of 7.9. Second most abundant metal, constituting 4.6 per cent of the Earth's crust. Generally referred to as iron ore.

Price

Price is generally set in US cents per dry tonne unit (mtu) free on board (FOB). One unit is equal to 1 per cent.

Lump ore: US 230¢ per mtu.

Fine ore: US 144¢ per mtu.

Pellets: US 290¢ per mtu.

Therefore, 60 per cent Fe lump ore would be priced at US$138 per tonne. Previously sold on evergreen contracts with volumes and prices renegotiated around April of each year, but now has changed to a quarterly index price for separate grades of iron ore.

In December 2008 spot lump ore prices reached US$2.30 per metric tonne unit (see figure 20.5) before falling during the GFC. Subsequently prices recovered strongly on the back of increasing demand from China.

Contracted prices are currently at a premium of US$0.60 per mtu to spot FOB prices, while spot iron ore including cost and freight (CFR) to China is at a premium of US$0.20 per mtu.

Figure 20.5: iron ore prices, 2001–11

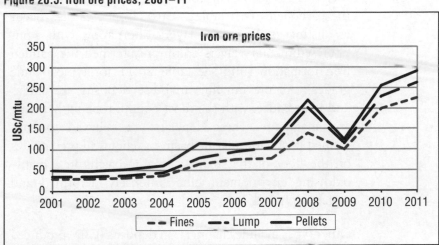

Supply/ demand

In 2011 world mine production totalled approximately 2800 million tonnes. Some 950 million tonnes is exported internationally.

Australian annual production is 480 million tonnes, of which 20 million tonnes is consumed domestically and the rest exported, primarily to Japan. Brazil is another major exporter with annual production of 390 million tonnes.

Other major producers include China (1200 million tonnes), India (240 million tonnes) and Russia (100 million tonnes). Iron ore is used in the manufacture of pig iron, from which all grades of iron and steel are derived.

World reserves of ore are 170 billion tonnes with primary reserves in Australia (21 per cent), Brazil (17 per cent), Russia (15 per cent), China (14 per cent) and the US (4 per cent).

Geology

Iron is found native in meteoritic masses and in eruptive rocks. The chief ores of iron are primarily the oxides and the carbonates (see table 20.10). Iron ores also occur as distinct sedimentary layers alternating with iron-poor sedimentary layers commonly termed the banded iron formation (BIF; see table 20.11 for typical mine grades). All ore minerals in these deposits are oxides and hydroxides, with the most common being hematite and magnetite. These deposits are believed to have formed in shallow marine basins as chemical precipitates on the floor of the shallow oceanic basins in a highly oxidising environment often intensely deformed and metamorphosed.

Other types include channel iron deposits (CID) produced through weathering and alluvial concentrations of lateritic soils that have good sintering properties. Detrital iron deposits (DID) occur when BIF and CID deposits have been eroded and deposited in drainage channels.

Table 20.10: iron oxides

Iron ore	Iron oxide	Iron content (%)
Magnetite	Fe_3O_4	72.4
Haematite	Fe_2O_3	70.0
Goethite	$Fe_2O_3H_2O$	62.9

Table 20.11: typical iron grades for some Australian iron ore mines

Mine	Lump (Fe%)	Fines (Fe%)
Tom Price	65.0	63.3
Paraburdoo	63.5	62.2
Marandoo	62.2	61.9
Hamersley	64.7	62.7

Characteristics

Several forms of iron ore are commonly traded:

» *Fine ore.* Fine size ore can occur naturally or result from the mining and handling of ore, or may be produced by the intentional grinding of ore.

» *Pellet.* Due to the inherent difficulty in handling fine ores, they may be formed into pellets. The pellets are created by rolling or balling the fines into spheres of 16 to 20 mm in diameter with a suitable binder and in some cases with a flux to aid later smelting. The pellets are then fired in a kiln to sinter the particles into hard spheres. Energy usages are around 350Mj/t for magnetite, 850Mj/t for hematite and 1 100Mj/t for limonite.

» *Sinter*. Fist-sized pieces are made by burning a mixture of fine iron ore and a flux, such as limestone or dolomite, and then breaking into pieces.

» *Lump*. Usually classified as run of mine ore with a size range of between 6 and 30 mm. Some fines will be present due to the handling of the ore.

» *Concentrate*. Usually produced from low-grade magnetite deposits of around 25 per cent to 35 per cent. Ore is crushed and magnetically separated to form a higher-grade concentrate of up to 70 per cent Fe with low impurities.

Specification

High iron content is desirable with as low as possible levels of alumina (less than 2.2 per cent) and silica (8 per cent), and low (less than 0.1 per cent) levels of sulphur (S) and phosphorus (P). Moisture content of around 1 per cent is preferred subject to the amount added through dust suppression and plant operation.

Hematite ores

Lump ore: 30 to 6 mm, min. 62 per cent Fe, max. 0.05 per cent S, max. 0.06 per cent P. Bulk density of 3.2 to 3.8 t/m^3.

Fines: less than 6 mm, min. 61 per cent Fe, max. 0.05 per cent S, max. 0.07 per cent P. Bulk density of 2.7 t/m^3.

Pellets: 16 to 9 mm, min. 62 per cent Fe, max. 0.03 per cent S, max. 0.06 per cent P.

Limonite ores

> *Sinter fines*: less than 9.5 mm, min. 56.5 per cent Fe max. 0.05 per cent S, max. 0.05 per cent P.

> *Pellets*: 16 mm to 9 mm, min. 62.5 per cent Fe, max. 0.01 per cent S, max. 0.05 per cent P.

Direct shipping ores (DSO) are normally obtained from BIF deposits and only require crushing and screening to produce saleable lump and fines.

Steel-making

The first process in steel-making is the production of pig iron from iron ore. There are two general approaches to its manufacture:

» *Blast furnace*. Iron ore is smelted in a blast furnace, where it is mixed with pre-heated air and coke as a reductant to remove the oxygen that is chemically bound to the Fe. The liquid iron or pig iron is then purified to steels of different grades in an oxygen converter.

» *Direct reduction*. In this process the oxygen is removed directly from the iron ore (direct reduced iron, DRI) while it is in a solid state, producing a sponge-like form of iron. The sponge is then generally made into hot briquette iron (HBI) to seal the surface and prevent oxidation.

Lead

Commodity

Symbol: Pb, specific gravity of 11.34 and melting point of 327°C.

Price

US$1980/t. LME forward markets are available for up to 27 months.

Supply/ demand

Western world mine production is approximately 4.5 million tonnes per annum, with a similar amount recovered from recycling, predominantly from lead batteries.

Consumption in 2011 of around 10.3 million tonnes of refined lead was primarily for batteries (80 per cent of consumption), pigments and alloys. Australian annual production is approximately 560 000 tonnes, while China produces 2.2 million tonnes, the US 335 000 tonnes and Peru 240 000 tonnes. World reserves are 85 million tonnes. Reserves are mainly located in Australia (34 per cent), China (16 per cent), Russia (11 per cent), Peru (9 per cent) and Mexico (7 per cent).

Geology

Found rarely as native lead, but primarily in sulphide minerals such as galena (PbS). Zinc and silver are often associated with galena and therefore lead is often a by-product of zinc mining. Ores are usually found as lodes or veins.

Average grades

Economic mine grades can vary subject to the level of associated zinc and silver. Typical grades vary from 4 to 15 per cent, predominantly mined from underground mines.

Metallurgy

First stage of recovery at the mine site is the production of a concentrate by froth flotation (see chapter 7).

The concentrate grade is generally required to be greater than 50 per cent to be acceptable to smelters, although lower grade sulphide concentrates can be processed at a price penalty. Examples of concentrate grades for several mines are listed in table 20.12. Lead is generally recovered by first sintering and then smelting in a reverberatory or blast furnace. See Zinc section on page 490 for more details.

Table 20.12: typical lead concentrate production grades for selected Australian mine sites

Mine site	Feed grade (%)	Concentrate grade (%)
Mt Isa	5.51	45.5
Elura	5.56	49.1
Rosebery	3.2	61.3
Hellyer	7.0	60.0

Refining charges

For the sale of lead concentrates to a smelter the typical terms include a reduction in the metal payable and a treatment charge (TC). A price participation (PP) formula is included to increase the TC if the metal price is above a set level and to decrease the TC if the metal price is below a fixed level. Refining charges may also be applicable for any precious metals and penalties for undesirable (dirty) elements such as antimony, bismuth, arsenic and mercury.

» *Payable metal.* 95 per cent of lead content (minimum deduction of 3 per cent), 95 per cent of gold content (minimum deduction of 1.5 g/dmt) and 95 per cent of silver content (minimum deduction of 50 g/dmt).

» *TC.* The treatment charge is generally quoted as a fixed deduction per tonne of concentrate. This charge has fluctuated widely in the past, with current charges at around US$200/t for 'clean' (65 per cent) concentrates. 'Dirty' concentrates can attract an additional charge of US$50/t. PP—US$1/t for each additional US 1¢ increase in the lead price above a base price of US$1.0/lb.

» *Refining charges and penalties*. Refining charges for payable gold can be of the order of US$3 to US$6 and for silver US$0.25 to US$0.35. Penalties are varied and negotiable. For example, in the case of arsenic there is an additional charge of US$3 for each 0.1 per cent above 0.1 per cent content in the concentrate.

Lithium

Commodity

Symbol: Li, specific gravity of approximately 0.5 and melting point of 181°C.

Price

Not traded on the open markets. A spot price is quoted in the *Metal Bulletin* with January 2012 around US$720 to US$770/t for spodumene (more than 7.25 per cent Li_2O), and US$190 to US$300 for Petalite (4.2 per cent Li_2O). Prices are also quoted per tonne of lithium carbonate equivalents (LCE), which contain 0.1879 tonnes of lithium metal. Most production is sold on long-term contracts.

Supply/ demand

Global production is some 34 000 tonnes of Li_2O. Lithium is the lightest known metal and is used as a raw material in the glass, ceramic and metallurgical industries. It is used in the making of heatproof cookware, glass ceramics, glass containers, television tubes and fibreglass, and in combination with numerous fluxing powders. Lithium batteries, particularly rechargeable ones, are also a major area of application. The amount of lithium required for storage batteries is around 0.6 kg per kWh.

The world's largest deposit is located at the Greenbushes mine in Western Australia with other major producers located in Canada and Zimbabwe. The major lithium chemical producers are in Chile, Argentina, China, Russia and the US. World reserves are some 13 million tonnes mainly located in Chile (58 per cent), China (27 per cent), Australia (7 per cent) and Argentina (7 per cent).

Geology

Lithium doesn't occur in a free state, but only as rare compounds in minerals associated with pegmatite. The Greenbushes mine in Western Australia produces 64 per cent of world lithium demand as spodumene mineral.

Average grades

For pegmatite operations like Greenbushes, the reserve grade is of the order of 1 per cent Li_2O per tonne of ore. Plant recoveries are of the order of some 40 to 45 per cent.

The plant can produce four spodumene ($LiAlSi_2O_6$) products, depending on market demand: fine grain (less than 125 microns) at 7.3 per cent Li_2O; intermediate (45–500 microns); chemical grade (less than 500 microns) at 6.5 per cent Li_2O; and glass grade (less than 850 microns) at 4.8 per cent Li_2O.

Magnesium (Magnesite)

Commodity

Symbol: Mg, specific gravity of 1.74 and melting point of 651°C. Magnesia (magnesium oxide) has the formula M_gO and is primarily sourced from magnesite (M_gCO_3). A number of different magnesium products are described in more detail, with approximate pricing shown in table 20.13 (overleaf).

Table 20.13: magnesium product pricing

	Price (US$/t)	World production
Magnesium	3 100	0.8 million tonnes
Magnesia		
Dead burned	750	7.3 million tonnes
Caustic calcine	615–630	1.6 million tonnes
Fused	950–1250	600 000 tonnes
Magnesite	80	20 million tonnes

Supply/ demand　World production in 2011 of magnesite ($MgCO_3$), which is the major source of magnesia, was approximately 20 million tonnes. The majority of production now takes place in China, Turkey, North Korea, Russia and Austria. Synthetic magnesia is obtained from seawater and brine.

Geology　Magnesium is not found in a natural state, but is produced using a number of different technologies from magnesia (MgO) or magnesium chloride $MgCl_2$. Magnesium represents some 2.7 per cent of the Earth's crust and is found in 60 minerals.

The primary source of magnesia is magnesite ($MgCO_3$). Other minerals include dolomite ($MgCa(CO_3)_2$), which is used as a building material and a source of carbon dioxide, and epsomite ($MgSO_47H_2O$), which is used in chemical manufacture.

Magnesia　Three types of magnesia (MgO) can be produced from the processing of magnesite ($MgCO_3$):

» *Caustic calcine magnesia (CCM)*. Produced by heating magnesite to 800°C–1000°C. Some 75 per cent of the world's production comes from naturally occurring magnesite. The low-quality product is used for agriculture, construction and mining, while the higher quality product is used in chemicals, pharmaceuticals and environmental applications.

» *Dead-burned magnesia (DBM)*. Produced by heating magnesite at temperatures of 1600–2000°C. DBM is used primarily in the steel industry for furnace linings. Synthetic magnesia accounts for approximately half of the higher grade market, but is more energy intensive than natural magnesite production.

» *Electro-fused magnesia (EFM)*. Produced by heating magnesite at temperatures of at least 2750°C in electric arc furnaces.

The EFM is used in more specialised applications such as high wear refractories and electric insulation in heating elements

Magnesium Magnesium (Mg) metal's principal attribute is its combination of lightness and diecastability. Magnesium is the lightest of all commonly used structural metals, being one-third lighter than aluminium and four times lighter than steel. Magnesium metal production is typically a complex, energy-intensive chemical process. Two types of process for magnesium production are currently in commercial use:

» *Silicothermic*. Thermal reduction of MgO using ferrosilicon at high temperature and low pressure; most commonly used in China.

» *Electrolytic*. Reduction of $MgCl_2$ in an electrolytic cell which follows the removal of water from hydrous magnesium chloride.

Manganese

Commodity

Symbol: Mn, specific gravity of approximately 7.21 and melting point of 2061°C. The most common ore is pyrolusite, which is mainly MnO_2. Other minerals include hausmannite (Mn_3O_4), polianite (MnO_2), maganite ($Mn_2O_3H_2O$) and braunite ($3Mn_2O_3MnSiO_3$).

Price

Current prices are approximately US$1500/t for ferromanganese (high carbon) and silicomanganese. Most production is sold on long-term contracts. Manganese ore with 48 per cent Mn is priced around $5.40/mtu.

Supply/demand

Major producers of mined manganese are South Africa (24 per cent), China (20 per cent), Australia (17 per cent) and Gabon (9 per cent).

Total production of manganese ore for 2011 was some 40 million tonnes for the production of 7.7 million tonnes of silicomanganese, 5.2 million tonnes of ferromanganese and 1 million tonnes of manganese metal. Manganese content typically ranges from 35 to 54 per cent for manganese ore and from 74 to 95 per cent for ferromanganese. Ferroalloys, consisting of various grades of ferromanganese (FeMn) and silicomanganese (SiMn), are essential to iron and steel production due to their sulphur-fixing, deoxidising and alloying properties.

Eighty-five to 90 per cent of total demand is for the manufacture of steel with an approximate consumption of 9 kg/t of steel. Manganese is also a key component of certain aluminium alloys and, in oxide form, dry cell batteries. As ore, manganese is also used for non-metallurgical purposes as plant fertilisers, animal feed and colourants for brick.

Mining

Mining is usually by conventional open cut methods. Ore is crushed (less than 150 mm) and washed to remove clays; it is also screened.

Lump ore is greater than 10 mm, while fine ore is between 10 and 0.5 mm. Heavy media may be used to separate lump from waste, while a heavy media cyclone can separate fine ore from waste material.

Metallurgy

Some Mn ores will not respond to beneficiation and if they are too high in phosphorus are not saleable. High-grade ores are processed by crushing, screening and washing. Medium- and low-grade ores may require beneficiation such as gravity separation.

Ore processing is very similar to iron metallurgy, although a higher temperature of 1200°C is required for reduction. High carbon (standard) FeMn contains more than 76 per cent manganese and 7 per cent carbon, and can be produced in a blast furnace or electric furnace.

Medium-grade ferromanganese of 1 to 1.5 per cent carbon is produced in the ladle or in a converter.

Lower carbon grade requires silicomanganese (SiMn), which is made by heating a mixture of manganese oxide, silicon dioxide (SiO_2), and iron oxide (Fe_2O_3), with carbon in a furnace.

The standard grade SiMn contains 14 to 16 per cent of silicon, 65 to 68 per cent of manganese and 2 per cent of carbon, while low carbon grade SiMn has carbon levels from 0.05 to 0.10 per cent.

Geology

Occurs widely disseminated in igneous rock, soils and sedimentary rock, but to be economic must be concentrated in a supergene environment by dissolving and re-depositing in more favourable locations.

Ore often occurs in distinct sedimentary layers as oxides and hydroxides, having formed in shallow marine basins in a highly oxidising environment.

As they are very ancient, most of these deposits have been intensely deformed and metamorphosed. Manganese nodules containing 30 per cent Mn can be found in deep ocean locations. Formed on a nucleus (shark tooth or whale's ear bone), they grow 1 mm per million years to sizes of 25 to 250 mm with estimates of 100 000 tonnes per square mile of sea floor.

Natural gas

Commodity

Natural gas is made up of hydrocarbons that occur as a gas at atmospheric temperature and pressure. The major gases are methane (CH_4) and ethane (C_2H_6). LNG is the liquefaction of methane by freezing to a temperature of 171°C, for ease of transportation to overseas markets. LPGs are propane (C_3H_8) and butane (C_4H_{10}), which are gases at atmospheric pressure and temperature, but are liquefied at moderate pressure (800 kPa or 120 psi).

Price

Natural gas (methane) is generally sold in Australia on a contract basis with CPI adjustment.

In the US, gas prices vary for different regional centres, but on NYMEX natural gas futures contracts are traded where the price is based on delivery at the Henry Hub in Louisiana, the nexus of 16 intra- and interstate natural gas pipeline systems. The most recent traded price was around US$2.40 per thousand cubic feet (mcf) or million British thermal units (mmBtu). The largest importer of LNG is Japan with some 83.5 billion cubic metres or 31 per cent of world trade. The average landed price (CIF—that is including cartage, insurance and freight) in Japan for 2010 was US$10.91 per mmBtu, compared with the energy-equivalent OECD crude price of US$78 per barrel.

Comparative natural gas prices per mmBtu were US$8.01 for the Germany, US$6.56 for the UK, US$4.39 for Henry Hub and US$3.69 for Alberta, Canada. More recently, with the increases in energy prices, contracts for LNG delivery to Japan have been set on new formulas that reflect near energy parity with the oil price. Energy equivalence can range from, say, 6.67 to 6.06; therefore, for oil prices of, say, US$100 per barrel the LNG price would be US$14.99 to US$16.50 per mcf of gas plus transport. Per tonne of gas, this would equate to US$688 to US$757.

LPG prices can be quite volatile subject to international supply and demand, and are influenced by the landed price of LPG from Saudi Arabia with current prices at around US$880 per tonne (oil price US$100/bbl).

**Supply/
demand**

World natural gas production for 2010 was 3193 billion cubic metres (2881 million barrels of oil equivalent (mmboe)), the major portion coming from Europe and Eurasia (33 per cent), North America (26 per cent), Asia–Pacific (15 per cent), the Middle East (14 per cent), Africa (7 per cent) and South America (5 per cent). World consumption was 3169 billion cubic metres (2858 mmboe), predominantly in Europe and Eurasia (36 per cent), North America (27 per cent), Asia–Pacific (18 per cent), the Middle East (12 per cent), Africa (3 per cent) and South America (4 per cent).

Proven reserves are some 187.1 trillion cubic metres with 40.5 per cent in the Middle East, 33.7 per cent in Europe and Eurasia, 8.7 per cent in Asia–Pacific, 7.9 per cent in Africa, 5.3 per cent in North America and 4 per cent in South America. Exports of LNG during 2010 were 297.6 billion cubic metres, primarily from Middle East (34 per cent), Africa (20 per cent), Indonesia (11 per cent), Malaysia (10 per cent) and Australia (9 per cent).

Geology

Gas originates from the burial and decomposition of plant and animal matter in a sedimentary basin. Temperature and time are important components in the successful creation of gas. Gas migrates from the source rock to reservoir rocks that exhibit adequate porosity (pores in the rock where the gas can accumulate) and permeability (the ability for the gas to move through the rock).

Porosity in the rock can vary between 1 and 40 per cent, and permeability between 1 and 1000 millidarcies. It is also necessary for economic volumes of gas to be trapped in the reservoir due to some form of seal that prevents the continued migration of the gas.

There are three basic types of trap: structural, which relate to structural movements such as folds (anticlines), faults or salt domes; stratigraphic, where the seal is due to an alteration process rather than to crustal movements; and a combination of both structural and stratigraphic. See appendix D for more details.

Nickel

Commodity Symbol: Ni, specific gravity of 8.9 and a melting point of 1455°C.

Price US$11 500/t. Forward nickel markets are quoted on the LME up to 27 months ahead. It is possible to obtain limited forward cover up to five years.

Supply/demand World mining production for 2011 was approximately 1.8 million tonnes.

Major producers included Russia (16 per cent), Philippines (12 per cent), Indonesia (13 per cent), Canada (11 per cent), Australia (10 per cent) and New Caledonia (8 per cent).

Reserves are 80 million tonnes, primarily in Australia (30 per cent), New Caledonia (15 per cent), Brazil (11 per cent), Russia (8 per cent), Cuba (7 per cent), Canada (4 per cent) and. South Africa (5 per cent). Major uses of nickel are for the production of alloys and, in particular, stainless steel (9 per cent nickel).

Geology Never occurs as a native, but as deposits divided into veins, nickeliferous pyrrhotite and nickeliferous pentlandite and serpentines.

More general descriptions relate to sulphides and lateritic ores. Sulphides are more commonly higher grade and mined underground, while laterites are low grade and generally restricted to open cut mines.

Average grades Economic mine grades can vary from 6 to 20 per cent for sulphide ores and 1 to 3 per cent for lateritic ores.

Metallurgy *Sulphide ores.* Amenable to flotation to reduce concentrates grading from 5 to 0 per cent Ni. The better concentrate can be smelted to produce a high-grade matte (75 per cent Ni) and leached, and the metal refined by electrolysis. Approximately the equivalent of 1 tonne of sulphuric acid is produced for each tonne of concentrate.

Laterite ores. Not amenable to flotation. Hence the ore (1.5 to 2.0 per cent) is smelted to produce ferronickel, or more commonly (for grades less than 1.5 per cent) leached (ammonia or acid) and then electro-won.

For pressure acid (sulphuric) leach, where magnesia is low, acid consumption should not be greater than 400 kg per tonne of ore treated.

Mill recovery Ferronickel from laterites 93 per cent, nickel oxides 90 per cent, reduced nickel oxides 95 to 99 per cent nickel.

Roast/ammonia leach, 90 per cent for high iron limonite to 65 per cent for low iron silicate ores, cobalt 50 to 75 per cent recovery.

Pressure acid leach, recovery of nickel 90 to 95 per cent and 80 to 90 per cent for cobalt. Nickel flotation at Leinster (Western Australia), feed grade 2.1 per cent Ni, concentrate grade 10.7 per cent Ni with a recovery of 80 per cent.

Smelting charges	On-site nickel metal production may require no further refining. For the sale of nickel sulphide concentrate to a smelter, the typical terms may include a reduction in the metal payable and a treatment and refining charge (TC/RC). TC is US$175/t of concentrate (30 per cent Ni). RC is US$0.70 per pound of Ni.

A price participation (PP) formula is included to increase the TC/RC if the metal price is above a set level and decrease it if the metal price is below a fixed level. PP is 10 per cent of any price increase above reference price of US$6 per pound.

Cobalt paid at 15 per cent of the published price. Copper paid for, less 0.5 per cent of contained grade at 45 per cent of the current copper price. Penalties can also apply for arsenic and magnesia.

Oil and oil shale

Commodity	Crude oil can vary greatly in terms of appearance and qualities, from location to location, but all are made up of hydrocarbons.
Price	*West Texas*: US$100/barrel is the world benchmark, with the price set in Oklahoma, the US.

Brent: US$115/barrel, price set for North Sea production.

Tapis: US$119/barrel, the Indonesian price that is a common benchmark for Australasian crudes. Forward oil markets are quoted on NYMEX up to seven years ahead.

**Supply/
demand**

World oil production for 2010 averaged 82.1 million barrels per day, the major portion coming from the Middle East (30.3 per cent), Europe and Eurasia (21.8 per cent), North America (16.6 per cent), the Asia–Pacific (10.2 per cent), Africa (12.2 per cent) and South America (8.9 per cent).

World consumption was 87.4 million barrels per day, predominantly in the Asia–Pacific (31.5 per cent), North America (25.8 per cent), Europe and Eurasia (22.9 per cent), the Middle East (8.9 per cent), South America (7.0 per cent) and Africa (3.9 per cent).

Reserves are 1.38 trillion barrels, with 54.4 per cent in the Middle East, 10.1 per cent in Europe and Eurasia, 9.5 per cent in Africa, 10.1 per cent in South America, 5.4 per cent in North America and 3.3 per cent in the Asia–Pacific.

Geology

Oil originates from the burial and decomposition of plant and animal matter in a sedimentary basin. Temperature and time are important components in the successful creation of oil. Petroleum then migrates from the source rock to reservoir rocks, which exhibit adequate porosity (pores in the rock where the oil can accumulate) and permeability (the ability for the oil to move through the rock).

Porosity in the rock can vary between 1 and 40 per cent, and permeability between 1 and 1000 millidarcies. It is also necessary for economic volumes of oil to be trapped in the reservoir due to some form of seal that prevents the continued migration of the oil.

There are three basic types of traps: structural, which relate to structural movements such as folds (anticlines), faults or salt domes; stratigraphic, where the seal is due to an alteration process rather than to crustal movements; and a combination of both structural and stratigraphic. See appendix D for more details.

Quality of oil

Crude oils can vary considerably in their quality. There are three types of classifications:

» *Paraffins*. These crudes provide good yields of high-grade lubricating oils and are mainly composed of isomers and paraffin.

» *Asphalts*. These crudes contain little in the way of paraffin and are mainly composed of naphthenes. These crudes yield predominantly lubricating oils

» *Mixed*. Commonly, these crudes consist of a mixture of paraffin and asphalt crudes, plus some aromatic hydrocarbons.

The impurities that can be present include sulphur and hydrogen sulphide, and of lesser importance, carbon dioxide, nitrogen and oxygen. A common index used by the industry is the API (American Petroleum Institute) gravity in degrees, where: API = (141.5/specific gravity at 60°F) − 131.5, so that an oil with a specific gravity of one would have an API of 10 degrees. Crude oil in Australia generally has APIs of around 35 to 45 degrees. The higher the API the lighter the oil and hence the lower the specific gravity.

Capital cost

Subject to size and location of the field. Rule-of-thumb estimates are around US$5 to US$25 per recoverable barrel of oil.

Operating costs
Variable and subject to location and project type, although they are relatively low once the oil is brought into production. Rule-of-thumb estimates are around US$2 to US$10 onshore and US$5 to US$25 per barrel of oil off shore.

Refining
The refining of oil in its simplest form consists of distillation at different temperatures (see table 20.14).

Table 20.14: distillation products of oil

Temperature (°C)	Fraction
Less than 32	Butanes and lighter
32 to 104	Gasoline
105 to 157	Naphtha
158 to 232	Kerosene
233 to 426	Gas oil
427 and higher	Residue

Oil shale
As the name implies, oil shales are shale deposits that contain significant levels of oil; that is, 100 to 200 litres of oil per tonne of shale.

The crucial issues for the successful development of a shale deposit are the quantity of oil, the ability to mine large volumes and the technology to extract the oil. The process of extracting the oil initially consists of mining, crushing and drying the oil shale. This can then be followed by a number of different technologies, but predominantly the oil shale is heated in a kiln to 500°C, where the high molecular weight hydrocarbons (kerogen) are turned to oil vapour and hydrocarbon gas.

The vapour and gas are then taken to an oil recovery section, where they are condensed into different fractions of fuel oil and light oil.

Phosphate

Commodity   Generally refers to a rock with high concentrations of phosphate minerals, commonly of apatite with the general formula $Ca_5(PO_4,CO_3)_3(F, OH, Cl)$.

Price $190/t based on 31 per cent to 33 per cent P_2O_5.

Supply/demand   Ninety per cent of phosphate mined is used to produce chemical fertilisers. Major producers include China (38 per cent), US and Morocco (15 per cent each), and Russia (6 per cent). World reserves are 71 million tonnes located in Morocco (70 per cent), Iraq (8 per cent), China (5 per cent) and Algeria (3 per cent).

Characteristics   For fertiliser, phosphate rock or its concentrates preferably have levels of 30 per cent phosphorus pentoxide (P_2O_5), reasonable amounts of calcium carbonate (5 per cent), and less than 4 per cent combined iron and aluminium oxides.

Geology   The most economically significant deposits are marine sedimentary deposits of phosphorites, which are sandy sediments containing stratified concentrations of calcium phosphate, mainly as apatite.

Other deposit types are apatite-rich igneous rocks (20 per cent of world production), and modern and ancient guano (bird droppings) accumulations.

Processing   Ammonium phosphate fertiliser (or di-ammonium phosphate, DAP) is produced from mined phosphate rock that is converted to phosphoric acid using sulphuric acid and then granulated (typically with ammonia) to create DAP.

Platinum group metals (PGMs)

Commodity   The PGMs display extraordinary physical and chemical properties, which were first discovered by Indian craftsmen in Ecuador over 1000 years ago. The Spaniards named the metal *platina* or little silver when it was first encountered in Colombia. The six PGMs are:

» *Platinum*: Pt, specific gravity of 21.45 and melting point of 1772°C

» *Palladium*: Pd, specific gravity of 12.02 and melting point of 1554°C

» *Iridium*: Ir, specific gravity of 22.65 and melting point of 2410°C

» *Osmium*: Os, specific gravity of 22.61 and melting point of 3045°C

» *Rhodium*: Rh, specific gravity of 12.41 and melting point of 1966°C

» *Ruthenium*: Ru, specific gravity of 12.45 and melting point of 2310°C.

Platinum, iridium and osmium are the heaviest metals known. Ruthenium and osmium are hard and brittle, unworkable in a metal state with poor oxidation resistance, but are often used as additions to other PGMs and catalysts. Rhodium and iridium are less brittle but still difficult to fabricate; however, they are valuable alone and as catalysts, particularly rhodium. Platinum and palladium are soft and ductile like gold and silver, and are resistant to oxidation and high temperature erosion.

It is as catalysts, either singly or in combination in complex metallic or chemical forms in industry, that the six PGMs stand out.

Price

Platinum: US$1625/oz — it is possible to obtain limited forward cover up to 10 years

Iridium: US$1085/oz

Osmium: US$400/oz

Palladium: US$700/oz

Rhodium: US1475/oz

Ruthenium: US$120/oz.

Supply/demand

Platinum makes up 60 per cent of PGM production, with 2011 production estimated at 192 000 tonnes.

Major production of platinum takes place in South Africa (72 per cent), Russia (14 per cent), North America (7 per cent) and Zimbabwe (5 per cent). Platinum's versatility comes from alloying with other metals such as 40 per cent rhodium platinum, which produces one of the strongest high-temperature alloys, which is used in the form of gauze to catalyse the partial oxidation of ammonia to yield nitric acid.

Platinum catalysts are also used in the refining of crude oil, in catalytic reforming and in the production of high-octane gasoline. Another major area of use due to its ductile nature is jewellery (40 per cent of the demand).

Palladium is the second most abundant of the PGM reserves with annual world production of about 207 000 tonnes. Major palladium producing countries include Russia (41 per cent), South Africa (38 per cent), North America (15 per cent) and Zimbabwe (4 per cent).

Palladium is less resistant to tarnish than platinum, but superior to silver and does not oxidise at temperatures below 400°C.

A 40 per cent silver palladium alloy produces one of the most cost-effective electrical contact materials; palladium is alloyed with gold for use in dentistry and with platinum to produce white gold for the jewellery business.

Rhodium at a 1:20 ratio to platinum represents only some 3 per cent of total world PGM production, primarily from South Africa and Russia.

It is more ductile than iridium, but can't be cold worked unless forged above 800°C. It is usually used as an alloy with other PGMs at 10 to 40 per cent content, which becomes highly resistant to corrosion and deformation for the use in equipment for glass and glass fibre manufacture.

Rhodium has excellent catalytic activity, especially in the organic chemicals industry and with platinum in vehicle exhaust emissions.

Iridium represents only 1 per cent of PGM reserves. It is a difficult metal to work and needs heat treatment around 1400°C to make use of its excellent properties of strength and corrosion resistance. Its particular use is in the manufacture of crucibles in which special materials are melted at over 2000°C to produce pure and defective-free crystals.

Iridium–platinum alloys are used in jewellery, electrical contact applications and calibration of the standardisation of the kilogram.

Osmium accounts for less than half a per cent of PGM reserves and is the densest metal, with the highest melting point of the PGMs. It is virtually unworkable, but is important as a catalyst as small quantities impart harness to alloys for use in electrical contacts and fountain pen nibs.

Geology

PGMs occur together in nature as native metal or alloys, the most abundant being platinum. Platinum occurs in a number of ways: disseminated as small grains in basalt and ultra-basic igneous rocks (Urals), in chrome-rich layers (Bushveld), in quartz veins (Transvaal), and in many copper deposits. Another source of platinum is sperrylite (PtAs2) from Sudbury (Ontario, Canada).

Average grades

Average grades range between 2.5 and 5 grams combined PGM (60 per cent Pt, 30 per cent Pd plus others).

Metallurgy

Zimplats is the operator of the Selous Metallurgical Complex, which has a flow sheet comparable with South African platinum ore-processing operations. The 2.2 mtpa process entails two-stage milling and flotation of run of mine ore grading around 3.2 g/t (82 per cent recovery), yielding a concentrate of about 75 g/t of PGM that is dried before smelting in a submerged arc furnace to produce a green matte containing sulphides and PGM.

The green matte then undergoes conversion to reduce iron (less than 1 per cent) and sulphur, to produce a granulated white matte that contains 44 per cent nickel, 33 per cent copper, 21 per cent sulphur and 1500 g/t PGM plus gold.

The white matte is then milled to a grade that is 80 per cent minus 45 microns and subjected to atmospheric and pressure leaching with copper and nickel recovered by electro-winning, leaving a high-grade PGM residue. This is sent to a PGM refinery for further refining into its constitute parts.

Potash

Commodity

Symbol: K (potassium), specific gravity of 0.862 and melting point of 63.38°C.

Price

US$500/t MOP FOB Vancouver. There are no open markets available for pricing.

Supply/demand

Potash is primarily used as agricultural fertiliser by providing potassium and is produced from mined products and salts that contain water-soluble potassium.

World production in 2011 was 37 million tonnes. The major producers were Canada (30 per cent), Russia (20 per cent), Belarus (15 per cent), Germany (9 per cent) and China (9 per cent).

Reserves are 9.5 billion tonnes, located in Canada (46 per cent), Russia (34 per cent), Belarus (8 per cent), Brazil (3 per cent) and China (2 per cent).

Geology

Most of the world's reserves were deposited in ancient inland seas, which evaporated, and the potassium salts crystallised into beds of potash ore. Potash usually describes the muriate of potash (MOP) that is potassium chloride (KCL) and another is sulphate of potash (SOP), which is potassium sulphate (K_2SO_4). The grade of potassium products is usually expressed in potassium oxide (K_2O), where the conversion factor from KCL to K_2O is 0.6317.

Rare earths

Commodity

There are 17 rare earth metals made up of 15 lanthanides, plus scandium and yttrium. Although not strictly rare earths, these last two elements are often found in the same ore deposits and exhibit similar chemical properties. As figure 20.6 (overleaf) shows, rare earths are not all that rare when it comes to their proportion of the Earth's crust, but economic deposits of the minerals are very few, leading to the terminology of rare earths.

Figure 20.6: crustal abundance of minerals

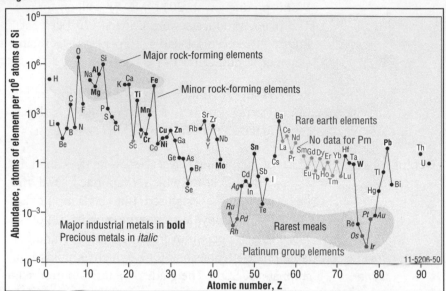

Source: 'The major rare-earth-element deposits of Australia: geological setting, exploration, and resources' by Dean M. Hoatson, Subhash Jaireth & Yanis Miezitis, 2011, Geoscience Australia, GeoCat 71820 p. 17.

Price   Prices are generally not quoted on open markets and are commonly obtained from trade journals such as *Metal Bulletin*. Table 20.15 provides some indicative prices for rare earth oxides and areas of major commercial usage.

Table 20.15: rare earth elements, oxides, prices and uses

Metal	Symbol	Oxide formula	Price as oxides (US$/kg)	Uses
Scandium	Sc	SC_2O_3	—	Mercury vapour lamps, aluminium–scandium alloy
Yttrium	Y	Y_2O_3	55	Lasers, superconductors microwave filters

Commodity profiles

Metal	Symbol	Oxide formula	Price as oxides (US$/kg)	Uses
Lanthanum	La	La_2O_3	52	Catalytic crackers, battery electrodes, high refractive glass, camera lenses
Cerium	Ce	CeO_2	45	Catalytic crackers, oxidising agent, yellow glass, flints for lighters
Praseodymium	Pr	Pr_6O_{11}	170	Magnets, lasers, carbon arc lighting
Neodymium	Nd	Hd_2O_3	200	Magnets, lasers, violet glass
Promethium	Pm	—	—	Nuclear batteries
Samarium	Sm	Sm_2O_3	280	Magnets, lasers, masers
Europium	Eu	Eu_2O_3	3800	Mercury vapour lamps, lasers, red and blue phosphors
Gadolinium	Gd	Gd_2O_3	200	Magnets, lasers, high refractive glass, X-ray tubes, computer memories
Terbium	Tb	Tb_4O_7	2820	Lasers, green phosphorus, fluorescent lamps
Dysprosium	Dy	Dy_2O_3	1485	Magnets, lasers
Holmium	Ho	Ho_2O_3		Lasers
Erbium	Er	Er_2O_3	105	Lasers, vanadium steel
Thulium	Tm	Tm_2O_3	—	X-ray machines
Ytterbium	Yb	Yb_2O_3	—	Lasers, reducing agent
Lutetium	Lu	Lu_2O_3	—	PET scan, high refractive glass

Supply/demand World mine production in 2011 was approximately 130 000 tonnes; nearly all came from China and small amounts from India, Brazil and Malaysia. Reserves were 110 million tonnes, located in China (19 per cent), Russia (14 per cent), US (13 per cent), India (11 per cent) and Australia (10 per cent).

Geology Economic concentrations of rare earths are associated with uncommon alkaline or carbonatite igneous rocks and also placer deposits. Only 527 carbonatites are known worldwide.

Silver

Commodity Symbol: Ag, specific gravity of 10.5 and melting point of 960.5°C.

Price US$30/oz. Forward silver markets are quoted on the LME and COMEX up to 27 months ahead. It is possible to obtain limited forward cover up to 10 years.

Supply/ demand World mine production in 2011 was approximately 765 million ounces, while consumption was around 1100 million ounces, with the difference made up of scrap.

Refined silver is primarily used for industrial applications: electronics, photography, batteries, mirrors and in the manufacture of coinage, plate and jewellery.

Major producers in 2011 were Mexico (19 per cent), Peru (17 per cent), China (17 per cent) and Australia (8 per cent), primarily from lead zinc production and, to a far lesser extent, copper and gold.

Reserves in 2011 were 17 billion ounces, located in Peru (23 per cent), Poland (16 per cent), Chile (13 per cent), Australia (13 per cent) and China (8 per cent).

Geology   Silver can be found in a native state occasionally up to 99 per cent pure.

Siliceous ore can be mined primarily for its silver content, but most world production comes as a by-product from the smelting of metalliferous ores, particularly those of lead, zinc, copper and gold.

Average grades   As a by-product of lead zinc mining, grades can be quite variable, but are important in enhancing the value of the orebody. Typical average silver grades are listed in table 20.16.

Table 20.16: typical silver concentrate grades for selected mines in Australia

Mining operation	Average silver grade g/t
Mt Isa (Qld)	149.0
Broken Hill (NSW)	50.0
Eulura (NSW)	124.0
Rosebery (Tas.)	100.0
Hellyer (Tas.)	160.0

Metallurgy   Silver in gold ores is recovered within the gold dore and later separated when the gold is refined.

Silver can be recovered from silver ores by cyanidation or by cupellation. For silver that reports primarily to the lead bullion, the desilverising process consists (under continuous conditions) of:

1 bullion flowing into a kettle of molten zinc forming an enriched zinc silver gold lead alloy and a solution of zinc in lead

2 a temperature gradient of 600°C to 330°C maintained in the kettle with zinc silver rich alloy crystals forming at the top

3 the alloy being distilled in a retort to remove the zinc (average grade of alloy Ag 15 per cent, Au 150 g/t, Zn 60 per cent, Pb 20 per cent and Cu 0.4 per cent)

4 the alloy being melted in a furnace where sodium nitrate is used to concentrate (cupellation) a final dore (average grade of alloy Ag 99.5 per cent, Au 1000 g/t, Pb 0.07 per cent and Cu 0.14 per cent)

5 electrolysis with dore anodes, stainless steel cathodes and silver nitrate electrolyte. Silver is deposited on the cathodes.

Mill concentrate Typical lead–silver concentrate production is as shown in table 20.17.

Table 20.17: typical lead–silver concentration grades for selected Australian mines

Mine site	Feed grade (g/t)	Concentrate grade (g/t)	Recovery (%)
Mt Isa	149.3	2270	66.2
Elura	94	835	36.7
Rosebery	104	1424	70.6

Refining charges Where silver is refined as part of gold bullion (dore), then the refining charge is approximately $2.00 to $6.00/oz. The refinery will pay for between 95 and 99 per cent of the silver content. Gold dore delivered to the refinery generally needs to be 70 per cent or higher gold content, and penalty rates apply for deleterious elements such as iron, lead, tellurium and nickel. The refining charge for silver is approximately US$0.5/oz.

Tantalum

Commodity

Symbol: Ta, specific gravity of 16.64 and melting point of 2850°C.

Price

Not traded on the open markets. CIF price in Rotterdam for tantalite (minimum 25 per cent Ta_2O_5) estimated at US$180 per pound. Most production is sold on long-term contracts.

Supply/demand

Global consumption is 6 million pounds of tantalum pentoxide Ta_2O_5. Tantalum processor production was 2000 tonnes of Ta with some 40 per cent as capacitor powder, 15 per cent superalloys and 10 per cent for wire. The major importers are the US, Japan and Germany. The metal is ductile, resistant to corrosion, superconductive and has a low coefficient of thermal expansion. Some 30 per cent of supply comes from reprocessed tin slags and tantalum scrap generated from the manufacture of capacitors.

The primary use is in the electronics industry, accounting for 60 per cent of world consumption for the production of electrolytic anode capacitors and their connecting wires, with a further 10 per cent for strengthening steel for application in turbine blades.

Primary production of 1.8 million pounds of tantalum was from Brazil (23 per cent), Mozambique (15 per cent), Rwanda (14 per cent) and Australia (10 per cent).

Geology

Rarely found in its natural form tantalum is often associated with tin and is considered an impurity. It is found in approximately 15 per cent of the world's pegmatites (the residual portion of magmas that contain concentrated valuable minerals).

The world's largest source is found at the Greenbushes and Wodgina tantalum mines in Western Australia, where Wodgina produces annually around 1.4 million pounds of Ta_2O_5 in concentrates containing 8 per cent to 10 per cent Ta_2O_5.

Average grades

As a by-product of tin, economic grades are not relevant, but for pegmatite operations such as Greenbushes the reserve grades are of the order of half a pound of Ta_2O_5 per tonne of ore.

Metallurgy

When tin concentrates are smelted, the tantalum reports to the reduced slag. With declining tin production, tantalum has increasingly come from tantalite deposits, particularly from Australia and Africa, each supplying some 25 per cent of global demand.

The pegmatites are ground and gravity concentration is used to produce a primary tantalum concentrate of approximately 17 per cent Ta_2O_5.

Metallurgy

Secondary concentrating is then used to increase the saleable product to 40 per cent Ta_2O_5 before shipping.

Tin

Commodity

Symbol: Sn, specific gravity of 7.3 and melting point of 232°C.

Price

US$20 900/t. Forward tin markets are quoted on the LME to 27 months ahead. It is possible to obtain forward cover up to 3 years.

Supply/demand   World mine production is approximately 270 000 tonnes per annum, from China (41 per cent), Indonesia (19 per cent), Peru (13 per cent), Bolivia (8 per cent) and Australia (7 per cent). World reserves are some 4.8 million tonnes; China (31 per cent), Indonesia (17 per cent), Brazil (12 per cent), Bolivia (8 per cent) and Russia (7 per cent).

Consumption is primarily for tin plate and alloys. Tin plate is sheet iron with a thin coating of tin for the production of cans.

Geology   Found rarely as native tin, but primarily in oxide minerals such as cassiterite (SnO_2). Ores are usually found as lodes or veins or as alluvials.

Average grades   Economic mine grades can vary from a low of 0.1 per cent per tonne for alluvial mines up to 2.0 per cent per tonne in underground mines such as Renison in Tasmania.

Metallurgy   First stage of recovery at the mine site is the production of a concentrate primarily by gravity concentration. This may result in a grade of around 70 per cent tin, although it can vary from as low as 30 per cent to as high as 75 per cent. A typical example is provided in table 20.18 (overleaf).

The concentrate is then reduced in a reverberatory furnace for about nine hours, using anthracite or petroleum coke (10 per cent by weight) as fuel and a small amount of limestone as a flux, producing a rough tin metal. The tin metal can then be refined by electrolysis, or 'boiling' the tin with compressed air to separate free tin.

Table 20.18: typical concentration grade for Renison tin mine in Tasmania

Grade	Tin (%)
Head grade	1.71
Concentrate grade	53.5
Concentrate recovery	72.9

Refining charges   The smelting and refining terms are complex and highly variable throughout the industry. This is particularly true given the large range of concentrates sold.

The smelter will therefore generally apply a unit deduction based on the difference between the grade of concentrate and the base concentrate grade. The deductions from the concentrate grade vary between 1.5 and 3.5 per cent.

The treatment charge is made up of a fixed charge and a variable charge, again based on the grade of the concentrate. An indicative figure was around 10 per cent of the ruling tin price for concentrates around 50 per cent tin content. Penalties are also applied, particularly for high levels of iron and wolfram.

These penalties take the form of tin deductions and increased treatment charges per tonne of concentrate.

Tungsten

Commodity   Symbol: W, specific gravity of 19.25 and melting point of 3422°C. Tungsten has the highest melting point of all the non-alloyed metals and is second to carbon.

Price　　　　　　Not traded on the open markets. The spot price for ore (min. 65 per cent WO_3) is quoted each week in the *Metal Bulletin* with current prices around US$140 per metric tonne unit (mtu). APT quoted at US$430 per mtu. Most production is sold on long-term contracts.

Supply/ demand　　Nearly 83 per cent of the world's 2011 mine production of 72 000 tonnes of tungsten takes place in China with minor production in Russia, Canada and Austria. China holds 61 per cent of world reserves of 2.9 million tonnes. Approximately 60 per cent of world production is used in the cemented carbides or hard-metals industry; 23 per cent in steels and alloys; 10 per cent in various chemical applications such as catalysts and pigments; and 7 per cent in the so-called mill-products industry, including lamp filament and various electrical uses. Cemented carbides, or hard metals, are materials made by 'cementing' very hard tungsten monocarbide grains in a binder matrix of tough cobalt metal by liquid phase sintering that results in hardness close to that of diamonds.

Geology　　　　Tungsten occurs in the form of chemical compounds with more than 20 tungsten-bearing minerals known, but only two are important for industrial use: wolframite $(Fe,Mn)WO_4$ (containing 76.5 per cent WO_3) and scheelite $CaWO_4$ (containing 80.5 per cent WO_3).

Average grade　　Most deposits grade at less than 1.5 per cent WO_4.

Metallurgy　　　The ore is crushed and milled and concentrated at on-site plants. Scheelite is concentrated by gravity methods, often combined with froth flotation, while wolframite ore is concentrated by gravity and also sometimes in combination with magnetic separation.

　　　　　　　　Tungsten ores can be treated with alkalis to produce WO_3 as an intermediate in the production of tungsten metal.

A metric tonne unit (mtu) of tungsten trioxide (WO_3) contains 7.93 kilograms of tungsten. More commonly, tungsten concentrates are processed chemically to ammonium paratungstate (APT).

Wolframite concentrates can also be smelted directly with charcoal or coke in an electric arc furnace to produce ferrotungsten, which is used as alloying material in steel production. Pure scheelite concentrate may also be added directly to molten steel.

Uranium

Commodity   Symbol: U, specific gravity of 18.7. However, mine production is by way of yellowcake, which is U_3O_8.

Price   Spot price of US$52/lb of U_3O_8. Spot markets have become increasingly important and volatile, given the large supply of uranium which is now brokered from Russia.

Supply/ demand   World mine production is approximately 54 000 tonnes per year. Consumption is for the production of fuel assemblies for nuclear power plants. Major producers include Kazakhstan (33 per cent), Canada (18 per cent), Australia (11 per cent) and Namibia (8 per cent). World resources are 5.5 million tonnes with the largest proportion in Australia (23 per cent), Kazakhstan (15 per cent), Russia (10 per cent), South Africa (8 per cent) and Canada (8 per cent).

Geology   Uranium is not found as a native mineral, but as a constituent of a number of rare minerals, including pitchblende, carnotite, torbernite and autunite.

Average grades   Economic mine grades can vary from a low of 0.15 per cent per tonne for open cut mines up to 0.50 per cent per tonne for underground mines.

Metallurgy   Yellowcake is normally produced on the mine site. The process is made up of the following steps:

1 After grinding of the ore (to approximately 700 μm) and thickening to approximately 50 per cent solids, it is leached in concentrated sulphuric acid. Consumption is approximately 40 kg of sulphuric acid per tonne of ore. For ores containing greater than 12 per cent limestone, grinding to 75 μm is required and leaching with an alkaline solution.

2 The pregnant liquor containing some 0.6 g/l of U_3O_8 is clarified and mixed with a tertiary amine solvent in a kerosene diluent.

3 The loaded solvent (4 g of U_3O_8 per litre of solvent) is stripped with ammonia solvent (to 20 g of U_3O_8 per litre of solvent) and neutralised with ammonia gas to precipitate ammonium diuranate.

4 The precipitate is washed, centrifuged and placed in a furnace at 700°C to produce triuranium oxide (yellowcake) containing 97 per cent U_3O_8.

5 The typical recoveries and concentrate grade are shown in table 20.19 (overleaf).

The steps that are undertaken to produce fuel rods (not in Australia) include:

» refining the yellowcake to nuclear grade uranium trioxide (UO_3)

» converting uranium trioxide to uranium hexafluoride (UF_6)

» enriching uranium hexafluoride from a natural level of about 0.7 per cent U 235 to 3 to 4 per cent uranium 235.

Table 20.19: typical uranium recoveries and concentrate grade for Ranger and Olympic Dam mines in Australia

	Ranger Mine	Olympic Dam
Mill head grade	0.3% U_3O_8	0.09% U_3O_8
Product grade	98.71% U_3O_8	98% U_3O_8
Mill recovery	85.51%	97%

Zinc

Commodity Symbol: Zn, specific gravity of 7.15 and melting point of 419°C.

Price US$1980/t. Forward zinc markets are quoted on the LME up to 27 months ahead. It is possible to obtain limited forward cover up to seven years.

Supply/demand World mine production in 2011 was approximately 12.4 million tonnes. Major producers include China (31 per cent), Australia (11 per cent) and Peru (11 per cent). World reserves are 250 million tonnes, primarily in Australia (22 per cent), China (17 per cent), Peru (8 per cent) and Mexico (6 per cent).

Consumption Primarily for anti-rust coatings (galvanising) and alloys such as brass, and as pigments.

Geology Found rarely as native zinc, but primarily in sulphide minerals such as sphalerite (ZnS). Sphalerite or blende often occurs in large quantities with galena (lead sulphide). Lead and silver are often by-products of zinc mining.

Average grades Economic mine grades can vary from a low of 5 per cent up to 20 per cent per tonne.

Mill concentrate Examples of different concentrate grades are shown in table 20.20.

Table 20.20: typical zinc concentrate grades for selected Australian mines

Mine site	Feed grade (%)	Concentrate grade (%)	Recovery (%)
Mt Isa	7.0	49.6	69.5
Broken Hill	8.2	49.9	88.7
Elura	8.5	50.3	70.4
Rosebery	10.0	52.7	89.1
Hellyer	13.0	50.0	82.9
Scuddles	15.1	50.6	88.3

Metallurgy The first stage of recovery at the mine site is the production of a concentrate by froth flotation. The concentrate grade can be 10 to 30 times greater than the grade of the ore.

The most common approach for the production of zinc metal is for roasted zinc sulphides to be leached in sulphuric add and then electrolysed between aluminium cathodes and insoluble lead anodes. The imperial smelting process (ISP) treats mixed lead and zinc concentrates. Concentrates are roasted in updraft sinter machines, where the sulphur is removed and converted to sulphuric acid.

The feed from the sinter plant is mixed with coke and placed into a furnace from which zinc metal and lead bullion is produced. The zinc is then further refined by way of distillation (see table 20.21, overleaf).

Table 20.21: typical imperial smelting process (ISP) metal recoveries

	Zn	Pb	Cd	S	Ag	Cu
In products %	91.5	95.0	90.0	95.0	96.0	78.0
Loss to slag %	7.0	2.0	—	—	—	—

Refining charges   Electrolytic processes require higher grade zinc concentrates (Zn > 50 per cent) and low levels of combined Cu and Pb. The ISP route requires some lead, therefore it can use bulk Zn, Pb concentrates.

Payable metal. 85 per cent of zinc content; 70 per cent of silver and cadmium content; ISP deduct 7 units of zinc; 95 per cent of lead with a minimum of 3 units; 25 per cent of copper after deducting 1.5 units; 70 per cent of gold after deducting 1g/t.

TC. For clean (> 53 per cent) concentrates, current charges are around US$230/t. ISP charges are approximately US$15 to US$35/t higher.

PP. Negotiable with base price at US$2500/t and adjustment of plus or minus US$0.10 TC per tonne of concentrate for each US$1 per tonne of metal price movement.

Refining. Refining charge of US$0.50/oz of associated silver.

Penalties. Penalties of the order of US$1 to US$1.5/t for excess increments in arsenic, magnesia, mercury, iron, manganese and silica.

Other commodity prices

Table 20.22 lists a number of minor commodities with indicative prices sourced from the *Metal Bulletin* and some of their more important commercial uses. Prices include cartage, insurance and freight (CIF) to deliver to the buyer.

Table 20.22: prices for minor metals

Metal	US$ (CIF unless otherwise indicated)	Uses (in descending order of importance)
Antimony	12 000 to 12 500/t	(99.65%) flame retardant, transport, ceramics and glass
Arsenic	1545 to 1765/t	(min. 99.99%) wood preservative, mineral flotation agents
Bismuth	22 000 to 24 500/t	(min. 99%) chemicals and pharmaceuticals, alloys and metallurgical additives
Cadmium	2200 to 2750/t	(99.99%) batteries, pigments and alloys
Germanium	1100 to 1200/kg	(99.99%) fibre optics, infrared systems, semiconductors and detectors
Indium	540 to 600/kg	(99.97%) thin film coatings, solders and alloys and electrical components
Mercury	2000 to 2200/flask	(99.99%) batteries, electronic and electrolytes (flask = 34.5 kg)
Selenium	132 to 145/kg	(99.5%) electronics, photocopiers, glass and chemicals
Silicon	3150 to 3195/t	(98%) alloy with aluminium and chemicals

Source: *Metal Bulletin* (23 January 2012), *Minerals Handbook* (March 1998).

APPENDIX A
Sources of information

Information is the most valuable asset for anyone attempting to determine the fundamental value of a project or company. For investors and management, the decision to invest in a company or project will be derived from analysis of financial and technical data. For management most information for their own project(s) will be in-house and generally not available to the public. However, large number of primary sources of information are available to the public.

Stock exchange releases

Stock exchanges throughout the world require different levels of disclosure by companies to keep the market informed. In Australia, the ASX requires the directors of companies to keep an informed market and to release market-sensitive information, although exemptions can be sought if the information is of a commercial nature and its disclosure would be detrimental to the commercial interests of the company.

Standard releases in Australia include:

» *Quarterly production and working capital reports.* All resource companies are required to provide a report for each quarter that details their exploration and, if applicable, production figures. Exploration companies are also required to provide a working capital report showing current cash and the next quarter's exploration budget. Some companies also supply quarterly profit and loss figures.

» *Half-yearly or interim results.* All resource companies, except pure exploration companies, are required to provide their half-yearly financial results.

» *Full-year results.* All resource companies are required to release their full-year financial results and provide an annual report to shareholders that summarises the company's activities and corporate objectives.

Prospectuses and information memorandums

For the float of a new public company or in some cases the raising of additional capital, it is normal for some form of prospectus or information memorandum (IM) to be issued to new and existing shareholders to provide sufficient information for investors to make informed decisions. Prospectuses and IMs are a valuable source of information, as an independent valuation of the assets is often included, which will provide information that may not be forthcoming in later company releases.

Takeover response or scheme of arrangement

Whenever a takeover offer is made for a public company it will generally respond and may include an independent expert's opinion on the fairness and reasonableness of the offer. Again, these reports are an excellent source of information about the current operations and they give detail (although quite variable between different experts) on the value of the company's assets.

Journals, newspapers and broker reports

A large number of mining journals are published throughout the world that can provide basic information on projects, markets for commodities, and current plans and activities for resource companies. Newspapers are also, at times, excellent sources of information, with news gleaned by reporters from company management. Commodity and company studies produced by stockbrokers and commercial agencies can be very helpful, but are more difficult or expensive to acquire.

The internet

Increasingly, a large amount of information is becoming available on the internet as resource companies, associations and government agencies use it to disseminate information. A small selection of relevant websites is given in the following table.

A selection of internet sources

Organisation	Website	Comment
Department of Resources, Energy and Tourism	<ret.gov.au>	Australian commodity information
Alternative Investment Market (AIM)	*See* London Stock Exchange	Listed company information
Australian Coal Association	<australiancoal.com.au>	Facts on coal
Australian Gas Association	<gas.asn.au>	Natural gas facts and figures
Australian Institute of Mining and Metallurgy	<ausimm.com.au>	Mining codes and ethics
Australian Institute of Petroleum	<aip.com.au>	Fact sheets on petroleum
Australian Securities & Investments Commission	<asic.gov.au>	Australian mining company filings
Australian Stock Exchange	<asx.com.au>	Company information
BP Statistical Review of World Energy	<bp.com>	Energy facts
Canadian Institute of Mining & Metallurgy	<cim.org>	Information on Canadian mining
Canadian Securities Administrators	<sedar.com>	Canadian mining company filings
Infomine	<infomine.com>	Commercial mines database
London Metal Exchange	<lme.co.uk>	News, facts and data on metals
London Stock Exchange	<londonstockexchange.com>	Listed company information
Minerals Council of Australia	<minerals.org.au>	Media releases and fact sheets
NSW Minerals and Petroleum	<dpi.nsw.gov.au/minerals>	State legislative information
NT Minerals and Energy	<nt.gov.au/d/Minerals_Energy>	State legislative information
NYMEX/COMEX	<cmegroup.com>	Current and historical metal price data
Queensland Mining and Safety	<mines.industry.qld.gov.au>	State legislative information

(*continued*)

A selection of internet sources (*cont'd*)

Organisation	Website	Comment
Society of Mining Engineers	<smenet.org>	Information on US mining
Society of Petroleum Engineers	<spe.org>	US gas and oil info at a price
South Australian Minerals	<pir.sa.gov.au/minerals>	State legislative information
South African Institute of Mining & Metallurgy	<saimm.co.za>	Mining codes and ethics
Mineral Resources Tasmania	<mrt.tas.gov.au>	State legislative information
Toronto Stock Exchange	<tsx.com>	Company information
Australian Uranium Association	<aua.org.au>	Fact sheets on uranium
US Geological Survey	<usgs.gov>	Extensive information on commodities
US Securities & Exchange Commission	<sec.gov>	Filings for US listed companies
Victoria Department of Primary Industries	<dpi.vic.gov.au/earth-resources>	State legislative information
Western Australia Dept of Mines & Resources	<dmp.wa.gov.au>	State legislative information
World Gold Council	<gold.org>	General information on world gold markets

Journals and publications

A list of useful journals and publications is given in the following table.

Journals and publications

Publication	Comment
Australian Journal of Mining	Metals, coal, industrial minerals and commodity profiles
Australian Mines Handbook	Summary of mines, prospects, projects and companies
Australia's Mining Monthly	Excellent journal that covers gold, coal, energy, and general mining and technology

Appendix A: Sources of information

Publication	Comment
Engineering and Mining Journal	Weekly news service
Gold & Minerals Gazette	Monthly coverage of commodity markets
Gold Mining Journal	Monthly news on Australian goldmining companies
NSW Coal Industry Profile	State government publication with statistics on coal
Western Australia Oil & Gas Review	WA Department of Resources Development
Oil & Gas Gazette	Monthly journal covering the oil and gas industry
Oil & Gas Journal	International petroleum news and technology
Mining Journal	Weekly newspaper
Register of Australian Petroleum	Annual summary of permits, prospects, projects and pipelines
Register of Australian Mining	Excellent annual summary of mines, projects and mining companies
Resource Information Unit	Email: <riu.com.au>

APPENDIX B
Australian Native Title

There are two issues to consider, one under common law and the other under statute:

1 *Common law.* Under *Mabo v Queensland* the High Court held that native title endures if there is a continuing connection with the land and unless displaced or extinguished in a way consistent with Commonwealth law—that is, freehold title. The Wik decision went further and confirmed that native title persists over pastoral leases as the intention was not to extinguish title.

2 *Statute.* The *Racial Discrimination Act 1975* requires compensation to traditional owners if the land was taken from them after 1975. The *Native Title Act 1993* established the framework for resolution of native title claims, including the establishment of the National Native Title Tribunal (NNTT) to implement the procedure.

The Wik decision on 23 December 1996, in summary, meant that:

» native title rights may coexist with a pastoral lease, although the rights of the pastoralist prevail

» native title claims can proceed over pastoral lease land

» it was incorrect to assume that native title was extinguished by the grant of a pastoral lease after January 1994

» titles granted before January 1994 are valid.

The government therefore introduced a 10-point plan to amend the *Native Title Act* to address the following:

1 *Validation.* The plan validates actions by government, such as the granting of mineral exploration licences, during the period between the *Native Title Act* on 1 January 1994 and the High Court decision on 23 December 1996.

2 *Confirmation.* The plan confirms permanent extinguishment of native title over 'exclusive tenure', such as freehold, residential, commercial and public works. Agricultural leases would be covered by the grant of a permit if exclusive possession was intended.

3 *Services.* The plan ensures that federal and local government services can continue without impediment from native title.

4 *Pastoral leases.* Pastoralists will be given security so that they can operate and manage their primary production, notwithstanding any native title that might be claimed or found to exist.

5 *Access rights.* Continued access rights of Aborigines will be confirmed until their native title claim is determined by the court.

6 *Mining activity.* For mining on vacant crown land the amendments will mean a tougher registration test for claimants seeking the right to negotiate. Mining projects will be covered by a single 'right to negotiate' process (covering mining) with native titleholders or registered claimants (rather than by separate negotiations for different stages of the project) and no negotiations on exploration. For mining on other tenures such as pastoral leaseholds, the right to negotiate would continue unless the state or territories provided a statutory regime acceptable to the Commonwealth. The regime would need to include procedural rights at least equivalent to other parties with an interest in the land and compensation that can take account of the nature of coexisting native title rights (where they are proven to exist).

7 *Government and commercial development.* The right to negotiate over vacant crown land and remnant pastoral leases within towns and cities will no longer apply, but compensation may be payable. On vacant Crown land outside towns and cities there would be a higher registration test to access the right to negotiate except for the purposes of government-type infrastructure.

8 *Water resources.* The ability of governments to regulate and manage surface and sub-surface water, offshore resources and air space, and the rights of those with interests under any such regulatory or management regime, would be put beyond doubt.

9 *Management.* Registration tests for native title will be strengthened and handling of claims will be speeded up and a sunset clause introduced.

10 *Agreements*. Resolution of native title issues through mutually beneficial agreements will be encouraged to reduce reliance on the native title process.

11 In August 2002 the High Court handed down a decision on the Miriuwung Gajerrong case with key findings as follows:

- If a right to minerals and petroleum had been established then it would have been extinguished by state legislation.

- Native title is not a single set of rights, but a number of rights with a question of fact in each case.

- Each right under native title can be extinguished independently.

- Western Australian pastoral leases don't extinguish all native title rights, but do extinguish rights and interest to control access to or use of land.

  Western Australian mining leases extinguish native title rights.

In December 2002 the High Court concluded in a claim by the Yorta Yorta people that:

» rights and interests possessed in the present are founded on traditional laws and customs which existed at the time of the acquisition of sovereignty

» there must be continuity of acknowledgement and observance of those laws and customs.

ILUAs

Indigenous land use agreements (ILUAs) are custom-made agreements developed through negotiation between native title claimants and those seeking land use for alternative purposes, such as the granting of exploration licences or mining leases. ILUAs enable parties to enter into binding agreements with respect to doing any future act in order to avoid the uncertainties and difficulties inherent in the NTA.

APPENDIX C
Royalty rates[1]

Africa

Botswana

Ad valorem (a percentage of defined revenue) 3 to 10 per cent. Precious stones 10 per cent, precious metals 5 per cent, other 3 per cent.

Ghana

Ad valorem 5 per cent.

Mozambique

Ad valorem 3 to 12 per cent. Diamonds 10 to 12 per cent, other 3 to 8 per cent; rate negotiable; artisanal miners exempt.

Namibia

Ad valorem 5 to 10 per cent. Uncut precious stones 10 per cent, other maximum 5 per cent.

South Africa

Ad valorem 1.5 to 4 per cent. Lower rates apply to refined product.

Tanzania

Ad valorem 0 to 5 per cent. Diamonds 5 per cent, cut and polished gemstones 0 per cent, other 3 per cent.

---

1 Sources: <www.un.org/esa/ffd/tax/2007DRM_SEG/02AnnexMiningComparisons.ppt>.

Zambia

Ad valorem 2 per cent. Small miners exempt; no royalty for local processing.

Asia and Pacific

China

Specific (fixed amount per tonne) + ad valorem 1 to 4 per cent. Combined royalty; specific rates vary.

India

Specific/ad valorem 0.4 to 20 per cent. Specific rates vary.

Indonesia

Production ad valorem rates. Coal open cut 3 to 7 per cent, underground 2 to 6 per cent; nickel 4 to 5 per cent; zinc, tin and iron 3 per cent; silver 3.25 per cent; gold, iron sand and bauxite 3.75 per cent; copper 4 per cent.

Mongolia

Ad valorem 5 per cent for coal and minerals sold outside of Mongolia, 2.5 per cent for internal sales. Additional 30 per cent for copper ore when copper price greater than US$3150 per tonne; additional 15 per cent for copper concentrate when price greater than US$1800 per tonne; additional 5 per cent for copper metal when price greater than US$900 per tonne. Price hurdles vary for different minerals.

Papua New Guinea

Ad valorem 2 per cent.

Philippines

Specific/ad valorem 2 per cent. Ad valorem generally applies with specific royalty on coal; small miners exempt.

Australia

New South Wales

Coal

7.2 per cent ex-mine value for underground mines, 6.2 per cent for deep underground mines and 8.2 per cent for open cut mines.

Specified minerals

$0.35 to $0.70 per tonne.

Non-specified minerals (metals)

4 per cent of ex-mine value, which includes the deduction of processing or treatment to produce saleable product.

Petroleum

Nil first five years increasing to 10 per cent of well-head value at end of year 10.

Northern Territory

Minerals

18 per cent of net value of production (NVP). First $50 000 is exempt from royalty.

$$NVP = GR - (OC + CRD + EEE + AD)$$

where:

GR = gross realisation from the product

OC = operating cost excluding tax and royalties

CRD = allowance for capital investments incorporating long-term bond rate plus 2 per cent over useful life

EEE = eligible exploration expenditure

AD = additional deduction approved by the minister.

Petroleum
10 per cent of the gross value at the well-head.

Queensland

Bauxite
Export: higher of 10 per cent of its value or $2 per tonne. Domestic 75 per cent of export rate or $1.50 per tonne.

Coal
7 per cent up to $100 per tonne of coal's value then 10 per cent thereafter.

Gemstones
2.5 per cent of value.

Iron ore
Where price less than A$100/t to A$1.25/t, if price greater then A$100/t then A$1.25 plus 2.5 per cent of value above A$100/t.

Mineral sands
5 per cent of value.

Manganese
2.5 per cent of value.

Prescribed minerals
Cobalt, copper, gold, lead, nickel, silver and zinc: variable rate between 2.5 and 5 per cent (varying in 0.02 per cent increments), depending on average metal prices.

Non-prescribed minerals
$0.50 to $1.80 per tonne.

Onshore oil and gas
10 per cent of the well-head value.

South Australia

Base metals, gold and iron ore
5 per cent of assessed saleable value.

Refined metalic products
3.5 per cent of assessed saleable value.

Extractive minerals
$0.35 per tonne of material sold or extracted.

Onshore oil and gas
10 per cent of net post well-head sales value.

Geothermal
2.5 per cent of well-head value.

Tasmania

$$\text{Royalty} = (0.016 \times N) + ((0.4 \times P^2) / N)$$

where:

N = yearly net sales of the mineral

P = yearly profit if any

Maximum royalty payable is 5 per cent of net sales. If mineral sales are less than $100 000, then royalty is only 1.6 per cent.

Prescribed minerals (industrial)
From $0.66 to $2.64 per tonne.

Onshore oil and gas and coal seam gas
12 per cent of well-head value.

Victoria

Gold
No royalty.

Prescribed minerals
2.5 per cent of value unless average market price exceeds set limits.

Coal
The higher of 7 per cent of value or royalty rate = 7 per cent + ((AP–100)/ AP × 3%) where AP is average price per tonne of coal.

Brown coal
To be determined per gigajoule ($0.0239 per gigajoule).

Industrial minerals
From $0.50 to $1.80 per tonne.

Bauxite
The highest of 10 per cent of value or $2 per tonne.

Marble
$8.07 per cubic metre or $3.23 per tonne.

Other minerals
2.5 per cent of net market value.

Onshore oil and gas
10 per cent of the well-head value.

Western Australia

Gold
2.5 per cent of sales value excluding first 2500 ounces.

Iron ore

Lump ore 7.5 per cent, fine ore 5.625 per cent and beneficiated ore 5 per cent.

Mineral sands

5 per cent of realised value (certain minimums apply).

Coal

Domestic $1 per tonne, export 7.5 per cent.

Bauxite

7.5 per cent of value.

Diamond and precious stones

7.5 per cent of value.

Nickel

$R per tonne of product sold where R = P ÷ 100 × 2.5U ÷ 100.

P = gross nickel price per tonne FOB in A$

U = number of units per hundred of nickel metal in product sold.

Magnetite

5 per cent of concentrate value.

Base metals

2.5 per cent of realisable metal sales or 5 per cent of realisable concentrate sales.

Onshore oil and gas

10 per cent primary, 12.5 per cent secondary production of the well-head value.

Federal government

Offshore oil and gas beyond coastal waters

Petroleum Resource Rent Tax (PRRT):

» tax assessed on a project basis

» all exploration expenditure is an eligible deduction

» applies at 40 per cent of net income after deduction of project expenditure and exploration expenditure from other PRRT areas

» undeducted exploration expenditure can be compounded forward at Australian long bond rate plus 15 per cent while general expenditure at bond rate plus 5 per cent (provided they were incurred less than five years before the production licence commenced) for deduction against future receipts from the project

» project closing down and environmental costs are deductible

» PRRT payments are deductible for company tax purposes.

Minerals resource rent tax (MRRT)

» From June 2012 MRRT is applicable to iron and coal mines with revenues in excess of $100 million.

» It is a profit-based cash flow tax with a rate of 22.5 per cent, which is deductible for corporate tax purposes.

» MRRT applies only to profits upstream of the taxing point, which has been defined at the run of mine stockpile.

» Negative cash flows are carried forward and uplifted by an interest rate defined as the long-term bond rate (LTBR) plus 7 per cent.

» If a mining company's operations were in existence as at 1 May 2010, then they are entitled to a starting base allowance based on their existing investments, further reducing their mining profit.

Canada

Alberta

12 per cent profit tax after full cost recovery; 1 per cent prior to full cost recovery.

British Columbia

13 per cent profit tax; 2 per cent ad valorem is minimum tax (fully deductible against profit royalty); losses can be carried forward under profit royalty.

Manitoba

10 per cent profit tax for less than $50 million, 15 per cent for $55 million to $100 million, 17 per cent for greater than $105 million.

New Brunswick

2 per cent of net revenue, 16 per cent net profit tax where profits exceed $100 000.

Newfoundland and Labrador

15 per cent of taxable income.

Northwest Territories

Sliding scale: no tax if income below $10 000; 5 per cent $10 000 to $5 million; 6 per cent $5 million to $10 million; increasing by 1 per cent for each additional $5 million to maximum of 14 per cent.

Nova Scotia

2 per cent of net revenue or 15 per cent of net income, whichever is the greater.

Ontario

10 per cent profit tax; 5 per cent for remote areas. No tax if income below $500 000.

Quebec

16 per cent profit tax.

Saskatchewan

5 per cent profit tax up to 1 million ounces gold or 1 million tonnes base metals sold; 10 per cent thereafter. Ten-year holiday on new mines.

United States

Arizona

Minimum ad valorem of 2 per cent. Commissioner to set rate, usually between 5 and 6 per cent.

Michigan

Ad valorem 2 to 7 per cent. Sliding scale.

Nevada

2 per cent to 5 per cent profit tax. Sliding scale.

Latin America

Argentina

Ad valorem up to 3 per cent. Most jurisdictions do not apply a royalty; federal government imposes a maximum rate of 3 per cent.

Bolivia

Ad valorem 1 to 6 per cent. Sliding scale based on price; rate is 60 per cent lower for domestic use.

Brazil

Ad valorem 0.2 to 3 per cent.

Chile

Ad valorem 0 to 5 per cent. Rates for copper with sliding scale based on annual sales; other rates not available.

Mexico

None.

Peru

Ad valorem 1 to 3 per cent. In late 2011 the Peruvian Government proposed a new royalty system with a sliding scale of 1 per cent to 12 per cent of operating profit for miners that had not negotiated a tax stability agreement in the 1990s.

Venezuela

Ad valorem 3 to 4 per cent.

APPENDIX D
Economic geology primer

Hard rock deposits

The theory of mineral deposition is both complex and still open to some debate. The criteria used to define mineral deposits are therefore varied and the following pages are only intended to provide a broad overview. The processes that form rocks that are part of the Earth's crust are ongoing and ore deposits are very special types of rock—ones that are economic to mine and provide the raw materials our society needs. Ore deposits can be associated with specific rock types and geological environments, and it is their physical description that allows us to place them into several categories, according to a generally accepted hypothesis on how those deposits are formed. Mineral deposits may also undergo numerous episodes of deformation and metamorphism over geological time, which may change them from their original form. There are two primary types: syngenetic and epigenetic.

Syngenetic deposits are formed at the same time as the waste rock that encloses them. Examples include the following:

» *Magmatic deposits* (orthomagmatic) are formed by the separation of metal sulphides or oxides within a magma chamber before the magma solidifies and crystallises. The heavier metal-rich liquids sink to the bottom of the chamber or intrusion, while the lighter silicates tend to rise to the top. Magma tends to solidify before reaching the surface, producing igneous rocks such as granite. Common metals include Cr, Ti, Fe, Cu, PGMs and also diamonds.

» *Volcanic or extrusive deposits* are associated with volcanic processes and are found only within the volcanic rocks themselves. The largest deposits are known as volcanogenic massive sulfide deposits (VMS) and are massive (80 per cent plus sulphides) accumulations *on or near the sea floor* containing combinations of Cu, Pb, Zn, Ag and Au.

» *Sedimentary deposits* are mineralised layered zones formed at the same time (geologically) as the surrounding layers, one on top of another, in lakes or seas. Due to their age, most deposits have been intensely deformed and metamorphosed (through heat and pressure). Typical examples include iron ore deposits that occur as distinct sedimentary layers commonly termed banded iron formation (BIF).

Epigenetic deposits are formed much later than the enclosing waste rock. For example, rock may be broken along a fault zone resulting in additional open spaces along the fault due to the brittle nature of the rock. Hydrothermal fluids might then migrate up the fault and precipitate the ore and gangue in the spaces or veins that are younger than the host rock. Examples include:

» *Hydrothermal deposits* consist of different types, but all come from hot circulating water-rich fluids that have dissolved metals such as Cu, Pb, Si, Fe or Au. These are then participated out of solution due to a significant change, such as temperature, to form a new deposit. Epithermal (Au and Ag) are shallow deposits that are formed by hydrothermal fluids at temperatures of 230°C–260°C that initially fracture the host rock and then act as channels for the hydrothermal fluids. Mesothermal deposits are those formed at intermediate depth and pressure while the hydrothermal deposits themselves are at the greatest depth and pressure.

» *Porphyry* is a large low-grade deposit of widely dispersed mineralisation associated with porphyry intrusions. The mineralisation may occur in country rock that may be older or of a similar age as the intrusion itself, which is all highly fractured. It is distinguished by its large size and structural control such as veins, vein sets, stockworks, fractures and breccias. Porphyry deposits are an important source of Cu and Mo, as well as Au, Ag and Sn; and account for about 50 to 60 per cent of world Cu production and more than 95 per cent of world Mo production.

» *Skarns* are formed from the replacement of calcareous sediments such as limestone by hydrothermal fluids usually from intrusive bodies containing combinations of Cu, Pb, Zn, Ag, Au, Sn, W, PGMs and Fe. Generally, Sn and W are associated with deeper and older deposits, while Pb, Zn and PGMs are shallower and the youngest.

» *Vein deposits* can often extend over large depths and lateral strike lengths, but are often very narrow. Deposition of minerals can be hydrothermal (Cu and Au) and mesothermal (Cu, Pb, Zn, Ag and Au).

For more information visit <www.amonline.net.au/geoscience/earth/geological_ore.htm>.

Oil and gas accumulations

Natural oil is believed to be derived from the decay of organic material in an anaerobic environment in fine-grained sediments, which, with metamorphic rocks (altered sedimentary rocks), make up 75 per cent of exposed surface rocks, but only 5 per cent of the Earth's crust by volume. The sedimentary rocks were formed, as the name implies, from the deposition, compaction and consolidation of sediments, either from the erosion of rocks (detrital), or from chemical processes (by evaporation or by organisms). The sedimentary units or layers have spaces or pores between the particles that create the rock's porosity with levels from 1 to 40 per cent. The degree of interconnection between the pores and their size is referred to as the permeability, which is a measure of how easily fluids will pass through the rock, commonly measured in millidarcies (1 mD) to many darcies, 1000 mD = 1D, the larger the number the greater the permeability).

The deeper the source rocks, the higher the prevailing temperature that transforms any organic matter (kerogen) into oil (110°C to 130°C) and gas at higher temperatures. Time is also a factor in generation, with geologically younger rocks requiring temperatures at the higher end of the desired range. Once petroleum generation has begun, the source rock is considered mature and may be termed the 'source' or 'hydrocarbon kitchen'. Natural gas is a mixture of hydrocarbons, predominantly methane, but may also contain small amounts of ethane, propane, butane, pentane and impurities such as sulphur dioxide, carbon dioxide, nitrogen and helium. Natural gas may be found associated with oil or on its own.

After the oil (gas) has formed in the source bed, it moves or migrates to more porous and permeable carrier beds with a lower formation pressure due to the heavy overburden weight of the more permeable beds above. The oil then continues its upward migration due to its density and hence buoyancy compared with the denser water within the layers. Due to tectonic forces, sedimentary layers may have been twisted, folded and faulted over time, producing structures or traps that may be covered by an impermeable layer of rock or a seal. Over many millions of years, oil may have accumulated in these traps within reservoir rock.

The types of traps referred to include the following:

» *Structural* traps, which in their simplest form are like a large underground dome or hill, are where the hydrocarbon (oil and/ or gas) can enter from any side and collect at the top, held in by the underlying water and 'top' seal, or fill all the structure with any surplus hydrocarbons moving beyond the structure. Fault traps are formed when the migration of hydrocarbons is stopped by a fault (a vertical or near vertical displacement of the beds along a surface known as a fault plane) that acts as a seal to the truncated reservoir.

» *Stratigraphic* traps are formed where the seal is due to depositional or alteration processes rather than to structural movements of the Earth's crust. Although potentially larger than structural traps they are more difficult to find due to their subtle nature. They may include buried and sealed high-porosity coral reefs, a truncation that is formed when sediments are deposited directly on top of older eroded structures that act as a seal, and when sandy lenses such as riverbeds or sandy beaches are surrounded by more finely grained impervious sediments.

As described previously, electromagnetics, geophysics and geochemistry can also be used to define likely hydrocarbon targets in sedimentary basins. However, the layering of sediments with different densities provides the opportunity to employ seismic surveys. The process involves creating an energy pulse (by explosives or vibration if a seismic survey on land) or a pneumatic pulse if the survey area is covered by water, particularly at sea, that sends a signal into the ground. The time for the reflections from layers of different density and interval velocity to reach the surface is measured and translated into depth, using estimates of the relative density of the sedimentary sequences and resultant velocity of the signal to provide an image of the underground layers and structures. Initially, cheaper and less definitive 2D surveys might be undertaken followed by more detailed 3D surveys. When a field is in production, multiple surveys may be undertaken over time to determine how the reservoir is draining. They are referred to as 4D seismic surveys.

Other types of deposits

There are also a number of economic secondary deposits that are transformations of the primary deposits as listed below.

» *Placer deposits* are concentrations of relatively high specific gravity minerals such as gold, PGMs, gemstones, tin, rutile, monazite and zircon. They occur as a result of the weathering of hard rock deposits and as minerals are remobilised through rivers and along coastlines. Deposits can be classified into the following:

- *alluvial*—material that is transported by a river and deposited along the riverbed itself or on its floodplain

- *colluvial*—material transported by gravity action such as on steep slopes

- *eluvial*—material still at or near its point of formation.

» *Residual deposits* are formed through a chemical weathering process more commonly in tropical regions where the zone down to the base of the water table is leached of relatively mobile ions such as sodium, potassium, calcium, magnesium and, under the right conditions, silica. In very tropical and hot climates a lateritic soil may be formed of primarily iron and aluminium oxides termed bauxite. In some cases a laterite may develop from ultrabasic rocks with relatively high concentrations of nickel.

» *Clay deposits* are formed either by settling of clay particles in sedimentary basins or through intense weathering of volcanic and granitic rocks. The most common clay minerals mined are kaolinite (china clay) and montmorillonite (fuller's earth).

» *Evaporite deposits*, such as salts, gypsum and nitrates, are formed through the evaporation of saline water.

» *Phosphatic deposits* are phosphate rocks formed through compaction of fine-grained mixtures of various calcium phosphates of three main types:

- *marine phosphate deposits*—all marine sediments contain some phosphate, and if in sufficient quantities can make the deposits commercial

- *bone beds*—these are localised accumulations of fossil deposits of bones that may be thick enough to form economic deposits

- *guano*—these are ancient and/or fossil deposits of bird or bat excreta.

APPENDIX E
Project details

Black coal

Project	Status	Production	Capital cost	$/t
Bengalla expansion stage 1	Expansion, under construction	2.1 Mt ROM	$179m	85
Boggabri open cut	Expansion, under construction	3.3 Mt thermal	$400m	121
Hunter Valley operations expansion	Expansion, under construction	6 Mt thermal and semi-soft coking	$252m	375
Metropolitan longwall	Expansion, under construction	1 Mt hard coking	$68m	68
Mount Arthur (RX1)	New project, under construction	4 Mt thermal (ROM)	$388m	97
Narrabri (stage 2)	Expansion, under construction	4.5 Mt thermal	$300m	67
Ravensworth North	Expansion, under construction	8 Mt thermal and semi-soft	$1.36b	163
Ulan West	Expansion, under construction	7 Mt thermal	$1.07b	153
Wilpinjong	Expansion, under construction	2–3 Mt thermal	$87m	35
Austar underground (stage 3)	Expansion, govt approval received	3.6 Mt ROM hard coking	$80m	22
Cobbora	New project, EIS under way	12 Mt thermal	$1.3b	108
Maules Creek	New project, EIS under way	10.5 Mt semi-soft coking and thermal	$651m	62
Moolarben (stage 2)	Expansion, EIS under way	12 Mt open cut; 4 Mt underground, thermal	$120m	10

(*continued*)

Black coal (*cont'd*)

Project	Status	Production	Capital cost	$/t
Mount Pleasant	New project feasibility study under way	8.5 Mt thermal	$1.3b	153
Mt Penny	New project, feasibility study under way	5 Mt thermal	$440m	110
South East open cut	Expansion, feasibility study under way	3.6 Mt thermal	$83m	23
Wallarah underground longwall	New project, govt approval not granted, second EIS under way	5 Mt thermal	$700m	140
Caval Ridge/Peak Downs expansion	New project, committed	8 Mt coking	$4.1b	525
Curragh Mine	Expansion, under construction	Increase to 8.5 Mt	$286m	34
Daunia	New project, committed	4.5 Mt coking	$1.55b	356
Ensham bord and pillar underground mine	Expansion, under construction	1.5t–2.5 Mt thermal	$166m	83
Kestrel	Expansion, under construction	1.7 Mt coking	$1.9b	1118
Lake Vermont	Expansion, under construction	4 Mt	$200m	50
Middlemount (stage 1)	New project, under construction	1.8 Mt coking (ROM)	$500m	278
Newlands Northern underground	Expansion, under construction	3 Mt	$146m	49
Oaky Creek (phase 1)	Expansion, under construction	1 Mt coking	$87m	87
Alpha Coal (incl. mine, port and rail)	New project, EIS under way	30 Mt thermal	$7.5b	250
Baralaba expansion	Expansion, feasibility study under way	3.5 Mt of PCI and thermal	$350m	100

Appendix E: Project details

Project	Status	Production	Capital cost	$/t
Belvedere underground	New project, pre-feasibility study completed	7 Mt hard coking	$2.8b	400
Colton	New project, EIS under way	0.5 Mt coking	$84m	168
Eagle Downs (Peak Downs East underground)	New project, EIS under way	4.5 Mt coking	$1.25b	278
Elimatta	New project, EIS under way	5 Mt thermal	$580m	116
Grosvenor underground	New project, feasibility study under way	4.3 Mt hard coking	$1.26b	302
Jellinbah East	Expansion, pre-feasibility study under way	1–2 Mt coking	$50–100m	50
Middlemount (stage 2)	Expansion, EIS under way	2.7 Mt semi-hard coking and PCI	$500m (includes stage 1 and 2)	185
Minyango	New project, feasibility study under way	4.5 Mt thermal and coking	$750m	167
Monto coal mine (stage 1)	New project, feasibility study under way	1.2 Mt thermal	$35m	34
Moranbah South	New project, pre-feasibility study under way	6.5 Mt coking	$971m	149
Orion Downs	New project, pre-feasibility study under way	2.5 Mt thermal	$65m	26
Springsure Creek	New project, feasibility study under way	11 Mt thermal (ROM)	$1.1b	100
The Range	New project, EIS[1] under way	7 Mt thermal	$500m	71

(*continued*)

1 Environmental Impact Statement

Black coal (*cont'd*)

Project	Status	Production	Capital cost	$/t
Washpool	New project, feasibility study completed	2.6 Mt hard coking	$368m	142
Wongai	New project, approval processes under way	1.5 Mt coking	$500m	333
Canning Basin	New project, feasibility study under way	2.5 Mt thermal	$199m	80

Coal seam gas

Project	Status	Production	Capital cost	$/PJ
Camden Gas (stage 2)	Expansion, planning approval received	12 PJ pa	$35m	3
Gloucester coal seam gas project	New project, feasibility study under way	15–25 PJ pa	$200m	10
Narrabri coal seam gas project	New project, feasibility study under way	20 PJ pa (initially) 150 PJ pa (ultimately)	$1.3b	9

Liquefied natural gas (LNG)

Project	Status	New capacity	Capital cost	$/t
Australia Pacific	New project, committed	4.5 Mt LNG	$13.6b	3022
Gladstone	New project, under construction	7.8 Mt LNG	$15.5b	1987
Gorgon	New project, under construction	15 Mt LNG, 110 PJ pa domestic gas	$43b	2867
Pluto (train 1)	New project, under construction	4.3 Mt LNG	$14.9b (incl. site works for train 2)	3465
Wheatstone	New project, committed	8.9 Mt LNG	$29b	3258

Project	Status	New capacity	Capital cost	$/t
Fisherman's Landing project (train 1)	New project, gas source studies under way, environmental approval received	1.5 Mt LNG	$782m	521
Queensland Curtis	New project, under construction	8.5 Mt LNG (12 Mt ultimately)	$14.6b	1718
Fisherman's Landing project (train 2)	Expansion, FEED studies under way, environmental approval received	1.5 Mt LNG	$291m	194
Timor Sea	New project, prefeasibility study under way	3 Mt LNG	$2b	667
Dandenong plant	Expansion, committed	25 kt LNG	$65m	2600
Micro plant	New project, awaiting govt approval	20 kt LNG	$100m	5000
Newcastle gas storage facility	New project, EIS under way	70 kt LNG processing, 30 kt LNG storage	$300m	4286

Natural gas

Project	Status	New capacity	Capital cost	$m/kbpd
Balnaves	New project, committed	30 kbpd	$425m	14
Coniston (tie back to Van Gogh)	Expansion, under construction	22 kbpd	$521m	24
Montara/Skua oilfield	New project, under construction	35 kbpd oil	$680m	19
Condensate processing facility	New project, feasibility study under way	Processing 60 kbpd of condensate to produce gasoline, diesel, jet fuel and fuel oil	$689m	11
Crux liquids project	New project, FEED studies completed	39 kbpd condensate at peak	$1.2b	31

(continued)

Natural gas (*cont'd*)

Project	Status	New capacity	Capital cost	$m/ kbpd
Macedon	New project, under construction	75 PJ pa gas	$1.45b	19
NWS North Rankin B	Expansion, under construction	967 PJ pa gas	$5b	5
Reindeer gas field/ Devil Creek gas processing plant (phase 1)	New project, under construction	78 PJ pa gas	$1.05b	13
Spar	New project, committed	18 PJ pa	$117m	7

Uranium

Project	Status	New capacity	Capital cost	$m/kt
Bigrlyi	New project, prefeasibility study completed	0.6 kt U3O8, 0.55 kt V2O5	$70m	117
Four Mile	New project, awaiting mineral lease	2.3 kt U3O8	$210m	91
Mulga Rock	New project, pre-feasibility study completed	1.2 kt U3O8	$260m	217
Valhalla	New project, on hold	2.7 kt U3O8 initially; 4.1 kt U3O8 eventually	$400m	148
Westmoreland	New project, on hold	1.36 kt U3O8	$317m	233
Wiluna	New project, environmental approval under way	0.8 kt U3O8	$250m	313

Bauxite

Project	Status	New capacity	Capital cost	$m/t
Bauxite Hills	New project, pre-feasibility study completed	2 Mt initially, 10 Mt ultimately	$200–250m (initially)	113
South of Embley	Expansion, EIS under way	22.5 Mt bauxite	$570m	25

Copper

Project	Status	New capacity	Capital cost	$m/t
DeGrussa	New project, under construction	77 kt Cu, 36 koz Au	$384m	4987
Kanmantoo	New project, under construction	20kt Cu, 10 koz Au, 180 koz Ag (all in concentrates)	$144m	7200
Osborne	New project, under construction	21 kt Cu, 34 koz Au	$137m	6524
Cloncurry	New project, feasibility study/ EIS under way	25 kt Cu, 19 koz Au	$200m	8000
Copper Hill	New project, feasibility study under way	37 kt Cu, 69 koz Au	$420m	11351
Einasleigh	New project, feasibility study completed	15 kt Cu, 3500 oz Au, 500 koz Ag	$108m	7200
Kalkaroo	New project, feasibility study completed	25 kt Cu, 75 000 oz Au	$360m	14400
Mt Dore	New project, feasibility study under way	19 kt Cu cathode	$00m	4368
Mutooroo	New project, approval processes under way	10 kt of Cu, 1.2 kt of Co, 550 ktpa H2SO4	$75m	7500
Pilbara VMS Province	New project, feasibility study under way	20 kt of Cu, 40 kt of Zn	$135m–145m	7000
Redbank	New project, feasibility study under way	30 kt Cu	$55m	1833

(*continued*)

Gold

Project	Status	New capacity	Capital cost	$m/oz
Duketon (Garden Well)	Expansion, under construction	180 000 oz	$109m	606
HBJ (SKO expansion stage 1)	Expansion, committed	100 000 oz	$25m	250
Mt Magnet	Redevelopment, under construction	91 000 oz	$28m	308
Nullagine Gold	New project, under construction	72 000 oz	$72m	1000
Tropicana Joint Venture Project	New project, under construction	330 000– 350 000 oz	$640m–690m	2077
Woods Point	Redevelopment, under construction	25 000 oz	$32m	1280
Agate Creek	New project, feasibility study under way	100 000 oz	$60m	600
Barlee	New project, feasibility study under way	50 000 oz	$30m	600
Bundarra	Expansion, on hold	91 500 oz (over life of project)	$25m	273
Carosue Dam (Red October)	Expansion, feasibility study under way	130 000–140 000 oz	$40m	296
Central Murchison	Redevelopment, feasibility study under way	120 000 oz	$100m	833
Central Tanami	Redevelopment, feasibility study under way	70 000 oz	$35m	500
Charters Towers	Expansion, awaiting final investment decision	310 000 oz	$230m	742
Cowal	Expansion, pre-feasibility study under way	400 000 oz (over life of mine)	$58m	145

Appendix E: Project details

Project	Status	New capacity	Capital cost	$m/oz
Gullewa (Deflector gold–copper project)	New project, feasibility study under way	50 000 oz Au, 2kt Cu, 35 koz Ag	$52m	104
Hera	New project, feasibility study under way	50 000 oz Au	$73.5m	1470
Laverton (Summit)	Expansion, feasibility study under way	50 000–70 000 oz	$33m	550
Leonora Gold	New project, feasibility study under way	53 000 oz	$35m	660
Majors Creek	New project, awaiting government approvals	50 000oz	$42m	840
Meekatharra	Redevelopment, feasibility study under way	100 000–120 000 oz	$37m	336
Mt Carlton (Silver Hill)	New project, feasibility study complete	95 000 oz Au, 1.7 Moz Ag, 2.4 kt Cu	$127m	1337
Mt Todd	Expansion, feasibility study under way	270 000 oz	$656m	2430
Murchison	New project, feasibility study under way	100 000 oz	$75m	750
Norseman Gold	New project, on hold	100 000 oz	$65m	650
Paddington (Enterprise)	Expansion, feasibility study under way	55 000 oz	$28m	509
Phillips River	New project, feasibility study completed	360 000 oz Ag, 30 000 oz Au, 3.5 kt Cu, 2.1 Kt Pb, 2.8 kt Zn	$133m	369
Rover 1	New project, feasibility study under way	60 000 oz	$100m	167
Tomingley (Wyoming) gold	New project, feasibility study completed	50 000 oz	$90m	1800

(*continued*)

Iron ore—mining projects

Project	Status	New capacity	Capital cost	$m/kt
Chichester Hub (55–95 mtpa)	Expansion, under construction	40 Mt	$1.07b	28
Extension Hill Direct Shipping Ore (DSO) project	New project, under construction	3.0 Mt hematite ore	$90m	30
Hamersley Iron Brockman 4 project (stage 2)	Expansion, under construction	18 Mt	$1.07b (incl. West Turner Syncline)	61
Hope Downs 4	New project, under construction	15 Mt	$2.0b	140
Jimblebar mine and rail (WAIO)	New project, under construction	35 Mt	$3.3b	97
Karara	New project, under construction	8 Mt magnetite concentrate, 2 Mt hematite ore	$2.6b	260
Koolyanobbing	Expansion, under construction	2.5 Mt	$280m	112
Sino Iron	New project, under construction	28 Mt (concentrates and pellets in total)	$6.1b	218
Solomon Hub (stage I)	New project, under construction	60 Mt	$2.7b	45
Wilcherry Hill (stage 1)	New project, under construction	2 Mt DSO	$26m	13
Yilgarn (stage 1) (Carina)	New project, under construction	4 Mt hematite	$120–130m	31
Balla Balla (phase I)	New project, govt approval received	6 Mt iron concentrates, 280 kt TiO_2	$1.3b	217
Balla Balla (phase II)	New project, feasibility study under way	4 Mt iron concentrates, 190 kt TiO_2, 7 kt FeV	$720m	180
Balmoral South magnetite (stage 1)	New project, feasibility study under review	12 Mt (5 Mt iron concentrate, 7 Mt pellets)	$3.3b	275

Project	Status	New capacity	Capital cost	$m/kt
Cape Lambert magnetite	New project, government approval under way	15 Mt concentrates	$3.7b	247
East Pilbara (Robertson Range and Davidson Creek)	New project, feasibility study under way	15 Mt	$960m	64
Eradu Iron	New project, pre-feasibility study under way	1 Mt pig iron	$720m	720
Extension Hill magnetite	New project, govt approval received	10 Mt magnetite concentrates	$2.9b	290
Hardey	New project, pre-feasibility study completed	10 Mt	$1.6b	160
Hawks Nest magnetite	New project, feasibility study under way	6–10 Mt concentrates	$1b	125
Hawsons	New project, feasibility study under way	5 Mt initally (20 Mt ultimately)	$2.9b	58
Irvine Island	New project, feasibility study under way	17 Mt	$700m	41
Jack Hills (stage 2)	Expansion, feasibility study under way	25–35 Mt	$2b	67
Marillana	New project, feasibility study under way	17–20 Mt hematite	$1.9b (incl. 80 km rail spur)	103
Nammuldi expansion	Expansion, feasibility study under way	26 Mt	$1.53b	62
Parker Range iron ore	New project, feasibility study completed	6 Mt	$164m	27
Peculiar Knob	New project, govt approval granted	3.3 Mt hematite ore	$170m	52
Pilbara	New project, feasibility study under way	5 Mt (up to 15 Mt)	$488m (for 5 Mt)	98
Ridley magnetite	New project, pre-feasibility study completed	15 Mt	$2.8b	187

(*continued*)

Iron ore—mining projects (*cont'd*)

Project	Status	New capacity	Capital cost	$m/kt
Roper River Iron Ore	New project, feasibility study under way	4–5 Mt	$95m–180m	36
Southdown magnetite	New project, feasibility study under way	10 Mt concentrates	$2.6b	260
Turner River Hub	New project, feasibility study under way	10 Mt DSO	$178m	18
Weld Range	New project, feasibility study completed	15 Mt hematite	$2b	133
West Pilbara	New project, feasibility study completed	30 Mt hematite	$5.8b (incl. infrastructure)	193
Wilcherry Hill (stage 2)	Expansion, prefeasibility study completed	5–6 Mt concentrates	$300m	55
Yilgarn iron ore project (stage 2) (Carina)	New project, feasibility study under way	5 Mt hematite	$120–130m	25

Iron ore—infrastructure projects

Project	Status	New capacity	Capital cost	$m/kt
Cape Lambert port and rail expansion	Expansion, under construction	53 Mt (to 133 Mt)	$3.07b	58
Dampier Port expansion	Expansion, under construction	5 mtpa (to 230 mtpa)	$276m	55
Port (55–155 mtpa)	Expansion, under construction	100 mtpa (to 155 mtpa)	$2.3b	23
Rail (55–155 mtpa)	Expansion, under construction	100 mtpa (to 155 mtpa)	$2.1b	21
WAIO Inner Harbour	Expansion, under construction	20 Mt (to 240 Mt)	$2.1b	12
Anketell Point port	New project, EIS under way	30–40 mtpa	$3.1b	89
Cape Lambert port expansion	Expansion, feasibility study under way	50 Mt (to 183 Mt)	$3.2b	64

Project	Status	New capacity	Capital cost	$m/kt
Darwin iron ore berth	Expansion, feasibility study under way	5–6 Mt	$300m	55
Port Bonython	New project, awaiting govt approval	20 Mt	$600m	30
Port Hedland	Expansion, feasibility study under way	50 Mt	$2.7b	54
Port Spence (Sheep Hill)	New project, feasibility study under way	18 Mt	$250m	14

Lead–zinc–silver

Project	Status	New capacity	Capital cost	$m/t
George Fisher mine	Expansion, under construction	1 Mt of ores and concentrates	$310m	310
Handlebar Hill	Expansion, under construction	80 kt Zn, ?? kt Pb	$40m	364
Lady Loretta	New project, committed	126 kt Zn 40 kt Pb	$246m	1482
Potosi (stages 2 and 3)	Expansion, under construction	45 kt Zn, Pb	$58m	1289
Rasp	New project, committed	70–90 kt Zn, 40–60 kt Pb in concentrate	$136m	1046
Admiral Bay	New project, pre-feasibility study completed	846 kt Zn, 1 Mt Pb, 18.97 Moz Ag	$997m	540
Dugald River	New project, EIS under way	200 kt Zn, 25 kt Pb, 1 Moz Ag	$850–950m	3889
Kempfield	New project, feasibility study under way	82.8 kt Zn, 25.5 kt Pb, 20.8 Moz Ag, 0.336 Moz Au (life of mine)	$100m	943
Koongie Zinc Copper	New project, feasibility study under way	43 kt Zn, 33 kt Cu, 7 koz Au, 296 koz Ag (life of mine)	$59m	776
Lennard Shelf	Redevelopment, feasibility study under way	49 kt Zn, 68 kt Pb	$219m	1872
McArthur River (phase 3)	Expansion, feasibility study under way	200 kt Zn in concentrate	$270m	1350

(*continued*)

Lead–zinc–silver (*cont'd*)

Project	Status	New capacity	Capital cost	$m/t
Sorby Hills Lead–Silver	New project, feasibility study under way	7.4 Moz Ag, 140 kt Pb, 13 kt Zn	$100m	654
Sulfur Springs	New project, feasibility study under way	50 kt Zn, 20 kt Cu, 0.5 Mt Pyrite	$242m	3457
Webbs Silver	New project, pre-feasability study under way	5.2 Moz Ag, 1.3 kt Cu, 4 kt Pb, 6.2 kt Zn	$65m	5652
Woodlawn Retreatment	Redevelopment, FEED study & EIS under way	151 kt Zn, 27 kt Pb, 25 kt Cu, 36 koz Au, 4 Moz Ag (life of project)	$66m	327

Mineral sands

Project	Status	New capacity	Capital cost	$m/t
Coburn	New project, feasibility study completed	90 kt ilmenite, 40 kt zircon, 9 kt rutile, 7 kt leucoxene	$180m	1233
Donald	New project, feasibility study under way	70 kt zircon, 106 kt ilmenite, 73 kt leucoxene	$282m	1133
Keysbrook	New project, govt approval under way	80 kt of zircon and leucoxene	$20m	250

Nickel

Project	Status	New capacity	Capital cost	$m/t
Ravensthorpe	Refurbishment, under construction	28 kt Ni	$200m	7143
Spotted Quoll (underground)	Expansion, under construction	10 kt Ni	$98m	9800
Barnes Hill	New project, feasibility study under way	2.2 kt Ni	$50m	22727
Canegrass	New project, pre-feasibility study under way	20 kt Ni, 1.4 kt Co	$865m	40421

Project	Status	New capacity	Capital cost	$m/t
Cosmos Project (includes Alec Mairs 2 deposits)	Expansion, feasibility study under way	10 kt Ni	$150m	15 000
Diggers South	New project, feasibility study completed	5–6 kt Ni	$100m	1 818
Gladstone Nickel (stage 1)	New project, environmental approval received, on hold	63 kt Ni, 6.2 kt Co	$4.1b	59 249
Kalgoorlie Nickel	New project, on hold	36.7 kt Ni, 3 kt Co	$2b	50 378
Lucky Break	New project, feasibility study completed	0.66 kt Ni	$12.4m	18 788
Mt Windarra (phases 1 and 2)	Refurbishment and expansion, feasibility study under way	10 kt Ni	$53m	5 300
New Morning/ Daybreak	New project, pre-feasibility study under way	4 kt Ni	$40m	10 000
NiWest Nickel Laterite heap leach project	New project, feasibility study under way	30 kt Ni, 1.4 kt Co	$660m	21 019
Nornico (stage 1) (Greenvale deposit)	New project, pre-feasibility study under way	6 kt Ni, 0.5 kt Co, 40–75 t Sc	$477m	7 571
Sherlock Bay	New project, pre-feasibility study under way	9 kt Ni	$34m	3 778
Wingellina	New project, EIS under way	40 kt Ni, 3 kt Co	$1.8b	41 860

Rare earths

Project	Status	New capacity	Capital cost	$m/t
Mt Weld (phase 2)	Expansion, feasibility study completed	11 kt rare earth oxides	$170m	15 455
Nolans Bore	New project, feasibility study under way	20 kt rare earth oxides	$250m	12 500

(*continued*)

Tin

Project	Status	New capacity	Capital cost	$m/t
Mt Garnet	New project, pre-feasibility study under way	5 kt Sn	$124m	24 800
Mt Lindsay	New project, feasibility study under way	8 kt Sn, 7 kt WO3, 7–8 kt magnetite	$162m	7 200
Renison expansion (Rentails)	Expansion, feasibility study under way	5 kt Sn metal, 2 kt Cu	$200m	28 571

Vanadium

Project	Status	New Capacity	Capital Cost	$m/t
Barrambie	New project, feasibility study completed	6.3 kt ferrovanadium, 11.2 kt V_2O_5	$489m	27 943

Other commodities

Project	Status	New capacity	Capital cost	$m/t
Gemco Phase 2 expansion	Expansion, committed	600 kt manganese ore	$271m	452
Kooragang Island ammonia	Expansion, on hold	65 kt of ammonia	$110m	1 692
Moranbah ammonium nitrate	New project, under construction	330 kt ammonium nitrate	$935m	2833
Mt Marion lithium	New project, under construction	200 kt of spodumene concentrate	$40m	200
Ammonium nitrate emulsion plant	New project, feasibility study under way	100 kt	$40m	400
Anduramba molybdenum	New project, on hold	950 t Mo, 0.14 kt Cu	$86m	91

Appendix E: Project details

Project	Status	New capacity	Capital cost	$m/t
Big Hill tungsten	New project, feasibility study under way	6 kt W	$112m	18 667
Burrup ammonium nitrate plant	New project, awaiting govt approval	350 kt ammonium nitrate	$600m	1 714
Dolphin tungsten	Redevelopment, feasibility study under way	3600 tonnes WO3 in concentrates	$45–50m	13 194
Dubbo zirconia	New project, feasibility study under way	6–15 kt zirconium, 4–10 kt rare earths	$200–400m	17 143
Kingsgate molybdenum–bismuth	New project, feasibility study completed	800 tonnes $(NH_4)2MoO_4$, 100 kt SiO_2, 260 t Bi	$81m	101 250
Kooragang Island ammonium nitrate facility	Expansion, feasibility study under way	320 kt of ammonium nitrate	$600–750m	2 109
Merlin molybdenum–rhenium (Cloncurry)	New project, feasibility study under way	5.3kt Mo, 7.5t Re	$337m	6 358
Mount Carbine	New project, pre-feasibility study under way	2.4 kt tungsten concentrate	$50m	20 833
Paradise phosphate	New project, feasibility study completed	600–1200 kt ammonium phosphate, 15 kt AlF_3	$1.73b	1 922
Spinifex Ridge molybdenum–copper	New project, feasibility study completed	4.7 kt Mo, 5.9 kt Cu (in concentrates)	$485m	45 755
Swan River (Kerrigan) kaolin	New project, on hold	250 kt processed kaolin	$36m	144

(*continued*)

Minerals processing facilities

Project	Status	New capacity	Capital cost	$m/t
Alumina				
Worsley refinery	Expansion, under construction	1100 kt	$3.4b inc. Marradong mine and co-gen unit	3091
Yarwun refinery	Expansion, under construction	2000 kt	$2.2b	1100
Rare earths				
Rare Earths Complex	New project, feasibility study under way	20 kt rare earth oxides, 500 kt Gypsum, 80 kt phosphoric acid 150 t U_3O_8	$1b	1667
Crude iron and steel				
Gladstone Steel Plant (stage 1)	New project, EIS under way	5 Mt billets	$1.4b	280
Magnesium				
Hazelwood magnesium	New project, feasibility study under way	5 kt of magnesium ingots	$20m	4000

Source: Based on 'Mining Industry Major Projects–Projects Listing', published by the Bureau of Resources and Energy Economics www.bree.gov.au

Note: the author's calculations in the final columns of the tables in this section are based on BREE data.

APPENDIX F
Exchange rates and CPI

Australian dollar exchange rates and Consumer Price Index June 1990–December 2011

Date	US	UK	CPI
Dec 11	1.0216	1.5208	179.4
Sep 11	0.9664	1.6131	179.4
Jun 11	1.0719	1.4975	178.3
Mar 11	1.0327	1.5520	176.7
Dec 10	1.0231	1.5261	174.0
Sep 10	0.9672	1.6250	173.3
Jun 10	0.8407	1.7780	172.1
Mar 10	0.9175	1.6547	171.0
Dec 09	0.8973	1.8024	169.5
Sep 09	0.8826	1.8111	168.6
Jun 09	0.8066	2.0414	167.0
Mar 09	0.6914	2.0717	166.2
Dec 08	0.7027	2.0816	166.0
Sep 08	0.7922	0.4448	166.5
Jun 08	0.9586	0.4811	164.6
Mar 08	0.9134	0.4603	162.2
Dec 07	0.8752	0.4409	160.1

(continued)

Australian dollar exchange rates and Consumer Price Index June 1990– December 2011 (*cont'd*)

Date	US	UK	CPI
Sep 07	0.8878	0.4336	158.6
Jun 07	0.8494	0.4229	157.5
Mar 07	0.8089	0.4110	155.6
Dec 06	0.7891	0.4027	155.5
Sep 06	0.7460	0.3984	155.7
Jun 06	0.7435	0.4022	154.3
Mar 06	0.7163	0.4123	151.9
Dec 05	0.7344	0.4263	150.6
Sep 05	0.7624	0.4319	149.8
Jun 05	0.7622	0.4254	148.4
Mar 05	0.7730	0.4089	147.5
Dec 04	0.7810	0.4072	146.5
Sep 04	0.7279	0.4019	145.4
Jun 04	0.6989	0.3839	144.6
Mar 04	0.7668	0.4154	143.7
Dec 03	0.7528	0.4212	142.8
Sep 03	0.6810	0.4097	142.1
Jun 03	0.6736	0.4070	141.3
Mar 03	0.6047	0.3821	141.3
Dec 02	0.5617	0.3486	139.5
Sep 02	0.5428	0.3458	138.5
Jun 02	0.5636	0.3675	137.6
Mar 02	0.5333	0.3740	136.6

Appendix F: Exchange rates and CPI

Date	US	UK	CPI
Dec 01	0.5088	0.3497	135.4
Sep 01	0.4918	0.3336	134.2
Jun 01	0.5114	0.3612	133.8
Mar 01	0.4857	0.3432	132.7
Dec 00	0.5588	0.3742	131.3
Sep 00	0.5428	0.3679	130.9
Jun 00	0.5967	0.3934	126.2
Mar 00	0.6077	0.3810	125.2
Dec 99	0.6571	0.4067	124.1
Sep 99	0.6525	0.3960	123.4
Jun 99	0.6667	0.4226	122.3
Mar 99	0.6344	0.3936	121.8
Dec 98	0.6126	0.3683	121.9
Sep 98	0.5936	0.3494	121.3
Jun 98	0.6200	0.3700	121.0
Mar 98	0.6622	0.3956	120.3
Dec 97	0.6503	0.3951	120.0
Sep 97	0.7257	0.4484	119.7
Jun 97	0.7455	0.4527	120.2
Mar 97	0.7856	0.4793	120.5
Dec 96	0.7943	0.4632	120.3
Sep 96	0.7914	0.5054	120.1
Jun 96	0.7873	0.5073	119.8
Mar 96	0.7815	0.5119	119.0
Dec 95	0.7437	0.4793	118.5
Sep 95	0.7554	0.4771	117.6
Jun 95	0.7091	0.4447	116.2
Mar 95	0.7345	0.4528	114.7

(*continued*)

Australian dollar exchange rates and Consumer Price Index June 1990– December 2011 (*cont'd*)

Date	US	UK	CPI
Dec 94	0.7764	0.4955	112.8
Sep 94	0.7395	0.4692	111.9
Jun 94	0.7277	0.4712	111.2
Mar 94	0.7017	0.4727	110.4
Dec 93	0.6793	0.4600	110.0
Sep 93	0.6461	0.4317	109.8
Jun 93	0.6665	0.4468	109.3
Mar 93	0.7048	0.4654	108.9
Dec 92	0.6885	0.4558	107.9
Sep 92	0.7132	0.3993	107.4
Jun 92	0.7478	0.3925	107.3
Mar 92	0.7693	0.4429	107.6
Dec 91	0.7595	0.4066	107.6
Sep 91	0.7990	0.4560	106.6
Jun 91	0.7670	0.4762	106.0
Mar 91	0.7704	0.4369	105.8
Dec 90	0.7722	0.3984	106.0
Sep 90	0.8255	0.4410	103.3
Jun 90	0.7935	0.4500	102.5

APPENDIX G
Continuous discounting and annuities

The common procedure in determining the NPV is to discount end-of-year lump sum cash flows. In practice, cash flows, both positive and negative, are over shorter time frames. For example, the payment of wages could be fortnightly, while the receipts from the sale of product could be monthly. Further, interest can also be based on a continuous discounting basis rather than on an annual basis. It is therefore possible to discount on a continuous basis on the assumption that the year's cash flow is received as a lump sum, but the interest is continuous: that is, in infinitely small increments. The new equation is:

NPV (discount rate i) = $\Sigma CF_n/e^{in}$

In practical terms it is simpler to discount on a yearly basis, although for analysis purposes for listed equities, half-yearly or perhaps quarterly discounting might be used if the company provides sufficient information to warrant that depth of analysis. Remember to adjust the discount rate where appropriate. For example, if half-yearly discounting is used when the annual discount rate is 10 per cent, then the biannual discount rate (ib) equals:

$(1 + ib)^n = 1 + i$, where n = the number of periods; therefore:

$(1 + ib)^2 = 1 + 0.1$ and ib = $(1.1)^{0.5} - 1 = 4.88\%$

Reversing the process, the compound effect of two six-monthly periods at 4.88 per cent equals 1.488 multiplied by 1.488 equals 10 per cent over a 12-month period.

Another important issue is the period in time over which the discount rate is calculated. Once all the cash flows are discounted to one point in time (generally the beginning of the cash flow period), the NPV will remain positive, or negative, irrespective of what other point in time is selected. As all discount rates are positive, the NPV sign will not change if it is discounted or inflated to a different point in time, but the absolute value will change. In terms of a decision process the point in time is not critical, but in valuing or applying a value to a project or company the point in time is critical. In the case of an IRR, it is possible to have more than one value if there is more than one change in the sign of the cash flow series. In other words, for the case where the project's yearly cash flow goes from negative to positive only once during the project's life only one IRR value is possible, but if the cash flow goes from negative to positive to negative and then back to positive, then there are three changes and therefore it is possible to have up to three different IRRs. In these cases it is best to rely on the NPV for valuation purposes.

When yearly cash flows are equal and therefore can be considered as an annuity A per annum, the present value is PV, the future value FV, interest rate (or discount) is i and the number of years for the annuity is n, then:

$$PV = A \times ((1 + i)^n - 1)/(i \times (1 + i)^n)$$

or $PV = A \times (1 - e^{-in})/(e^i - 1)$ on a continuous interest basis assuming end-of-year payments

$$FV = A \times ((1 + i)^n - 1)/i$$

or $FV = A \times (e^{in} - 1)/(e^i - 1)$

Additionally:

$A = FV \times i/((1 + i)^n - 1)$, often termed the sinking fund

$A = PV \times (i \times (1 + i)^n)/((1 + i)^n - 1)$, often termed the capital recovery factor

If we know PV and FV and n, we can solve for i by:

$i = \text{antilog} ((\log(FV) - \log(PV))/n) - 1$

A shorthand way of calculating the approximate number of years needed to double an investment is to divide 72 by the interest rate. For example, if the interest rate is 10 per cent then 72/10 = 7.2 years. The method is more accurate for smaller interest rates, say less than 15 per cent.

APPENDIX H
Abbreviations, conversions and energy factors

Carbon table

Dry gas

Methane	$C H_4$
Ethane	$C_2 H_6$

LPG

Propane	$C_3 H_8$
Butane	$C_4 H_{10}$
Condensate	
Pentane	$C_5 H_{12}$
Hexane	$C_6 H_{14}$

Crude oil

Heptane	$C_7 H_{16}$
Octane	$C_8 H_{18}$
Nonane	$C_9 H_{20}$
Decane	$C_{10} H_{22}$

Units and abbreviations

Units		Abbreviations	
B	billion	ad	air dried
T	trillion	Ag	silver
p (pico)	10^{-12}	Au	gold
n (nano)	10^{-9}	A/m2	amperes per square metre
u (micro)	10^{-6}	API	American Petroleum Institute
m (milli)	10^{-3}	BCF	billion cubic feet
k (kilo)	10^{3}	bbl	barrel
M (mega)	10^{6}	bhp	break horsepower
G (giga)	10^{9}	boe	barrels of oil equivalents
T (tera)	10^{12}	bopd	barrels of oil per day
P (peta)	10^{15}	BTU	British Thermal Unit
		cal	calorie
E (exa)	10^{18}	J	Joule
		hp	horsepower
		W	watts
		kW	kilowatts
		kWh	kilowatts per hour
		lb	pound weight
		LNG	liquefied natural gas
		LPG	liquefied petroleum gas
		mcf	thousand cubic feet
		mmbbl	millions of barrels
		NGL	natural gas liquids
		tpa	tonnes per annum
		mcfgpd	thousand cubic feet of gas per day
		WTI	West Texas Intermediate

Conversions

Length		Area	
1 metre	39.3701 inches	1 square metre	10.7639 square feet
	3.2808 feet	1 hectare	2.417 acres
1 inch	2.54 cm		
1 kilometre	0.6214 miles	1 square kilometre	247.105 acres
	0.540 nautical miles		0.386 square miles

Volume		Weight	
1 cubic metre	1000 kg of water	1 tonne	2204.62 pounds
	35.3147 cubic feet		1.102 short tons
	219.969 imperial gallons		0.984 long tons
	264.172 US gallons	1 ounce (troy)	31.1 grams
	1.308 cubic yards	1 pound	0.4536 kilograms

Pressure		Temperature	
1 lb per sq inch (psi)	6.895 kilopascals (kPa)	Celsius	(Fahrenheit 32) × 5/9
1 atmosphere	14.7 psi		

Power		Energy	
1 hp	745.7 W	1 kJ	0.9478 BTU
1 ft-lb/s	1.356 W		238.846 cal
			0.000278 kWh

Crude oil and condensate			
1 barrel	42 US gallons	tonne crude	7.8616 barrels
	34.9726 imperial gallons		46.3 Gj
	0.158987 kilolitres	1 tonne condensate	8.2 barrels

Natural gas			
1 TJ	847 mcf (North West Shelf)	1 cu ft gas	1000 BTU

(*continued*)

Conversions (*cont'd*)

Natural gas

943 mcf (Cooper Basin)	1 cu m gas	9000 k calories
948 mcf (Surat Basin)	1 tonne Ethane	26 800 cubic feet
953 mcf (Bass Strait)	1 boe	5875 cubic feet (approx.)

Liquefied petroleum gas (LPG)

1 tonne LPG	11.60 barrels		
Propane	50.0 MJ/kg	Butane	49.5 MJ/kg
	25.4 MJ/1 litre		28.7 MJ/litre
	93.3 MJ/cubic metres		124.0 MJ/ cubic metre
	1960 litres/tonne		1720 litres/tonne
	12.33 bbls/tonne		10.82 bbls/tonne
	0.51 kg/litre		0.58 kg/litre

Liquefied natural gas (LNG)

1 tonne LNG	45.9 mcf gas
	1333 cubic metres at 0°C
	1.242 tonnes of oil equivalent
	54.4 GJ

Calorific equivalents

1 boe	0.1272 tonnes oil	1 therm	100 000 BTUs
	1.0690 barrels condensate	1 Kjoule	0.9478 BTUs
	0.1360 tonnes condensate		238.846 calories
	1.3986 barrels LPG	0.2778 Watt-hours (Wh)	
	0.1182 tonnes LPG	1 GJ	277.8 kilo Watt-hours (kWh) (100 per cent efficiency)

Calorific equivalents		
0.1134 tonnes Propane		294 kilo Watt-hours (kWh) (100 per cent efficiency)
0.1293 tonnes Butane	1 mcf	
6000 cubic feet gas		
0.1024 tonnes LNG	1 bhp	0.746 kW
0.1908 tonnes coal	1 calorie	4.186 joules

Energy factors

Energy content of solid fuels

Black coal	GJoule per tonne
Export coking	29.0
Export steaming	27.0
Electricity generation	23.4
Steelworks	30.0
Washed steaming coal	27.0
Unwashed steaming coal	23.9
Queensland	
Export coking	30.0
Export steaming	27.0
Electricity generation	23.4
Other	23.0
South Australia	
Steaming coal	13.5
Western Australia	
Steaming coal	19.7

(continued)

Energy content of solid fuels (*cont'd*)

Black coal	GJoule per tonne
Tasmania	
Steaming coal	22.8
Victoria	
Brown coal	9.8
Briquettes	22.1
Coke	27.0
Wood (dry)	16.2
Bagasse (sugar cane)	9.6

Energy content of liquid fuels

	By volume MJoule/litre	Specific volume litres/tonne	By weight GJoule/tonne
LPG			
Propane	25.3	1960	49.6
Butane	27.7	1750	49.1
Mixture	25.7	1928	49.6
Naturally occurring	26.5	1866	49.4
Automotive gasoline	34.2	1360	46.4
Power kerosene	37.5	1230	46.1
Heating oil	37.3	1238	46.2
Automotive diesel oil	38.6	1182	45.6
Industrial diesel fuel	39.6	1135	44.9
Fuel oil			
Low sulphur	39.7	1110	44.1
High sulphur	40.8	1050	42.9
Crude oil			
Indigenous	37.0	1250	46.3
Imports (average)	38.7	1160	44.9
Liquefied natural gas	25.0	2174	54.4

Energy content of gaseous fuels

Natural gas	GJoule per tonne
Victoria	38.8
Queensland	38.2
South Australia, New South Wales	38.3
Western Australia	38.9
Northern Territory	40.6
Ethane	57.5
Town gas	
Synthetic natural gas	39.0
Reformed gas	20.0
Tempered LPG	25.0
Tempered natural gas	25.0
Coke oven gas	18.1
Blast furnace gas	4.0

Australian power generation (1995–96)

	Power generated (GWh)	Tonnage (mt)	Power/ tonnes (MWh/t)	Energy content (TJ)	Efficiency (%)
Coal/steam					
New South Wales	57 109.1	22.70	2.52	546 195	37.6
Victoria (brown coal)	38 573.5	50.18	0.77	398 010	34.9
Queensland	32 165.0	13.98	2.30	312 492	37.1
South Australia	6 747.4	12.50	0.54	35 189	69.0
Western Australia*	11 370.91	4.74	2.40	92 351	44.3
Gas turbines					
New South Wales (oil)	1.292	507	2.55	23	20.2
Victoria	543	—	—	28 171	6.9
Queensland (oil)	0.44	204	2.16	9	17.6

(*continued*)

Australian power generation (1995–96) (*cont'd*)

	Power generated (GWh)	Tonnage (mt)	Power/ tonnes (MWh/t)	Energy content (TJ)	Efficiency (%)
Western Australia	1 029.3	—	—	42 710	8.7
Oil/Internal combustion					
New South Wales	1.586	548	2.89	25	22.8
Queensland	55.021	13 294	4.14	567	34.9
South Australia	19.761	5 643	3.50	253	28.1
Western Australia	295.4	67 342	4.39	3 098	34.3

* Includes higher level of fuel oil and natural gas additions.

Source: Electricity Supply Association of Australia.

Power plant carbon emissions, 2011

Generator type	Fuel	Capacity (MW)	Thermal efficiency (%)	Emission factor (kg CO_2 equiv/ GJ of fuel)	Fugitive emission factor (kg CO_2 equiv/GJ of fuel)
Gas turbine	Natural gas	166	32.0	0.0513	0.0142
Gas turbine	Liquid fuel	50	28.0	0.0697	0.0053
Cogeneration	Natural gas	176	41.0	0.0513	0.0142
Steam turbine	Black coal	720	35.4	0.0895	0.0087
Steam turbine	Brown coal	560	27.2	0.0915	0.0003

Source: Electricity Supply Association of Australia.

GLOSSARY

ABARE   Australian Bureau of Agricultural and Resource Economics.

accrual accounting   the net payment or receipt in each period is accrued and recorded as an adjustment to income or expense.

adit   a horizontal opening into a mine, started from a hillside.

ADR   asset depreciating range.

ad valorem   a royalty or tax based on value, often as a percentage of defined revenue.

aeromagnetic survey   a survey made from the air for the purpose of recording magnetic characteristics of rocks.

AFC   armoured face conveyor used in underground longwall operations for the transport of coal from the face of the coal panel.

Ag   chemical symbol for silver.

Al   chemical symbol for aluminium.

air core drilling   an air blast drilling technique with a limited coring capability.

All Industrials Index   index of aggregate market capitalisation for selected industrial stocks on the ASX.

All Ordinaries Index   index of aggregate market capitalisation for selected industrial and resource stocks on the ASX.

All Resources Index   index of aggregate market capitalisation for selected resource stocks on the ASX.

alluvial gold   gold transported and deposited by river action, and mined from the river sediments; also termed placer gold.

altered   referring to physical or chemical change in a rock or mineral subsequent to its formation.

American-style option an option that may be exercised at any time up to its expiry date.

amine solvent formed from ammonia.

amortisation to extinguish goodwill and exploration expenditure by periodic (annual) amounts debited against profits.

anomaly zone or point in the soil or underlying rock determined by exploration methods to be different from its general surroundings.

anticline a fold in rock strata that is convex upward—that is, bent into an upward bow or hill—with a core of older rocks.

API American Petroleum Institute; standard for measuring the specific gravity of oil.

arbitrage trading a security or commodity to profit from differences in price between two or more markets.

As chemical symbol for arsenic.

ash inorganic residue remaining after the incineration of coal.

ash fusion test ash softening temperature, in °C.

Asian or average option payoff depends on an average of prices for the underlying commodity over a period of time, rather than the price of the commodity on a single date.

ASIC Australian Securities and Investments Commission.

assay valuable metals test.

ASX Australian Stock Exchange.

Au chemical symbol for gold.

auger screw-like drilling or boring tool most commonly used for shallow soil samples.

auriferous containing gold.

autoclave a cylindrical vessel which is constructed to withstand high temperatures and pressures in processing material; for example, to oxidise sulphide ore.

BAC base acquisition cost.

backfill material used to fill mined-out stope voids.

backwardation when the future price for a commodity is lower than the spot price.

bacterial leaching leaching through the use of simple micro-organisms.

ball mill a rotating cylindrical mill using iron balls to reduce broken ore to powder to assist the release of constituent minerals.

banded iron formation iron formation with distinct banding. Generally of iron-rich minerals and chert.

barge motored or motor-less vessel used to carry products often along a river. Barges vary in capacity, mainly from 1000 to 5000 tons.

barrel (bbl) standard volume of oil equal to 158.99 litres, 42 US gallons or 34.97 imperial gallons.

basalt a fine-grained basic volcanic rock.

basement generally refers to the older rocks below the sedimentary base or solid rock underlying superficial weathered rock or soil.

base metals the more common and chemically active non-precious metals—for example, lead, copper, zinc and nickel.

basic term used to describe igneous rocks containing less than 55 per cent silica.

basis point one-hundredth of a per cent, or one ten thousandth of the total.

bcf billion cubic feet; volume of rock before mining.

bcm bench cubic metres

bcmpa bench cubic metres per annum

bedrock unweathered rock below soil and cover.

beam stage loader (BSL) transfers coal from the face to the longwall panel conveyor.

bench the horizontal floor along which mining progresses in a pit; also used to describe the horizontal segment between two such floors.

The thickness of such a segment is referred to as the bench height. As the pit progresses to lower levels, safety benches are left in the walls to form a safety batter (slope).

beneficiation the upgrading of a mineral by concentration processes.

beta the extent to which a rate or price follows movements in the overall market.

Bi chemical symbol for bismuth.

binomial model incorporates a binomial tree, which describes the evolution of a random variable over a series of time steps with given probabilities for a rise or fall in the variable.

bioleach a metallurgical practice to leach minerals from rock using biological processes.

bituminous coal that coal which by the effects of time/pressure/temperature has been metamorphosed to a state that it has coking properties. Classified by chemical properties and energy value.

Black & Scholes model an option-pricing model.

blast hole stoping an underground mining method by which ore is extracted using large diameter holes for blasting.

block model the term applied to the final output of a computer-based process to reflect the likely configuration of the mineralisation and the surrounding material.

board and pillar a method of mining that forms pillars of coal which are then extracted.

bolting machine used to install bolts into roof, sides or floor of a mine for increased ground stability.

bond a bond issuer agrees to pay the full amount of the loan plus all due interest on or before a specific date in the future (maturity).

BOOT build, own, operate and transfer.

bopd barrels of oil per day.

box cut initial opening to access coal seam in open cut.

breaker line supports (BLS)   hydraulic powered mobile roof supports for continuous coal miners during secondary extraction.

bright coal   vitrinite rich coal.

British Thermal Unit (BTU)   standard unit of measurement of the amount of heat required to increase the temperature of a pint of water by one degree Fahrenheit (3412 BTUs = 1 kWh or 1 BTU = 1055.06 joules).

bulk density   weight per cubic metre.

bullion   gold or silver in bars or ingots.

calcining   to reduce to a powder or friable state by heat.

call option   a contract that gives the buyer the right to take delivery of a commodity or share at some time in the future at a set price (strike) from the seller.

calorie   heat required to raise one gram of water by 1°C.

capital cost   the cost of acquiring or building capital equipment and operating plant.

CAPM   capital asset pricing model, which estimates the equity holders' expected rate of return on investment.

carbonaceous   containing carbon or coal, especially shale or other rock containing small particles of carbon distributed throughout the whole mass.

carbon-in-leach (CIL) process   this process is used to recover gold into activated carbon during the agitation leach process. The CIL system then follows the normal carbon-in-pulp procedures. This process is used to improve gold recoveries when naturally occurring carbonaceous materials are present in the ore that will compete for gold values and reduce normal gold recoveries.

carbon-in-pulp (CIP) process   this process is used to recover gold that has been dissolved after cyanide leach agitation. After cyanidation, the pulp is contacted in a series of agitators with coarse activated carbon particles. Carbon is moved countercurrent to the pulp, absorbing gold as it passes through the circuit. Loaded carbon is removed by screening from the first agitator. Gold is recovered from the loaded carbon by stripping at an elevated temperature and pressure in a caustic cyanide solution. This high-grade solution is passed through an electrolytic cell, where gold is deposited on a steel wool cathode, which is later smelted to produce dore.

carbon reactivation the high temperature and acid washing process applied to the carbon following removal of absorbed gold. This reactivates the carbon allowing it to be reused in the gold recovery process.

carbon sequestration the underground capture and long-term storage of CO_2.

cash-and-carry arbitrage a strategy to generate a risk-less profit by selling a futures contract and buying the underlying to deliver into it.

cash costs total direct operating costs at the mine excluding abnormal items, depreciation and amortisation, exploration costs and income tax.

cathode electronegative pole.

chain pillar pillar of coal remaining between adjacent longwall panels.

chalcocite a copper sulphide mineral.

chalcopyrite a sulphide of copper and iron.

circuit in a mineral processing plant this refers to the sequence of processing that the ore will undergo.

circulating fluid bed roaster a furnace in which finely ground ore or concentrate is roasted to eliminate sulphur.

Co chemical symbol for cobalt.

coal handling and preparation plant (CHPP) plant used to upgrade coal through crushing, sizing and drying.

coal measures sedimentary rocks containing coal seams.

coal rank a measure of the metamorphic grade of coal measured by vitrinite reflectance.

coke oven enclosed vessel where coking coal is converted to coke for steel making.

coking coal coal that is used for producing blast furnace or foundry coke by carbonisation.

column flotation a method of mineral separation in which a froth created in water by a variety of reagents floats finely crushed minerals, whereas other minerals sink.

COMEX New York Commodity Exchange, now affiliated with NYMEX.

comminution circuit crushing and grinding to reduce ore to small particle size.

concentrate material that has been processed to increase the content of contained metal or mineral relative to the contained waste.

concentrator a plant for recovery of valuable minerals from ore in the form of concentrate. The concentrate must then be treated in some other type of plant, such as a smelter, to effect recovery of the pure metal.

condensate in the form of hydrocarbon gas in the reservoir, but when subjected to atmospheric conditions it becomes liquid.

conditional simulation a geostatistical modelling technique that reflects the variability of the grade (metal content) in a deposit.

conglomerates a corse-grained sedimentary rock in which rounded to sub-angular fragments greater than 2 mm in diameter are cemented in a fine-grained matrix.

contact metamorphism change in a rock-type state due to heating by an intrusive.

contango when the price for forward or future delivery of a commodity is higher than the spot price.

continuous miner a machine that mines coal in development headings or in pillar extraction workings.

core sample of rock produced by diamond drilling.

correlation the degree of relationship between two variables where a correlation coefficient of 1 is perfect, while no correlation has a value of 0.

cost of capital the expense incurred in obtaining funds used as capital assets.

countercurrent the clarification and concentration of slurry material by the use of several thickeners in series, with the washing solution flowing in the opposite direction to the slurry.

CPI Consumer Price Index, which quantifies inflation rates.

Cr chemical symbol for chromium.

crack spread refined product price per barrel less the price per barrel of oil.

crosscut an underground opening generally driven to cut across a mineralised vein or structure.

cross-section a diagram or drawing that shows features transected by a vertical plane drawn at right angles to the longer axis of a geological feature.

crown pillar a horizontal block of rock left in place to stabilise ground after removal of ore by underground mining.

crystal a mineral grain with faces developed that reflect the internal atomic structure.

crude oil oil produced, but not yet subjected to any type of refining or chemical processes.

c/t carats per tonne.

Cu chemical symbol for copper.

cupellation separation of base metals from precious metals by oxidation and absorption of the metal oxides in a dish of bone ash.

cut-and-fill stoping a stoping method in which the ore is excavated by successive flat slices, working upward from the level. After each slice is blasted, all broken ore is removed and the stope is filled with waste up to within a metre of the back before the next slice is taken out.

cutoff grade the estimated lowest grade of ore that can be mined and treated profitably in a mining operation.

cut through a driveage that joins two headings (underground roadways).

cuttings samples of rock produced by percussion and rotary drilling methods such as reverse circulation drilling.

cyanide leach the dissolution of minerals and metals into a weak solution of cyanide.

cyclonic separation separating different size particles by the application of a centrifugal force.

darcy a unit measure of permeability where rock permeability is usually expressed in millidarcies (mD) — 1 mD is equal to 0.001 darcy.

DCF discounted cash flow.

debt to equity ratio net debt compared to market capitalisation of a company.

decline downward-sloping tunnel providing road access from the surface to underground mine operations.

decline rate annual rate at which hydrocarbon production will reduce due to weaker natural drive and/or increasing amounts of associated water.

deep lead auriferous alluvials buried by younger rocks.

delta sensitivity of an option price to changes in the price of its underlying instrument.

depreciation to extinguish, by periodic (annual) amounts debited against profits, capital expenditure whose value decreases with age or wear and tear.

derivatives securities that have no real value of their own, but whose value depends on, or is derived from, some other value such as a prevailing market price, stock value or market index.

detrital coal coal fragments.

development mining carried out to gain access to ore.

development heading a mine driveage used to set up a board and pillar working on longwall headings.

diamond drilling rotary drilling using diamond-set or diamond-impregnated bits, to produce a solid continuous core sample of rock.

dilution reduction of ore grade by contamination with waste material.

diorite a coarse-grained intrusive rock of intermediate composition.

dip   the angle at which layered rocks, foliation, a fault, or other planar structures, are inclined from the horizontal. True dip is perpendicular to strata.

discounting   financial method used to determine present or future values of investments or expenses.

disseminated   descriptive of mineral grains that are scattered throughout the host rock.

dmt   dry metric tonne.

dolerite   medium-grained basic igneous rock with a composition similar to basalt.

downstream   activities from an oil or gas refinery onwards.

dore   unrefined gold and silver bullion bars that will be further refined to almost pure metal.

drift   a tunnel driven from the surface to the coal seam, or between seams.

drill cross-section   a section perpendicular to strike on which the trace of drill holes are plotted.

drilling   in mineral exploration, boring a hole into prospective ground to recover cuttings indicative of rock types and grades of mineralisation.

drilling traverses   series of drill holes in a line.

drillstem test   a test tool that is lowered into an oil well to test for formation fluids.

drill intercepts   the intersections (usually of the target mineralisation) made within an exploration drill hole.

drill string   lengths of drill pipe that are screwed together.

drive   an underground opening driven along the bedding planes of country rock or driven along strike.

DSCR   debt service coverage ratio is the ratio of cash available to service interest, principal and lease payments.

DSRA   debt service reserve account provides a buffer for periods when cash available for debt service is not sufficient.

dwt dead weight tonnes; in shipping, the weight of cargo carried by a ship.

dyke a tabular igneous intrusion that cuts across the bedding or other planar structures in the country rock.

earnings before interest and taxes (EBIT) revenues less cost of goods sold and selling, general and administrative expenses (earnings) before the deduction of interest and income taxes.

EBITA earnings before interest and tax and amortisation.

EBITDA earnings before interest, tax, depreciation and amortisation.

EBT earnings before tax.

EBTDA earnings before tax, depreciation and amortisation.

EIS environmental impact statement.

EL exploration licence.

ELA exploration licence application.

electro-winning recovery of metal from solution by electrolysis.

elusion the process of desorption (taking of gold from carbon).

embedded derivatives an instrument that is combined with a non-derivative host contract to form a single hybrid instrument.

EMV expected monetary value.

en-echelon parallel structural features (veins, faults and so on) that are offset.

enterprise value (EV) market capitalisation plus net debt.

EPCM an arrangement with a contractor to provide equipment, procurement, construction and management contract.

epithermal a term applied to those mineral deposits formed in and along fissures or other openings in rocks at shallow depths from ascending solutions at low to moderate temperatures (100° to 200°C).

EPS earnings per share.

European option an option that may be exercised only on its expiration date.

EVA   economic value added.

evergreen contract   ongoing contract where terms and conditions are renewed yearly.

exchange traded option   an option traded and cleared on an organised securities or derivatives exchange.

exercise   process of converting an options contract into a futures or physical position.

exploration   the act of investigating the location of undiscovered mineral deposits.

extract or retreat mining   recovery of coal pillars once a longwall panel has been developed.

extrusive   igneous rock that is deposited on the surface of the earth, such as lava or tuff.

facies   a general term denoting the sum of the rock type characteristics.

fault   a break in rock strata continuity with strata remaining parallel, but displaced relative to one another on either side; strata on opposite sides of a fault may be displaced vertically and/or laterally relative to their original position.

Fe   chemical symbol for iron.

feasibility study   a technical and financial study of a project at a sufficient level of accuracy and detail to allow a decision as to whether the project should proceed.

feed size   the size of mineral particles entering a processing section.

feldspar (felspar)   a very abundant group of rock-forming silicate minerals in which calcium, sodium and potassium are in combination with aluminium.

fire assay   an assay procedure involving heating the sample in a furnace to ensure complete extraction of all the contained precious metal.

fixed carbon   100 per cent less moisture percentage less volatile matter percentage less ash percentage.

flotation   a milling process by which some mineral particles are induced to become attached to bubbles of froth and float, and others to sink, so that the valuable minerals are concentrated and separated from the gangue.

fluidity   a measure of a coal's fluid properties as it is heated.

Free on Board (FOB)   price paid at the mine site or port that excludes freight or shipping and insurance costs.

fold   a bend in strata or any planar structure.

footwall   a geological or mining term meaning the rock below a fault, or underlying a natural feature.

force majeure   term or clause in a contract to protect a contracting party against uncontrollable events such as natural disasters, wars or climatic conditions that could prevent the fulfilment of some or all of the terms of the contract.

FPSO   floating production storage and offtake facilities.

fracture breaks   breaks in rocks due to intensive folding or faulting.

free gold   gold not chemically or physically entrapped and hence amenable to relatively simple extraction processes.

free milling   descriptive of ore which can readily be ground so as to release the valuable constituents for separation.

futures contract   an agreement to acquire goods or services on the futures market.

GAAP   Generally Accepted Accounting Principles; refers to a standard guideline for financial accounting in a particular jurisdiction.

galena   a lead sulphide mineral.

gamma   sensitivity of an option's delta to changes in the price of the underlying futures contract.

gamma ray   a measure of natural radioactivity of strata in a bore hole. Shales tend to be more radioactive than sandstones.

gangue   waste rock.

gas lift   where natural gas is sent to the bottom of an oil production well to help increase the oil flow rate.

gasoil   European designation for No. 2 heating oil and diesel fuel.

gate roads   development either side of a longwall block.

GDP   gross domestic product (total value of goods and services produced by labour and property).

geochemical   a prospecting technique that measures the content of certain metals in soils and rocks, and defines anomalies for further testing.

geochemistry   study of variation of chemical elements in rocks.

geological mapping   recording of geological information.

geophysical   a prospecting technique that measures the physical properties (magnetism, conductivity, density and so on) of rocks and defines anomalies for further testing.

geostatistics   a computer-based methodology wherein particular relationships between sample points are established and employed to project the influence of the sample points for grade estimation and variability.

geotechnical   referring to the physical behaviour of rock under stress.

geothermal   pertaining to the heat of the Earth's interior.

gigawatt (GW)   one billion watts.

gigawatt-hour (GWh)   one billion watt-hours.

GJ   gigajoule; one thousand million (10^{-9}) joules.

goaf   space left behind following extraction of longwall coal where roof is allowed to collapse.

gold equivalent   the conversion of non-gold ounces of economically valuable mineral commodities to a gold equivalent by taking account of the commodity price and the gold price.

GOR   gas oil ratio.

gossan   rock composed of hydrated oxides of iron that forms a superficial cover over sulphides of iron and/or other metals.

graben   down-thrown area between two faults.

grade   quantity of metal per unit weight of host rock.

grade control   a general term that describes the many measures required to maximise mining recovery of the valuable mineral while minimising dilution.

granite   a coarse-grained igneous rock consisting largely of quartz and feldspar.

grassroots estimation   initial stages of a mineral exploration program involving a preliminary assessment of potential.

gravimetric survey   survey that measures differences in the Earth's gravity field as an indicator of a mineral resource.

gravity concentration   a metallurgical process that separates metals from gangue using the specific gravity differential between the metal and the gangue.

grid   a method of systematically marking a study area.

grinding   reducing mineralised rock to the consistency of fine sand by crushing and abrading in a rotating steel grinding mill.

gross working interest   the interest being used prior to it being reduced for services rendered.

grouting   the process of injecting cement or chemicals into the earth to fill cavities or to stabilise broken ground.

g/t   grams per tonne, equivalent to parts per million (ppm).

gyratory crusher   a crusher that reduces the size of mined rock by passing it between a stationary outer shell and a gyrating central cone.

ha   hectares.

hanging wall   a geological or mining term meaning the rock above a fault, or overlying a natural feature.

head grade   a general term referring to the grade of ore delivered to the processing plant.

heap leach   method of extracting metals from ore dumped on a prepared pad by applying a solution, usually by irrigation via sprinkling or by dripping.

hedging contract   used to establish a predetermined price that will be paid for a given amount of product.

hematite, haematite   a common iron oxide mineral.

Henry Hub   natural gas price for delivery in Louisiana.

HGI   Hardgrove Grindability Index is a standard test to measure ease of grinding.

host rock   the rock containing a mineral or an orebody.

hp   horsepower.

hydrocarbon   class of compounds containing only carbon and hydrogen, generally referring to natural gas and petroleum products.

hydrothermal   pertaining to heated water, particularly of magmatic origin associated with the formation of mineral deposits or the alteration of rocks.

IFRS   International Financial Reporting Standards are principles-based standards, interpretations and frameworks adopted by the International Accounting Standards Committee.

igneous   a molten rock formed by the solidification of a mineral-rich molten liquid that is intruded into sedimentary rock or erupted from a volcano.

indicated mineral resource   a mineral resource sampled by drill holes, underground openings or other sampling procedures at locations too widely spaced to ensure continuity, but close enough to give a reasonable indication of continuity and where geological data are reliably known. An indicated mineral resource estimate will be based on more data, and therefore be more reliable, than an inferred mineral resource estimate.

induced polarisation   a geophysical exploration method that measures changes in magnetic and electrical fields induced in the earth by the application of an electrical current to the ground.

inferred mineral resource   mineral resource inferred from geoscientific evidence, drill holes, underground openings or samplings where the lack of data is such that continuity cannot be predicted with confidence.

inferred resources class 1 (coal)   resources for which the points of observation allow an estimate of the coal thickness and general coal quality to be made, and the geological conditions indicate continuity of seams between the points of observation. Points of observation should generally be not more than 4 km apart. Extrapolations of trends should extend not more than 2 km from the points of observation.

inferred resources class 2 (coal)   resources for which there is limited information and as a result the assessment of this type of resource may be unreliable. Provided the coal thickness can be determined, the order of magnitude may be expressed within the following ranges:

1 to 10 million tonnes

10 to 100 million tonnes

100 to 500 million tonnes

500 to 1000 million tonnes

greater than 1000 million tonnes.

injection well   a well used to force gas, water or other fluids into the reservoir in order to maintain reservoir pressure in secondary recovery projects or for conservation purposes.

in situ   in its natural position.

interest expense   total cost of interest charges as an operating expense.

inter-bedded   two or more lithologic types bedded in close association (for example, sandstone or shale).

interest coverage ratio   the ratio of annual net income to annual interest on outstanding debts.

internal rate of return (IRR)   interest rate where the net present value (NPV) of a cash flow series is equal to zero.

in-the-money   where the underlying futures price is above a call option's strike price, or below a put option's strike price.

intermediate   in geology, igneous rocks with composition between acid (granites and so on) and basic (basalts and so on) groups containing between 52 and 66 per cent SiO_2.

intrusive   plutonic rock formed by intrusion of molten magma, below the surface, where it cooled and crystallised to form a solid rock.

inverse distance weighting   a relationship applied for resource estimation, whereby the influence of a particular sample is inversely weighted according to, for example, the square or cube of the distance from another point.

IP anomaly   anomalous readings detected by a particular surface electrical geophysical surveying method.

IPO   initial public offering.

ISP   imperial smelter process.

JORC   Joint Ore Reserves Committee; common reference to the Australasian code for reporting of exploration results, mineral resources and ore reserves.

joule   unit of work done.

kbpd   kilo (thousand) barrels per day.

Kcal   kilocalories.

kilowatt (kW)   one thousand watts.

kilowatt-hour (kWh)   one thousand watts being used continuously for a period of one hour.

kimberlite   a silica-poor intrusive igneous rock, normally found in pipes, which can contain diamonds.

km²   square kilometre.

Knelson concentrator   a rotating concentrator used to separate minerals on the basis of differences in their specific gravities.

kPa kilopascals.

kriging a mathematical means of projecting grades into resource blocks from a range of sample points to provide unbiased weighted estimation of a block value when the geostatistical special relationship is identified.

kt kilotonnes.

kWh/t kilowatt hours per tonne.

laterite a strongly leached, iron- and aluminium-rich rock, formed at the surface by weathering in tropical conditions.

leachate solution extracted from a leaching process.

leaching the dissolution of mineral components from ore by appropriate chemicals.

leach kinetics description of the speed of recovery of gold or mineral products and the process response to the addition of reagents in an established heap leach.

lens a geological deposit that is thick in the middle and thin towards the edges.

Lerchs Grossmann modelling technique used to determine the open cut depth for a given set of parameters.

Li chemical symbol for lithium.

LIBOR London Inter-Bank Offer Rate is the average interst rate set by leading London banks when lending to other banks.

limestone a sedimentary rock consisting chiefly of calcium carbonate (mainly as calcite).

limonite a type of iron oxide.

lineament lines on the Earth's surface discernible in photos or satellite images that could be the surface expression of faults or other linear geological structures.

lithology the physical characteristics of rock.

liquefied natural gas (LNG) natural gas converted to a liquid by chilling for ease of transport and storage.

liquefied petroleum gas (LPG) light hydrocarbon composed mainly of propane and butane occurring naturally in crude or from refining processes. LPG is gaseous at normal temperature and pressure, but liquefied at moderate pressure and reduced temperature for transport and storage.

LLCR loan life cover ratio.

LME London Metal Exchange is a non-ferrous metals market that offers futures and option contracts.

lode a tabular or vein-like deposit of valuable mineral between well-defined walls of country rock.

long-hole stoping this method of stoping involves the drilling of blast holes generally exceeding 15 metres in length, and is normally only practical for large orebodies or wide regular veins with strong country rock to minimise waste dilution.

longwall blocks areas of coal to be extracted by the longwall mining method.

longwall mining a high-productivity mechanised mining system for extracting longwall blocks.

longwall mining unit a coal-cutting machine with a coal conveyor and hydraulic shields.

longwall panel an area containing the longwall development roadways and the coal to be extracted by longwall.

LTCC Longwall Top Coal Caving method that employs two AFCs to increase productivity and extract thicker seams.

MACRS modified accelerated cost recovery system is the current tax depreciation system in the USA.

mafic an igneous rock of low silica with high magnesium and iron content, usually dark in colour.

magma liquid molten rock.

magmatic pertaining to processes and rocks involving magma.

magnesia magnesium oxide; MgO.

magnetic survey a geophysical technique that measures variations in the Earth's magnetic field in order to define the distribution of values that may be indicative of different rock types, formations and so on.

magnetite a magnetic iron oxide mineral (Fe_3O_4).

maingate the heading adjacent to the longwall block containing all the electrical and water services, and usually the conveyor belt.

mantle the portion of the Earth's interior below the crust from a depth of 35 to 2900 km.

margin amount of money or collateral deposited by a customer for the purpose of insuring against adverse price movement on open futures contracts.

marked-to-market the value of a financial instrument at current market prices.

mbcm million bench cubic metres.

mboe thousand barrels of oil equivalent.

mcf thousand cubic feet of gas.

megawatt (MW) one million watts.

megawatt-hour (MWh) one million watt-hours.

Mlb million pounds.

mmBtu one million British thermal units (one dekatherm), equal to approximately one thousand cubic feet of natural gas.

mmcf million cubic feet of gas.

measured mineral resource a mineral resource intersected and tested by drill holes, underground openings or other sampling procedures at locations that are spaced closely enough to confirm continuity and where geoscientific data are reliably known. A measured mineral resource estimate will be based on a substantial amount of reliable data, interpretation and evaluation that allows a clear determination to be made of shapes, sizes, densities and grades.

Merrill Crowe precipitation   a process utilised to recover dissolved gold and silver values from a sodium cyanide leaching solution. The gold and silver metals are precipitated by zinc dust after the leaching solution is clarified and deoxygenated under vacuum.

mesothermal   descriptive of ore minerals of hydrothermal origin formed at medium temperatures.

metallogenic   used in describing the study of the origin of mineral deposits.

metallurgical recovery   percentage of the mineral presented to the metallurgical process that is recovered to a saleable product.

metallurgy   the science and technology of metals, usually pertaining to the processing of metals and minerals in mining.

metamorphic   term applied to pre-existing sedimentary and igneous rocks that have been altered in composition, texture or internal structure by processes involving pressure, heat and/or the introduction of new chemical substances.

methane   gaseous compound of carbon and hydrogen emitted from coal.

Mg   chemical symbol for magnesium.

mill   a rotating machine used for reducing the size of ore particles, although the term has come to cover the broad range of machinery inside the treatment plant where the economically valuable minerals are separated from the ore.

mill feed grade   the grade of material feed or equivalent received at the mill.

millidarcies   measure of permeability. See darcy

milling   the comminution of the ore.

mine call factor   an adjustment derived from comparing the tonnes and grade of gold actually mined from a section of a deposit and the original ore reserve projections.

mineral   a natural, inorganic, homogeneous material that can be expressed by a chemical formula.

mineral deposit a mineralised body that has been delineated by appropriate drilling and/or underground sampling to support a sufficient tonnage and average grade of metal(s).

mineralisation the process by which minerals are introduced into a rock. More generally, a term applied to accumulations of economic or related minerals in quantities ranging from anomalous to economically recoverable.

mineralised zone a volume of rock that contains anomalous to economically recoverable quantities of mineral.

mineralogy the science of minerals.

mineral resource an identified in situ mineral occurrence from which valuable or useful minerals may be recovered. Subdivided into inferred, indicated or measured categories in accordance with JORC.

mining dilution the incorporation of uneconomic material with economic material that occurs in the process of mining.

mining recovery the amount of the ore that is recovered in the mining process, usually expressed as a percentage.

mining tenement an authority for exploration or mining purposes.

ML mining lease.

Mn chemical symbol for manganese.

Mo chemical symbol for molybdenum.

Monte Carlo refers to the simulation process to estimate a probabilistic distribution of an outcome such as a project's net present value.

mPa megapascals.

MSP mineral separation plant.

mt million tonnes.

mtpa million tonnes per annum.

naked option an option that is purchased or sold without an offsetting position in the underlying asset.

native naturally occurring and may be relatively pure.

natural gas that part of petroleum production that exists as a gas at atmospheric temperature and pressure. The major constituent is methane.

net asset value (NAV) the sum of all asset values and liabilities.

net present value (NPV) the sum of discounted future negative and positive cash flows.

net revenue interest that portion of income directly payable to the owner. Working, royalty and overriding royalty interest owners each have a net revenue interest.

net smelter returns the value received for a mineral after refining, less the cost of transporting the mineral to the refinery and the cost of refining.

net working interest usually refers to the interest used for normal operations in the joint interest billing after a promoter has been paid.

New York Mercantile Exchange (NYMEX) world's largest physical commodity exchange, consisting of two divisions — the NYMEX Division and the COMEX Division.

NGL natural gas liquids.

Ni chemical symbol for nickel.

nominal cost, dollars based at a particular time not accounting for inflation.

nomogram a graphical geometric presentation of relationships between quantities where a value may be found by the drawing of straight lines.

non-refractory ore ore that is relatively easy to treat for recovery of the valuable substances.

normal distribution bell-shaped histogram of a statistical occurrence.

NPAT net profit after tax.

Organisation of Petroleum Exporting Countries (OPEC) its 13 members are Algeria, Angola, Ecuador, Indonesia, Iran, Iraq, Kuwait, Libya, Nigeria, Qatar, Saudi Arabia, United Arab Emirates (Abu Dhabi, Dubai, Ras al Khaimah Sharjah) and Venezuela.

O&M   operation and maintenance.

open cut (open pit)   surface mining in which the ore is extracted from a pit. The geometry of the pit may vary with the characteristics of the orebody.

operating cash flow per share   cash flow (comprising operating profit before tax, depreciation and amortisation, exploration/evaluation expenditure expense and provisions, less income tax paid) divided by issued shares.

operating expenses   costs of doing business that do not include interest and debt payments.

OP   option price.

option   contract that gives one party the right but not the obligation to buy something at a given price some time in the future.

ore   mineral-bearing rock that contains one or more minerals, at least one of which can be mined and treated profitably under current or immediately foreseeable economic conditions.

orebody   a continuous, well-defined mass of material of sufficient ore content to make extraction economically feasible.

ore grade   the average amount of the valuable metal or mineral contained in a specific mass of ore.

ore pass   a chute or opening through which broken ore passes to a lower levels.

ore reserve   that part of a mineral resource that could be mined, together with dilution, economically under conditions existing at the time of reporting.

ounces (oz)   troy ounces of 31.103 grams, or 1.097 avoirdupois ounces.

outbye   a non-hazardous zone underground.

outcrop   that part of a rock formation exposed on the surface.

out-of-the-money   for calls, an option that has an exercise price above the market price of the underlying future. For puts, an option that has an exercise price below the futures price.

overburden rock that has to be removed to access the coal seam in open cut mining.

overcast ventilation device that allows stale return air to pass over or cross fresh air intake without contamination in underground mines.

over-the-counter (OTC) customised derivative contract, usually arranged with an intermediary as opposed to a standardised derivative contract traded on an exchange.

OWC oil–water contact in hydrocarbon accumulation.

oxide ore ore that has been oxidised by exposure to air and circulating ground waters. During this process, sulphide minerals break down to iron and other metal oxide minerals.

pantechnicon a train of sleds incorporating longwall services, including power.

partial extraction continuous miner systematic removal of some parts of coal pillars.

pathfinder in geochemical exploration, an element that occurs in close association with the element being sought.

payback period time it takes for positive cash flows received to cover the cost of capital investment.

pay zone the sub-surface geological formation where a deposit of oil or natural gas is found in commercial quantities.

PCFR price to cash flow ratio.

PCI pulverised coal injection; fine pulverised coal injected into the blast furnace—used to reduce the usage of coking coal.

PE price to earnings ratio; the share price divided by the earnings per share, or alternatively the total market capitalisation of the company divided by the after-tax earnings (net profit).

percussion drilling drilling method that utilises a hammering action under rotation to penetrate rock while the cuttings are forced to the surface by compressed air.

petrology study of formation of rock.

PF   project finance.

PGM   platinum group metals.

pH   a measure of the degree of acidity or of basicity of a solution.

pillar   column of ore or waste remaining after primary extraction.

pillar quartering   secondary mining involving formation of smaller size pillars for improved recovery of coal.

pit shell   designed outline of an open pit mine containing all the open pit ore reserves.

PJ   petajoules.

placer gold   *see* alluvial gold

plat   an excavation on a shaft to provide access to underground level workings.

PLCR   project life coverage ratio.

plug   a more or less cylindrical intrusive body of igneous rock.

plugged and abandoned   refers to a well that was filled with cement and abandoned; sealing the well with plugs will not allow communication of fluids or gases between different geological horizons.

plunge   the angle from the horizontal of a geological feature in a vertical plane.

polygons, polygonal   the derived shape of the mineralisation on a particular cross-section that provides the basis for projecting the mineralisation to the next section and thus estimating the tonnage.

porphyry   any igneous rock in which relatively large, conspicuous crystals (called phenocrysts) are set in a fine-grained ground mass.

porphyry copper   copper deposit in which copper minerals are widely disseminated.

portal   the entrance to a tunnel or decline.

pound (lb)   measure of weight equal to 0.4536 kilograms.

PP&E   property, plant and equipment.

ppb   parts per billion (1000 million).

ppm   parts per million (the same as grams per tonne, g/t).

pre-feasibility study   a relatively comprehensive analysis that is qualified by the availability and accuracy of fundamental criteria and assumptions to the degree that it cannot be the basis for final decisions.

present value   present sum of discounted future values.

pressure oxidation   the use of elevated temperature and pressure to promote the oxidation of sulphides.

pressure transient analysis   the utilisation of pressure data in mathematical formulae to estimate reservoir characteristics. This type of analysis can be used to estimate the original oil in place, recovery factors and completion efficiency.

pre-stripping   removal of overburden (waste rock) in advance of beginning operations to remove ore in an open pit operation.

PRI   political risk insurance.

primary ore   ore that has not been affected by near-surface oxidising processes.

probable ore reserve   an ore reserve that has been based, after application of mining recovery and dilution factors, on an in situ identified resource that has been categorised as 'indicated'.

probability distribution   a statistical representation of the likelihood of outcome for various parameter values.

product size   the size of mineral particles leaving a crushing or grinding circuit.

profit   income remaining after all business expenses are paid.

proved reserve   an ore reserve that has been based, after application of mining recovery and dilution factors, on an in situ identified resource that has been categorised as 'measured'.

psi   pounds per square inch

Pt   chemical symbol for platinum.

pulp   a mixture of ground ore and water capable of flowing.

put option   a contract that gives the buyer the right but not the obligation to deliver a commodity or shares at some time in the future at a set price (strike) to the seller for a one-time payment.

pyrite   a common iron sulphide mineral; FeS_2.

quartz   a mineral composed of silicon dioxide; SiO_2.

RAB drilling   rotary air blast; rotary drilling, a technique in which the sample is returned to the surface outside the rod string by compressed air.

radiometric   pertaining to the measurement of radiation produced by the spontaneous decay of certain atoms.

raise   a vertical or inclined underground opening that is constructed from the bottom upwards.

RC drilling   reverse circulation drilling; percussion drilling using a method in which the sample is brought to the surface inside the drill rods, thereby reducing contamination.

reagent   a chemical or additive used in processing.

real discount rate   the nominal discount rate adjusted for inflation.

real price   price that has been adjusted to remove the effect of inflation.

reconnaissance   a general examination or survey of a region with reference to its main features, usually as a preliminary to a more detailed survey.

recovery   the percentage of metal in an ore extracted by the metallurgical process.

reef   mineralised rock, particularly gold-bearing quartz.

refining   the final stage of metal production in which impurities are removed from the molten metal by introducing air and fluxes. The impurities are removed as gases or slag.

refractory rock   rock that is difficult to treat for recovery of the valuable minerals. Most commonly treated by roasting the rock in a furnace.

reserve   an ore estimate based, after application of mining recovery and dilution actors, on an in situ identified resource. Mineral reserves are divided into proven and probable categories according to JORC.

reserves (hydrocarbons) estimated volumes of hydrocarbons anticipated to be commercially recoverable from known accumulations.

resource an identified in situ mineral occurrence from which valuable or useful minerals may be recovered. Mineral resources are divided into inferred, indicated and measured categories according to JORC.

return on equity (ROE) profit earned by a company in comparison with shareholder equity on its balance sheet.

revenue total amount of money received from sales of products and/or services, gains from the sale or exchange of assets, interest and dividends earned on investments, and other increases in the owner's equity, except those arising from capital adjustments.

RFT repeat formation test; small samples are collected from the bottom of an oil well to test for hydrocarbons.

rib sidewalls of an underground coal roadway.

rift a trough bordered by two faults.

RL relative level.

RLCR reserve life coverage ratio.

roadway primary access for the supply of man, materials, ventilation and conveyance of coal to surface.

rock mineral matter of various compositions.

rock chip sampling collection of rock samples by breaking chips off a rock face, usually for chemical analysis.

ROM run of mine; ore produced from the mine available for processing.

room-and-pillar stoping the system of mining in which ore is mined in rooms separated by pillars left at intervals.

royalties payments generally either as a fixed amount per unit of production or a percentage of revenue or profits.

SAG semi-autogenous grinding mill; a large-diameter rotating tube that grinds crushed rock to separate mineral particles using the rock itself as the main grinding medium.

sampling   taking small pieces of rock at intervals along exposed mineralisation for assay (to determine the mineral content).

sandstone   sedimentary rock comprising sand-size grains (> 0.06 mm, > 2.0 mm).

scat   a coarse particle of rock discharged from the milling process that is often crushed and recycled through the mill.

SCF   standard cubic feet.

scheelite   an ore of tungsten.

seam   informal name for a coal sequence; usually describes the mining profile.

sediment   formed of particles deposited from suspension in water, wind or ice.

sedimentary rock   rock formed from solid particles, whether mineral or organic, that has been moved from its position of origin and redeposited.

seismic survey   pertaining to shock waves that pass through the earth which are used to map underground sedimentary structures.

self-advancing hydraulic supports   used to support immediate face area where coal is mined at a longwall.

semi-anthracite   high-quality rocks, low volatile coal, with high carbon content.

shaft   a vertical or steeply inclined passage from the surface by which a mine is entered and through which ore is transported.

shale   a fine-grained laminated sedimentary rock formed from clay, mud and silt, splitting into distinct layers with grain size > 0.0025 mm.

shear   zone in which rocks have been deformed by lateral movement along parallel planes similar to a fault.

shearer   a machine used to cut and load coal from a longwall face.

shoot   a general term describing lens-like bodies of mineralisation defined by grade/thickness parameters.

shrinkage mining   a method of mining where ore is mined using successive slices moving upwards from a level. After each slice is blasted, about 40 per cent of the ore is removed from the working place to provide a working space between the blasted ore and the back of the stope. When the mining has been completed to the top of the ore zone, the remaining 60 per cent of the ore is drawn out to empty the stope.

shut in   a well that has been temporarily shut down due to either economic or mechanical problems.

sieve size   size at which particles will pass through the meshed or perforated bottom of a sieve.

siliceous   descriptive of rocks having a high silica content.

sill   a tabular intrusion of igneous rock that is concordant with the structure of the enclosing rocks.

sintering   to agglomerate particles of a metal or mixture of substances to just below melting point by the application of heat and pressure.

skarn   a thermally metamorphosed limestone often containing sulphide minerals.

slate   a compact, fine-grained metamorphic rock that possesses cleavage and hence can be split into slabs and thin plates.

slurry   a fluid comprising fine solids suspended in a solution (generally water containing additives).

smelting   thermal processing whereby molten metal is liberated from beneficiated ore or concentrate with impurities separating as lighter slag.

SML   special mining lease.

SMU   selective mining unit; theoretically, the block size at which the grade and tonnage recovered in mining operations match the orebody model; in practice, the block size that can be mined selectively.

Sn   chemical symbol for tin.

solvent extraction   a method of transferring mineral values from an impure solution into a more pure solution using specialised solvents.

SPE   Society of Petroleum Engineers.

specific gravity (SG) the density of a substance relative to water.

sphalerite a zinc sulphide mineral.

spot market the price quoted on terminal markets for the immediate delivery of a commodity.

SPV special purpose vehicle.

standard deviation measure of the degree to which an individual value in a probability distribution tends to vary from the mean of the distribution.

STB stock tank barrels.

steaming coal coal used for steam raising, usually in a power station.

steel-chained armoured face conveyor (AFC) machine used to tranfer coal across the face of a longwall.

stochastic process where the evolution of some random variable is over some parameter such as time.

stockpile material mined and piled for future use.

stope an underground opening in a mine from which ore has been or is being extracted.

stratigraphy composition, sequence and correlation of layered rocks in the Earth's crust.

stress direction direction of stress acting on an area.

strike the direction or bearing of a bed or layer of rock in the horizontal plane.

strike length distance along strike (at right angles to dip).

strip (or stripping ratio) the tonnage or volume of waste material that must be removed to allow the mining of one tonne of ore in an open pit.

stripping removal of metal from material on which it has precipitated or been absorbed; for example, gold from carbon or copper from cathodes.

structure the general disposition, attitude, arrangement or relative positions of rock.

subduction the process of movements in the Earth's crust when one crustal plate slides under another.

subsidence movement of strata resulting from the extraction of coal.

sulphide ore ore characterised by the inclusion of metal in the crystal structure of a sulphide mineral. This type of ore is often refractory.

supergene concentration of minerals by secondary processes involving percolation of water from the surface downwards.

surface depletion leaching of minerals from near the surface lithologies by descending ground waters.

SX-EW processing solvent extraction and electro-winning processing. Recovery of a metal from an ore by means of acid leaching and organic extraction, combined with electrochemical processes.

syncline a sequence of rocks flexed downwards into a valley shape with a core of younger rocks.

t tonnes.

Ta chemical symbol for tantalum.

tailgate the heading used for ventilation of return air on the opposite side of the coal panel to the main gate.

tailings finely ground waste materials rejected from a treatment plant after the recoverable valuable minerals have been extracted.

tailings dam structure that holds back the storage of tailings.

take-or-pay obligation to pay for a specified amount of product whether this amount is taken or not.

TC/RC treatment and refining charge to produce high-grade metal product from concentrates.

TCF trillion cubic feet.

tectonic geological setting involving movements of the Earth's crust.

tenement an area of land defined by the relevant government authority over which an approved applicant may conduct exploration or mining activities.

Ti   chemical symbol for titanium.

tonne (t)   1000 kilograms.

top cut   an upper assay limit to which all abnormally high assays in a population are reduced to restrict their influence on the average grade of the resource.

total moisture   moisture as sampled (free plus inherent).

total sulphur   total inorganic and organic sulphur contained.

tpa   tonnes per annum.

tpd   tonnes per day.

tph   tonnes per hour.

transition zone   in a mineralised body, usually refers to a zone between the oxidised zone and the primary zone.

tuff   rock type sometimes above or below a coal seam often associated with difficult ground conditions.

turbidite   a sedimentary rock formed by mass slumping of material down submarine slopes.

U   chemical symbol for uranium.

ultimate analysis tests   analysis expressed in terms of carbon, hydrogen, nitrogen, sulphur and oxygen.

ultrabasic   igneous rocks containing very high magnesium and iron, and generally containing less than 45 per cent silica.

uphole benching   an underground mining technique where mining progresses upwards.

upstream   oil and gas exploration and production, as opposed to downstream areas of refining and marketing.

variogram   a geostatistical tool involving the measurement of the spatial continuity of a parameter such as grade.

vein   a thin sheet-like infill of a fissure or crack, commonly bearing quartz.

ventilation raise opening through which air passes to reach underground workings.

viscosity the resistance of liquids, semi-solids and gases to movement or flow.

vitrinite bright coal, formed from woody plant material; one of the main coal components that imparts coking properties.

volatile matter loss in mass other than water lost on heating; often organic components.

volatility measure of the variability of a market factor.

volcanic rocks formed from the solidification of lava extruded on or erupted at the Earth's surface. Also includes pyroclastic rocks.

volumetric analysis the process used to determine oil or gas reserves when lithologic characteristics and properties of the reservoir fluids are known. This type of analysis is usually referred to as the indirect method of valuation since exact lithologic characteristics and fluid properties are not usually known.

WACC weighted average cost of capital as a percentage, used as a discount rate.

wacker drilling a simple portable drill rig capable of driving a sampling tube a short distance into soft ground.

wall rock in mining, the host rock to the mineralisation.

washed coal coal that has passed through the wash plant.

wash plant plant for separating waste rock and coal.

waste dump site for the placement of waste rock.

waste rock material other than ore excavated during a mining operation.

waste to ore (stripping) ratio tonnage/volume of waste material that must be removed to allow the mining of one tonne/cubic metre of ore in an open cut.

watt unit of power equal to 1 joule/second.

weathered mineralisation mineralisation showing a high degree of weathering.

weathering near-surface alteration of minerals and rocks by exposure to the atmosphere and ground water.

well (oil & gas) circular drilled hole that provides access to underground hydrocarbon reservoirs.

West Texas Intermediate (WTI) US Oklahoma crude oil used as a benchmark for pricing much of the world's crude oil production.

Wh (watt-hour) work done in one hour by an agent working at a constant rate of 1 watt.

winze a vertical or inclined opening in an underground mine developed from the top downwards.

WPC World Petroleum Council.

yield the proportion of the total that is recovered; or the dividend return on an investment as a percentage.

Zn chemical symbol for zinc.

BIBLIOGRAPHY AND REFERENCES

Agricola, G 1556, *De re Metallica*, trans HC Hoover & LH Hoover 1912, New Ed 1950, Dover Publications, ISBN 0 486600 06 8, p. 638, New York.

AIME 1976, *Economics of the mineral industries*, 3rd edn, p. 863, New York.

AusIMM 1980, *Mining and metallurgical practices in Australia*, Monograph No. 10, ISBN 0 909520 55 0, p. 947, Melbourne.

AusIMM 1982, *Field geologist's manual*, Monograph No. 9, ISBN 0 909520 69 0, p. 301, Melbourne.

AusIMM 1993, *Australasian mining and metallurgy*, Monograph No. 19, ISBN 0 949106 76 3 2, volume set, p. 1571, Melbourne.

AusIMM 1993, *Cost estimation handbook for the Australian mining industry*, Monograph No. 20, ISBN 0 949106 87 9, p. 412, Melbourne.

Australian Gas Association 1992, *Gas supply and demand study*, 3rd report, ISBN 187552101 1, p. 104, Canberra.

Australian Mining Consultants 1997, *Minesite — the mining reference guide*, <www.minesite.aust.com>.

Brailsford, T, Handley, J & Maheswaran, K, 2007, *A re-examination of the historical equity risk premium in Australia*, Accounting & Finance, Melbourne.

Camus, JP 2002, *Management of mineral resources: creating value in the mining business*, SME, ISBN 0 87335 216 5, p. 107, Colorado.

Crowson, R 1996, *Minerals handbook 1996–97*, Stockton Press, ISBN 1 561591 91 2, p. 455, London.

Gastineau G.L. 1979, *The stock options manual*, McGraw-Hill Book Co., ISBN 0 070229 70 8, p. 389, New York.

Joint Ore Reserve Committee 2004, *Australasian code for reporting of exploration results, mineral resources and ore reserves*, Melbourne.

Hathaway, N 2005, *Australian market risk premium*, Capital Research Pty Ltd, Melbourne.

Kernot, C 1999, *Valuing mining companies*, Woodhead Publishing Ltd, p. 241, Cambridge.

Kodukula, P and Papudesu, C 2006, *Project Valuation Using Real Options*, Ross Publishing, Fort Lauderdale

KPMG, 2008 *Portman Mining Limited Independent Expert Report*.

Lane, KF 1988, *The economic definition of ore*, Mining Journal Books Ltd, ISBN 0 900117 45 1, p. 149, London.

Lonergan, W 2006, *The valuation of mining assets*, Sydney University Press, ISBN 1920898267, p. 215, Sydney.

Mackenzie, BW and Bilodeau, ML 1984, *Economics of mineral exploration in Australia*, WMC, ISBN 0 908039 44 1, p. 171, Melbourne.

Mular, AL 1982, CIM special vol. 25, Montreal.

Mular, AL and Bhappu, RB 1978, *Mineral processing plant design*, Port City Press Inc, Maryland.

Officer, RR & Bishop, S 2009, *Market risk premium: further comments*, Energy Networks Association.

Parks, RD 1957, *Examination and valuation of mineral property*, Addison-Wesley Publishing, p. 507, Reading.

Parliament of the Commonwealth of Australia 2011, *Exposure draft Minerals Resource Rent Tax* <www.treasury.gov.au/documents/2157/PDF/MMRT_exposure_draft.pdf>.

Reed, HH 1971, *Rutley's elements of mineralogy*, Allen & Unwin Ltd, Second imp. ISBN 0 0454900 06 6, p. 560, London.

RSM Bird Cameron 2010, *Control Premium Study*.

Rudenno, V 1985, *Mining economics*, 2nd edn. UNSW, ISBN 0 959103 70 8, Sydney.

Runge, IC 1998, *Mining economics and strategy*, Society for mining, metallurgy and exploration Inc., p. 295, Littleton.

Sloan, DA 1983, *Mine management*, Chapman & Hall Ltd, ISBN 0 412240 70 X, p. 495, London.

South Australian Centre for Economic Studies 2006, *Market risk premium for Australian regulatory decisions*. Adelaide.

Stermole, FJ and Stermole, JS 1987, *Economic evaluation and investment decision methods*, Investment Evaluations Corporation, ISBN 0 9603282 8 9, p. 479, Golden, Colorado.

Tarring, T and Pinney, G 1989, *Trading in metals*, Metal Bulletin Books Ltd, ISBN 0 94767129 3, p. 275, Worcester Park, UK.

Torries, TF 1998, *Evaluating mineral projects applications and misconceptions*, Society for Mining, Metallurgy and Exploration Inc., p. 153, Littleton, Colorado.

Wanless, RM 1983, *Finance for mine management*, Chapman and Hall Ltd, ISBN 0 412240 60 2, p. 208, London.

Welker, A J 1985, *The oil and gas book*, SciData Publishing, ISBN 0 87614 279 7, p. 258, Tulsa.

Wilkinson, R 1997, *Speaking of oil & gas*, 2nd ed. BHP Petroleum Pty Ltd, ISBN 0646 24557 0, p. 112, Melbourne.

Willcox, E 1949, *Mine accounting and financial administration*, Pitman Publishing Corporation, p. 489, New York.

Woodcock, JT (ed.), 1980, *Mining and metallurgical practices in Australasia*, Australasian Institute of Mining and Metallurgy, Melbourne.

INDEX